Francophone Studies

Other titles in *The Essential Glossary* series

Forthcoming

Francophone Studies
The Essential Glossary

Edited by

Margaret A. Majumdar

A member of the Hodder Headline Group
LONDON
Distributed in the United States of America by
Oxford University Press Inc., New York

First published in Great Britain in 2002 by
Arnold, a member of the Hodder Headline Group,
338 Euston Road, London NW1 3BH

http://www.arnoldpublishers.com

Distributed in the United States of America by
Oxford University Press Inc.,
198 Madison Avenue, New York, NY10016

British Library Cataloguing in Publication Data
A catalogue record for this book is available from the British Library

Library of Congress Cataloging-in-Publication Data
A catalog record for this book is available from the Library of Congress

ISBN 0 340 80696 6 (hb)
ISBN 0 340 80697 4 (pb)

1 2 3 4 5 6 7 8 9 10

Typeset in 10 on 12 pt Minion by Phoenix Photosetting, Chatham, Kent
Printed and bound in Great Britain by MPG Books, Bodmin, Cornwall

What do you think about this book? Or any other Arnold title?
Please send your comments to feedback.arnold@hodder.co.uk

Contents

Preface

This glossary is designed to provide an introduction to the global area of Francophone Studies and a route-map for further study, providing students as well as a wider public with the tools to deepen their knowledge of specific aspects of this field.

The field of Francophone Studies is a relatively new area of study. It has only come into its own in French departments in the English-speaking world over the last two decades, since when it has proven a popular option for undergraduate and postgraduate studies. In most cases, and despite some notable exceptions, it has been introduced in piecemeal fashion into the curriculum, with a corresponding lack of a global approach. It is hoped that this glossary will be of assistance in this respect, with the coverage of a wide array of topics, including the history, politics, economies, societies, as well as the cultures of the different societies concerned.

Definitions of Francophone Studies are themselves problematical. On the one hand, the communality of the French language has been taken as the main criterion for the definition of the Francophone community. If taken to its logical conclusion, this should include French-speakers in the 'Hexagon' on an equal footing with French-speakers from elsewhere. However, in French academic circles, Francophone Studies normally means the study of French-language literature and other genres produced by authors and artists who are non-French, or originate from outside metropolitan France. There is clearly some inconsistency here, with the further complication that this binary divide in French-language literature and culture tends to create an illusory homogeneity in the camps on either side of the divide. Moreover, an emphasis on the unifying force of the French language has tended to obscure the real linguistic and cultural diversity that exists in countries which normally come under the Francophone banner, even where there exists only a minority of French speakers.

A second approach has been based on the institutional definition of *La Francophonie*, including those countries which are official members of at least one of the *Francophone* institutions. Given the way in which *Francophonie* has evolved over recent years to embrace a policy and discourse promoting pluralism and diversity, this might seem to offer a more solid basis for a credible definition. This approach would include France as a member country; however, at the same time, it would exclude a number of countries, most notably the DOM-TOM and Algeria.

In an attempt to go beyond these difficulties, this glossary adopts a broader, more inclusive approach, in which 'Francophone Studies' is defined as the study of any aspects of the society and culture of non-European countries which, because of a variety of historical and/or current economic, political, social and cultural factors, have been marked by French influence.

Given that the basis of this definition is the *relation* to France and French influence, this glossary does not include entries relating primarily and solely to France itself. These are covered elsewhere in the glossary series. The potential vastness of the material to be covered means that it has also not been possible to include entries relating to other European Francophone countries, such as Belgium, Luxembourg and Switzerland. The focus is on the post-1945 historical period, though references to events and individuals from earlier periods are included where they still have major contemporary significance. Even with these restrictions, we cannot claim to have provided entries on every topic that might have been included. We hope that we have none the less provided a menu which gives a taste of the essentials, while stimulating the appetite for further reading and research.

The longer entries of the glossary present overviews of important topics and issues, individual countries, aspects of different societies and cultures, key institutions and figures. The shorter entries provide brief outlines of other topics, profiles of significant figures, events and cultural phenomena. Cross-connections are indicated and suggestions offered for further reading and investigation. Wherever possible, details of English translations of literary works are given – usually citing the earliest known version.

The contributors to the glossary come from a variety of different backgrounds and countries and have been chosen for their expertise, but also to reflect the truly international dimension of this subject. The aim has been to ensure that a diversity of perspectives is maintained, within an overall cohesive framework. Names of contributors are shown at the end of each entry and further information about each of them is provided in the Notes on Contributors. All unattributed material is the work of the editor.

Guide to the glossary

The glossary has been designed as a handbook, which may be used in a number of different ways.

Use it as a dictionary to look up items, which are arranged in alphabetical order from A (Aba) to Z (Zoreille). You will find concise, easy-to-follow explanations of some of the key names and keywords in Francophone Studies.

Use it to explore further by following up the cross-references (marked by small capitals in the text) to similar topics, using these entries to build up a broader knowledge of the subject area.

Use the thematic index of entries to explore entries related to particular areas of the French-speaking world and cultures, or to explore particular themes across the different areas.

Use it as a guide for your further reading by consulting some of the books, articles or websites suggested at the end of the entries. You will find the full bibliographical details of all of these in the bibliography at the end of the book.

Thematic index of entries

General concepts, issues and debates in Francophone Studies

Afropessimisme; anticolonialism; antiracism; *assimilation/intégration/insertion*; centre–periphery; citizenship; colonial policy; *coopération*; cultural identity; cultural imperialism; decolonisation; democracy/democratisation; diglossia; diversity/difference; economic relations; élites; ethnography; Eurocentrism; *exception culturelle*; exoticism; Francophone discourse; French language; GATT; gender issues; globalisation; hybridity; language policy; memory; migration; modernity and tradition; nationhood/nationalism; neo-colonialism; NGOs; orientalism; postcolonialism; postmodernity; race/ethnicity; racism; science and technology; secularism and religion; universalism.
Césaire; Fanon; Glissant; Senghor.

General historical topics

Colonialism and anticolonialism

Anticolonialism; Bandung Conference; Brazzaville Declaration; colonial policy; decolonisation; nationhood/nationalism; *Communauté française*; *Union française*.
Césaire; de Gaulle; Fanon; Ho Chi Minh; Memmi; Senghor.

Postcolonialism

Afropessimisme; c*oopération*; democracy/democratisation; DOM-TOM; economic relations; GATT; globalisation; Lomé Convention; migration; nationhood/nationalism; neo-colonialism; NGOs; Non-Aligned Movement; postcolonialism; Yaoundé Convention.
Foccart.

History of La Francophonie

Charte de la Francophonie; Francophone discourse; Francophone summits; *Francophonie*, birth and development.
Bourguiba; Boutros-Ghali; Chirac; Mitterrand; Reclus; Senghor; Sihanouk.

Francophone institutions

ADELF; AFAL; *Agence intergouvernementale de la Francophonie*; AIMF; *Alliance française*; APF; AUF; CILF; CMF; CONFEJES; CONFEMEN; CPF; *Délégation générale à*

la langue française; DOM-TOM; FFA; FIPF; Francophone institutions; Francophone summits; *Haut Conseil de la Francophonie*; *Jeux de la Francophonie*; OIF; TV5; *Université Senghor*.
Boutros-Ghali; Josselin.

The Maghreb and Middle East

Economy and politics

Algeria; Algerian Elections, 1991; Barcelona Agreement; Berber Spring; Egypt; *Ennahda*; *Ettahaddi*; economy; EuroMed policy; FFS; FIS; FLN; GIA; Green March; GSPC; *Hizb al IstiqLal*; Kabylia; Lebanon; Mauritania; MCB; Morocco; Neo-Destour; PAGS; Pan-Arabism; PCA; Polisario; RCD; science and technology; SONATRACH; Syria; Tunisia; UGTA; UMA; Western Sahara; *Wilaya*; women's movements.
Abdel Aziz; Abdesselam; Aït Ahmed; Aslaoui; Basri; Ben Ali; Benhadj; Benjedid; Boudiaf; Bouteflika; Hanoune; Harbi; Hassan II; Madani; Malek; Messaoudi; Mohammed VI; Saadi; Serfaty; Taleb Ibrahimi; Zeroual.

Geography, history, people and society

Algeria; Algerian National Charter; Algerian War of Independence; ALN; Battle of Algiers; Berbers; Blum–Violette; Casbah of Algiers; Charter of Algiers; Egypt; ENA; Evian Agreements; family; family codes; FLN; food; GPRA; Green March; *hammam*; *harem*; *Harkis*; Kabylia; Lebanon; *Manifeste du Peuple Algérien*; Mauritania; Mediterranean; Morocco; MTLD; November 1st 1954; OAS; *pieds noirs*; Polisario; Sahara; Setif Uprising; Syria; veil; Western Sahara.
Abbas; Abdelkader; Aït Ahmed; Alleg; Bastien-Thiry; Belkacem; Ben Barka; Ben Bella; Bidault; Bitat; Boudiaf; Bouhired; Boumedienne; Boupacha; Bourguiba; Challe; Fanon; Farès; Hadj; Harbi; Jouhaud; Jugurtha; Kahina; Khider; Lacoste; Mernissi; Mohammed V; Mollet; Oufkir; Ramdane; Saint Augustine; Salan; Soustelle.

Language, culture and religion

Arabian Nights; Arabisation; Battle of Algiers; cinema; Islam; Koran; Lebanon; literature; *Missionnaires d'Afrique*; *Moudjahidin*; music; North African Jewish culture; orality; *Oulema*; *Pères Blancs*; PPA; *Raï*; Sherazade; *Souffles*; sport; *Tamazight*.
Aba; Ait Mansour; Allouache; Alloula; Amrouche; Baccouche; Béji; Bekri; Benaissa; Bencheikh; Ben Jelloun; Bensoussan; Bouabaci; Boudjedra; Boulmerka; Bouraoui; Camus; Cardinal; Cheb Hasni; Cheb Mami; Cheikha Remitti; Choukri; Chraïbi; Dib; Djabali; Djaout; Djebar; Djemaï; Farès; Feraoun; Gallaire; Ghachem; Haddad; Houari; Jugurtha; Kahina; Kateb Yacine; Khadda; Khaïr-Eddine; Khaled; Khatibi; Laâbi; Lakhdar-Hamina; Laroui; Lounes; Maalouf; Mammeri; Mechakra; Meddeb; Memmi; Mimouni; Mokkedem; Morsy; Pélégri; Pontecorvo; Roblès; Roy; Said; Sebbar; Sebti; Sefrioui; Sénac; Serhane; Tengour; Zemmouri.

Sub-Saharan Africa

Economy and politics

Bénin; Burkina Faso; Burundi; Cameroon; CEDEAO; Central African Republic; CFA; Chad; Congo, République de; Côte d'Ivoire; Democratic Republic of Congo; Djibouti; ECOWAS; Franc Zone; Franco-African summits; Gabon; Guinea; Lomé Convention; Mali; Niger; OAU; Pan-Africanism; RDA; Rwanda; Senegal; Togo; Yaoundé Convention.

Thematic index of entries

Biya; Bongo; Boukassa; Compaoré; Diori; Diouf; Foccart; Guèye; Houphouët-Boigny; Jospin; Kabila; Kagamé; Konaré; Lamizana; Mitterrand; Mobutu; Sankara; Tombalbaye; Wade.

Geography, history, people and society

AEF; AOF; Bénin; Brazzaville Declaration; Burkina Faso; Burundi; Cameroon; Central African Republic; Chad; Congo, République de; Côte d'Ivoire; Dahomey; Democratic Republic of Congo; Djibouti; Gabon; Guinea; Mali; Niger; Rwanda; Senegal; Togo; Upper Volta.
Boukassa; Diori; Houphouët-Boigny; Lumumba; Mobutu; Sankara; Senghor; Soundiata; Touré.

Language, culture and religion

Audio-visual media; cinema; education; Griot; Jeune Afrique; literature; Missionnaires d'Afrique; music; négritude; Pères Blancs; popular culture; Présence Africaine; press; religion; sport; visual arts.
Adiaffi; Bâ; Bebey; Beyala; Bhêly-Quénum; Blondy; Boni; Cissé; Dadié; Diabaté; Dibango; Diop; Dongala; Fall; Fantouré; Franco; Hazoume; Hondo; Kaboré; Kane; Karoné; Keïta; Ken Bugul; Konaté; Kourouma; Laye; Lopes; Ly; Mambety; M'Fouilou; Milla; Monénembo; Mongo Beti; Mudimbe; Nanga; N'dour; Ngal; Nganang; Ngandu Nkashama; Ngoye; Ouédraogo; Ouologuem; Oyono; Sadji; Sassine; Sembene; Senghor; Socé; Sony Lab'ou Tansi; Sow Fall; Tadjo; Tati-Loutard; Tchicaya U Tam'si; Touré Kunda; Werewere Liking.

Canada and North America

Economy and politics

Lake Meech Accord; NAFTA; Parti Québécois; Politics; Quebec; Révolution tranquille
Bouchard; Bourassa; Chrétien; Duplessis; Lévesque; Mulroney; Parizeau; Trudeau.

Geography, history, people and society

Acadia; Cajun; Louisiana; New Brunswick; Ontario; Quebec; Saint-Pierre-et-Miquelon.

Language, culture, religion

Audio-visual media; Cajun; Charter of the French Language; cinema; CODOFIL; Hiawatha; joual; language/language policies in Quebec; Law 101; literature; theatre; Révolution tranquille.
Aquin; Arcand; Beaulieu; Blais; Brossard; Cardinal; Carle; Carrier; Charlebois; Desjardins; Dion; Ducharme; Ferron; Garneau; Godbout; Grandbois; Hébert; Huston; Julien; Jutra; Langevin; Leclerc; Lepage; Maillet; Mankiewitz; Micone; Miron; Nelligan; Perrault; Poulin; Renaud; Roy; Tremblay; Vigneault.

Caribbean

Economy and politics

Guadeloupe; Guiana; Haiti; Marronnage; Martinique; Tonton Macoutes.
Aristide; Césaire; Duvalier; Larifla; Michaux-Chevry.

Geography, history, people and society

Antillanité; Békés; Francophone Black Atlantic; Guadeloupe; Guiana; Haiti; Marronnage; Martinique; race/population.

Language, culture, religion

Antillanité; Creoles; *créolité*; education; food; Francophone Black Atlantic; literature; mangrove; music; roots/rhizome.

Alexis; Bébel-Gisler; Bernabé; Boukman; Brival; Capécia; Césaire; Chamoiseau; Condé; Confiant; Damas; Depestre; Fanon; Frankétienne; Glissant; Gratiant; Hazaël-Massieux; Hyvrard; Juminer; Maran; Maximin; Menil; Orville; Palcy; Pepin; Pineau; Placoly; Roumain; Saint-John Perse; Schwarz-Bart; Tirolien; Zobel.

Indian Ocean

Economy and politics

Comoros; economy; Madagascar; Mauritius; Mayotte; Reunion; Seychelles.

Geography, history, people and society

Comoros; daily life; Madagascar; Mauritius; Mayotte; Reunion; Seychelles.

Language, culture, religion

Creoles/*créolité*; education; language policy; literature; media; music; popular culture; religion; theatre.

Albany; Aubry; Azéma; Cabon; Chazal; Cheynet; Devi; Gamaleya; Gauvin; Humbert; Marimoutou; Masson; Maunick; Rabéarivelo; Rabémananjara; Rakotosen; Sam-Long; Souza; Vaxelaire; Virahsawmy.

Pacific Ocean

Economy and politics

CFP; economy; FCFP; FLNKS; Mururoa; New Caledonia; nuclear testing; Pacific Islands Forum; Polynesia; *Rainbow Warrior*; RPCR; Tahiti; Vanuatu; VP; Wallis & Futuna.

Carlot; Flosse; Lafleur; Lini; Machoro; Néaoutyine; Pouvanaa a Oopa; Stephens; Temaru; Tjibaou.

Geography, history, people and society

Caldoche; *Kanak*; New Caledonia; daily life; Polynesia; Tahiti; Vanuatu; Wallis & Futuna.

Language, culture, religion

Art and culture; daily life.

Gorodé; Hiro; Mariotti.

Asia

Economy and politics

Boat people; Cambodia; Khmer Rouge; Laos; Vietnam.

Bao Dai; Diem; Ieng Sary; Khieu Samphan; Pham Van Dong; Pol Pot; Sihanouk.

Geography, history, people and society

Cambodia; Chandernagore; Dien Bien Phu; Geneva Agreement; Indochina War; Laos; Pathet Lao; Pondicherry; Viet Cong; Viet Minh; Vietnam.

Ho Chi Minh; Giap.

Notes on contributors

Kay Adamson is a political sociologist working at the University of Sunderland. Her specialist area is France and Algeria and the links between colony and metropole. She has published *Algeria: A Study in Competing Ideologies* (London: Cassell, 1998) and *Political and Economic Thought and Practice in Nineteenth-Century France and the Colonization of Algeria* (Lewiston, NY: Edwin Mellen Press, 2002).

Robert Aldrich, who teaches at the University of Sydney, Australia, is the author of *The French Presence in the South Pacific, 1842–1940* (London: Macmillan, 1989); *France and the South Pacific since 1940* (Macmillan, 1993); and *Greater France: A History of French Overseas Expansion* (Macmillan, 1994). He is co-author, with John Connell, of *France's Overseas Frontier: Départements et Territoires d'Outre-Mer* (Cambridge: Cambridge University Press, 1992) and *The Last Colonies* (Cambridge University Press, 1998).

Mahfoud Amara is a doctoral student in the Institute of Sport and Leisure Policy at Loughborough University. He is researching on global culture and local identity, with a case study of the Algerian government's project for professional sport. Research interests also include the relation between sport, nationalism and nation-state building, sport in colonial/postcolonial history and modern/postmodern discourse, and Olympism.

François-Emmanuël Boucher recently completed a PhD in French Literature at McGill University on 'The Religions of Temporal Salvation in France (1750–1848)'. He is a Professor at the Royal Military College of Canada. He has publications in the journal *Religiosité* (2001, 23), *Social Discourse* (forthcoming) and a collective work (Louvain: Peeters, forthcoming). Memberships include Collège de Sociocritique de Montréal; Conseil International d'Etudes Francophones.

Tony Chafer is Principal Lecturer in French and African Studies at the University of Portsmouth (UK). He has written widely on Franco-African relations in the colonial and postcolonial period and is the author of *The End of Empire in French West Africa. France's Successful Decolonization?* (Oxford/New York: Berg, 2002).

Beïda Chikhi is Professor of Francophone Literature at the Université Marc Bloch, Strasbourg. Her research encompasses various aspects of Francophone studies. Her books include *Problématique de l'écriture dans l'oeuvre de Mohammed Dib* (Algiers: OPU, 1989), *Les Romans d'Assia Djebar* (OPU, 1989), *Maghreb en textes* (Paris: L'Harmattan, 1996), *Littérature algérienne: désir d'histoire et d'esthétique* (L'Harmattan, 1997), *Les Filières de la fantaisie dans la littérature algérienne* (Strasbourg: Presses Universitaires de Strasbourg, forthcoming).

Patrick Corcoran studied French at King's College, London, and the Ecole Normale Supérieure, Paris. He is currently Principal Lecturer in French at the University of Surrey Roehampton and President of ASCALF (Association for the Study of Caribbean and African Literature in French). He has published widely on Francophone African literature, notably on Ferdinand Oyono, Ahmadou Kourouma and Henri Lopes.

Gordon Cumming began his career in the Africa Research Department of the Foreign and Commonwealth Office. He is now a Lecturer in French at Cardiff University. He has published widely on French and British foreign and development policies. He is the author of *Aid to Africa: French and British Policies from the Cold War to the New Millennium* (Aldershot: Ashgate, 2001).

Abdelkader Djeflat, Algerian scholar and researcher, holds a PhD from the University of Bath. Full Professor at the University of Oran (Algeria) for several years, he is currently at the University of Lille I in France working on the issues of science and technology for development. He is Chairman of the MAGHTECH (Maghreb Technology) network, which he founded in 1994.

Marianne Durand graduated from Portsmouth University in 1998 with a First Class Honours degree in French Studies. She is currently pursuing a European doctorate on Algerian nationalist violence during the Sétif revolt, 8 May 1945, from the University of Glamorgan, UK. She is the postgraduate representative of the Association for the Study of Modern and Contemporary France.

Moha Ennaji, Professor of Language and Linguistics at Sidi Mohamed Ben Abdellah University (Fez, Morocco), is author of *Contrastive Syntax* (Würzburg: Königshausen & Neumann, 1985), co-author of *Introduction to Modern Linguistics* (Casablanca: Afrique-Orient, 1992) and *Applications of Modern Linguistics* (Afrique-Orient, 1994), and editor of thematic issues on 'Maghreb sociolinguistics' (1991), 'Moroccan sociolinguistics' (1995), and 'Berber sociolinguistics' (1997) for *International Journal of the Sociology of Language*. He is Director of the international journal *Languages and Linguistics*.

Charles Forsdick is James Barrow Professor of French at the University of Liverpool. His research interests include exoticism, colonial literature, travel writing and the Francophone dimensions of postcolonial theory. Recent publications include *Victor Segalen and the Aesthetics of Diversity* (Oxford: Oxford University Press, 2000) and *Travel and Exile: Postcolonial Perspectives* (Liverpool: ASCALF, 2001). He is currently co-editing a forthcoming volume on Francophone Postcolonial Studies for Arnold.

Susan Fox is engaged in PhD research into Francophone Jewish literature of the Maghreb at Lancaster University. She is also interested in the Francophone Arabic and Berber cultures of the Maghreb. She has worked in Burkina Faso and Israel, and travelled extensively throughout the Maghreb.

Mary Gallagher teaches at University College Dublin and works principally on Caribbean Literature in French. She is the author of *La Créolité de Saint-John Perse* (Paris: Gallimard, 1998) and of *Soundings in French Caribbean Writing 1950–2000: The Shock of Space and Time* (Oxford: Oxford University Press, forthcoming). She is currently editing *Ici-Là: Place and Displacement in Caribbean Writing in French* (Amsterdam/New York: Rodopi, forthcoming).

Denise Ganderton lectured in French at the University of North London from 1967 until her retirement in 1995. She became secretary of ASCALF in 1994. She has written entries for the *Bloomsbury Guide to Women's Literature* (London: Bloomsbury, 1992) and has been an occasional contributor to the *ASCALF Bulletin*. She belongs to the British Translators Association.

Sharif Gemie is a Reader in History at the University of Glamorgan. He has published *Women and Schooling: Gender, Authority and Identity in the Female Schooling Sector, France, 1815–1914* (Keele: Keele University Press, 1995); *French Revolutions, 1815–1914: An Introduction* (Edinburgh: Edinburgh University Press, 1999); plus more than thirty articles on topics including anarchism, orientalism and literature. He is currently studying Breton identity.

Marie-Annick Gournet is Senior Lecturer in Languages and European Studies at the University of the West of England (Bristol). Born in Guadeloupe, brought up in France, she has lived in the UK since 1989. She is completing a thesis on *Identity and Choice of Language in Poetry of the Caribbean*. Marie-Annick has published reviews of books written in French, English and Creole and contributed to programmes on Caribbean identity for RFI, BBC Radio 3, RFO, and TV Guadeloupe.

Geoff Hare is a Senior Lecturer in French at Newcastle University. He has published extensively on French radio and television. More recently he has written on French sport in society (particularly French football and the World Cup) and on the impact of television on sport. He is a Vice-President of the British Federation of Alliance Française.

Alec G. Hargreaves is Director of the Winthrop-King Institute for Contemporary French and Francophone Studies at Florida State University. His publications include *Voices from the North African Immigrant Community in France: Immigration and Identity in Beur Fiction* (Oxford/New York: Berg, 1991; 2nd edition, 1997) and *Postcolonial Cultures in France* (London/New York: Routledge, 1997), co-edited with Mark McKinney.

Peter Hawkins teaches French at the University of Bristol, specialising in Francophone postcolonial cultures of Africa, the Caribbean and the Indian Ocean: he is currently preparing a book on the latter. He has taught at the University of Benin, Nigeria (1997–9) and the Université de la Réunion (1994–7). He was President of ASCALF – Association for the Study of Caribbean and African Literature in French – in 1989–94 and 1997–2000.

Susanne Heiler teaches Romance literatures at the Universities of Heidelberg and Münster. Publications include her PhD on the Moroccan novel, *Der marokkanische Roman französischer Sprache* (Berlin: Neue Romania 1990) and numerous articles on Maghrebian literature. She is currently preparing a history of the Maghrebian novel. Her doctoral thesis (Heidelberg, 1998) concerns the reception of the Spanish picaresque novel in Italy.

Marie-Anne Hintze (L. ès Lettres, DES, Lille) was formerly a Fellow in French at the University of York and is now a Senior Lecturer in French at the University of Leeds. Her research interests lie in the field of historical linguistics, sociolinguistics and phonetics. Her publications include *The French Language Today* (London/New York: Routledge, 2001).

Nicki Hitchcott is Senior Lecturer in French at the University of Nottingham. Her recent publications include *Women Writers in Francophone Africa* (Oxford/New York: Berg, 2000), *Francophone Literatures: A Literary and Linguistic Companion* (with Offord *et al.*, London/New York: Routledge, 2001), and *Gender and Francophone Writing* (*Nottingham French Studies*, 40:1, 2001). She is currently preparing a book on Calixthe Beyala.

Jim House lectures in French at the University of Leeds. He has published on the history of antiracism and racism in France, and on French colonial and postcolonial representations of Algerians. He is currently working with Neil MacMaster (University of East Anglia, Norwich) on a study of the 17 October 1961 massacre of Algerians in Paris (Oxford: Oxford University Press, forthcoming).

Laïla Ibnlfassi is Senior Lecturer in French at London Guildhall University. She has published extensively on Francophone Maghrebian writers. She is co-author (with M. Offord, N. Hitchcott, S. Haigh and R. Chapman) of *Francophone Literatures* (London/New York: Routledge, 2001) and co-editor (with N. Hitchcott) of *African Francophone Writing* (Oxford/New York: Berg, 1996).

Debra Kelly is Senior Lecturer in French, Director of the Group for War and Culture Studies, University of Westminster; Associate Fellow, Institute of Romance Studies, London University. She is the author of *Pierre Albert-Birot* (Madison, NJ: Fairleigh Dickinson University Press/London: Associated University Press, 1997), co-editor of *France at War in the Twentieth Century* (Oxford/New York: Berghahn, 2000), and editor of *Remembering and Representing the Experience of War in Twentieth-Century France* (Lampeter/Lewiston, NY: Edwin Mellen Press, 2000). She has published on North African writing in French and is currently working on a book on autobiographical discourses by Maghrebian writers (Liverpool University Press, forthcoming).

Naaman Kessous is a Lecturer in French Studies at the University of Lancaster. He has published on colonial and postcolonial studies, Frantz Fanon and African-Americans, and French politics. He is author of *Two French Precursors of Marxism: Rousseau and Fourier* (Aldershot: Avebury Press, 1996) and he is currently working on the *Historical and Biographical Dictionary of the Algerian War*.

Raymond Lalonde received a degree in Political Science at Laurentian University in Sudbury, Ontario. He has lived in many of the Canadian provinces as well as abroad. He is a father, a teacher, a social activist and a chef, and is currently learning Catalan in the south of France.

Peter Langford has taught continental philosophy and social theory at the Institute of Philosophy, Wroclaw University, Poland, and English at the Centre de Télé-Enseignement Universitaire (Nancy II), France. He is currently working on a study of the 1994 genocide in Rwanda which focuses upon the role and character of the Rwandan postcolonial state.

Rachael Langford is Lecturer in French at Cardiff University. She researches and teaches on nineteenth-century French literature and culture, and Francophone African litera-ture, film and culture. She has published widely on both of these specialisms. Within Francophone Studies, she is particularly interested in the relationship between French colonial ideology and the aesthetics of Francophone African film and literature.

Béatrice Le Bihan is a tutor at the Open University and works in industry delivering training and consultancy in French using the latest technology. Her interests and publi-cations are in the field of French and English sociolinguistics.

Cathie Lloyd is Senior Research Officer at the International Development Centre, University of Oxford. Her work focuses on antiracist and democratic movements in Europe and North Africa. Recent publications include *Discourses of Antiracism in France* (Aldershot: Ashgate, 1998); 'Organising Across Borders: Algerian women's associations in a period of conflict', *Review of African Political Economy*, 26: 82 (1999); 'The Global and the Local: the cultural interfaces of self-determination movements', co-edited with S. Dudley and F. Stewart, *Oxford Development Studies* (June 2002).

Ian Lockerbie is Emeritus Professor of French, University of Stirling. He is the author of articles on Quebec cinema, theatre and literature, and the editor of a volume on theatre and cinema in Quebec and Scotland. He is the first recipient of the Prix du Québec in the UK for research on Quebec themes.

Margaret Majumdar is Honorary Secretary of the Association for the Study of Modern and Contemporary France. She has published widely on Francophone colonial/post-colonial theory and discourse, Algerian national identity, Leïla Sebbar, Azouz Begag, Mohammed Dib, Aimé Césaire and other Caribbean writers. Books include *Althusser and the End of Leninism?* (London/East Haven, CN: Pluto, 1995), and *Algeria into the*

New Millennium: Transitions and Challenges, co-edited with Mohammed Saad (Exeter: Intellect, forthcoming).

Bill Marshall is Professor of Modern French Studies at the University of Glasgow. His most recent book is entitled *Quebec National Cinema* (Montreal: McGill-Queen's University Press, 2001).

Simon Massey is a member of the African Studies Centre at Coventry University. His main research area is the theoretical and moral bases for peacekeeping operations in Sub-Saharan Africa. He has published articles on this subject as well as on the politics of Chad and Guinea-Bissau.

Maeve McCusker lectures in French Studies in Queen's University, Belfast. She wrote her doctorate on the work of Patrick Chamoiseau, and specialises in the Caribbean novel in French. She has published articles examining issues of space and history in the Caribbean, and is a member of the editorial committee for the *ASCALF Bulletin*.

Mark McKinney is Associate Professor of French at Miami University, Ohio. He co-edited, with Alec G. Hargreaves, *Postcolonial Cultures in France* (London/New York: Routledge, 1997). He has contributed to *Immigrant Narratives in Contemporary France*, *Feminist Encyclopedia of French Literature*, *Encyclopedia of Contemporary French Culture*, *Women, Immigration and Identities in France*, *Modern and Contemporary France*, *Sites*, and *Minorités ethniques anglophones et francophones*.

Daniela Merolla works at Leiden University and is a researcher with the Netherlands Organisation for Scientific Research. She specialises in the construction of group identities through imaginative productions, particularly those of Berber minorities in North Africa and Europe, involving orality, literacy and new media. Her publications include *Gender and Community in the Kabyle Literary Space: Cultural Strategies in the Oral and in the Written* (Leiden: CNWS University Publications, 1996).

Roshni Mooneram was born in Mauritius. She completed her PhD at Leeds University in 2001, with her thesis 'Creative Writing in Mauritian Creole: The emergence of a literary language and its contribution to standardisation'. She has published on theatre in Creole in Mauritius and in Reunion and intends further research on language and development in the context of linguistic globalisation.

David Murphy is Lecturer in French at the University of Stirling. He is the author of *Sembene: Imagining Alternatives in Film and Fiction* (Oxford: James Currey, 2000), and has published numerous articles on African literature and cinema. He is currently preparing a major study on culture and national identity in Senegal.

Samantha Neath is a doctoral student at the University of Westminster, conducting research on the Muslim diaspora in Britain and France. She teaches at the Paris Institut Supérieur d'Interprétation et de Traduction and has published 'La musique

Raï: 100 per cent Arabica?' in the *Bulletin of Francophone Africa* (2000), and co-edited with M. Bray and A. Cook, *Rwanda: Perspectives* (London: Marylebone Publications, 1997).

Christine O'Dowd-Smyth lectures in French and Francophone Studies at Waterford Institute of Technology, Waterford, Republic of Ireland. She is currently writing up a doctoral thesis on North African Francophone literature. She is the editor of the WIT Francophone Literatures Conference Proceedings: *Littératures francophones: la problématique de l'altérité* (Waterford: WIT School of Humanities Publications, 2001).

Yvette Rocheron is currently a Lecturer in French at the University of Leicester. She has held teaching posts in secondary and higher education in France and Britain. As a sociologist, she has published on a wide range of issues: sexism in British schools, the mass media and AIDS, health and ethnicity in Britain. Other publications cover French television culture, immigration, mixed families and multiculturalism.

Fatima Sadiqi is Senior Professor of Linguistics and Gender Studies at the University of Fes, Morocco. She has written extensively on Berber, linguistics, and gender: *Studies in Berber Syntax* (Würzburg: Königshausen & Neumann, 1986), *Grammaire du Berbère* (Paris: L'Harmattan, 1997), *Introduction to Modern Linguistics* (with Moha Ennaji, Casablanca: Afrique-Orient, 1992) and *Applications of Modern Linguistics* (with Moha Ennaji, Afrique-Orient, 1994). Her latest book is *Women, Gender and Language in Morocco* (Leiden: Brill, forthcoming).

Kamal Salhi is Director of the Centre for Francophone Studies at the University of Leeds and editor of the *International Journal of Francophone Studies*. His interests include African cultural/language policies. He has written a number of articles and is the author of *The Politics and Aesthetics of Kateb Yacine* (Lampeter/Lewiston, NY: Edwin Mellen Press, 1999); and the editor of *African Theatre for Development* (Exeter: Intellect, 1997), *Francophone Voices* (Exeter: Elm Bank, 1999), *Francophone Studies: Discourse and Identity* (Exeter: Elm Bank, 2000).

Zahia Smail Salhi lectures in Arabic and Middle Eastern Studies at the University of Leeds. Her research interests include Maghrebian literature and gender issues in the Arab world. She is reviews editor for the *British Journal of Middle Eastern Studies* and a member of the editorial board of the *International Journal of Francophone Studies*. She has published a number of articles and a book, *Politics, Poetics and the Novel* (Lampeter/Lewiston, NY: Edwin Mellen Press, 1999).

John Kristian Sanaker is Professor of French Literature at the University of Bergen. He is a specialist in the areas of Quebec film and literature. His publications include books on Marivaux and the cinema, as well as articles on Anne Hébert, Jacques Poulin, Denys Arcand and Quebec cinema (the theme of identity and the importance of the spoken word).

Notes on Contributors

Max Silverman is Professor of Modern French Studies at the University of Leeds. He is a specialist in the areas of immigration, race, nation and citizenship; the city; cultural theory and debates; colonial and postcolonial theory and cultures. His most recent monograph is *Facing Postmodernity: Contemporary French Thought on Culture and Society* (London/New York: Routledge, 1999). At present he is editing a new collection of essays on Frantz Fanon's *Peau noire, masques blancs* (Manchester: Manchester University Press).

Ingse Skattum is Associate Professor of Francophone Studies at the Department of Classical and Romance Studies, University of Oslo. Her doctoral thesis (University of Oslo, 1991) was: *De Bakoroba Koné à Camara Laye. La répétition comme trait d'oralité dans la littérature mandingue traditionnelle et moderne.* She was the guest editor of 'L'école et les langues nationales au Mali', *Nordic Journal of African Studies*, 9:3, 2000.

Andy Stafford is Lecturer in French Studies at the University of Lancaster, specialising in the intersections between literature, politics and cultural/critical theory. He has published on Barthes (Edinburgh: Edinburgh University Press, 1998), Morin, Ousmane, Césaire and Glissant. He is a member of the editorial board of ASCALF, and is currently working on the French Black Atlantic, and on the relationship between photography and the essay.

Keith Sutton is Senior Lecturer in the Department of Geography, University of Manchester. He has conducted extensive research and published numerous articles and chapters on economic development and rural settlement in Algeria. More recently he has focused on electoral geography and environmental degradation in Algeria and on urban planning and urban heritage conservation in Cairo.

Antony Walsh read his BA French and Philosophy at the University of Exeter and MA in Contemporary French Studies at the British Institute, Paris, whilst teaching at l'Université de Versailles-St Quentin-en-Yvelines. He gained his PhD from the University of Leeds with a dissertation on *Egalité, complémentarité et solidarité: The politics of Francophonie and development aid to culture in Francophone Africa.* His research interests include the political structures of the Francophone movement; the evolution of French development aid institutions to Sub-Saharan Africa.

Salah Zaimeche is Honorary Research Fellow in the Department of Geography, University of Manchester. He originally trained as a historian and then taught at the University of Constantine. His recent research has focused on environmental degradation in North Africa and on heritage conservation in the Islamic World.

Acknowledgements

This glossary would not have been possible without the contributions from all those who have collaborated in this publication. My sincere thanks go to all the contributors who have given their expertise, energy and time to the difficult task of producing concise and clear entries within the constraints of the volume. Their efforts have certainly provided me with a more complete picture of this wide-ranging and diverse field. I would also like to thank Eva Martinez of Arnold, for her patience and support, as well as Elena Seymenliyska, who initiated the project. There are others whose names do not appear elsewhere who have none the less made a contribution and provided support. They include many scholars and researchers in the field of Francophone Studies, who have shared their insights with me over the years and also provided the opportunity for dialogue and support. I would also like to thank Jonathan Forbes for his help; Babuni and Mike, for allowing me to take over their computer for much of last summer; the OMs, for providing me with a roof and a desk for some of the time I was involved with this volume; and, last but not least, Anne, Aurindam and Kalyan for their forbearance, understanding and critical awareness.

Margaret Majumdar
London, 2002

Aba, Noureddine   Born Setif, 1922; died 1996. Algerian writer. He began his career as a journalist, including coverage of the Nuremberg trials. His political commitments included the Algerian nationalist cause (NATIONHOOD/NATIONALISM), that of the Palestinians and of the BERBERS. He taught and lectured in the USA, Canada and elsewhere. His work covered different genres, including essays, poetry (*La Toussaint des énigmes*, 1963, *Montjoie Palestine*, 1968), plays (*La Récréation des clowns*, 1980, *Le Dernier Jour d'un nazi*, 1986, *L'Aube à Jérusalem*, 1979, *Gazelle après minuit*, 1979, *Tell El Zaatar s'est tu à la tombée du soir*, 1976, *L'Annonce faite à Marco*, 1981). Prizes include Afrique Méditerranée 1979, Amitié Franco-Arabe 1981, Charles Oulmont (Fondation de France) 1985. In 1990, he created the Noureddine Aba Foundation to honour Algerian intellectuals for their contribution to Algerian culture, which has awarded prizes to, among others, Tahar DJAOUT (1992), and the Association of Algerian Journalists (1993).

Abbas, Ferhat   Born Taher, ALGERIA, 1899; died Algiers, 1985. He is known as one of the first 'Young Algerians' to graduate from Algiers University. Although he was a doctor of pharmacy, he is more famous as a political leader, whose political demands shifted from his plea for ASSIMILATION to the ending of colonisation, the rejection of 'assimilation' as a lie and demands for Algeria's political autonomy. This shift caused him to be arrested and indicted for jeopardising French sovereignty. In 1955 he joined the FLN. In 1958, he wrote *La Nuit coloniale* in Rabat (MOROCCO). In 1962, he was elected President of the Algerian National Assembly. He retired from politics in 1963. (Zahia Smail Salhi)

Further reading

Abbas (1931), (1962).

Abdel Aziz, Mohammed   Leader of the POLISARIO and head of state of the disputed Democratic Republic of Sahara (WESTERN SAHARA).

Abdelkader   Born Mascara, 1807; died Damascus, 1883. Algerian military leader, man of letters and theologian. The Emir Abdelkader led Algerian resistance against the French invasion of 1832, until his surrender to the Duc d'Aumale, in 1847. He was famous not only as a military leader whose exploits became legendary, but also for his intellectual and spiritual prowess. He was placed under house arrest for three years in the château d'Amboise. After his release by Napoleon III in 1852, he went to live in Bursa, Turkey, before going to Damascus, where he died in 1883. While in Damascus, he saved the life of many Christians during religious riots in 1860, offering them shelter in his house. He was himself a disciple of the *soufi* doctrine, and was buried near Ibn Arabi, whom he considered his spiritual father. In 1967, President

BOUMEDIENNE had his ashes brought back to ALGERIA and a ceremony was held in his honour. The 'Fondation Emir Abdelkader' came into being shortly afterwards, with the mission of disseminating knowledge of Abdelkader and his heritage. Considered the founder of the first Algerian state, he figures in Algerian literature as one of the emblematic heroes of the nationalist movement, alongside such figures as JUGURTA and KAHINA. (**Beïda Chikhi**)

Abdesselam, Belaïd   Born 1928. Algerian politician. Architect of the 'industrialising industry' policy under BOUMEDIENNE. He was Prime Minister in 1992–93.

Acadia   Territory in eastern Canada settled by French colonists from the sixteenth century. Called *Nova Scotia* from 1713, when France lost the colony to England by the Treaty of Utrecht. In 1755, the 10,000 French-Acadians were deported (e.g. to LOUISIANA), but this ethnic cleansing failed, as many returned. Their descendants, the Acadians of today, represent a small minority of the populations of Prince Edward Island and Nova Scotia, and about 30 per cent of NEW BRUNSWICK. They look upon themselves as a people, with their own flag (the French tricolour with a yellow star) and national holiday (15 August). (**John Kristian Sanaker**)

Further reading

Maillet *et al.* (1984) – contributions by leading representatives of Acadian culture.

ACCT   See *AGENCE INTERGOUVERNEMENTALE DE LA FRANCOPHONIE*.

ADELF *Association des Ecrivains de Langue Française* (Association of Francophone Writers). Created in 1926, ADELF aims to promote the expansion and knowledge of Francophone literature, through publications (e.g. the review *Lettres et Cultures de Langue Française*), literary prizes (e.g. Afrique méditerranéenne/ Maghreb, Afrique noire, France–Québec etc.), conferences and other activities. The current president is Edmond Jouve.

Adiaffi, Jean-Marie   Born 1941. Ivorian novelist, poet and playwright. He is best known for his novel *La Carte d'identité* (1980; *The Identity Card*, 1983), which presents the tribulations of an African prince with the bureaucracy of a colonial state as an allegorical quest for true African identity and spiritual enlightenment. His writing in this cyclical narrative is recognisably post-modern and resolutely experimental in this and subsequent works, such as *Silence! On développe* (1990). (**Peter Hawkins**)

AEF *Afrique Equatoriale Française*   The name given in 1910 to France's colonial possessions in Equatorial Africa following the decision to decentralise colonial administration to two large government generals (the other area being the AOF – *Afrique Occidentale Française*). The AEF area was made up of GABON, Middle CONGO (now Republic of Congo), Oubangui Chari (now CENTRAL AFRICAN REPUBLIC) and CHAD. Its capital was Brazzaville (Middle Congo), which, during the Second World War, was declared capital of Free France when used as the headquarters of the Free France Forces led by General DE GAULLE. (**Antony Walsh**)

AFAL *Association Francophone d'Amitié et de Liaison* (Francophone Friendship and Collaboration Association). AFAL was formed in 1974, as an international association of non-governmental organisations, with the objective of defending and promoting FRENCH LANGUAGE and culture. See website: http://site.voila.fr/afal_france

African Union See OAU.

Afrique Equatoriale Française See AEF.

Afrique Occidentale Française See AOF.

Afropessimisme A pessimistic view of Africa today. Though achieving independence during post-war DECOLONISATION, African countries have since regressed in terms of economic self-sufficiency. Francophone Africa, largely tied to the French Franc, has seen its living standards continually fall. Monocultural economies (producing so-called 'cash-crops') and falling market prices, IMF 'restructuring' and spiralling debt, and the dramatic spread of AIDS, do not augur well. Talk of an 'African renaissance' has to be balanced with the estimate that only 5 per cent of world trade passes through Africa. Both DEMOCRACY and peace have been the casualties, as today's COTE D'IVOIRE and the DEMOCRATIC REPUBLIC OF CONGO (ex-Zaire) amply illustrate. (**Andy Stafford**)

Agence de coopération culturelle et technique See AGENCE INTERGOUVERNEMENTALE DE LA FRANCOPHONIE.

Agence de la Francophonie See AGENCE INTERGOUVERNEMENTALE DE LA FRANCOPHONIE.

Agence intergouvernementale de la Francophonie **(previously ACCT)** The *Agence de coopération culturelle et technique* (ACCT) was the first intergovernmental FRANCOPHONE INSTITUTION created after French DECOLONISATION and has played a significant role in instigating educational and cultural programmes amongst French-speaking countries and communities around the world.

Created in 1969, the ACCT's first 28 members (in majority made up of states from Sub-Saharan and North Africa together with states from South East Asia) had the common objective of intensifying cultural and technical CO-OPERATION between member states and promoting their respective cultures with French.

Although beset by Franco-Canadian rivalries throughout the 1970s and the early 1980s the organisation underwent reforms to make it more efficient whilst defining specific areas for projects associated to development. In the period from the organisation's founding to 1981, 15 new states or countries joined the Agency.

1986 was the main turning-point for the organisation when it took its place as the main operating agency for the decisions of the first FRANCOPHONE SUMMIT, held in Versailles. From 1991, the Agency would oversee the activities of the four other main agencies – TV5, AUPELF-UREF (see AUF), *UNIVERSITÉ SENGHOR* and AIMF – in implementing main summit policy decisions.

Throughout the organisation's history, the promotion of a diverse range of cultural activities has been a main concern of the ACCT and it has organised a number of music, dance and theatre festivals, of which the most significant has been the MASA (*Marché des arts du spectacle africain*, Trade Fair for African Performing Arts), established in 1993 in order to promote African musicians and dancers and assist them in gaining recording and performance contracts both in Africa and overseas. Another significant ACCT event has been the FESPACO (*Festival pan-africain de cinéma de Ouagadougou* (Ouagadougou Pan-African Film Festival), which is held in Burkina Faso and show-cases African cinematic talent every two years. (**Antony Walsh**)

Further reading

There is very little secondary literature on the ACCT/*Agence intergouvernementale de la Francophonie*. To understand how it has developed, readers will find the organisation's own history an invaluable starting point: Mworoha (1995).

Agence Universitaire de la Francophonie   See AUF.

AIMF *Association Internationale des Maires et responsables de capitales et métropoles partiellement ou entièrement Francophones*. See Francophone institutions and the association's website: http://www.aimf.asso.fr

AIPLF *Association/Assemblée Internationale des Parlementaires de Langue Française.* See APF.

Aït Ahmed, Hocine   Born Kabylia, Algeria, 1919. Algerian politician. He was one of nine nationalist leaders who planned and co-ordinated the struggle for independence against France, which began in 1954. After Algerian independence in 1962, he opposed the dictatorial rule of the Ben Bella and Boumedienne regimes, founding a new political party, the Socialist Forces Front (FFS) and organising dissident groups in Algeria and abroad. Since 1989, the FFS has been a viable democratic party under Aït Ahmed's leadership. He withdrew his candidature from the 1999 presidential elections, concluding that fraud had taken place. (**Susan Fox**)

Further reading

Aït Ahmed (1983), (1989).

Ait Mansour, Fadhma (Marguerite Amrouche)   1882–1967. Algerian writer. Mostly known for her *Histoire de ma vie* (1968; *My Life Story*, 1989), Fadhma Ait Mansour is the first Maghrebi woman to have published an autobiography. Her work is an expression of deep alienation. Being the illegitimate child of a young widow, she was persecuted by her tribe and her mother had to place her in the care of missionaries, who converted her to Catholicism. After her marriage to another convert, she had to emigrate to Tunisia, where she lived in exile, longing for the return 'home'. The couple returned in the 1950s, but after her husband's death in 1959, Fadhma Ait Mansour emigrated to France, where she died in 1967. (**Zahia Smail Salhi**)

Further reading

Ait Mansour (1968).

Albany, Jean   1917–84. Reunionese poet. Albany's first collection of poetry *Zamal* (1951) – the title refers to locally grown cannabis – uses a creolised French that marked the beginning of the CREOLE revival in REUNION, which reached its peak in the 1970s. His poetry is a light and playful celebration of the sensuous beauty of the island, rooted in a strong sense of Creole identity. (**Peter Hawkins**)

Alexis, Jacques-Stephen   Born Gonaïves, HAITI, 1922. Haitian writer and medical doctor, whose family has played a prominent role in Haiti's political and cultural history. He was involved with literary and cultural groups and magazines. Exiled for many years. In 1959 he founded the Marxist *Parti de l'Entente populaire*. In 1961 he tried to enter Haiti secretly from Cuba with other DUVALIER opponents; they were all seized and probably executed. Alexis promoted the concept of '*réalisme merveilleux*' in Haitian literature. Key texts: *Compère Général Soleil* (1955; *General Sun, My Brother*, 1999); *Les Arbres musiciens* (1957); *L'Espace d'un cillement* (1959); *Romancero aux étoiles* (1960). (**Susanne Heiler**)

Further reading

Laroche (1978); Mudimbe-Boyi (1992) – for a new perspective.

Algeria   North African country, central to the Maghreb and bordering the MEDITERRANEAN Sea, Algeria is divided into a northern Tell section and a vast southern Saharan section (see SAHARA). Coastal plains and Tell Atlas ranges give way southwards to the High Plains/Plateaux, followed by Saharan Atlas ranges and then inhospitable desert. Climate rather than relief is Algeria's major geographical factor. The Tell's Mediterranean climate is restricted to the northern fringe. Precipitation diminishes southwards and also in the western Tell, south of Oran. Forest cover of holm oak and cork oak has been greatly reduced and replaced by garrigue scrub. Esparto grass covers part of the steppes of the High Plateaux.

More than four-fifths of the population of 29.3 million (1998 census) is ethnically Arab, the other fifth being BERBER, largely Kabyles, or Chaouïa in the Aurès region, Mozabites around Ghardaia, and Tuaregs in the Saharan Hoggar region. Arabic became the official national language in 1990 following a policy of ARABISATION to replace French, the legacy of colonialism. Berbers still seek proper linguistic recognition. Both linguistic groups are Islamic, largely Sunni Muslim. The largest urban settlements – Algiers, Oran, Annaba, Constantine – are coastal or in the Tell region. Recently interior towns such as Batna, SETIF, and Saida have grown more quickly, as have Saharan oasis towns. Population growth was high in the 1970s but by the mid-1990s demographic transition was apparent. A long tradition of out-MIGRATION to France maintains the link between the two countries. While a major attempt at industrial development occurred in the 1970s and 1980s, with steel production, petrochemical products, and consumer durables, Algeria's economy remains heavily dependent on oil and gas for over 90 per cent of export earnings. Pioneering sub-

Mediterranean pipelines convey gas directly to European markets. Relatively, agriculture has stagnated so that Algeria is a food deficit country. Viticulture has markedly declined, though horticultural production has expanded significantly.

Once the westernmost province of the Ottoman Empire, Algeria was a French colony from 1830 to 1962 when independence followed a fiercely fought struggle (see ALGERIAN WAR OF INDEPENDENCE). Militarily France won but politically they were condemned worldwide. One-party FLN rule under BEN BELLA, BOUMEDIENNE and Chadli BEN DJEDID eventually gave way to multi-party local and national elections in 1990–91. The threat of an elected FIS government precipitated a military *coup*, followed by a decade of civil war, assassinations and atrocities. These included the killing of up to 100,000 Algerians, including President BOUDIAF, the writer–journalist Tahar DJAOUT, and a number of prominent singers, academics and sports personalities. (**Keith Sutton**)

Further reading

Côte (1996); Entelis and Naylor (1992).

Algerian cinema   See CINEMA, ALGERIA.

Algerian Communist Party   See PCA.

Algerian elections, 1991   Late 1980s economic liberalisation in ALGERIA encouraged political pluralism in this one-party state. From 1989 new political parties could be established and local elections in June 1990 handed municipal power in most of Algeria to the FIS (*Front Islamique du Salut*), which sent shock waves through the Maghreb. The FLN, in power since 1962, endeavoured to gerrymander the 1991 national elections with smaller rural and interior seats and through proxy voting. When the first multi-party national elections took place on 26 December 1991, following the French two-rounds voting system, 41 per cent of electors abstained, and spoilt ballot papers increased this rate to 52.8 per cent, despite 48 parties contesting the elections. With 47.3 per cent of the votes, FIS won 188 seats. The FLN's election result was disastrous – 23.4 per cent of the votes and just 16 seats in the first round. The regionally more concentrated FFS (*Front des Forces Socialistes*) won 25 seats, and Independents 3 seats. The FIS's electoral success was especially strong in the northern regions, taking over 75 per cent of those seats decided in Oran, Mascara, Chlef, Ain Defla, Medea, Jijel, Mila and Constantine. In many other WILAYATE in central and eastern Algeria, the FIS captured over 50 per cent of the seats decided in round one. Significantly, the FIS were best placed for the second round in 144 constituencies out of 198. Hence their victory seemed highly probable unless the abstentions voted overwhelmingly against the FIS in round two. However, the Algerian army stepped in, cancelled the second round of voting, due for 16 January 1992, and suspended the short-lived democratic revival.

France and the adjoining Maghreb states were concerned about the active spread of Islamic fundamentalism from an elected Islamic Algerian Government, and France feared an influx of political refugees. Would an FIS government permit any future multi-party elections, especially with the participation of socialist or secularist parties? WOMEN'S MOVEMENTS and BERBER organisations were similarly concerned. Many accusations of electoral irregularities and inefficiencies were made. The military *coup* of 11 January 1992 was bloodless and replaced President BENDJEDID with the historic FLN leader, Mohamed BOUDIAF. The FIS leaders and many of their militant followers were arrested soon after and non-democratic governments prevailed well into the 1990s, though other political parties were allowed to organise. (**Keith Sutton**)

Further reading

Kapil (1994); Sutton and Aghrout (1992).

Algerian family   See FAMILY, ALGERIA.

Algerian National Charter   Adopted in 1976 under the BOUMEDIENNE regime, the National Charter established a new Constitution for ALGERIA, in which the state was proclaimed a Socialist Republic, with ISLAM as its official religion and Arabic as its national language.

Algerian Revolution   See ALGERIAN WAR OF INDEPENDENCE.

Algerian War of Independence   As political action failed to make progress, the *Comité Révolutionnaire d'Unité et d'Action* (CRUA) started military action on 31 October 1954 in the Aurès region. The CRUA, re-named *Front de Libération Nationale* (FLN), spread guerrilla activity especially to the KABYLIA mountains and later to the cities, such as Skikda, where nearly 100 Europeans were killed in August 1955. French forces quickly built up to 500,000 troops. After the FLN's Soummam Valley congress in August–September 1956, ALGERIA was divided up into six autonomous zones (*WILAYATE*), each led by a significant guerrilla commander. More effective guerrilla activity probably occurred in the capital with the BATTLE OF ALGIERS in 1956, which resulted in harsh French searches of the CASBAH and other districts and the detainment and torture of many FLN activists. Pacification of the FLN's rural strongholds included the 1959 *Plan Challe* and the *Opération Pierres Précieuses* in Lesser Kabylia, which involved free-fire zones, scorched earth policies and massive population resettlement to controlled *centres de regroupement*. FLN armies in exile developed in MOROCCO and TUNISIA after their independence. However, a planeload of FLN leaders travelling from Morocco to Tunis was diverted by the French and BEN BELLA and others were captured. The French fortified Algeria's borders with Tunisia and Morocco, effectively blocking incursions and assistance from the FLN armies in exile. In February 1958 the French bombed the Tunisian frontier village of Sakiet Sidi Youssef, causing an international outcry.

Within Algeria a settler uprising contributed to the return of DE GAULLE to power in France, which brought about a more positive government attitude towards eventual Algerian independence and a more developmental approach to winning hearts and minds through the building of schools, hospitals, etc. under the 1958 Constantine Plan. French settler reaction culminated in uprisings led by Generals Raoul SALAN and

Maurice Challe, previously commanders-in-chief, but these soon collapsed to re-emerge as the destructive OAS terrorist uprising in early 1962. Negotiations between France and the GPRA (Provisional Government) from May 1961 until March 1962 resulted in an agreed independence in July 1962. French military losses are estimated at 27,000 killed, while Algerian casualties range from 300,000 to 500,000. Resettlement by the French army displaced upwards of 2.35 million people and from March to July 1962 over 90 per cent of the French settler population of about one million departed precipitately back to France, so ending French occupation of Algeria. (**Keith Sutton**)

Further reading

Horne (1987); Sutton (1999); Talbott (1980).

Alleg, Henri (Henri Salem)   Born London, 1921. Journalist. A European Jew, he emigrated to France, then Algeria (1939). After 1940 he lived semi-clandestinely, disguising his Anglo-Jewish origins with the pseudonym 'Alleg'. He joined underground militant Communists (1941), editing *La Jeune Algérie*, and then the PCA (Algerian Communist Party) in 1942. He became editor (1951) of the anticolonial paper *Alger Républicain*, banned in 1955. He went underground in 1956, and was arrested in 1957 and tortured for a month by French paratroopers. His book *La Question* (1958; *The Question*, 1958) was banned in France because it exposed the systematic use of torture by French forces in Algeria. (**Marianne Durand**)

Further reading

Alleg (1958) – Henri Alleg's personal account of his imprisonment, interrogation and torture at the hands of French paratroopers during the summer of 1957; Berchadsky (1994) – readable account of Henri Alleg's career, dealing with the context surrounding his arrest and torture, making clearer the impact his book had in France.

Alliance Française   Recognised by the French government as an important arm of French cultural presence overseas, the '*Alliance*' is the largest French language teaching network in the world, particularly prominent in Latin America. Founded in Paris in 1883 as a non-profit-making organisation, with its headquarters at 101 boulevard Raspail, Paris 6ᵉ, it consists, in 2001, of around 1100 centres in 138 countries, with nearly 400,000 members and students worldwide. National *fédérations* have a large measure of local autonomy, but benefit from organisational support from Paris and, often, an administrative officer (*détaché* or *coopérant*) paid for by the Foreign Ministry. (**Geoff Hare**)

Further reading

Bruézière (1983).

Allouache, Merzak   Born 1944. Algerian film-maker. His work is influenced by a radical political commitment, but is also characterised by a keen sense of humour. Amongst the first students of the Algerian National Cinema Institute, before moving on to IDHEC in Paris, Allouache came to the attention of the public with his first feature film *Omar Gatlato* (1976), a humorous, but realistic view of young people's lives in a working-class suburb of Algiers. *Les Aventures d'un héros* (1978) and *L'Homme* *qui regardait les fenêtres* (1982) followed, then *Un Amour à Paris*, made in France in 1983. Subsequently he made several documentaries in ALGERIA, which constitute a picture of a country in crisis, in which women are demanding a voice: *L'Algérie en démocratie*; *Femmes en mouvement*. *Bab El-Oued City* (1993) represents a return to the feature film, but one which is deeply rooted in the realities of Algeria's political crisis. Other films include *Salut cousin* (1996), *Alger-Beyrouth pour retour* (1998), *A Bicyclette* (1999).

Alloula, Abdelkader Born El Ghazaouet, north-west ALGERIA, 1939. Algerian actor, director and playwright. He went to primary school in Aïn El Berd, and then studied at secondary schools in Sidi-bel-Abbès and Oran. He gave up studies in 1956 and began working in the theatre, leading the company Echabab d'Oran. Until 1960 he went on many training courses and performed in numerous plays. In 1962 he staged his first play, *El Asra*, a version of Plautus's *The Captives*, and was also recruited as an actor when the TNA (Algerian National Theatre) was formed. He continued to prove himself a true man of the theatre, as administrator as well as actor, adapter, director and writer. The highly sophisticated nature of his work ensured him popularity abroad as well as in Algeria. He adapted many plays, including Gogol's *The Diary of a Madman* (as *Hom Salim*) and Goldini's *A Servant of Two Masters*, and he wrote several challenging scripts dealing with postcolonial issues: *El Khobza* (Bread), *Hammam Rabi* (The Good Lord's turkish baths), *Al-Agwal* (The statements), *Al-Ajwad* (Generous people) and *Al-Litham* (The veil). He was attacked in Oran on 10 March 1994, while on his way to a debate about drama, and died at Val-de-Grâce, Paris, three days later. (**Kamal Salhi**)

Further reading

Ouvrage collectif (1997).

ALN Armée de Libération Nationale Founded in July 1954 by the CRUA (*Comité Révolutionnaire pour l'Unité et l'Action*, which became the FLN in November 1954), the ALN was the military arm of the revolutionary movement that started the Algerian war of national liberation in November 1954 (see ALGERIAN WAR OF INDEPENDENCE). Numbering 25,000 in 1954 and poorly equipped, it applied guerrilla warfare tactics against a superior French army. The primary concern of the commanders of the six WILAYATE (military zones) was to create a field force of insurgent fighters and auxiliaries. Re-organised and legalised as a belligerent army by the Soummam Conference (20 August 1956), the ALN was forced to combine hit-and-run operations in the mountains with urban terrorism (the BATTLE OF ALGIERS). One of the major problems was the uneven supply of arms caused by the sealing of the Tunisian and Moroccan frontiers in 1958. By March 1962, the ALN numbered 40,000 troops, based in TUNISIA and MOROCCO (the *Armée des Frontières*), while its internal forces operating inside ALGERIA amounted to 20,000. After Independence, the ALN was renamed *Armée Nationale Populaire* (ANP). (**Naaman Kessous**)

Amazigh See BERBERS.

Amrouche, Jean (El Mouhouv)   Born 1906. Algerian writer. He was the son of Fadhma AIT MANSOUR, and the brother of Taos AMROUCHE. All three were pioneering writers in different ways, making their experience of cultural and political exile their main theme. Jean was the first Algerian poet to write in French. During his time in TUNISIA, he worked as a teacher and started his career as a poet, publishing *Cendres*, *Etoile secrète* and *Chants berbères de Kabylie*. He later turned to journalism, creating a literary/cultural journal, *L'Arche*, in which his outstanding essay 'L'Eternel Jugurtha' was published in 1946. This essay is an expression of his identity crisis, created by several factors which made the poet an outcast – the colonisation of ALGERIA, his parents' conversion to Christianity and his life in exile. 'L'Eternel Jugurtha' attempts to explain the Algerian soul through the character of the Berber hero JUGURTHA. Jean asserts that, despite all, he remained Algerian, an identity he casts in a frame of diversity. He died prematurely in Paris in 1962. (**Zahia Smail Salhi**)

Further reading

Marty (1998); Giono (1990); Mauriac (1981).

Amrouche, Marguerite   See AIT MANSOUR, FADHMA.

Amrouche, Marguerite Taos   Born Tunis, 1913; died St-Michel-l'Observatoire, France, 1976. Algerian novelist and singer. She was the daughter of Fadhma AIT-MANSOUR and sister of Jean AMROUCHE, in a kabyle family converted to Catholicism. She was the first Algerian woman to publish a novel in French, *Jacinthe noire* (1947). She wrote an autobiographical novel, *Rue des tambourins* (1960), and collected and translated BERBER tales, poems, songs, proverbs, *Le Grain magique* (1966). Her recordings of traditional Berber songs are an important record of the oral tradition of the Kabyle Berber people: *Florilège de chants berbères de Kabylie*; *Chants de processions, méditations et danses sacrées berbères*; *Chants de l'Atlas: Tradition millénaire des Berbères d'Algérie*. (**Debra Kelly**)

Anelka, Nicolas   Born Versailles, 1979. Footballer. He arrived at Arsenal, completely unknown, soon after Wenger took over the London club. After poor initial showings he burst with fire and power in the second half of 1998 to help Arsenal beat Manchester United, top the league and win the Cup in the same year. Anelka's career seemed destined to great heights when he was transferred to Real Madrid for over £20 million. He failed to impress there, however, and the club sold him to Paris St-Germain, who then sold him to Liverpool. Although he gained a position on the French national team, Anelka still had to fight stiff competition for that coveted place. (**Salah Zaimeche**)

Anticolonialism   The movement against French colonialism was an uninterrupted extension of resistance to the original invasions. In ALGERIA, resistance was always present beneath the surface after 1830 (Djebar, 1989). It took physical and cultural forms, through the use or refusal to use the FRENCH LANGUAGE (some intellectuals, notably KATEB YACINE, saw their excellence in the French language as a way of proving their superiority), the veiling and withdrawal of women, go-slows and other forms of sabotage. The ALGERIAN WAR OF INDEPENDENCE (1954–62) was marked by extreme violence, torture and divisions (Alleg, 1958). Although born in MARTINIQUE, Frantz FANON is associated with Algeria's struggle for independence. His analysis of the conflict (Fanon, 2001) and more general critique of colonialism influenced the wider international, anticolonial and other emancipatory movements (Fanon, 1975; 1991).

Similarly, in VIETNAM, anti-French resistance was uninterrupted from the occupation in the mid-nineteenth century, taking different political forms, e.g. a Vietnamese offshoot of the Kuomintang, then the 1930s Nghe Tinh soviets, which led to the first declaration of independence by a colony, in 1945. Crucially, the national movement drew on the resources of the international Communist movement, with material support from the USSR and China, but also gained solidarity from the left in France and even within the French expeditionary forces. Later, during the USA's neo-colonial intervention, this international solidarity movement also drew powerfully on the New Left, civil rights movement, and 'third world' activists in the USA. Showing the primacy of the political over the military, the 'Tet' uprising was a military failure, narrowly viewed, but in fact heralded the political defeat of the USA.

MIGRATION provided an important external base for the anticolonial movement, enabling leaders such as HO CHI MINH to exchange ideas with intellectuals from the French Caribbean, and North and West Africa. Students from the colonies formed important relationships, too, within the French intelligentsia and artistic milieu. This alliance organised opposition to the Colonial Exhibition of 1931 and supported PAN-AFRICANISM and *NÉGRITUDE*, inspired by Léopold SENGHOR and Aimé CÉSAIRE. This developed international dimensions, connected to the Harlem Resistance in the USA and other struggles against racial oppression (Dewitte, 1985). (**Cathie Lloyd**)

Further reading

Alleg (1958); Dewitte (1985); Djebar (1989); Fanon (1975), (1991), (2001); Macey (2001).

Antillanité Derived from Antilles ('*ante illum*', or 'before the continent'), *antillanité* is the geo-political vision of Caribbean CULTURAL IDENTITY proposed by Edouard GLISSANT, principally in the essays of *Le Discours antillais* (1981). The suffix -*ité* suggests an essentialism that Glissant would now disavow in favour of a poetics of relation, Creolisation, and global circulation (*tout-monde* or *chaos-monde*). *Antillanité* signals an effort to re-localise Caribbean identity in the Americas, after ASSIMILATION and *NÉGRITUDE* had alienated it from its own space. Resonating with the aims of independence and pan-Caribbean federation, it reverberates also in the writing of Simone SCHWARZ-BART, Daniel MAXIMIN, and in the *CRÉOLITÉ* movement. (**Mary Gallagher**)

Antilles-Guyane The name of the French Caribbean territories: GUADELOUPE, GUIANA and MARTINIQUE.

Antiracism Contemporary antiracism often synthesises a number of initially distinct political traditions: opposition to anti-semitism (a key element of republican antiracism) developed in France during the Dreyfus Affair of the 1890s, and resurfaced during antifascism (1930s). However, opposition to colonial RACISMS often drew on the existing counter-cultures of resistance to colonial governance (e.g. NÉGRITUDE, pro-independence nationalisms, see NATIONHOOD NATIONALISM) (House, 2002). French republican antiracist groups (e.g. the MRAP – *Mouvement contre le Racisme et pour l'Amitié entre les Peuples*) began to oppose colonial racism due to the growing anti-Algerian racism of the 1950s. Today, these organisations co-exist alongside the newer antiracist associations and movements that have emerged since the late 1970s, as postcolonial migrants and their descendants have mobilised against racial violence, discrimination, immigration policies and racial stereotyping (see MARCHE POUR L'ÉGALITÉ ET CONTRE LE RACISME, BEURS, SANS-PAPIERS, SOS-RACISME).

In the 1990s, antiracism became subject to major theoretical debate, following Taguieff's argument that antiracism is simply the opposite or 'double' of racism: for example, where racism posits immutable ('racial' or 'cultural') 'DIFFERENCES' between groups, antiracism would respond with a 'UNIVERSALIST' discourse, stressing all that humans have in common. This remains the principal form of antiracism in metropolitan France. Where racism on the other hand demands ASSIMILATION to the dominant group, antiracism will highlight the 'right to difference' of minority groups (Taguieff, 1987). Antiracist groups have re-thought their strategies accordingly, notably since racist groups have recuperated the 'right to difference' discourse to 'defend' a supposedly threatened 'French' identity. Indeed, the role of identity politics within antiracism in France remains a key and contentious issue. However, racism and antiracism seldom occupy binary 'universalist' or 'differentialist' positions in practice. Furthermore, antiracism as a social movement conveys demands for social justice, political agency, greater CITIZENSHIP and a recognition of cultural DIVERSITY going beyond any narrowly defined opposition to racism (Lloyd, 1998). (**Jim House**)

Further reading

Lloyd (1998) – an accessible historical overview of French antiracism since 1945 from both empirical and theoretical perspectives; Bonnet (2000) – usefully discusses antiracism as theory and practice, with several sections specifically on the French context.

AOF *Afrique Occidentale Française* was the term employed to refer to France's government general of her Western African territories from 1895. The area was made up of nine states: SENEGAL, MAURITANIA, Soudan (today MALI), UPPER VOLTA (today BURKINA FASO), French GUINEA, NIGER, IVORY COAST and Dahomey (now BÉNIN). Its capital was in Dakar (Senegal). (**Antony Walsh**)

APF *Assemblée Parlementaire de la Francophonie* Previously known as AIPLF – *Association Internationale des Parlementaires de Langue Française*, it was founded in 1967, and renamed in 1989 as *Assemblée Internationale des Parlementaires de Langue Française*, following the Dakar Summit, thus affirming its vocation to be the interparliamentary organ of the Francophone countries. Recognised at the Mauritius Summit of 1993 as FRANCOPHONIE'S consultative assembly, it adopted the name *Assemblée Parlementaire de la Francophonie*, APF, in 1998. A forum for the promotion of DEMOCRACY, human and political rights, it is part of the institutional life of

Francophonie. Presents motions and recommendations to the CMF and CPF. (Béatrice Le Bihan)

Further reading

See website: http://www.*francophonie*.org/apf

Aquin, Hubert 1929–72. QUEBEC novelist, film-maker and essayist, who in the 1960s was a leading political activist in the cause of Quebec independence. Despairing of the success of this cause, he committed suicide in 1972. Among his four novels, the best known is *Prochain Episode* (1965), a political allegory which takes the form of a poetic, highly charged espionage narrative. Among his critical and political writings, the essay on 'La fatigue culturelle du Canada Français' (included in *Blocs Erratiques*, 1977) is important. A critical edition of his complete works is in course of publication. (Ian Lockerbie)

Arab Maghreb Union See UMA.

Arabian Nights Known in Arabic as *The Book of the Thousand and One Nights*, this is a collection of stories told by a female narrator, SHERAZADE, to entertain King Shahrayar, and save herself and her like from being beheaded. The king has sworn an oath to have a virgin brought to him every night, only to behead her the next morning, but he is so diverted by Sherazade's tales that he breaks his custom, and indeed, Sherazade manages to wean the king from his habit altogether.

The tales belong to a late decadent period, and mainly due to their style they were not very popular in their time (ninth to twelfth centuries). As to the origins of this collection, critics agree that they contain Indian, Persian and Arabic stories. Their frame-tale was transmitted by the Indians to the Persians, who transmitted it to the Arabs under the title *Hazar Afsaneh* meaning 'A Thousand Tales'. The Arabs' additions to the tales belong to two periods and settings, the first additions were set in Baghdad around Haroun al-Rasheed's castle, and are known to be well constructed and usually short and simple stories; the second additions are the Egyptian picaresque stories, known for their clumsy construction and semi-colloquial Arabic.

The themes displayed in the *Arabian Nights* are varied. The book contains fairy tales, courtly love tales, animal fables, moral and historical anecdotes, religious tales, scholastic discussions, strange voyages and adventures, romances of epic nature and picaresque tales.

Although neglected in their time, the *Arabian Nights* have gained much popularity in modern times. Their fame in Europe was due to the work of the French Antoine Galland who presented a twelve-volume book to the French readers between 1704 and 1717. This translation was reprinted several times and translated into the main Western European languages. An anonymous English translation appeared in 1707 and several revisions of it were carried out between 1785 and 1811. (Zahia Smail Salhi)

Further reading

Erwin (1994); Hovannisian and Sabagh (1997).

Arabisation   Arabisation has two major aims: the modernisation/standardisation of Arabic vocabulary and structure (corpus Arabisation) – hundreds of new terms have been coined/ borrowed, and adapted to Arabic paradigms; secondly, the introduction of Arabic in all walks of life, with the goal of supplanting French by Standard Arabic (Arabisation as policy). Corpus Arabisation has been relatively successful. The domains in which Standard Arabic is employed have hugely increased since the 1960s. It is now in competition with French in education and administration, and used for science teaching in schools all over North Africa. Arabisation as policy has, however, been confronted with difficulties, mainly because French still predominates in higher education, government and the private sector. It is none the less favoured by many people, for Standard Arabic is associated with the national CULTURAL IDENTITY and used as a sign of sociocultural independence. Language-planners have also adopted Standard Arabic–French bilingualism, as a means of immersing in modern culture, thought, science and technology. Although contested by Arabic purists for ideological reasons, this bilingualism is valued by most of the modern intelligentsia as a necessary tool for socioeconomic progress. It also serves the purpose of Arabisation, since this language contact is beneficial for the modernisation of Standard Arabic, which borrows massively from French.

There are two major attitudes toward Arabisation: that of the *Arabisants* (traditionally Arabic-educated intellectuals and politicians) and that of the *Francisants* (French-educated ÉLITE). *Arabisants* are generally Arabic or Islamic Studies teachers, lawyers or administrators. They advocate total Arabisation and the exclusion of French from all active sectors. This type of discourse goes back to the anticolonial struggle, when Arabic was used as a crucial weapon, along with Islam, to rally the masses. Muslim fundamentalists go even further, claiming that only Classical Arabic is worth teaching/learning because it reflects Muslim tradition, beliefs, and values; foreign languages are to be banned because they express corrupt Western values, while the local vernaculars, Dialectal Arabic and BERBER, are to be eradicated, as divisive, perpetuating ethnic hostilities. The opposite attitude is held by the *Francisants*, generally decision-makers and intellectuals, with positions in higher education, public administration and the private sector. They have a moderate, pragmatic attitude toward Arabisation, favouring French–Standard Arabic bilingualism. For them, Classical Arabic alone cannot replace French in all domains, e.g. science and technology, because it is not yet fully prepared and modernised. (**Moha Ennaji**)

Further reading

Ennaji (1988); Grandguillaume (1991).

Arcand, Denys   Born 1941. QUEBEC film-maker. One of the most successful of his profession, he became known in the 1970s for hard-hitting documentaries, and feature films, such as *Réjeanne Padovani* (1973), which exposed corruption in Quebec society. He achieved worldwide fame with *Le Déclin de l'Empire Américain* (1986), a satirical sex comedy which lampoons the Quebec intellectual class for abandoning the ideals of Quebec NATIONALISM. His masterwork is *Jésus de Montréal* (1989), in which he combines his customary denunciation of social decadence with a picture of more positive values, through the transposition of the Biblical story of Jesus to contemporary Montreal. (**Ian Lockerbie**)

Aristide, Jean-Bertrand   Born 1953. Political leader, formerly a priest. He worked as a priest in the slums of Port-au-Prince, and was elected President of HAITI in 1990, although he was ousted by a military *coup* in 1991 and returned into exile. Shortly after American intervention in 1994, he returned to power, with the support of his movement, *La Famille Lavalas* (Avalanche). In accordance with the Haitian constitution, he stepped aside in 1996, when René Préval took over the presidency, but returned in 2000. His initial popularity has been largely dissipated in the face of Haiti's continuing economic, social and political problems.

Armée de Libération Nationale   See ALN.

Art and Culture, Pacific   The creative culture of traditional Melanesian and Polynesian populations concentrated on sculpture and architecture, and the transmission of oral literature and genealogies. Baskets, shields, ornaments for houses, jewellery and statues were made from wood, sea shells, mother of pearl, pandanus fibres, jade and other materials often invested with a cultural significance. Among the most impressive works are the *flèches faitières*, carvings which decorate houses in parts of NEW CALEDONIA, the large wooden slit-drums of VANUATU and *ti'i* (wooden statues) of the Marquesas islands, as well as the *marae* (stone altars) common throughout French POLYNESIA. Belief systems included creation myths, stories of ancestors and legendary voyages, and family histories retold in Polynesian and Melanesian languages (of which there are several hundred in Vanuatu and New Caledonia). Westerners for long dismissed local cultures as primitivism, but from the 1920s ethnologists, such as the pioneering Maurice Leenhardt in New Caledonia, began to valorise the cultural patrimony of Oceania.

The islands attracted many Western writers and artists, whose works now also form part of their cultural heritage. French Polynesia inspired Pierre Loti's *Le Mariage de Loti* (1880) and Victor Segalen's *Les Immémoriaux* (1907), which described (and popularised) the EXOTICISM of the islands while lamenting the ravages of European incursions. The painting of Paul Gauguin (1848–1903), who died in the Marquesas islands, illustrated the same themes of luxuriant landscapes and alluring Polynesians, but also the deleterious effects of culture contact on this 'paradise lost'.

Recent years have seen attempts to preserve and develop traditional cultures, including forms such as dance and tattooing (censured by the missionaries who converted most of the South Pacific populations to Christianity), and to expand into new media. The opening of the Jean-Marie TJIBAOU Cultural Centre in New Caledonia in 1998 represented a state-sponsored attempt to foster traditional and modern cultures. (**Robert Aldrich**)

Further reading

Margueron (1989) – a study of novels and other creative works written about French Polynesia; Oliver (1989) – a comprehensive two-volume survey of traditional island cultures.

Aslaoui, Leila Born 1950. Algerian lawyer, writer and human rights activist. The assassination of her husband, a Casbah dentist, in 1994 was viewed as a strike against her. A practising Muslim herself, she was opposed to any compromise with the FIS (*Front Islamique du Salut*) so long as it espoused violence. In 1995 she resigned from her post as Minister for Family and National Solidarity in protest about the dialogue between the government and the FIS. She is president of the Association of the Victims of Terrorism and a prominent member of the Algerian Union of Democratic Women. (**Susan Fox**)

Assemblée Parlementaire de la Francophonie See APF.

Assimilation/intégration/insertion Concepts denoting models of ethnic relations, particularly in situations arising from international population movements. *Assimilation* is generally understood to mean a process whereby weaker groups abandon their existing cultural forms and adopt the forms of a dominant ethnic group. During the colonial period, it was frequently claimed that France pursued an assimilationist policy through its so-called *mission civilisatrice* ('civilising mission'), whereby the cultures of indigenous peoples were to be replaced by the norms imported by French colonists. In practice, France provided few of the educational resources which would have been required to make a reality of these claims for most of the population, though small French-speaking ÉLITES of indigenous origin did emerge.

After DECOLONISATION, international MIGRATION led to the settlement of postcolonial minorities within France, where broadly assimilationist policies were pursued. But partly because of its colonial connotations, the word 'assimilation' was seldom used. During the early 1980s, the Socialist Party briefly championed the ideas of *insertion* and *le droit à la différence* ('the right to be different'), according to which immigrant minorities would be incoporated socially and economically alongside the majority ethnic population without renouncing their cultural distinctiveness. Attacked on the grounds that they resembled 'Anglo-Saxon'-style multiculturalism, these ideas were largely abandoned in the face of the electoral successes of the anti-immigrant FRONT NATIONAL. During the early 1990s, a somewhat ambiguous consensus emerged among most political parties in favour of *intégration*. For some right-of-centre politicians, *intégration* was a euphemism for *assimilation*, while some on the left saw it as a new label for *insertion*. More generally, *intégration* serves to mark a halfway house between *assimilation* and *insertion*, with the main emphasis on ensuring that minority ethnic groups live harmoniously with the rest of the population. (**Alec G. Hargreaves**)

Further reading

Wieviorka (1996) offers an incisive guide to recent debates in France.

Association des Ecrivains de Langue Française See ADELF.

Association des Universités Partiellement ou Entièrement de Langue Française See AUF.

Association Francophone d'Amitié et de Liaison   See AFAL.

Aubry, Gilbert   Born 1942. Poet and Catholic Bishop of Reunion. The poetry of Monseigneur Aubry, in collections such as *Rivages d'alizé* (1971), celebrates the natural environment and cultural diversity specific to the Mascarene islands through the ideal domain of '*Créolie*' of which he is the natural spiritual leader. (**Peter Hawkins**)

Audio-visual media, Canada and North America   Francophone television viewers in Quebec have access to four main generalist channels, all based in Montreal, as well as to the international TV5. SRC (*Société Radio Canada*) is pan-Canadian, the Francophone arm of the CBC founded in 1936, its programming funded out of general taxation and advertising. It also runs the 24-hour cable news channel RDI (*Réseau des informations*). Despite the federal jurisdiction over broadcasting, with its regulatory body the CRTC (Canadian Radio-Television and Telecommunications Commission), there is also a channel owned and run by the province of Quebec, Télé-Québec, which has an educational and cultural brief. The private sector is dominated by large multimedia corporations in a market with a high penetration of cable. In 2001 the CRTC approved Quebecor's acquisition of the cable distributor Videotron, and of the largest private generalist channel TVA. As Télé-Métropole, TVA in 1961 broke SRC's TV monopoly, enjoyed since 1952, and set out to produce programmes with a distinct Quebec address. A condition of the CRTC's 2001 ruling was that Quebecor shed its interest in the smaller TQS (*Télévision Quatre Saisons*), founded in 1986. The corporation that dominates pay TV is Astral Media, which owns the movie channels *Super Ecran* and *Canal Indigo*, and several other specialist stations. Television in Quebec plays a much more developed and central role in the culture than in France, with viewing figures for programmes far outstripping those for indigenous fictional products in English Canada, where, as in Quebec, most of the population have easy access to US stations. Elsewhere, TFO (*Télévision franco-ontarienne*) and TVNB (*Télévision Nouveau-Brunswick*) add a regional programme offer to the SRC. The first national radio broadcast in Canada was in 1927. The dual language monopoly of CBC/SRC has for long been broken by a plethora of AM and FM stations in major centres. Here again Astral Media own a large proportion (9) including the most popular (*Radio Energie*). Outside Canada, the only significant Francophone output consists of certain hours of radio programming in Louisiana and also New York (for the Haitian community). (**Bill Marshall**)

Audio-visual media, Sub-Saharan Africa   All the countries of Francophone Sub-Saharan Africa have state-controlled national radio and television stations, usually dominated by the government currently in power, especially in the many states where the one-party system or the military dictatorship still dominate. In those where a measure of multi-party democracy has been established, there are sometimes independent radio stations, but less often television, because of the higher cost of television production and diffusion. Broadcasting is mainly in French, but a considerable proportion of airtime is usually given over to broadcasting in local African languages. Often the French satellite television channel RFO is also available, as is

17

Radio France International, sometimes providing the only independent source of news broadcasting. Local websites are still relatively uncommon, although in many African cities cybercafés provide access to the Internet. Surprisingly, given the relative poverty of most of their national economies, the countries of Francophone West Africa were the cradle of the African film industry. The Senegalese writer and film-maker SEMBENE OUSMANE was the first pioneering director of an African film: the short *Borrom Sarret* (1962). Sembene went on to establish himself as a leading African film-maker with a considerable body of politically committed social realist films in African languages, such as *Mandabi* (The Money Order) in 1968. The following year saw the first FESPACO bi-annual Pan-African Film Festival in Ouagadougou, BURKINA FASO. Directors such as Souleymane CISSÉ from MALI and Idrissa OUÉDRAOGO from Burkina Faso found international recognition and distribution for films such as *Finye* and *Ye'elen* (Cissé, 1982, 1987), *Yaaba* and *Tilai* (Ouédraogo, 1989, 1990). These were almost always filmed using local African languages, which gave them an advantage over the Francophone writing of these countries in reaching a wider African public. Their distribution was often restricted in African countries, however, where the local film circuits are most often dominated by American productions from Hollywood, sometimes international French hits, but also, more surprisingly, by Indian romances from Bollywood. (**Peter Hawkins**)

AUF *Agence Universitaire de la Francophonie* (Francophone University Agency). The successor to AUPELF (*Association des Universités Partiellement ou Entièrement de Langue Française* – Association of partially or wholly Francophone universities), created in 1961 in Montreal, where the AUF still has its headquarters. With around 400 institutions, it includes most universities in member countries of La FRANCOPHONIE. It exists to promote research, training, teaching, promotion of the FRENCH LANGUAGE, linguistic diversity and exchanges. It has set up UREF (*Université des réseaux d'expression française* – Francophone network university), bringing academics together from all over the Francophone world. It also supports collaboration through FICU (*Fonds international de coopération universitaire* – international fund for university cooperation). (**Béatrice Le Bihan**)

Further reading

See website: http://www/auf.org

Augustine See SAINT AUGUSTINE.

AUPELF See AUF.

Azéma, Jean-Henri Born 1913. Reunionese poet. Although he spent most of his life in exile, living in Europe and South America, Azéma's poetic inspiration drew on the oceanic landscapes of his native island, as in long poems such as *Olographe* (1978). (**Peter Hawkins**)

B

Bâ, Amadou Hampâté   1900–91. Writer from MALI. One of Africa's foremost scholars of traditional and Islamic wisdom, he was a member of the UNESCO board from 1962 to 1971. His are the words: 'In Africa, the death of an old person is a library that burns down.' His novel *L'Etrange destin de Wangrin* (1973; *The Fortunes of Wangrin*, 1987) tells of an interpreter in the colonial service, combining humour, narrative force and documentary interest (*Grand prix littéraire de l'Afrique noire*, 1974). His autobiography, *Amdoullel, l'enfant peul* (1991) aims at a public without prior knowledge of Africa. (**Ingse Skattum**)

Further reading

Jouanny (1992) – collection of articles, a good introduction; *Notre Librairie* (1984) – a good introduction to Malian literature.

Bâ, Mariama   Born SENEGAL, 1929; died 1981. Senegalese writer. She won the first Noma Prize for Publishing in Africa in 1980 for her first novel, *Une si longue lettre* (*So Long A Letter*, 1981). Her second novel, *Un chant écarlate* (*Scarlet Song*, 1985), was published posthumously in 1982. Widely recognised as a pioneer of Francophone women's writing in Sub-Saharan Africa, Bâ uses fiction to expose the divisions of gender and class inherent in contemporary Senegalese society. (**Nicki Hitchcott**)

Further reading

Grésillon (1986) – a student guide to *Une si longue lettre*; Hitchcott (2000) – a feminist reading of Bâ's novels.

Baccouche, Hachemi   Born 1917. Tunisian writer. He is a nephew of Salaheddine Baccouche, one of the last prime ministers (1952–54) of pre-independent TUNISIA. He is known principally for two novels, *Ma Foi demeure* (1958), which discusses his complex feelings towards the French colonial power, and *La Dame de Carthage* (1961), a historical novel, as well as a play, *Baudruche* (1959).

Bandung Conference   The Bandung Conference was a conference of African and Asian states which took place 18–24 April 1955 in the Indonesian city of that name. It brought together delegations from 29 countries, with representatives from France's three North African territories – ALGERIA, MOROCCO and TUNISIA – present as observers. The main motivations for holding the conference were dissatisfaction with Western powers' reluctance to consult with other countries on decisions affecting Asia, and opposition to the continuation of colonial rule, in particular to French rule in North Africa. The conference condemned colonialism in all its manifestations, declared its support for respecting the sovereignty and integrity of nations, for the equality of all races and nations, and for world peace and international co-operation. It advocated the resolution of international disputes by recourse to negotiation. SENGHOR welcomed the conference as marking the 'death of the inferiority complex of coloured peoples'. Hailed by the leaders of the newly independent nations as a symbol of the ideal of co-operation, peace and progress for Third World peoples, it was also seen as a symbol of hope by nationalist leaders, especially in France's colonial empire. It marked the birth of the notion of Asian–African solidarity and the beginning of the NON-ALIGNED MOVEMENT. (**Tony Chafer**)

Banlieue   Literally 'suburbs', although the term is increasingly synonymous with so-called 'inner-city' areas in the UK and North America. As a result of progressive industrialisation throughout the nineteenth century, the rural area around Paris was rapidly transformed into a ring of working-class towns, where factories and heavy industry were situated. Low-cost housing for workers was found in these suburbs, but a housing crisis following the First World War led to the districts' rapid politicisation by the French Communist Party. The *banlieue* began to acquire a reputation as marginal territories, separated from the city of Paris yet remaining a permanent political and social threat to it. This idea was consolidated in the 1970s when ethnic minority families were increasingly housed in publicly owned tower blocks in these peripheral urban areas. By the early 1980s, such areas were suffering from high unemployment, and social tensions (triggered in part by the rise of the National Front) led to violence between young people and the police. The suburbs of Paris and other major French cities (such as Lyons) became the focus of ongoing debates about IMMIGRATION, INTEGRATION and national IDENTITY. The term *banlieue* now designates a deprived urban area, usually associated by the media and politicians (i.e. in the imaginations of those who live elsewhere) with stereotypical ideas of immigration, delinquency and criminality. In response to the transformation of the *banlieue* into a falsely homogeneous and exclusively threatening territory, its inhabitants (e.g. Azouz BEGAG, Mehdi CHAREF, Mounsi) have written a series of novels and used hip-hop music (e.g. Lionel D, Suprême NTM, MC SOLAAR) to offer a more realistic portrait of everyday life. There has also been a series of *banlieue* films, of which the most influential was Kassovitz's LA HAINE (1995). Maspero, *Les Passagers du Roissy-Express* (1990) is the account of a Parisian narrator's journey through the *banlieue* along the RER-B line. Engaging with and undermining stereotypes of the suburbs, it goes beyond political and media stereotypes to underline the ethnic and social DIVERSITY of suburban areas. (**Charles Forsdick**)

Further reading

Hargreaves (1996); Rosello (2001); Stovall (2001).

Bao Dai   Born Hue, 1913; died Paris, 1997. Last emperor of VIETNAM. Bao Dai never enjoyed real power, his rule taking place first under the French occupation, then that of the Japanese during World War II. He abdicated in 1945 and left for exile, but returned in 1949, with the support of the French, who saw a role for him as puppet emperor. Upon the division of the country, he attempted to take control in South

Vietnam, but was outmanoeuvred by the Prime Minister, Ngo Dinh Diem, and ousted from the monarchy in 1955.

Barcelona Agreement   See also EuroMed policy. This is the name given to the agreement which was signed following a Conference held on the 27–28 November 1995 between foreign ministers of the EU and twelve Mediterranean countries (Algeria, Egypt, Jordan, Lebanon, Morocco, Syria, Tunisia, Turkey and the Palestinian Authority plus Israel, Cyprus and Malta with Libya having observer status). It led to the creation of what is referred to as the Euro-Mediterranean Partnership. It aims to ensure Europe's security in the Mediterranean, bring about economic development and develop human capital resources in the south. (**Kay Adamson**)

Further reading

Xenakis and Chryssochoou (2001) – Chapter 4 provides a detailed discussion of the Barcelona Agreement.

Basri, Driss   Born Settat, Morocco, 1938. Moroccan politician. Powerful figure in the regime of Hassan II. Interior Minister in control of national security for several decades, until his dismissal by Mohammed VI in 1999.

Bastien-Thiry, Jean-Marie   1927–63. French airforce colonel and a supporter of *Algérie française*, who was executed in 1963 for his part in the attempted assassination of de Gaulle at the Petit Clamart in 1962. Commemorated as a martyr by the French Extreme Right.

Battle of Algiers   This began in earnest on 7 January 1957, when General Jacques Massu, commanding the 10th paratrooper division of the French army, was given a free hand to wipe out the FLN networks, engaged in a violent guerrilla campaign of bombing and attacks in the Algiers area. The means employed were ruthless and brutal, including torture and summary executions. A few months later, Massu boasted of having won the Battle of Algiers, with 3000 or so suspects captured or killed, including Larbi Ben M'Hidi, Yacef Saadi and Ali-la-Pointe.

The Battle of Algiers   The historical film *The Battle of Algiers* (Pontecorvo, 1966) is a beautifully made film about the Algerian War of Independence (1954–62). Inspired by the testimony of eyewitnesses, the film recreates the historic moments that played a decisive role in this war of national liberation. It shows two forces clashing: the powerful French army represented by its élite soldiers, the parachutists, and the Algerian people, whose only weapons are their faith and determination. *The Battle of Algiers* is unique in being the vehicle for an account of the combat, singular reflections on the heroism of the common people and a film of the highest artistic quality, which has been the subject of many works of academic research in the areas of postcolonial studies and history. It is still highly relevant for the contemporary world, and many studies of Algerian culture have found that it provides the keys to an understanding of the country's colonial history and postcolonial theory. (**Kamal Salhi**)

Beaulieu, Victor-Lévy   Born 1945. Quebec writer. He is the most prolific writer in Quebec literature, and one of the most challenging. Not only does his work embrace a bewildering variety of idiosyncratic styles and genres, but most of his most significant novels offer a very black vision of life and society. His gallery of obsessive characters are usually lost in despair, the victims of a brutal childhood and an alcoholism which leads them to bouts of erotic fantasy and sexual violence. Feminist critics, especially, have objected to the misogyny and abuse of women that for them pervade his fictional world. Yet it is always evident that Beaulieu's turbulent writing is driven by the idealistic hope of eventually producing harmony from the ugliness and violence of the world – an ambition expressed in books he has devoted to his four great literary mentors, Hugo, Melville, Kerouac and Ferron, all exemplars of a mythopoeic vision he wishes to emulate. He has recently, however, gained a new, wider following through long-running television serials, *L'Héritage* and *Bouscotte*, subsequently transformed into novels. These show an ability to write inventively yet accessibly for a mass audience, and seem to point to a different literary approach. If one adds the exemplary role he has played in the promotion of literature in Quebec, notably through the founding of publishing houses which work to the highest standards, and his championing of cultural activity in the remote regions of the country against the metropolitan centralism of Montreal, a more rounded picture of his stature emerges. New readers might begin with the novel versions of *L'Héritage* (1992) and *Bouscotte* (2001) before proceeding to relatively accessible earlier works like *Race de monde* (1969) and *Les Grands-Pères* (1973). (**Ian Lockerbie**)

Bébel-Gisler, Dany   Guadeloupean sociolinguist and author. Her important study of the unequal power relations between French and Creole is entitled *La Langue créole, force jugulée* (1976, 1981). She is committed to celebrating the oral tradition of Guadeloupe. *Léonora: l'histoire enfouie de la Guadeloupe* (1985; *Léonora: The Buried Story of Guadeloupe*, 1994) is presented as the testimony of an elderly peasant woman, transcribed from oral to written form and translated from Creole into French. (**Maeve McCusker**)

Bebey, Francis   Born Douala, Cameroon, 1929; died Paris, 2001. Novelist, poet, jazz musician and film-maker. His work employed humour to struggle against racism. His novel *Le Fils d'Agatha Moudio* (Yaoundé, CLE, 1967; *Agatha Moudio's Son*, 1971) won the 1968 Literary Prize of Black Africa. Some of his poetry, such as *Concert pour un vieux masque*, was originally composed as pieces for solo guitar accompaniment. It is one of his few works to be currently available (L'Harmattan, 1980), as his work was chiefly published by small publishing houses. Bebey came to Paris in 1950 to study English at the Sorbonne and used English and French alongside Douala, pygmy polyphonics and Bantu songs in his composing and performing. He also worked for French radio and UNESCO. (**Kay Adamson**)

Further reading

Wake (1965) contains two of his poems.

Begag, Azouz   Born Lyons, 1957. French novelist and sociologist of Algerian origin, Azouz Begag is probably the best-known of Beur writers, in particular for the self-avowedly autobiographical *Le Gone du Chaâba* (1986), recounting the life of a young boy of Algerian parents growing up in a *bidonville* in Lyons in the mid-1960s. The symbolic violence of the French school system and the harshness of *bidonville* life are graphically depicted yet, as in most of Begag's fiction, humour (situational or linguistic, ironic or farcical) softens the pessimism. Begag's texts often portray young male protagonists of Algerian origin in France attempting to bypass and subvert cultural and racial stereotyping. (**Jim House**)

Further reading

Begag (1989) – the follow-up to *Le Gone du Chaâba* (1986) recounting the adolescence of the main protagonist in a Lyons public housing estate; Begag (1995) – a more sombre, allegorical text portraying a migrant community's revolt against racism.

Béji, Hélé   Born 1948. Tunisian writer. Her essay 'Désenchantement national' (1982) was an important polemical contribution to the debates about the DECOLONISATION experience. Refusing the separation of autobiography and ideas, her writing explores questions of women's relationship to TRADITION and MEMORY, as in the novel *Oeil du jour* (1985). Other texts include the satirical text *Itinéraire de Paris à Tunis* (1992), *L'Imposture culturelle* (1997).

Békés   Derived from the Igbo term for whites, the *békés* are the white Creole ascendancy class. The equivalent expression in Guadeloupe is '*grands blancs*'. Thanks to English occupation during the *Terreur*, the plantocracy of Martinique fared better than its Guadeloupean counterpart. Ethnographers like Jean Benoist and Michel Leiris have stressed the *békés*' colour and caste complex, and its protectionism and ambivalence regarding metropolitan France. In popular novels like *La Grande Béké* (1989) by Marie-Reine de Jaham, but also in more experimental works like Edouard Glissant's *Le Quatrième Siècle* (1964; *The Fourth Century*, 2001), Patrick Chamoiseau's *L'Esclave Vieil Homme et le molosse* (1997), or Raphaël Confiant's *Commandeur du Sucre* (1994), the *béké* is an important literary figure. (**Mary Gallagher**)

Bekri, Tahar   Born Gabès, Tunisia, 1951. Tunisian poet, literary critic and university professor. He was a political exile from Tunisia between 1976 and 1989. He writes both in French and in Arabic, and the poetry is marked by the themes of exile and wandering, MEMORY, tradition and MODERNITY. First major collection in French, *Le Laboureur du soleil* (1983), the most recent *Marcher sur l'oubli* (2000); also a number of illustrated editions of poetry. In addition, he has published works of literary criticism on Malek Haddad (1986), and more generally on Tunisian and North African literature in French. (**Debra Kelly**)

Belghoul, Farida   Born Paris, 1958. Maghrebi-French activist, writer and film director. Her family is from Kabylia, Algeria. Hargreaves (1992) describes how, after time in the *Parti Communiste* and university studies in economics, Belghoul came to national attention as an organiser of *Convergence '84*, a sequel to the MARCHE DES BEURS (1983). However, the experience convinced her that collaborating with activists having weak ties to the BANLIEUES was counterproductive, as she argued in speeches and articles. She therefore turned to fiction-writing. *Georgette!*, Belghoul's sole published novel (1986), is generally regarded as one of the best examples of Maghrebi-French fiction. She also made two films: *C'est Madame la France que tu préfères?* and *Le Départ du père*. (**Mark McKinney**)

Belhadj, Ali   See BENHADJ, ALI.

Belkacem, Krim   Born Douar Ait Yahia, 1922; died Frankfurt, 1970. Algerian political leader and activist. Krim Belkacem was a member of the Algerian People's Party (PPA) from 1946, going underground in 1947. He became responsible for the Movement for the Triumph of Democratic Liberties (MTLD) throughout KABYLIA. He became the sixth member of the internal leadership of the FLN in 1954 and was in charge of Kabylia when the NOVEMBER 1ST 1954 insurrection was launched. He joined the Committee for the Election of the Executive (CEE) following the Soummam Congress in 1956, and gained a dominant position within the ALN during 1958–59 as Vice-President of the GPRA and Minister for the Armed Forces. Krim left Algeria after the BATTLE OF ALGIERS. Minister for Foreign Affairs in 1960, Minister of the Interior in 1961, he opened negotiations with France at EVIAN. Following Algerian Independence he disapproved of BEN BELLA's policies, found himself excluded from political life and went into business. In the aftermath of the *coup d'état* of 19 June 1965 he became involved in the opposition again. Accused of having organised an attempt on the life of President BOUMEDIENNE, he was condemned to death in his absence. Krim Belkacem was found murdered in a hotel room in Frankfurt in October 1970. (**Kamal Salhi**)

Benaissa, Slimane   Born Guelma, 1943. Algerian playwright. He is from a BERBER part of the Aurès region, eastern ALGERIA. At school he learned French, but, unlike many of his generation, also gained a sound mastery of Colloquial Arabic and Berber. At 13 he went to technical college in Annaba, going on to work as an engineer. He gained a diploma in industrial technology, but gave up studies in 1961 at a time when the OAS was stepping up its activities against the civilian population. In 1963 he went to France to continue his technical training and returned to Algeria in 1967. In 1968 Benaissa studied mathematics at the University of Algiers. During this period he joined the group Theatre and Culture. Between 1969 and 1971 he took part in several plays. He produced *La Femme algérienne* and wrote his play *The People*. After completing his degree, Benaissa pursued a career in the theatre, becoming one of the most sophisticated playwrights working in North Africa, writing and directing several very popular original plays.

In Algeria, badly planned and poorly implemented policies, incompetent management and corruption created the disastrous situation that resulted in the insurrection of October 1988. Since then there has been a sharp polarisation of Algerian politics, marked by violent clashes between the Islamic fundamentalists and the military. The main victims have been the civilian population. Intellectuals and artists have found themselves targeted by both sides, and many have fled the country. Benaissa went into exile in February 1993 after receiving death threats from Islamic fundamentalists. He now lives and works in France, where he employs satire and a dark sense of humour to cope with homesickness and stave off despair. Since 1993 he has written several plays in French, which have been published and performed in France, Europe and the Middle East. (**Kamal Salhi**)

Further reading

Benaissa (1999), (1997).

Ben Ali, Zine al-Abidine   Born 1936. Tunisian politician. He became President in 1987, following the forced retirement of President Habib BOURGUIBA, during whose presidency he had been Deputy Secretary-General of the DESTOUR Party. Ben Ali, who had also had responsibility for national security, has taken a hardline approach to Islamists in TUNISIA and has frequently been accused of violating human rights, particularly after 1997. More recently, he has had to withstand the hunger strike of journalist Tawfik Ben Brik. Viewed favourably by the West, he has managed to combine pursuit of economic liberalism whilst maintaining a planned economy. (**Kay Adamson**)

Ben Barka, El Mehdi   Born 1920; died *c.* 1965. Moroccan political thinker. He was a leading member of the USFP (Socialist Union of Peoples' Forces) and hence opposed to the government of the former king, HASSAN II. His anti-monarchist views and political activities led to his imprisonment, torture, exile and famously, his kidnapping in October 1965 on the steps of a Paris café. He disappeared in a Moroccan jail – a victim of the then head of Moroccan security, General Mohammed OUFKIR, who was later convicted by a French court, in his absence, of Ben Barka's abduction and murder. His widow and other family members returned to MOROCCO for the first time in November 1999. (**Kay Adamson**)

Ben Bella, Ahmed   Born 1916. Algerian political leader. One of nine historic founder leaders of the FLN, who planned and launched the ALGERIAN WAR OF INDEPENDENCE. Drafted into the French army in 1939, he was awarded the *Croix Militaire* by DE GAULLE. After World War II, he returned to ALGERIA, joined the PPA and helped to found the underground paramilitary OS (*Organisation Spéciale*), a splinter group of the MTLD. Arrested by the French in 1950, he escaped in 1952 and fled to EGYPT, where he co-founded the FLN. Re-arrested by the French in 1956, he was released in 1962 and took part in the EVIAN negotiations that led to the end of the war. Prime Minister in 1962, elected President of the Republic in 1963, he was ousted by BOUMEDIENNE in a military *coup* in 1965. Freed in 1980, he went into exile in France and returned to Algeria in 1990. (**Naaman Kessous**)

Bencheikh, Jamel-Eddine   Born Casablanca, 1930. Professor of Medieval Arab Literature at the University of Paris IV. Literary critic, known for his work on the *Arabian Nights*. Also poet (*Le silence s'est déjà tu*; *Les Etats de l'Aube*) and political essayist. Publications include: *Poétique arabe* (1989); *D'Arabie et d'Islam* (1992); *Ecrits politiques* (2001).

Further reading

Chaulet-Achour (1994), (1998).

Benguigui, Yamina   Born Lille, 1957. Film-maker, screenwriter and television producer of Algerian origin. Benguigui's work has been devoted to the exploration of
memories and exile of the North African community in France. Her first major work
to receive public recognition was the 1997 documentary, *Mémoires d'immigrés*.
Divided into three sections (*les pères*, *les mères*, and *les enfants*), it represents a journey into 'immigrant' experience, and is made up of a collection of interviews with
North African exiles and their French-born descendants (including the authors
Azouz BEGAG and Mounsi). In 2001, Benguigui's first feature-length film was released.
Inch'allah dimanche, the story of an Algerian woman travelling to join her family in
Picardy (as part of the French policy of *regroupement familial*), received a series of
awards, including the Grand Prix at the International Film Festival in Marrakech.
(**Charles Forsdick**)

Further reading

Benguigui (1997) – for an account accompanying the film *Mémoires d'immigrés*.

Benhadj, Ali   Born Tunis, 1954. Algerian Islamist politician and preacher. Hardline
deputy leader of FIS. Held in prison since 1991.

Bénin, République du   Country in West Africa, formerly known as DAHOMEY.
Capital: Porto Novo (official), Cotonou (administrative/economic). Located
between Nigeria and TOGO (to the east and west) and BURKINA FASO (north), and with
a population of less than five million and a surface area of 112,000 sq. kilometres,
Bénin is one of the smallest countries in Africa. Its official language is French, though
the tribal languages of Fon, Yoruba, Bariba and Dendi are widely spoken. Its economy is attached to the CFA, exporting mainly coffee and cotton, as well as palm
products and groundnuts; external debt is currently estimated at £58m. Its religion is
mainly Christian, and minority Muslim, though animism is widely practised –
indeed Voodoo is said to have originated (and is still evident) in the coastal town of
Ouidah. It is officially a multi-party presidential republic, though the current Head of
State, the political maverick Mathieu Kérékou, has controlled, if not ruled, the country since the 1970s, via the *Parti de la Révolution Populaire du Bénin* (PRPB). Kérékou
seized power in 1972, rejecting the country's 'misbegotten French name' of Dahomey
in 1975. Surviving a 1977 *coup* attempt by the military (backed by MOROCCO, GABON
and France), Kérékou declared the country a socialist state, aligned with the Soviet
Union and then Libya. Though a recent opening out to the West, especially to France,
has led to economic investment, it has not been able to turn around an ailing and
debt-ridden economy that suffers from a desperate lack of infrastructure. Culturally,
on the other hand, Bénin has flourished. Cotonou was known for many years as the

'Latin Quarter' of Francophone West Africa, producing an impressive array of writers, such as Paul HAZOUMÉ, Félix Couchoro, and, more recently, Olympe BHÊLY-QUÉNUM, Jean Pliya, Florent Couao-Zotti, as well as the political and cultural theorists Albert Tevoedjre and Spéro Adotévi. (**Andy Stafford**)

Further reading

Notre Librairie (1995) - special number on Bénin.

Benjedid, Chadli   Born Sebaa, 1929. Algerian soldier and political leader. A relatively obscure army commander in charge of the eastern military region from 1964 to 1979, he took over the Algerian government in 1979 after the premature death of President BOUMEDIENNE. Initially viewed with some favour, as he appeared to liberalise aspects of the polity and the economy. However, he would also provoke opposition from women as his government succeeded in pushing through a restrictive FAMILY CODE in 1984. After riots in October 1988, he promised political and economic liberalisation, including a new multi-party constitution. The FIS was legalised in 1989, then won the 1990 municipal and communal elections, a precursor of the December 1991 general election (see ALGERIAN ELECTIONS, 1991). He was forced out of office in January 1992. (**Kay Adamson**)

Ben Jelloun, Tahar   Born Fez, 1944. Moroccan novelist, essayist and poet. After graduating in philosophy in Morocco he went on to study social psychiatry in France. His doctoral thesis, a study of North African immigrants' sexual dysfunction, was published in 1977 under the title *La plus haute des solitudes*. Earlier, in 1973, he published his first novel, *Harrouda*. Ben Jelloun is one of the most prolific and most daring writers in Francophone Maghrebian literature for his thematic exploration of religious and sexual taboos. His most acclaimed novels, *L'Enfant de sable* (1985; *The Sand Child*, 1988) and its sequel *La Nuit sacrée* (1987; *The Sacred Night*, 1989), for which he won the prestigious Prix Goncourt, depict a woman's journey to self-discovery. These novels narrate the ambiguous sexual identity of a woman who was forced to live as a man for the sole reason that her father wanted a male heir to carry his name. Ben Jelloun's writing is very rich, not only because of his innovative style but also because his work straddles two cultures. He uses the FRENCH LANGUAGE in a Maghrebian framework. He borrows his narrative style from the oral tradition and the popular tale, while at the same time subverting them and adding new dimensions. His style is unique in the way in which the real, the fantastic and the fantasmatic are made to interact. On a thematic level, Ben Jelloun has covered a great number of issues including religion, social behaviour, sexuality and philosophy. In general, his work is designed to shock, to transgress and to challenge unspoken assumptions. (**Laïla Ibnlfassi**)

Further reading

Elbaz (1996); Saigh Bousta (1999).

Bensoussan, Albert   Born Algiers, 1935. Author, literary critic, poet, translator. He emigrated to France after independence. Despite his current state of exile from

ALGERIA, he holds an enduring sense of identity with it, because his JEWISH upbringing in a Muslim environment in colonial Algeria, is a dominant theme of his literary works. Publications include: *Isbilia* (1970), poems and short stories; *L'Echelle de Mesrod* (1984), short stories; *La Ville sur les eaux* (1992), a novel. He contributes to several literary journals and is a translator between French/Spanish literary texts. (**Susan Fox**)

Further reading

Schousboe (1991).

Berber literature See LITERATURE, BERBER.

Berbers Berbers (*Imazighen* - sing. *Amazigh*) are the largest linguistic minority of the Maghreb. Berber (*TAMAZIGHT*), belonging to the Hamito-Semitic or Afro-Asiatic language family, is spoken all over the Maghreb. *Tamazight*-speakers are estimated at 12–15 million, about 20 per cent of Algerians (in KABYLIA, Aurès, Mzab) and 40 per cent of Moroccans (Rif, Central/South Atlas, Draa River area). TUNISIA has a small number on the Isle of Djerbaa and in the south (Chenini, Douz, Tozeur), Libya in the Nefousa Mountains and some oases (Ghadamès, Sokna, Awjila), EGYPT in the oasis of Siwa. About 500,000 Tuareg people also speak *Tamazight* in a wide area, throughout ALGERIA, Libya, MALI, NIGER.

The use of the term Berber in European languages, to describe these peoples, dates from the sixteenth century and was definitively consolidated after colonisation. Since it derives from Greek *barbaros*/Latin *barbarus*, i.e. extraneous, and carries with it the meaning of 'non-civilised', it has been recently rejected by those who prefer to call themselves *Imazighen*, 'free men', referring to their language as *Tamazight*. These terms were known in MOROCCO and Libya but not previously used north of the SAHARA, particularly in northern Algeria, where they are accepted today. The huge but scattered extension of *Tamazight*-speakers in the Maghreb leads some specialists to speak of Berber 'languages', underlining socio-linguistic differences among local variations. In the past, only a limited number of speakers were conscious of *Tamazight*'s linguistic unity, although broad areas of intercomprehension existed. The introduction of the terms *Amazigh*, *Imazighen*, *Tamazight* points to a changed social context: *Tamazight*/Berber-speakers have become aware of their linguistic unity and tend to assert their autonomy.

The present condition of *Tamazight* minorities varies politically, economically and socially. Berber is recognised as a national language in Mali and Niger, but the Tuaregs, once nomads, suffered most from the constitution of nation-states and their insurmountable borderlines, followed by years of armed rebellions and military and economic repression. In Morocco and Algeria, governmental denial and repression had lately made room for a more open attitude. However, neither recognise *Tamazight* as an official national language or provide it in school curricula. *Tamazight* was recognised as the second national language of Algeria in April 2002. In Algeria, demands for recognition of *Tamazight* in Kabylia are accompanied by ongoing repression. The issue of Berber minorities is intrinsically connected to demands for pluralism, DEMOCRATISATION and state decentralisation. (**Daniela Merolla**)

Further reading

Bougchiche (1997); Brett and Fentress (1997); Chaker (1989).

Berber Spring (*Printemps Berbère*)   Discussion of the BERBER problem was suppressed during the ALGERIAN WAR OF INDEPENDENCE, to come to the fore again after independence had been achieved. Even if conflicts and rivalries of clan chieftains have sometimes taken on a regionalist aspect, questions of language, identity and culture mark the claims put forward on behalf of the country's Berbers by Kabyle leaders. The increasing use of Arabic combined with opposition to any official usage of Berber since 1962 have brought the *Amazigh* problem to the surface, above all in university circles and among Algerian émigrés. The repressive approach adopted has made itself felt in official discourse, which interprets any criticism as subversion. In the run up to the popular explosion of April 1980 known as the *Printemps Berbère*, it was possible to distinguish two currents within the Berber Spring. The first was an activist Pan-Berber movement that recruited its members from the whole range of society and propagated a political discourse heavily influenced by anti-Arab sentiment and calling for the establishment of an *Amazigh* nation. The second current was based in the universities and generally more moderate, concentrating on the teaching of TAMAZIGHT, linguistic and cultural planning and the publication of relevant works. Given the increasingly repressive measures against Berber activists, including arrests, disappearances, torture and imprisonment, all legal channels for dialogue with the authorities appeared to be closed. These developments led to violent incidents in KABYLIA and Algiers in the spring of 1980 and the creation of a climate that radicalised the entire situation. As a result, the protagonists spent the entire 1980s engaged in constant antagonism; demands were met by repression, which in turn encouraged more extreme demands. The Berber Spring called into question the regimes that had ruled Algeria since 1962, and no serious study of the country can be considered comprehensive unless it considers the roots and genesis of the Berber Spring. Indeed, the old patterns continue to assert themselves. The bloody repression and murder of Kabyles by state forces since April 2001 have come to be known as the 'Black Spring'. (**Kamal Salhi**)

Bernabé, Jean   Born MARTINIQUE, 1942. Linguist, creolist, Professor of Languages and Cultures at the University of ANTILLES-GUYANE. He founded the *Groupe de Recherches et d'Etudes en Espace Créolophone* (GEREC, 1975) and the journal *Espace créole*, now *Espace créole, Espaces francophones*. Author of referential linguistic works on the CREOLES of Martinique and GUADELOUPE, in particular *Fondal-Natal* (1983). Equally known, alongside P. CHAMOISEAU and R. CONFIANT, as one of the authors of *Eloge de la créolité* (1989; *In Praise of Creoleness*, 1993), the manifesto of the literary and cultural movement of *créolité*. Recently, one of the most enthusiastic promoters of the Creole CAPES, a French educational qualification. (**Roshni Mooneram**)

Beti   See Mongo Beti.

Beurs   As a noun, *Beurs* (feminine *Beurettes*) refers to the descendants of Algerian, Moroccan and Tunisian migrants who have been born and/or raised in France. Of somewhat confused etymological origins (Durmelat 1998), the term 'Beur' originated in the late 1970s as a reversal and modification of the French term *Arabe* (Arab) according to the rules of VERLAN. The descendants of North African migrants initially chose to describe themselves as *Beurs* to avoid the often stigmatising label of *Arabes*, as part of a wider process of challenging RACISM. First appearing nationally in 1981 (see RADIO BEUR), the term was popularised in late 1983 during the antiracist social movement MARCHE POUR L'ÉGALITÉ ET CONTRE LE RACISME (March for Equality and against Racism) which the media called *la marche des Beurs* (the *Beurs*' march). The '*Beur* movement' of the 1980s also contained a number of radical counter-cultural projects (*Sans-Frontière* (1979–85), *Rock against Police* (1980)).

In the late 1970s, media discourse had spoken of the 'second generation' of immigrants to describe the '*Beurs*', many of whom had never migrated. Whilst significant structural changes had indeed occurred in migratory patterns from North Africa from the 1960s onwards (when family regrouping became increasingly widespread), sociologically speaking there was no homogeneous 'second generation': children of North Africans had been arriving in France since the 1950s. These simplifying media images of the 'second generation' were often negative, associating young males with criminality. '*Beur*', as an assertion of a simultaneously French and Arab–Berber hybrid identity, also contested dominant constructions of monolithic French identity. As the 1980s progressed, many descendants of North African migrants viewed the term '*Beur*' with suspicion, judging it to have been recuperated by the dominant (Parisian) political and media actors, and antiracist associations SOS-RACISME or FRANCE-PLUS. This explains why the term has now become largely discredited amongst descendants of North Africans. (**Jim House**)

Further reading

Begag and Chaouite (1990) – accessible and humorous sociological discussion of the key issues facing descendants of North Africans in the 1980s; Guénif Souilamas (2000) – an in-depth study of women descendants of North African origin in France.

Beyala, Calixthe   Born CAMEROON, 1961. Cameroonian writer. She now lives in Belleville, Paris. Author of ten novels, many of which have been translated into English, including *C'est le soleil qui m'a brûlée* (1987; *The Sun Hath Looked Upon Me*, 1996) and *Le Petit Prince de Belleville* (1982; *Loukoum: the Little Prince of Belleville*, 1995). She has also published two essays. A controversial figure who has twice been accused of plagiarism, most notably for her novel *Les Honneurs perdus* (1996), which in the year of publication was awarded a major literary prize by the Académie Française. (**Nicki Hitchcott**)

Further reading

Gallimore (1997) – a fairly wide-ranging introduction; Hitchcott (1997a) – postcolonial analysis of Beyala and her writing.

Bhêly-Quénum, Olympe   Born 1928. Novelist and journalist from the former DAHOMEY (now BÉNIN). He was educated in France and settled there. He has published several novels, the best-known being *Un Piège sans fin* (1960; *Snares Without End*, 1981), a moral and philosophical novel in which the influence of Sartre, CAMUS and Beckett can be detected. Its theme is the power of supernatural forces and the difficulty of escaping their influence, and this theme is picked up again in his later works, such as *Le Chant du lac* (1965) and a more autobiographical novel, *L'Initié* (1979). (**Peter Hawkins**)

Bidault, Georges   Born Moulins, 1899; died Cambo-les-Bains, 1983. French Christian Democrat politician. He succeeded Jean Moulin as head of the wartime resistance and was a member of the 1944 provisional government and Prime Minister 1949–50, but an unsuccessful presidential candidate in 1953. In 1955, with Jacques SOUSTELLE, René Dumont, and four ex-Governor-Generals of ALGERIA he called for a government of public salvation to retain a French Algeria. In the governmental crisis of May 1955, he called for DE GAULLE's return. Later he opposed de Gaulle's move towards an independent Algeria, campaigning for a French Algeria and a 'No' vote in de Gaulle's referendum. This allied him with LE PEN and the putschist generals – JOUHAUD, Zeller and CHALLE. After SALAN's arrest, he took over nominal control of the OAS. (**Kay Adamson**)

Bidonville   Shantytown of dwellings made of metal sheeting, tarpaulin and petrol drums (*bidons*). *Bidonvilles* grew around major metropolitan French cities from the late 1940s onwards (they were already commonplace in the colonies): France's urban economy excluded migrant workers and their families from suitable inner-city accommodation. *Bidonvilles* lacked basic drainage and sanitation, resulting in appalling living conditions. Self-contained societies of their own, larger *bidonvilles* contained shops providing essential services. Successive governments sought to remove *bidonvilles*: during the ALGERIAN WAR OF INDEPENDENCE, the Nanterre *bidonville* (on the outskirts of Paris) was considered an Algerian nationalist 'enclave' (Hervo, 2001). The remaining large-scale *bidonvilles* were dismantled in the 1970s, their former inhabitants usually being relocated to low-standard public housing. (**Jim House**)

Further reading

Lallaoui (1995) – well-illustrated, accessible account of history of *bidonvilles* and subsequent rehousing policy; Sayad with Dupuy (1995) – an in-depth analysis of the best-known *bidonville* by an expert on Algerian migration.

Bitat, Rabah   Born Aïn Kerma, Algeria, 1925; died Paris, 2000. One of the original six founding members of the CRUA/FLN in March 1954; he organised, until his arrest in March 1955, the first guerrilla campaign in Algiers. He was tortured at the Villa Susini, and held in prison until March 1962. After independence, he married the woman militant Zohra Driff. His closeness to Ben KHIDER meant that his political career had to wait until his appointment first as Minister of State and subsequently as Minister of Transport by BOUMEDIENNE, under whom he became an increasingly powerful political figure. Subsequently, he served as President of the Algerian National Assembly, resigning in 1990 and retiring as a deputy in 1992. (**Kay Adamson**)

Biya, Paul   Born Mvomeka'a, 1933. President of CAMEROON since 1982, after many years in the service of the previous president, Ahmadou Ahidjou. Although he instituted multi-party elections in 1992, his regime is often the object of criticism for its authoritarianism and abuse of human rights.

Biyaoula, Daniel   Congolese author and microbiologist. He now lives in Paris. His novels include *L'Impasse* (1996; Grand Prix Littéraire de Afrique noire) and *Agonies* (1998). They deal with the problems of corruption, poverty and alienation faced by Africans in the Paris suburbs. He has also contributed to a volume about Pushkin (*Pouchkine et le monde noir*).

Biyidi, Alexandre   See MONGO BETI.

Blais, Marie-Claire   Born 1939. QUEBEC novelist who shot to fame with her first novel, *Une Saison dans la vie d'Emmanuel* (1963; *A Season in the Life of Emmanuel*, 1966). The black picture this painted of a rural family sunk in poverty, ignorance and backwardness seemed an indictment of the state of Quebec before the RÉVOLUTION TRANQUILLE. Her later novels are more challenging in form, often being densely woven poetic monologues. But they continue to be marked by great social compassion, notably for the stresses placed by a materialist society on women and vulnerable young people. (**Ian Lockerbie**)

Blérald, Daniel   See BOUKMAN.

Blondy, Alpha   Born as Sedou Kone, CÔTE D'IVOIRE 1953. Reggae-style musician, heavily influenced by Bob Marley. Sings with an international band, The Solar System, with African, Caribbean and European members.

Blum–Viollette   The name given to the proposals by Maurice Viollette (Governor-General of ALGERIA, 1925–27, and Minister of State for Algerian affairs in Léon Blum's Popular Front government) to increase Muslim Algerian participation in political affairs. The most contentious, which was published in December 1936, proposed to offer French CITIZENSHIP to 25,000 Muslims (graduates, non-commissioned army officers, and civil servants) without loss of their personal status. There were also proposals to restrict the size of colonist properties. The colonists' opposition to the proposals dominated political discussion in Algeria until their withdrawal in 1939. (**Kay Adamson**)

Further reading

Viollette (1931).

Boat people Originally used for the Vietnamese 'boat people' who left VIETNAM after the fall of Saigon, often in small, unseaworthy craft, the term is now in general use to describe refugees fleeing from their homeland by sea.

Bongo, Omar Born 1935. President of GABON since 1967. Born Albert Bongo, he converted to Islam in 1973. Bongo has maintained his autocratic rule by means of censorship and corruption. There have been allegations of human rights abuses and financial impropriety. A 1999 US Senate investigation claimed that Bongo had amassed huge financial assets from Gabon's oil revenues. He was forced to introduce democratic reforms in 1990, following popular demand, but evidence that the 1993 and 1998 elections were rigged has only fuelled further demands for true reform. (**Susan Fox**)

Further reading

Auracher (2001).

Boni, Tanella Born CÔTE D'IVOIRE, 1954. Lecturer in Philosophy at the University of Abidjan. Has published two collections of poetry, a novel for children and two novels, *Une Vie de crabe* (1990) and *Les Baigneurs du lac rose* (1995). An experimental writer who, like Véronique TADJO and WEREWERE LIKING, mixes genres, registers and narrative voices. (**Nicki Hitchcott**)

Further reading

Hitchcott (1997b) – the only published study of *Une Vie de crabe*.

Bouabaci, Aïcha Born Saïda, 1945. Algerian writer and intellectual. She studied literature and international law in Algiers and the Netherlands, and subsequently taught French in Algiers and in German universities. Her novellas *Les Missionnaires de l'incertitude*, *Narcose réglementaire* and *L'Insoumis*, published in *Peau d'exil*, received first and third prizes from the *Comité des Fêtes de la ville d'Alger* in 1982, 1983 and 1984. *L'Aube est née sur nos lèvres: Poèmes* was published in 1985, *Peau d'exil* in 1990. She conceived the staging of several of her works with musical accompaniment and choreography and had them performed on several occasions in different places. Further works include *Le Désordre humain conté à mon petit-fils* (to be published in 2002); 'Les Secrets de la cigogne' (unpublished autobiography). (**Susanne Heiler**)

Further reading

Heiler (1996) – for an analysis of her poetry.

Bouchard, Lucien Born QUEBEC, 1938. Lawyer and French Canadian separatist leader. Originally a member of the Progressive Conservartive Party, Bouchard formed the *Bloc Québécois* in 1990, to complement the provincial *PARTI QUÉBÉCOIS* at the federal level. He became both *Bloc Québécois* leader and leader of the Opposition following the 1993 elections. Although credited with the near success of the separatists in the 1995 Quebec referendum, and the province's economic revival during his period as Quebec premier, Bouchard fell foul of separatist hardliners, who wanted a stronger push for independence, and resigned in 2001. (**Susan Fox**)

Further reading

Kaur (2000).

Boudiaf, Mohammed Born M'sila,1919; died Annaba, 29 June 1992. Algerian political leader. He was assassinated after having been recalled from a long exile to take over the presidency in January 1992 following the annulment of the elections. Boudiaf was one of the six founding members of the CRUA/FLN in March 1954. (See also Rabah BITAT.) He served as the general co-ordinator of FLN activities after the commencement of the armed struggle but like many of the FLN leaders spent much of the time in a French prison. Despite his status, he was arrested by President BEN BELLA. However, his death sentence was commuted and he spent the remaining years in exile when he was associated with Algerian radical left organisations in France. (**Kay Adamson**)

Boudjedra, Rachid Born 1941. Algerian novelist and poet. His considerable output can be considered as a cross between a linguistic '*violence du texte*' and New Novel-inspired experimentation with narrative. From *La Répudiation* (1969; *The Repudiation*, 1995) through *L'Insolation* (1972), to *Le Vainqueur de coupe* (1981), he treats themes of Algerian history, family upheaval and racial violence on immigrants in France obliquely via eroticism, madness and even football. Up until 1981 he wrote in French, but has insisted since on writing in Arabic and then translating into French. FLN activist during the ALGERIAN WAR OF INDEPENDENCE, he has recently roundly condemned the Islamists (1997). (**Andy Stafford**)

Bouhired, Djamila Born 1935. Algerian political activist. She was one of the *Moudjahidate* (women fighters) of the Algerian Independence struggle (see ALGERIAN WAR OF INDEPENDENCE). She joined the FLN in 1956, acting as liaison agent for the FLN commander in Algiers, Saadi Yacef. Bouhired's task was to plant bombs in specified parts of the European Quarter. Sentenced to death for terrorist activities by the French authorities, Bouhired was imprisoned in France. She was acknowledged internationally and in ALGERIA as being in the vanguard for the country's independence, following the defence of her actions in the book *Pour Djamila Bouhired* by Jacques Vergès and Georges Arnaud. (**Susan Fox**)

Further reading

Arnaud and Vergès (1957).

Boukassa, Jean Bedel Born 1921. Jean Boukassa became army chief-of-staff of the CENTRAL AFRICAN REPUBLIC in 1964. In a *coup d'état* on New Year's Eve 1965, he became President. In 1976 Boukassa transformed the Central African Republic into an empire, becoming Emperor Boukassa the First. In 1979, after riots in the capital,

Bangui, he ordered the mass arrest and killing of hundreds of children. Later in 1979, with Boukassa in Libya, France intervened militarily to end the empire. Boukassa went into exile, but, in 1986, returned. He was tried and sentenced to death in 1987. This was reduced, in 1988, to life imprisonment with hard labour. (**Peter Langford**)

Further reading

Titley (1997).

Boukman, Daniel   Born 1936, as Daniel Blérald. Martinican playwright. His best-known play, *Les Négriers* (1971), likened the contemporary exilic relocation of Black West Indians to France to the slave trade. Other plays have taken up the themes of RACISM, money and power, for example, *Ventres pleins, ventres creux* (1971), and have included a Marxist critique of NÉGRITUDE in his parody of Sartre's 1947 essay 'Orphée noir', called *Orphée nègre* (1969), extracts of which were first published in SOUFFLES, whilst Boukman was living in newly liberated ALGERIA. More recently he has published poetry in CREOLE (*Pawol*, 1999). (**Andy Stafford**)

Boulmerka, Hassiba   Born Constantine, ALGERIA, 1968. Woman athlete. In 1991, she was the first African woman to win a world title in the 1500m race at the Barcelona Olympics. Islamists in Algeria denounced her for 'displaying her nudity before the world'! She was also winner of the gold medal in the 1991 and 1995 World Athletic championships. Although she is now in her thirties, Hassiba continues to pose a challenge to younger runners. (**Susan Fox**)

Boumedienne, Houari   Born Guelma, ALGERIA, 1925; died 1978. He conducted guerrilla operations in the ALN (the FLN's military wing) against French forces, throughout the ALGERIAN WAR OF INDEPENDENCE. In 1962, he became Minister of National Defence in the new Algerian government under Ahmed BEN BELLA. Following the 1965 *coup* staged by Boumedienne, a civil–military autocracy emerged in the form of the Council of the Revolution as the predominant force in the new Islamic Socialist government, with Boumedienne ruling as effective head of state, until he formally accepted election as President in 1976. (**Susan Fox**)

Further reading

Minces (1992).

Boupacha, Djamila   Born 1938. Algerian political activist. During the ALGERIAN WAR OF INDEPENDENCE she acted as a liaison agent for the FLN and, aged 23, was imprisoned illegally by the French army. She was interrogated and tortured by officers, who deflowered her with a bottle in order to force her to talk. This was a common-enough method of dealing with female detainees at the time, but shocked liberal French opinion at a time when the terms of Algeria's independence were being negotiated. A Boupacha group led by the victim's Tunisian-born lawyer, Gisèle Halimi, and French writer Simone de Beauvoir, persuaded the French government that she should be released from military prison and the charges against the French military authorities investigated thoroughly. Thanks to Gisèle Halimi's campaign, the case eventually became a decisive victory for the pioneering French women's movement of the 1960s. (**Kamal Salhi**)

Further reading

Beauvoir and Halimi (1962).

Bouraoui, Hédi   Born TUNISIA, 1932. A Francophone poet, novelist and critic. He has lived in Toronto for over 30 years and teaches at York University. He participates in a number of reviews and is a member of the Academy of Literature and Humanities of the Royal Society of Canada. His poetry is a heady mix of linguistic invention and challenge to cultural categories. His novels *Retour à Thyna* (1997) and *La Pharaone* (1999) won him COMAR prizes. Other prizes include the Grand Prix de la Ville de Sfax (1996), the Nouvel-Ontario prize (1999) and the Toronto Book Fair Prize for his story 'Rose des sables' (1998). Other publications include: *Ainsi parle la Tour* (1999), *Bangkok Blues* (1994), *Eclate Module* (1971), *Haïtuvois, suivi de Antillades* (1980), *L'Icônaison* (1985), *Nomadaime* (1995).

Bouraoui, Nina   Born 1967. Algerian writer. Her first novel, *La Voyeuse interdite* (1991; *Forbidden Vision*, 1995), received much critical acclaim for its literary qualities and critique of masculine domination in ALGERIA. The narrator, a young woman in Algiers, is cloistered in the family apartment by her jealous father (and complicit mother), determined to control the sexuality of his daughters and wife. The outcome is a kind of death, as the narrator celebrates her wedding and leaves home to continue the cycle of women's oppression. Bouraoui's subsequent works include *Poing mort* (1992), *Le Bal des murènes* (1996), *L'Age blessé* (1998), *Le Jour du séisme* (1999) and *Garçon manqué* (2000). (**Mark McKinney**)

Bourassa, Robert   1933–96. QUEBEC politician. He became Liberal Prime Minister of Quebec just before the crisis known as 'October 1970', a major milestone in Quebec history. This resulted from the action of a militant political group, the QLF (Quebec Liberation Front), in abducting two prominent figures as hostages (one of whom was killed in the course of the crisis). Bourassa having requested his help, the federal Prime Minister, Pierre TRUDEAU, declared a national emergency and, to general consternation, dispatched tanks and armed soldiers to occupy the streets of Montreal. In addition, the authorities arrested and held without charge 468 people, including writers and intellectuals, arbitrarily suspected of being sympathetic to the QLF. These heavy-handed actions gave the crisis a resonance which went far beyond the events that precipitated it, and ensured its perpetuation in people's memory as a symbol of injustice towards Quebec.

A more productive achievement of Bourassa's early career was his launching of the James Bay hydroelectric project. Although this gigantic undertaking involved friction with the native peoples of the area, it became a symbol of national pride for its technological prowess and its production of environmentally friendly energy.

Bourassa returned as Premier of Quebec in 1985 and again provoked controversy by opposing a ruling of the Canadian Supreme Court which had declared illegal the provisions of the CHARTER OF THE FRENCH LANGUAGE concerning commercial signs. Using a let-out clause in the constitution, Bourassa fashioned a compromise which preserved French-only signs outside shops, but allowed limited use of English inside. This incident, and many similar compromises, revealed the dilemma of the Liberal Party of Quebec in matters concerning Quebec–Canada relations. Although ostensibly the leader of the major pro-federation party, resolutely opposed to the separatism of the PARTI QUÉBÉCOIS, Bourassa was driven by the force of public opinion to defend Quebec interests against the federal power with equivalent virulence, as the LAKE MEECH debate again showed. (Ian Lockerbie)

Further reading

McRoberts (1997) deals fully with the constitutional issues that Bourassa faced.

Bourguiba, Habib   Born Monastir, 1903; died 2000. Tunisian lawyer, journalist and politician. He was educated at the Sorbonne and trained as a lawyer, though he also worked as a journalist. His life was to be spent in organising the masses, seeking to fill them with enthusiasm for politics. At an early age he was active in the DESTOUR party, which advocated TUNISIA's political independence from France. An eloquent speaker in French and Arabic, he appealed to and influenced world opinion. At this time he advocated close co-operation with France (as he was later to promote the project of *la FRANCOPHONIE* alongside SENGHOR). However, he became a staunch nationalist, in 1934 forming the Neo-Destour party, which was banned by the French government several times on account of its anti-French agitation. Bourguiba faced exile, house arrest, imprisonment and, on one occasion, the probability of summary execution. He was deported for two years in 1934, jailed again in 1938, released in 1942, and continued to work for Tunisian independence after World War II. Arrested once more in 1952, he was in and out of prison until 1955, and subject to heavy surveillance whenever he was released. He became Tunisia's Prime Minister in 1956, when the country gained its independence, and was elected President in 1957, when Tunisia became a republic. Bourguiba was proclaimed life president of Neo-Destour at its Ninth National Congress in September 1974. The following March, the National Assembly also unanimously voted him President of the Republic for life. Bourguiba pursued a policy of political non-alignment, but maintained close relations with France and the US, generally taking a moderate position on the Arab–Israeli conflict. He was a strong advocate of women's rights and promoted social equality and secularism. As a result, Tunisia is one of the most prosperous and peaceful member states of the International Francophone Organisation. In November 1987 he was ousted by his newly appointed Prime Minister, Zine al-Abidine BEN ALI, who claimed Bourguiba was too ill and senile to govern. The new President took over a country that was well positioned culturally, socially and economically, with a strong degree of political stability. (Kamal Salhi)

Bouteflika, Abdelaziz   Born Oudja, Morocco, 1937 of an Algerian family. Military and political leader. He became President of ALGERIA in 1999. Bouteflika joined the

National Liberation Army (ALN), the FLN's military wing, in 1956. He was given command of Algeria's frontier zone with MALI, in order to secure the SAHARA as Algerian territory after independence. After independence in 1962, he was elected deputy for Tlemcen in the Constituent Assembly, and was appointed Minister for Youth and Sport in the BEN BELLA government. The following year he was appointed Minister for Foreign Affairs, remaining in this position during the regime of BOUMEDIENNE, of whom he was considered to be a close political associate. Boumedienne's death in 1978 left a political vacuum, which the FLN and its military backers moved swiftly to fill, choosing Chadli BENJEDID, a colonel in the now revamped ALN, the ANP, as President. Bouteflika, who had expected to succeed Boumedienne, was increasingly isolated from the governing élite, and left Algeria in 1981. Charges that he had misappropriated Foreign Ministry funds for personal use during his period of office were later dropped.

He returned to Algeria in 1989, after the implementation of a programme of political reform and a new constitution by the Benjedid government. In the ALGERIAN ELECTIONS OF 1991, Bouteflika stood as an FLN candidate, with the party winning 16 seats against the 188 taken by the Islamic Salvation Front (FIS). An army-led changeover of power blocked the FIS's legislative success. Since then, Algeria has experienced a wave of violence allegedly perpetrated by Islamic extremists, in which 100,000 people have been murdered. Bouteflika held ministerial office in the ZEROUAL government in 1994. He was sole candidate for the presidential election in 1999, following withdrawal of the others, who concluded that fraud had taken place. (**Susan Fox**)

Further reading

Lamchichi (1991).

Boutros-Ghali, Boutros Born Cairo, 1922. Egyptian statesman. Before his election as Secretary-General of the United Nations in 1992, Boutros Boutros-Ghali was Egyptian Deputy Prime Minister, in charge of foreign affairs. Present at the 1978 Camp David summit, he took part in the negotiation of the 1979 Camp David Accords signed by EGYPT and Israel. Professor of International Law and International Relations, Cairo University (1949–77); member of the Central Committee and Political Bureau of the Arab Socialist Union (1974–77); also Vice-President of the Socialist International. Founder and editor-in-chief of the publication *Alahram Igtisadi* and, until 1991, the quarterly *Al-Seyassa Al-Dawlia*, Boutros-Ghali won the Prix Méditerranée Etranger 1998 for the first volume of his memoirs, *Le Chemin de Jérusalem* (Fayard, 1997; *Egypt's Road to Jerusalem: A Diplomat's Story of the Struggle for Peace in the Middle East*, 1997), which described the negotiations leading up to the Camp David Accords. His second volume of memoirs, *Mes Années à la maison de verre* (Fayard, 1999; *Unvanquished: A US–UN Saga*, 1999), recounts his years at the head of the UN. He was elected Secretary-General of the Francophone Agency at the Seventh FRANCOPHONE SUMMIT at Hanoi in November 1997. (**Kamal Salhi**)

Brazzaville Declaration During the Second World War many of French Africa's élite aligned themselves with the Free French, and many Africans had joined the Free

French forces. There was a gradual political awakening in the region, and General DE GAULLE was among the first to recognise the need for a radical revision of France's relationship with the overseas territories. Late in 1944 he called a conference at Brazzaville that is regarded as the starting-point for the constitutional progress made in Black Africa after the war. Brazzaville laid down the lines for far-reaching social and economic reforms, and France invited French Africans to participate in the development of France's post-war constitution. The Declaration also provided for greater administrative decentralisation, the election of territorial assemblies with powers to deliberate over a wide range of subjects and the establishment of councils representing groups of colonies associated within federal structures. At Brazzaville General de Gaulle proclaimed the freedom of the colonised peoples and their right to choose their own destinies. This step prepared the way for France's acceptance of its colonies' moves towards independence. (**Kamal Salhi**)

Further reading

Pleven (1996); Grosser (1967).

Brival, Roland Born 1950. Martinican writer, composer, singer and painter. His writing is thematically varied and unmarked by affiliation to any specific Caribbean identity movement. His novels include *Les Tambours de Gao* (1985) and *Le Dernier des Aloukous* (1996), while his historical plantation novel *Montagne d'ébène* (1984) treats of slave resistance on a plantation in the 1840s and is centred on the relationship between a runaway slave and a planter's daughter. *Biguine Blues* (1999) is a poetic novel with historical resonance; it contrasts the peace of mind that comes with retirement to the hills and a life lived in harmony with traditional music, nature and spirituality, with the turmoil of a life adrift in the cacophony and social dysfunction of the town. Brival's most recent novel, *Robe rouge*, won the Prix RFO 2000. (**Mary Gallagher**)

Brossard, Nicole Born 1943. QUEBEC poet of the avant-garde. She is best known for her feminist convictions, and her disruption of traditional poetic forms. *Le Centre blanc* (1978) and *Amantes* (1980; *Lovers*, 1986) are among her well known poetry collections. Her novels *French Kiss* (1974; *French Kiss or A Pang's Progress*, 1986) and *Le Désert mauve* (1987; *Mauve Desert*, 1990) reveal her conviction that the future of humanity will be better served by 'emotional thought', associated with feminine values, than by the acquisitive drives typical of male attitudes. (**Ian Lockerbie**)

Burkina Faso (See also UPPER VOLTA). Landlocked West African state, bordered by MALI to the north and west, NIGER to the east, and BÉNIN, TOGO, Ghana and the CÔTE D'IVOIRE to the south. Population (*Burkinabé*) was estimated at 12 million in 2001. Capital city: Ougadagou (pop. 500,000: 1994 estimate). Official language: French; major indigenous languages: Mooré, Gourmatché, Dioula and Peul. Some 45 per cent of the population follow traditional religions, 43 per cent are of Islamic faith and 12 per cent Christian. The country consists of extensive plains, low hills, high savannah, and desert to the north. Predominantly agricultural, Burkina Faso suffers from a lack of water resources and fertile soil, and has been hit by recurring droughts in recent years as well as falling gold prices. Burkina Faso is culturally vibrant, particularly in the areas of music and cinema. It hosts biennially the renowned *Festival pan-africain de cinéma de Ougadougou* (FESPACO), showcase for the African film industry.

Mossi and Gurma peoples migrated to the lands making up modern-day Burkina Faso in the twelfth century and established kingdoms. In the precolonial period, Mossi kingdoms displayed remarkable social and religious cohesion, remaining politically stable right up until their conquest by the French. In the European scramble for Africa of the late nineteenth century, the French were keen to gain control of lands around the Niger, and in 1896 took Ougadougou. The Mossi kingdoms became French protectorates in 1897 and a separate colony called Haute Volta (Upper Volta) in 1919. The French invested little in their colony, which was heavily exploited for plantation manpower and conscripts in the two world wars. Indigenous resistance to colonisation was strong from the beginning. In 1960, Haute Volta gained its independence from France. Since independence there have been a series of military *coups*. The most recent of these saw the assassination of the politically and socially radical, non-aligned president, Thomas SANKARA, who gave the country its modern name of Burkina Faso ('Land of honest men'). His successor Blaise COMPAORÉ has won the approval of the World Bank but has been accused by the United Nations of involvement in illegal arms and diamond trading. (**Rachael Langford**)

Further reading

McFarland and Rupley (1998); Aicardi de Saint-Paul (1993).

Burundi   Burundi is a small, landlocked country with a population of about 6.5 million. Subsistence-level agriculture supports 90 per cent of the population and the state's revenue is based upon coffee, tea and cotton production and international aid. Under Belgian colonisation, from 1916 until independence on 1 July 1962, French became the official administrative language and the precolonial ethnic groups of Hutu, Tutsi and Twa were redefined as distinct, racial groups.

In 1966, Captain Micombero ended Burundi's constitutional monarchy and declared a Republic, installing a Tutsi ÉLITE based upon the one-party rule of the *Union pour le Progrès National* (UPRONA) and a Tutsi-dominated army. Between April and June 1972 interethnic massacres caused between 100,000 and 300,000 deaths and thousands of refugees. In 1976, Colonel Bagaza established the Second Republic after a *coup d'état*. A *coup d'état* ousted Bagaza in 1987 and Major Buyoya established the Third Republic. In August 1988, interethnic violence caused between 10,000 and 20,000 deaths and 60,000 refugees. Between October 1988 and April 1992, Buyoya began a slow process of change leading to the elections of 1993. These were won by the *Front Démocratique de Burundi* (FRODEBU), with Melchior Ndadaye elected President. In October 1993, President Ndadaye was killed in an attempted military *coup d'état*. This led to interethnic violence and army retaliation, causing thousands of refugees.

Between 1994 and Buyoya's *coup d'état* in July 1996, UPRONA gradually restored its political position and a civil war developed. International economic sanctions and pressure led, in 1998, to negotiations, mediated by the Tanzanian President Nyerere, in Arusha, Tanzania. In December 1999, Nelson Mandela became the new mediator and, on 23 July 2001, a power-sharing agreement was finally signed establishing a coalition government for a transition period of 36 months, after which elections would be held. (**Peter Langford**)

Further reading

For the period up to independence: Lemarchand (1970/ 1979). For the postcolonial period: Chrétien and Guichaoua (1988); Chrétien, Guichaoua and Le Jeune (1988); Lemarchand (1994); Chrétien (1997); Reyntjens (2000); *Réseau documentaire sur la région des Grands Lacs africains.*

Cabon, Marcel 1912–72. Mauritian jounalist, poet and novelist. Cabon is the author of novels such as *Namasté* (1965), and poems which illustrate the fusion of Francophone and Indian cultures particular to Mauritius, through the celebration of Indo-Mauritian peasant life and traditions. (**Peter Hawkins**)

Cajun The term Cajun (derived from *(A)cadien*) describes a descendant of French Canadians expelled by the British from the captured French colony of Acadia in 1755 (present-day Nova Scotia and adjacent areas). Many deportees to France returned to America between 1764 and 1788 and settled in the fertile lands of southern Louisiana. In the relative isolation of these areas, the close-knit communities of the Cajuns remained largely unaffected by external political and linguistic developments in Louisiana until the early twentieth century. However, the Mandatory Education Act of 1916, industrialisation and oil exploration, and the 1921 Constitution which established English as the sole official language of the state, were defining points for the Cajuns' language and culture since French was excluded from key domains such as education and religion. A rapid decline in the use of French in favour of English ensued: many parents ceased to transmit French actively to their children and the overwhelming majority of Cajun French speakers today are bilingual.

Linguistically, Cajun French stands as a distinct variety of French, different from Louisiana Creole, Louisiana French and Standard French – the international norm. It retains many dialectal features (lexical and structural) inherited from the French spoken by the initial settlers but, due to its independent evolution, it has also developed original features. It is, to this day, essentially a spoken and unstandardised language.

Since 1968, both Cajun French and culture have been promoted as positive symbols of Louisiana French identity. Actions taken by the CODOFIL (Council for the Development of French in Louisiana) have improved the legal status of Cajun French, developing educational and language codification programmes. The efforts of Cajun activists also seek to reconstruct a culturally defined Louisiana French identity, notably through music and literature, together with the commercialisation of the ethnic lifestyle and food largely defined by the ethic of *joie de vivre*. Major figures in this cultural revival include the musicians Zachary Richard and Michael Doucet, and the writers Revon Reed, Antoine Bourque and Richard Guidry. (**Marie-Anne Hintze**)

Further reading

Chapters by Henry and Brown in Valdman (1997) discuss the Louisiana French Movement and Cajun cultural revival. See also Ancelet (1991) for a presentation of Cajun musical revival and Barry (1989) on the literary renaissance.

Caldoche Term of recent origin, originally pejorative, used to describe people of Metropolitan French origin, living in New Caledonia.

Cambodia South-east Asian country, on the Gulf of Thailand, bordering Thailand, Vietnam and Laos. Main river: the Mekong. Population: 12.5m. Capital: Phnom Penh. Official language: Khmer. Mainly agricultural (rice), with timber and gemstone resources and a growing tourist industry. Home of an ancient civilisation, illustrated most notably in the temples of Angkor Wat.

A French protectorate from 1863, independence was gained in 1953. The king, Norodom Sihanouk, abdicated in 1955 in favour of his father, remaining in power, however, as Prime Minister, promoting a 'Buddhist Socialism' and heading the Popular Socialist Community party. He was overthrown in 1970 by General Lon Nol in a US-backed *coup*, in order to end Cambodian neutrality in the fight against communism. Nonetheless, the Cambodian Khmer Rouge forces, under Pol Pot, succeeded in taking Phnom Penh in 1975 and establishing a brutal regime, in which the urban population was evacuated to the countryside, with the death or execution of up to 2 million people. A Vietnamese invasion in 1978 sparked off 13 years of fighting. The economy and basic social infrastructure were practically annihilated as a result of the political turmoil. The situation only began to stabilise at the beginning of the 1990s, with the eclipse of Khmer Rouge power, the formation of a coalition government and elections in 1993. Sihanouk was restored as king, as part of a constitutional monarchy. Since then, coalition government, based on the two largest parties, FUNCINPEC and the Communists, has prevailed, with the king's son, Norodom Ranariddh, sharing power with Hun Sen, although this arrangement was temporarily disturbed by violence, following elections held in 1998, in what was effectively an attempted *coup d'état*.

Cambodia is a member of the OIF and has links with both France and other members of the Francophone world. Francophone influence, practically wiped out in the 1970s, is beginning to make its presence felt once again, mainly in higher education and co-operation projects (see COOPÉRATION), with the support of Sihanouk and other members of his generation, though there has been some resistance in favour of English by younger people. There is only a small minority of French speakers.

Further reading

Regaud and Lechervy (1996) – deal with conflict in the whole region; Delvert (1983) – for concise information on Cambodia; Lechervy (1993) – for a discussion of the political settlement and its prospects.

Cameroon   A central-African country bordered by Nigeria, CHAD, CENTRAL AFRICAN REPUBLIC, GABON and Equatorial Guinea; 14,303,010 inhabitants; capital Yaoundé. Originally colonised by the Germans in the late nineteenth century, it was divided between France and Britain after the First World War and remains Francophone in the north and east and Anglophone in the west. As such it belongs both to *FRANCOPHONIE* and the Commonwealth, although the Francophone culture is dominant and it maintains close economic ties with France, using the CFA franc as its currency. Over 200 ethnic groups speaking a similar number of African languages make up its population; over half practise traditional African beliefs, but a third are Christian, either Catholic or Protestant, and some 16 per cent Muslim. One of the economically more prosperous countries of the region, its relative wealth is generated by a varied agricultural output – coffee, cocoa, bananas, rubber, cotton and palm-oil for export, and corn, millet, sorghum, rice, yams, manioc and plantain for domestic consumption. The country also has considerable mineral resources – oil, bauxite, iron ore – and exports both crude and refined oil products through its coastal terminal at Kribi. Douala, the economic capital, is also the country's major port.

Culturally, Cameroon has produced several writers of an international stature, almost all Francophone: probably the best known, the novelist MONGO BETI (1932–2001) spent most of his career in France as a political exile, and was extremely critical of the corrupt and authoritarian regimes of the post-independence period. His contemporary Ferdinand OYONO (b. 1929), also a critic of the French colonial regime in his early novels, went on to represent his country as a diplomat. Other well-known figures of the post-independence generation are the poet and novelist Bernard NANGA (1934–85); the novelist, dramatist, artist and singer WEREWERE LIKING (b. 1950), who has lived for most of her artistic career in IVORY COAST; and the controversial novelist Calixthe BEYALA (b. 1961), who has made her name in France. (**Peter Hawkins**)

Camus, Albert   Born Mondovi, East ALGERIA, 1913; died Sens, France, 1960. French *pied-noir* writer. His parents were second-generation settlers. After the death of his father in 1914, his mother moved to Belcourt, a working-class quarter in Algiers, where Albert was brought up. He was forced to leave it at the age of seventeen, when he suffered his first attack of tuberculosis, and embarked on an independent and itinerant life. His illness prevented Camus from pursuing an academic career; instead he became a journalist and a regular contributor to the left-wing newspaper *Alger Républicain*. First published in October 1938, its principal aim was the creation of equal rights for all Frenchmen living in Algeria, Europeans and Muslims alike. Although Camus adhered to this objective and declared himself a proponent of the new spirit of political reform, he painfully lived the years of the ALGERIAN REVOLUTION. When, in 1957, he delivered a speech after being awarded the Nobel Prize for Literature, Camus was interrupted by an Algerian student who asked him why he did not condemn torture in Algeria. Camus replied that he loved justice, but if he had to choose between his mother and justice, he would then choose his mother. This remark put Camus in a difficult position: he was caught in a deep conflict over the question of belonging, for he knew no other homeland than Algeria, and the raging war between the French and the Algerians was far beyond reconciliation. This Camus expressed in his novel *L'Etranger* (1942; *The Outsider*, 1942). In fact, the foreigner in *L'Etranger* was no other person but Camus himself living through a deep identity crisis. Camus died in a car accident near Paris, in 1960, leaving behind him a wealth of literary output made up of novels, short stories, plays, essays and various articles in *Alger Républicain, Le Soir Républicain,* of which he was editor, *Combat* and other journals and newspapers. (**Zahia Smail Salhi**)

Further reading

Freeman (1971); Thody (1961).

Canada and North America   See Audio-visual media; cinema; Language and language policies; Literature; Politics; Theatre.

Capécia, Mayotte   Born Carbet, Martinique, 1916; died 1955. Martinican writer. Although Capécia's studies were curtailed by the outbreak of World War II, her early experiences made her a skilled novelist. Immediately after the war, she left her homeland for France in 1946, where she wrote her first novel. Her years of exile were interrupted by a single brief return trip in 1948. In France she devoted herself to literature. Following the completion of her second novel, she learned that she was suffering from cancer. She turned to painting as a form of art therapy, but died in 1955. She remains well known for her novels, *Je suis une Martiniquaise* (1948; *I am a Martinican Woman*, 1997), which combines a retrospective view of the main character's life with a certain amount of exoticism, and *La Négresse blanche* (1956; *The White Negress*, 1997), which explores the relationships between Europeans and West Indians in considerable depth. (**Kamal Salhi**)

Further reading

Makward (1999).

Cardinal, Marie   Born Algiers, 1929; died Avignon, France, 2001. Pied noir feminist writer. She studied at the University of Algiers and at the Sorbonne, after which she taught philosophy in Greece, Portugal, Austria and Canada. From 1961, she worked for the publishers Gallimard and Grasset and also as a journalist. She lived for many years in Quebec, where she was married to the dramatist Jean-Pierre Ronfard and also worked in the theatre herself. Prizes include the *Prix international du premier roman* (*Ecoutez la mer*, 1962), *Prix Lettré* (1976). Other novels include *La Clé sur la porte,* (1972), *Une Vie pour deux* (1978), *Amours...amours* (1998). She also published an emotional account of her early life in Algeria, *Au Pays de mes racines* (1980), along with autobiographical novels (*Les Mots pour le dire*, 1975; *Words to Say It*, 1983) and works which reflect on her experiences as a woman and a writer, such as *Autrement dit* (1977; *In Other Words*, 1995). Honorary life president of the *Syndicat des écrivains de langue française.*

Caribbean   See Education; Food; Francophone Black Atlantic; Literature; Music; Race/population.

Carle, Gilles Born 1929. Quebec film-maker, with a long list of box office successes, including *La Vie heureuse de Léopold Z* (1965), *Le Viol d'une jeune fille douce* (1968), *Red* (1969), *Les Mâles* (1970), *La Vraie Nature de Bernadette* (1972), *La Mort d'un bûcheron* (1973), *Fantastica* (1980), *Maria Chapdelaine* (1983). These films criticised flaws in Quebec society in a lively, freewheeling style, which occasionally borrowed from Hollywood, as in the use of an alluring female star, Carole Laure, but also parodied its techniques. His films since the 1990s, however, have been less popular. (**Ian Lockerbie**)

Carlot, Maxime Born 1942. Francophone Vanuatuan politician, with a platform of support for French-speaking interests. He was Prime Minister from 1991 to 1995, and again in 1996.

Carrier, Roch Born Sainte-Justine-de-Dorchester, Quebec, 1937. Quebec writer. He is best known for *La Guerre, yes sir* (1968; Eng. trans., same title, 1970), *Floralie, où estu?* (1969; *Floralie, where are you?* 1971) and *Il est par là, le soleil* (1970; *Is it the Sun, Philibert?* 1972). These, like *Il n'y a pas de pays sans grand-père* (1979; *No Country without Grandfathers*, 1981), depict in fantastic form the clash of values of old rural Quebec with those of the modern world. Later works continue to show an affection for village life and the rural scene, which has led some commentators to see his outlook as too fixedly nostalgic. But he is an effective storyteller and one of the most widely read of contemporary Quebec writers. (**Ian Lockerbie**)

Casbah of Algiers The Casbah of Algiers represents the pre-colonial medina, which in 1830 was a walled pre-industrial town composed of traditional houses and other buildings, such as mosques and *medersas*, which had evolved on Islamic urban principles. The hillside location resulted in often stepped narrow streets, lined with courtyard vernacular houses, usually with terraced roofs. French occupation in 1830 resulted in much destruction of the Lower Casbah, near the port, and the pushing through of new straight roads. Classification as an historic monument in 1887 did not do much to prevent degradation of this marginalised and largely indigenous district of a colonial dual city. Overpopulation and subdivision of vernacular houses furthered their degradation, sometimes to the point of collapse. The architect Le Corbusier was enthusiastic about the Casbah's traditional houses in the 1930s but proposed two immense modern structures, which would have dominated and ruined the district. By 1959, 85,000 were living in the Casbah at intolerably high densities. Independence in 1962 meant an influx of rural immigrants and the departure of middle-class residents to vacant ex-settler houses in the colonial town. Surveys in the late 1960s and 1970s, especially by the Atelier du Casbah, led to some intervention to restore some major buildings. By the 1980s, Lesbet reckoned that 1030 vernacular houses still existed out of 1750 houses in total. However, 30 per cent of them were insalubrious and 30 per cent needed major repairs. Rehabilitation of the Casbah required prior de-densification. Belatedly in 1992 the district was declared a UNESCO World Heritage Site but demolitions continued to outnumber restorations. However, the restoration of the Bastion 23, a waterfront outpost of eighteenth-century buildings, carried out in 1991–92, was an achievement. Other significant restored buildings include the sixteenth-century citadel, the Ketchaoua mosque and the Palace of the Dey.

In the ALGERIAN WAR OF INDEPENDENCE, the Casbah was an FLN stronghold from whence bombers hit the Cafeteria in September 1956 and other targets in the European part of the city. General Massu sought to reclaim the Casbah for the security forces in the BATTLE OF ALGIERS, with house-to-house searches culminating in the capture of Casbah guerrilla leader Yacef Saadi and the blowing up of Ali la Pointe. (**Keith Sutton**)

Further reading

Icheboudene (1997); Lesbet (1985); Sutton (1996).

CEDEAO *Communauté Economique des Etats de l'Afrique de l'Ouest*   Formed in 1975, the CEDEAO is known in English as the Economic Community of West African States (ECOWAS). The aim of the community was initially the economic integration of states with disparate historical, cultural, economic and political backgrounds with a view to the promotion of growth and development. These aims have only minimally been achieved. Latterly the CEDEAO has developed a capacity to intervene in regional conflicts. Both the economic and political ambitions of the community have been impeded by rivalry between the Francophone and Anglophone blocs. (**Simon Massey**)

Central African Republic (*Centrafrique***)**   Landlocked country, bordered by CHAD, Sudan, CONGO and CAMEROON. Under French rule it was known as Oubangui-Chari. Population approx. 3.3m, composed of Bandas, Gbaya-Manzas, Ngbandis, Zandés, Saras and other ethnic groups. Capital: Bangui, on Oubangui River. Official languages: French, Sango. Religions: Christianity (Protestants 40 per cent; Catholics 28 per cent); traditional (24 per cent); Islam (8 per cent). One of the poorest countries in the world with high youth unemployment. French aid represents 20–25 per cent GNP. Mainly agricultural, with significant diamond resources. Other exports include coffee, cotton, timber. Member of the Central African Customs Union, whose headquarters is in Bangui.

The French colony of Oubangui-Chari was formed, after lengthy military campaigns, in 1905, becoming part of AEF in 1910. Mainly under the control of concessionary companies, the colonised were subject to brutal treatment and forced labour, which provoked strong resistance, e.g. the Kongo-Wara War (1928–35). World War I saw many soldiers from the colony in the French Army. In World War II, it was one of the first colonies to support Free France. 1946 saw the abolition of forced labour and the election to the French National Assembly of Barthélemy Boganda, who created MESAN (*Mouvement de l'évolution sociale de l'Afrique noire*) in 1949. In 1958, after DE GAULLE's referendum, the République Centrafricaine was founded. A mysterious plane crash killed Boganda a year later. Independence came in 1960, with David Dacko as leader, and transformation to a one-party state in 1962. After a military *coup*, Jean BOUKASSA ruled from 1965 until his overthrow in 1979 by the French army, after a surfeit of excesses, including his coronation as emperor and bloody repression of popular revolt, even the massacre of children. Dacko was restored as leader, before another military *coup* put André Kolingba in power. A National Conference began the process of democratic reform in 1992, leading to Ange-Félix Patassé's election as President in 1993. Unrest has continued sporadically, provoking further French military intervention, along with the creation of a combined African military force to help maintain the peace.

The most notable literary figure is Pierre Makombo Bamboté. Other writers include Faustin-Albert Ipeko-Etomane, Pierre Sammy, Etienne Goyémidé, Cyriaque Yavoucka, Antonio-Gabriel Franck.

Centre–periphery   Cartography has traditionally depended on an imaginary construction of space – linked to what geographers call the 'omphalos syndrome', which places the mapmaker's culture at the centre of the world and others on its periphery. The gradual creation and consolidation of the French Empire depended on a similar ideological process that placed metropolitan France as a model to be emulated at the centre of power and civilisation. Relegating colonised cultures to a supposedly dark, exotic, powerless and uncivilised periphery, this binary and hierarchical division of the world provided the principal justification for the *mission civilisatrice* (civilising mission) central to French COLONIAL POLICY after the mid-nineteenth century. Although postcolonial literature and criticism have endeavoured to dismantle such binaries, certain aspects of NEO-COLONIAL practice and thought have ensured the perpetuation of a centre–periphery understanding of international relations. (**Charles Forsdick**)

Césaire, Aimé   Born 1913. Martinican poet, dramatist and politician. Theorist of NÉGRITUDE, co-founder in 1947 of PRÉSENCE AFRICAINE, member of parliament, celebrated by André Breton and the Surrealists. Co-founder in 1930s Paris of the journal *L'Etudiant noir* and educated in France's élite system, he assimilated the greats of French literature – Baudelaire, Rimbaud, Mallarmé. Breton described his epic poem *Cahier d'un retour au pays natal* (1939; *Notebook of a return to the homeland*, 1968) as 'the greatest lyric monument of our time'. Mixing Caribbean, African and European poetic traditions into a multi-voiced and troubling narrative, the *Cahier* is now a classic of Francophone Caribbean LITERATURE. Inspiration for the poem was his return to MARTINIQUE in 1935 to find a downtrodden people, who, through discovering their African and slave-revolt ROOTS, are shown to stand up and demand dignity and freedom. Other collections of poetry written in the same erudite, opaque and polemical style followed: *Les Armes miraculeuses* (1946), *Soleil cou coupé* (1948).

Elected in 1945 to represent Martinique in the new Constituent Assembly in Paris, he made a speech in 1950, *Discours sur le colonialisme* (*Discourse on Colonialism*, 1972), an indictment of European colonialism and a Communist tirade against American imperialism. However, he left the Communist Party over the 1956 invasion of Hungary, writing his famous *Lettre à Maurice Thorez* (*Letter to Maurice Thorez*, 1957). Continuing to publish prize-winning poetry (1960 and 1961), he founded the *Parti Progressiste et Martiniquais* (PPM) in 1958, wrote a biography of Haitian revolutionary leader Toussaint-Louverture (1961), and a series of plays, the most famous of which – *Une saison au Congo* (1967; *A Season in the Congo*, 1969) – deals with murdered Congolese leader Patrice Lᴜᴍᴜᴍʙᴀ. Recent critical reassessment of his achievements (Confiant, 1993) focuses on his failure to win Martinican independence and on his ignoring of Cʀᴇᴏʟᴇ language and culture. (**Andy Stafford**)

Further reading

Confiant (1993) – highly critical but balanced account of Césaire's politics in relation to his writing; Davis (1997) – accessible analysis of literary output.

CFA *Communauté Financière Africaine* (African Financial Community). Although the CFA is commonly used as an umbrella term to designate the African franc, there are in fact two distinct financial zones, each with its own currency and currency-issuing bank, although both are pegged to the French currency at the same level. The BCEAO (*Banque Centrale des Etats d'Afrique de l'Ouest*), based in Dakar, issues the *Franc de la Communauté Financière Africaine*, the currency of the UEMOA (*Union économique et monétaire ouest-africaine*) zone, whose current member states are: Bᴇ́ɴɪɴ, Bᴜʀᴋɪɴᴀ Fᴀѕᴏ, Cᴏ̂ᴛᴇ ᴅ'Iᴠᴏɪʀᴇ, Guinea-Bissau, Mᴀʟɪ, Nɪɢᴇʀ, Sᴇɴᴇɢᴀʟ, Tᴏɢᴏ. The BEAC (*Banque des Etats de l'Afrique centrale*), based in Yaounde, issues the *Franc de la coopération financière en Afrique centrale*, the currency of the CEMAC (*Communauté économique et monétaire de l'Afrique centrale*), whose current member states are Cᴀᴍᴇʀᴏᴏɴ, Cᴇɴᴛʀᴀʟ Aꜰʀɪᴄᴀɴ Rᴇᴘᴜʙʟɪᴄ, Cᴏɴɢᴏ (*République du Congo*), Gᴀʙᴏɴ, Cʜᴀᴅ, Equatorial Guinea. See Eᴄᴏɴᴏᴍɪᴄ ʀᴇʟᴀᴛɪᴏɴѕ; Fʀᴀɴᴄ ᴢᴏɴᴇ.

Further reading

For a useful factual and analytical briefing paper and bibliography by Africa Research Group at FCO, see 'Growing up with the umbilical cord attached', at http://files.fco.gov.uk/info/research/africafranc.pdf and also websites of the various institutions: www.Uemoa.int; www.Cemac.int; www.Banque-france.fr

CFP *Communauté financière du Pacifique* The Pacific Financial Community designates the currency zone of the CFP or Pacific franc (XPF). This zone includes the French Pacific territories of Nᴇᴡ Cᴀʟᴇᴅᴏɴɪᴀ, French Pᴏʟʏɴᴇѕɪᴀ and the Wᴀʟʟɪѕ & Fᴜᴛᴜɴᴀ islands. The currency is issued by the *Instutut d'Emission d'Outre-Mer* in Paris. With a fixed exchange parity against the French franc since 1949, it is now tied to the Euro.

Chad Central African country, to the south of Libya and sharing borders also with Nɪɢᴇʀ, Nigeria, Cᴀᴍᴇʀᴏᴏɴ, Cᴇɴᴛʀᴀʟ Aꜰʀɪᴄᴀɴ Rᴇᴘᴜʙʟɪᴄ and Sudan. Chad's postcolonial history has seen unremitting civil strife, interspersed with cyclical external interventions. Reasons for the conflict overlap in a complex web of ethnic, religious, economic and political motivations. On an elemental level, an animus between northern Muslim groups and the Christian and animist peoples of the south was exacerbated and entrenched by a negligent French colonial administration. However, the sociology of the conflict goes beyond crude dichotomies, with the many ethnic groups and sub-groups equally open to segmentation.

On 11 August 1960 Chad became an independent republic. The first President,

François Ngarta T OMBALBAYE, consolidated his rule using repression. In response, as early as 1966, a rebellion had coalesced behind the *Front de Libération Nationale de Tchad* (FROLINAT). In 1975 Tombalbaye was killed in a *coup d'état*. The conflict came to fit the 'warlord model', with its stress on regional centres of power based on personalised rule and military force. After three years of civil war, Hissène Habré, a northern warlord, emerged as the strongest faction leader. A ruthless dictator, Habré sought to extend his control beyond the capital N'Djaména using iron rule and the military support of France, which saw Chad as a bulwark against Libyan encroachment into West and Central Africa. However, in the light of its new pro-democracy policy for Africa, France did not intervene to support Habré when his erstwhile army commander, Idriss Deby, overthrew him in 1990.

Deby embarked on a protracted democratic transition. He was elected President in 1996 and re-elected in 2001. Both presidential and legislative polls were flawed. Although levels of civil violence have diminished under Deby, rebellion continues in the north. Human rights abuses are widespread. Although Chad remains very poor, the proposed exploitation of oil reserves in the south should greatly improve the standard of living in the country. (**Simon Massey**)

Further reading

Nolutshungu (1996) – by far the best and most readable account of Chad's postcolonial political economy.

Challe, Maurice   Born Pontet, 1905; died Paris, 1979. General of the French air force. Senior military commander. He entered the air force in 1925 after attending Saint-Cyr. Distinguished war record. M OLLET government's military representative to Britain during the Suez campaign (1956). Commander-in-chief of French forces in A LGERIA 1958–60. Executed military offensive called the 'Challe plan' against the FLN. After remaining loyal to troops defending French Algeria during the civil unrest of 'barricades week' (1960), Challe opposed DE G AULLE in an increasingly political manner, finally leading the failed military *coup* of April 1961, for which Challe was imprisoned for fifteen years. (**Marianne Durand**)

Further reading

Bromberger, Elgey and Chauvel (1960) – dramatic account of the role of the French military in the civil disturbances of 'barricades week' in Algiers 1960; Challe (1968) – Maurice Challe's personal account of his military command in Algeria.

Chamoiseau, Patrick   Born M ARTINIQUE, 1953. Most successful and versatile of the CRÉOLITÉ writers. His novels are experimental in form and language, subverting linearity and fusing French and C REOLE. They are usually set in urban Martinique. In their reconstruction of a forgotten and fragmented past, they celebrate privileged vectors of an increasingly threatened Creole culture: the marketplace of *Chronique des sept misères* (1986; *Chronicle of the Seven Sorrows*, 1999); the oral tradition, and particularly the central role of the storyteller, in *Solibo Magnifique* (1988; *Solibo Magnificent*, 1997); the popular neighbourhoods of Fort-de-France in the Goncourt-winning *Texaco* (1992; *Texaco*, 1997). Departing from this urban milieu, *L'Esclave vieil homme et le molosse* (1997) tells the story of a runaway slave. (**Maeve McCusker**)

Chandernagore   Former French colony, on the River Hooghly (Ganges), West Bengal, 30 km north of Calcutta and most important commercial centre of the '*Comptoirs de l'Inde*' (Chandernagore, Karaikal, Mahe, Pondicherry, Yanam (Yanaoun)), left to France after its unsuccessful struggle against its British rival in India. Its gates, inscribed with the French motto, *Liberté, Egalité, Fraternité*, provided a refuge from the British for Indian nationalists, especially those involved in its revolutionary wing, including Aurobindo Ghosh, who sheltered here in 1910, before leaving for Pondicherry. Chandernagore was ceded to India in the Treaty of Cession of Chandernagore, of 1952, and formally transferred in 1954. Now merged into the sprawl of greater Calcutta, it bears few signs of its original Frenchness, apart from its colonial architecture, including the governor's residence, where once Dupleix had stayed (now a cultural institute), and a French convent school, St Joseph's.

Charef, Mehdi   Born Maghnia, Algeria, 1952. Maghrebi-French writer and filmmaker, who has lived in France since childhood. He is best known for his novel portraying banlieue life, *Le Thé au harem d'Archi Ahmed* (1983; *Tea in the Harem*, 1989), and the film *Le Thé au harem d'Archimède* (1985). The titles' pun on the theorem of Archimedes symbolises the school system's failure to teach Maghrebi-French youths. His other movies are *Camomille* (1988), *Miss Mona* (1987, about a clandestin), and *Au Pays des Juliets* (1992, portraying three women prisoners, one a Maghrebian), *Marie-Line* (2000, about the FN and *clandestines*) and *La Maison d'Alexina* (2001). His subsequent novels are *Le Harki de Meriem* (1989), about racism and the memory of the Algerian War of Independence, and *La Maison d'Alexina* (1999). (**Mark McKinney**)

Charlebois, Robert   Born 1944. Singer–songwriter from Quebec. Charlebois came to prominence in 1965 and soon established a reputation in France, combining lyrical and personal songs in a nostalgic tone with sounds and rhythms borrowed from North American rock music. The lyrics are often provided by poets and writers such as Réjean Ducharme and Claude Péloquin. The consecration of his career came with a joint concert in Montreal in 1976 when he shared the stage with two other heroes of the *chanson québécoise* from earlier generations, Félix Leclerc and Gilles Vigneault. He remains one of the best-known exponents of Quebec popular song in both Canada and France. (**Peter Hawkins**)

Charonne   On 8 February 1962 French police killed nine anti-fascist protestors at and around the Charonne metro station (Paris). The mainstream Left, which in the four months preceding Charonne had unified against *Organisation armée secrète* (OAS) violence, police repression, and in support of peace in Algeria, organised a massive response – the national general strike (13 February), which marked the victims' funerals in Paris and represented the largest political mobilisation in France since 1934. Charonne's subsequent inscription within the political mythology of the left probably overlaid the memory of the October 1961 Paris massacre, when the dead were Algerian, not French. (**Jim House**)

Further reading

Heurgon (1994) – see Chapter 16, pp. 355–75, which provides a detailed and reliable examination of the political context from a key activist at the time.

Charte d'Alger   (Charter of Algiers). The name given to the set of texts adopted by the FLN at its first congress, in April 1964. Their aim was to bring together different strands within the independence movement under the umbrella concept of ALGERIA as both an Arab and a Muslim country. The Charter argued that it was this idea that had sustained the Algerian people throughout colonisation and enabled the revolution. Independence meant that the true identity of Algeria could be reasserted. The Charter also attempted to integrate the strategies of the planners with the aims of the advocates of the self-management (*autogestion*) movement. (**Kay Adamson**)

Further reading

Clegge (1971): see Appendix II (pp. 210–20), which gives a translation of a small section of the Charter, covering 'the ideological foundations of the Algerian Revolution', 'the socialist revolution' and the 'transition from capitalism to socialism'.

Charte de la Francophonie   (Francophone Charter). This is the text adopted by the tenth session of the CMF, acting as the general conference of the AGENCE DE LA FRANCOPHONIE at Hanoi on 16 November 1997. At this meeting the Francophone heads of state and government decided to elect a secretary-general, who was to be the keystone of the Francophone world's institutional system. It was also necessary to give this figure a legal framework lacked by the institutions set up following earlier summits. The heads of state and government were of the opinion that the *Charte de l'Agence*, which subsequently became known as the *Charte de la Francophonie*, provided a sufficient legal basis for the secretary-general's work. The aim of the Charter was to ensure the perpetuation of 'the Francophone ideal, the ideals of liberty and human rights, the ideals of justice and solidarity, and the ideals of democracy, development and progress'. (**Kamal Salhi**)

Further reading

Mworoha (1995).

Charter of the French Language   Often known as Law 101, the 1977 Charter made French the official language of QUEBEC, in defiance of Canada's bilingual legislation. It required all public signs and commercial material to be in French. Immigrant children had to be educated in French-language schools, businesses with more than 50 employees had to convert to working in French. Although amended in certain respects by the Supreme Court, the law has been successful in restoring French as the public language, without affecting the rights of the resident Anglophone community, who retained all their traditional English-language institutions. (**Ian Lockerbie**)

Chazal, Malcolm de   1902–81. Mauritian poet and painter. Chazal's collection of aphoristic prose poetry *Sens plastique* (1947; *Plastic Sense*, 1971) was discovered by

Jean Paulhan and André Breton and hailed as an example of an authentically spontaneous surrealist writing. Chazal's visionary celebration of the mystical geography of his native island was the theme of many subsequent volumes, such as *Petrusmok* (1951), in which he speculated on the cosmic forces that might have created the island's singular environment. (**Peter Hawkins**)

Cheb Hasni   Born Oran, 1968; died 1994. Algerian RAÏ singer whose daring duo (it blatantly mentions the taboo subject of illicit sex) with female artiste, Zahouania, brought him fame in 1987. In spite of death threats Hasni refused to flee the Algerian civil war. By the time of his assassination (which he predicted in the song 'Goulou Hasni mett' – They say Hasni's dead) he had recorded hundreds of often autobiographical songs conveying the difficulties of life and love for young people in ALGERIA and beyond. Divorced, he left behind a child and innumerable fans. His assassins remain at large. (**Samantha Neath**)

Cheb Mami   Born Mohamed Khelifati, Saida, 1966. Algerian RAÏ singer. The youngest of eight, nicknamed 'Mami' ('kid') because of his adolescent success in an Algerian television talent contest, he began singing at weddings and festivals, and recording cassettes. The first émigré RAÏ-man, he triumphed at the French *Festival de Bobigny* in 1986. Despite initial immigration problems and the public's resistance to songs in Arabic, he went on to make five internationally acclaimed albums. Credited by Sting as having the most beautiful voice in the world, he celebrated the twentieth year of his career in 2001 with a Bercy (Paris) concert in aid of Algerian flood victims. (**Samantha Neath**)

Cheikh Abbas Bencheikh El Hocine   Born 1912, Constantine *département* of ALGERIA. Muslim cleric. He became a senior figure in the reformist Muslim movements of the OULEMAS during the 1930s. During the ALGERIAN WAR OF INDEPENDENCE (1954–62), he became a diplomatic representative of the *Front de Libération Nationale* (FLN). Appointed Rector of the PARIS MOSQUE in 1982, he died in office seven years later after seeking to raise the profile of France's growing Muslim minority in a spirit of tolerance and dialogue. (**Alec G. Hargreaves**)

Further reading

The obituary by Laffifi (1989) covers both the spiritual and political dimensions of Cheikh Abbas's life.

Cheikha Rimitti   Born Algeria, 1920s. Algerian singer. This celebrated queen of *raï* began her career as a penniless orphan, joining the nomadic singers who entertained at religious festivals and wedding feasts. Rimitti, whose name derives from a request, in broken French, to fill her glass ('*remettez*'), cut her first record in 1954, and eventually moved to France in the late 1970s. In 2001, following successful concerts in the USA, she visited ALGERIA for the first time in over 25 years. The muted reception by the authorities precipitated her return to France, where, like MAMI and KHALED she continues her career. (**Samantha Neath**)

Cheynet, Anne Born 1938. Reunionese poet and novelist. She came to prominence with her first novel, *Les Muselés* (1977), set in the popular CREOLE milieu of REUNION, marginalised and disenfranchised by political corruption. Her concern for the outcasts and underdogs of Reunionese society is reflected in a more recent novel, *Rivages maouls* (1994). (**Peter Hawkins**)

Chibane, Malik Born Saint-Vallier, France, 1964. Film-maker. He was brought up in the Paris suburb of Goussainville. After training as an electronics engineer and working in the theatre, he became involved in organising community cultural events, mainly through the association IDRISS. His films *Hexagone* (1995), *Douce France* (1995), *Nés quelque part* (1997) look at BANLIEUE life with wit and humour, from an insider's viewpoint.

Chirac, Jacques (René) Born Paris, 1932. Chirac is France's leading centre-right politician. He studied at the *Institut d'Etudes Politiques* and saw military service in ALGERIA. He graduated from the *Ecole Nationale d'Administration* in 1959 and joined the civil service the same year.

In 1962, Chirac took charge of the private office of Prime Minister Georges Pompidou and earned the nickname 'Bulldozer' for his no-nonsense approach. He was elected to parliament in 1967 and held numerous cabinet posts before becoming Prime Minister in 1974. He resigned two years later and formed a neo-Gaullist movement, the *Rassemblement pour la République* (the Republican Rally). He became Prime Minister for a second time (1986–88) but failed in his first two bids for the Presidency (1981, 1988).

Chirac won the 1995 presidential contest but became instantly unpopular with voters. He salvaged his image by adopting a high profile foreign policy which, although more pragmatic than DE GAULLE's (e.g. his ending of conscription), was also deeply reminiscent of Gaullism (e.g. his resumption of NUCLEAR TESTING in the South Pacific). Nowhere was Chirac's Gaullist heritage clearer than in his efforts to extend French influence throughout the Francophone world. To this end, he visited VIETNAM and LEBANON and invited them to host the 1997 and 2001 FRANCOPHONE SUMMITS. He also paid frequent state visits to black Africa and oversaw significant increases in aid to former dependencies in North Africa.

Chirac remained in charge of foreign policy, despite the 1997 election of socialist Premier Lionel JOSPIN and despite damaging allegations of complicity in funding scandals dating back to his time as mayor of Paris (1977–95). He did, however, have to compromise and accept Jospin's radical reforms of French economic and miltary aid policies. He will wish to draw a line under these measures following his re-election in the 2002 presidential elections. (**Gordon Cumming**)

Further reading

AGIR ICI ET SURVIE (1995) – critical account of Chirac's relations with undemocratic African regimes; Giesbert (1995) – the standard political biography.

Choukri, Mohammed Born near Nadhor, 1935. Moroccan writer. He was illiterate until the age of 20 and now writes in Arabic. *For Bread Alone*, translated from

Moroccan Arabic into English by Paul Bowles (1973), describes his childhood, one full of privation and hunger, in the streets of Tangiers. The French version of the novel, *Le Pain nu* (1980), translated by Tahar Ben Jelloun, was forbidden in Morocco for many years because of its presentation of the misery of children forced to live in the streets. Key texts: *Jean Genet in Tangiers* (1974); *Tennessee Williams in Tangiers* (1979); *Jean Genet et Tennessee Williams à Tanger* (1992); *Le Fou des roses* (1993); *Le Temps des erreurs* (1994); *Jean Genet (Suite et fin)* (1996); *Zoco chico* (1996); *StreetWise* (1996); *Paul Bowles le reclus de Tanger* (1997). (**Susanne Heiler**)

Further reading

Mouzouni (1987) – pp. 149–81; Gontard (1993) – Chapter VI , 'Le récit tangérois', pp. 127–49. Both have in-depth analyses of the work of Tangiers authors Choukri, Charhadi and Mrabet.

Chraïbi, Driss   Born El Jadida, 1926. Moroccan writer and one of the founders of Francophone Maghrebian LITERATURE. Born into a wealthy mercantile family, he was one of the few privileged Moroccans, under French protectorate, to have had access to a French Lycée and education. After obtaining his baccalauréat from the prestigious Lycée Lyautey in Casablanca, he went to Paris in 1945 to pursue his studies. He graduated with a degree in chemistry. In 1954 he published his first novel, *Le Passé simple* (*The Simple Past*, 1990) – a novel which provoked an unprecedented scandal both in France and in Morocco. The caustic manner in which the author criticised the patriarchal and Muslim traditions of Morocco was seized by the French Right to justify and legitimise French rule over the country. On the national level, the novel provoked the fury of Moroccan people who, at the time of its publication, were fighting the French for Morocco's independence. In further novels, such as *Les Boucs* (1956; *The Butts*, 1983) and *La Civilisation, ma Mère!...* (1972; *Mother Comes of Age*, 1984), Chraïbi tackled the issues of IMMIGRATION and Moroccan civilisation to reinstate himself amongst the North African community in general and the Moroccan people in particular. In more recent years, Chraïbi has published a whole series of novels portraying the adventures of the unscrupulous, ignorant and womanising Inspector Ali. The endless humour in these novels is as much out of self-mockery as it is a sarcastic account of the societies in which his character evolves. In his novel *L'Homme du livre* (1994) Chraïbi re-establishes himself within the Arabo-Islamic tradition. In 2000, he published his autobiography under the title *Le Monde à côté*. (**Laïla Ibnlfassi**)

Further reading

Kadra-Hadjadji (1986).

Chrétien, Jean   Born 1934. Canadian Prime Minister. He studied law and was called to the Quebec Bar in 1958. He became a Liberal MP in 1963, subsequently holding various major ministerial portfolios. As Minister for Constitutional Negotiations, he enshrined the Charter of Rights and Freedoms in the 1982 Constitution Act. In 1990, Chrétien was elected Liberal Party leader, becoming Prime Minister after the federal elections in 1993. He pursues independence from US policy in order to emphasise

Canadian sovereignty and to reinforce Canada's Francophone commitments. Chrétien promotes global trade liberalisation and greater debt relief. (**Susan Fox**)

Further reading

Lawrence (1992).

CILF *Conseil International de la langue française* (International Council of the French Language). See FRANCOPHONIE, BIRTH AND DEVELOPMENT, and the Council's web site at http://www.cilf.org/

Cinema, Algeria After independence, successive organisations were established in ALGERIA to support the film industry: *l'Office national pour le commerce et l'industrie cinématographique* (ONCIC) organised the second Congress and manifesto of the Pan-African Federation of Film-makers in Algiers (1975). The *Cinémathèque Algérienne* remains an important forum. The state-run cinema celebrated the heroes of the anticolonial struggle: Chahine's *Djamila L'Algérienne* (1958), on the trial of Djamila BOUHIRED, and *Le Vent des Aurès* (Mohammed LAKHDAR HAMINA). Mohammed Bouamari won the Palme d'Or at the Cannes Festival for *Le Charbonnier*, 'the other Algeria, frustrated and precarious, invaded by industrialisation' (Lotfi Maherzi). The agrarian revolution was reflected in films like *Noua* (Abdelaziz Tolbi, 1972). Other films included 'a new feminist image' in *Leila et les autres* (Sid Ali Mazif, 1978); *Une femme pour mon fils* (Ali Ghanem, 1982); *La Nouba des Femmes du Mont Chenoua* (1978) and *La Zerda* (1980), by the novelist/ film-maker, Assia DJEBAR. Algerian cinema is rich in comedy: Merzak ALLOUACHE's *Omar Gatlato* (1976), on the frustrations of machismo, was followed by his *Aventures d'un héros* (1978) and *Bab El Oued City* (1993), before his exile in France. *La Montagne de Baya* portrayed the BERBER resistance to colonialism and documentary film-makers, notably Jean-Pierre Lledo, have made films chronicling how the 1990s conflict is played out in daily life: *Chroniques Algériennes, Femmes en Crue* and more recently films on Algerian migrant/exile identity. See also ZEMMOURI. (**Cathie Lloyd**)

Cinema, diaspora As a cultural manifestation indebted to colonisation and (post)colonial MIGRATION, Francophone diaspora cinema thematises issues of dislocation, displacement, homecoming and minority cultures. Diasporic connections are made between ancestral homelands and newfound homes. The link has been expressed as a journey into the heart of the former coloniser (e.g. France or Belgium), a return to ROOTS through a voyage to the ancestral homeland (Ngangura's *Pièces d'identité*, 1998), or a voyage to a third space, with possible connections between diasporas (e.g., French Arabs meet African-Americans in LOUISIANA: Bouchareb's *Bâton Rouge*, 1985). These movements evoke earlier colonial histories of migration that explain and legitimate ethnic minority presence in the (former) colonial metropolis ('we are here because you were there'), or, by contrast, suggest that a return to the ancestral homeland is the only real solution, given the history of (neo)colonial RACISM and oppression.

The provocative nature of these issues and their appeal to smaller audiences can be obstacles to financing. Still, some such films do encounter considerable success: Mehdi CHAREF's *Le Thé au harem d'Archimède* won a prize at the Cannes Film Festival, and Yamina BENGUIGUI's *Mémoires d'immigrés* had considerable success with majority and minority audiences in France. Interestingly, Charef's film was criticised by minority activist Farida BELGHOUL for having pandered to ethnic majority spectators, and Benguigui publicly acknowledged that she had eliminated the most shocking NEO-COLONIAL statements that she had gathered from French officials, regarding North African immigration.

An important transnational aspect of diaspora cinema is illustrated by the positive reception of *Mémoires d'immigrés* in North Africa. (**Mark McKinney**)

Further reading

Tarr (1997) provides an excellent, concise overview of diaspora cinema in France. Hennebelle and Schneider (1990) includes very useful critical articles and plot summaries.

Cinema, Morocco   Moroccan film-makers have received little significant state support. Hamid Benani's film *Traces* (1970) concerns an orphan boy with a strict Muslim adoptive father. Souhel Ben Barka made *A Thousand And One Hands* (1972) about the situation of dyeworkers, *The Petrol War Won't Happen* (1975) and *Amok* (1982). Films of poetic realism have been produced: in the 1970s *El Chergui* (Moumen Smihi, 1975) about the problems of a young wife; and Ahmed el Maanouni's *Oh les jours* (1978), a dramatised documentary about peasant life and the imagined promise of France. In the 1980s Mohamed Reggab's *The Hairdresser from a Poor District* (1982); Taieb Sakkiki's *Zeft* (1984); *The Great Voyage* by Abderrahmane Tazi (1981), Mustapha Derkaoui's *The Beautiful Days of Scheherazade* (1982) and Jilali Ferhati's *Reed Dolls* (1981), the tragic story of a young girl married against her wishes, widowed and deprived of her children by the law. (**Cathie Lloyd**)

Cinema, Quebec   Although there was some early film-making in French Canada, it was with the *RÉVOLUTION TRANQUILLE* of the 1960s that QUEBEC cinema became a powerful force. Its emergence was aided by the transfer in 1956 of the National Film Board of Canada from Ottawa to Montreal, where it became a training ground for a new generation of Francophone film-makers. In addition, since the 1960s, both Quebec and Canadian government agencies have subsidised film production in French on a generous scale.

Many of the young film-makers, like Pierre PERRAULT, made their mark in a new style of documentary film – Direct Cinema/*Cinéma Vérité*, a film form in which Quebec has excelled ever since – while others made the transition to feature films. The common preoccupation of all these film-makers was the affirmation of Quebec identity, but there was considerable diversity in their style of doing so. Some adopted the counter-cultural stance popularised by the hippie and protest movements of the 1970s, which chimed in with the Quebec mood of self-affirmation. This trend produced the remarkable low-budget films of Jean-Pierre Lefèbvre, and encouraged the emergence of women film-makers, such as Anne Claire Poirier, a hitherto stifled voice in cinema. Directors like JUTRA, CARLE, ARCAND, Beaudin and many others adopted an approach nearer the public taste, but still emphasising the problems and predicaments of Quebec as an emergent society. A distinctive flavour in all these films is the use of spoken Quebec French, whether JOUAL or more mainstream speech.

Since the early 1990s, there has been a prolonged period of transition as new directors have emerged, like François Girard (*Le Violon rouge*), reflecting a changing social context in Quebec. (**Ian Lockerbie**)

Further reading

Coulombe and Jean (2000) is the most up-to-date and accessible guide. Marshall (2001) is theoretically demanding, but illuminating.

Cinema, Sub-Saharan Africa The cinema of Sub-Saharan Africa emerged in the early 1960s and most major African directors have been from ex-French colonies – e.g. Ousmane SEMBENE (SENEGAL), Idrissa OUÉDRAOGO (BURKINA FASO), Med HONDO (MAURITANIA), Souleymane CISSE (MALI) – as the French authorities have been willing to invest in African films.

By the time of independence, the cinema was extremely popular in Francophone Africa but there were no Black African films. Africans thus began to make films about their own societies, setting out to tell African stories to an African audience. The biennial FESPACO film festival in Ougadougou was launched in 1969, and the Federation of African Film-makers (FEPACI) was formed the following year. In 1975, FEPACI committed itself to the development of an African cinema that would not only represent Africa from an African point of view but that would also reject commercial, Western film codes.

However, African film-makers have continued to struggle to finance their films (the main funding sources are African governments, the French authorities and European television stations), and these works are rarely shown in Africa (or outside of Western film festivals), as they are considered a financial risk. Indian films and Taiwanese Kung Fu movies now dominate the African market. African directors have retreated from the radicalism of the 1970s, worrying far more about the problems of forging a popular African cinema, and the creation of a viable African film industry. A new generation of talented Francophone African directors emerged in the 1990s – e.g. Balufu Bakupa-Kanyinda (Congo-Kinshasa), Adama Drabo (Mali) – but the future of African cinema remains precarious. (**David Murphy**)

Further reading

Givanni (2000) – an excellent theoretical overview of African cinema; Ukadike (1994) – a comprehensive historical overview of film-making in Sub-Saharan Africa.

Cinema, Tunisia The independent government of TUNISIA provided state sponsorship for the film industry, encouraging organisations such as the Tunisian Film Club Federation. In the mid-1960s, the Minister of Culture, Tahar Cheriaa, founded the Pan-African/Arab Carthage Film Festival. Tunisian film-makers were afforded generous financial support by the national film company. *Le Soleil des Hyènes* (Ridha

Behi, 1977) was presented at the Cannes Film Festival, followed by Abdellatif Ben Amar's *Aziza* (1979). Ferid Boughedir's early films, *Caméra d'Afrique* and *Caméra Arabe* won major awards and were followed by *Halfaouine* (1989) and *A Summer in La Goulette*. Nouri Bouzid's *Man of Ashes* (1987) was a study of masculinity and child abuse. The female director Moufida Tlatli made *Saimt el Qusur* (The silences of the palace, 1994) and *La Saison des Hommes*, exploring the relationships of different generations of women with men. (**Cathie Lloyd**)

Circulaire Bayrou In 1994 François Bayrou, as Minister of Education under the right-wing government of Prime Minister Edouard Balladur, directed teachers in the national school system to ban all ostentatious signs of religious belief (cf. Hargreaves, 1995). However, he made it clear that this only applied to headscarves worn by Muslim girls (mostly adolescents of North African and Turkish heritage), not to symbols of Christian and Jewish faiths. This launched a second, stigmatising 'HEADSCARF AFFAIR' (the first had been in 1989). Many girls who refused to remove their scarves were expelled from school, but courts annulled many of the expulsions. (**Mark McKinney**)

CISIA Comité international de soutien aux intellectuels algériens Set up in the early 1990s in Paris (followed by offshoots in other countries) with Pierre Bourdieu as president, with the aim of disseminating information and providing practical support for those affected by the Algerian crisis and the wave of attacks and assassinations targeting intellectuals.

Cissé, Souleymane Born 1950. Malian fim-maker. Surmounting the obvious difficulties of film production in one of the poorest countries in Africa, Cissé wrote and directed a series of films documenting the social and political conflicts of MALI, such as *Finye* (*The Wind*, 1982). His best-known film, *Ye'elen* (1982), is an imaginative and symbolic epic tale of initiation into the mysteries of traditional animist beliefs, and won many international festival awards. His more recent film, *Waati* (1994), although politically and artistically ambitious, embracing the political problems of the African continent, did not achieve the same success, and has had difficulties securing international distribution. (**Peter Hawkins**)

Citizenship Citizenship refers to the rights and duties that define an individual's membership of the political community. The first French revolution (1789–99) transferred political allegiance from the monarchy to the nation, henceforth theoretically ruled by its citizens. A contract linked the individual citizen and the nation, the citizen enjoying rights on condition that certain duties were performed (e.g. taxes paid, military service accomplished). Yet not all won the right to vote: a minority of politically 'active' citizens could vote, and 'passive' citizens (all women, most men) could not.

The Second French Republic (1848–51) ensured universal male suffrage in metropolitan France and some colonial contexts (e.g. ANTILLES-GUYANE, GUIANA, REUNION), and partial male enfranchisement elsewhere (SENEGAL). Opponents of the further extension of political rights stated that the colonised were 'insufficiently educated'. However, the fact of the matter is that enfranchising colonial subjects would have fatally compromised French rule: in no French colony did the colonisers ever represent more than 14 per cent of the population (ALGERIA), hence only a fraction of colonial subjects were allowed to acquire full French citizenship. After 1918, anticolonial movements highlighted how France had made colonial subjects liable for military service whilst it refused to grant full citizenship rights in return. Pressure for political reform became irresistible after 1945, and colonial subjects (and metropolitan French women) became full citizens, although unfair electoral systems fuelled radical pro-independence movements.

Citizenship remains a significant political issue. Since the 1880s in metropolitan France, nationality and citizenship have gone together. Consequently, non-French residents in France cannot vote (EU nationals resident in France can now vote in local elections). In 1981, MITTERRAND had promised the right to vote in local elections for non-nationals, a promise that never materialised. Antiracist campaigns since the 1980s have suggested separating nationality and citizenship, the latter to be conditional instead upon residency in France. This new citizenship (*nouvelle citoyenneté*) has gained added support in the context of European integration (see SANS-PAPIERS). (**Jim House**)

Further reading

Bouamama (2000) – stimulating analysis of both historical and contemporary dynamics of citizenship from a proponent of new citizenship; Rosanvallon (1992) – a wide-ranging historical overview that usefully combines analysis of citizenship in metropolitan France with the various colonial contexts.

Clandestins Typically working class people residing in a country (e.g. France, Belgium) without official permission, *clandestins* are subject to harassment, exploitation and expulsion. The semi-official encouragement of illegal IMMIGRATION by the French government during the post-war boom period (1944–74), ended with the oil crisis of 1974 and subsequent economic downturn. *Clandestins* include recent arrivals, but also people who have spent most of their life in France. Resistance by *clandestins* has taken the form of hunger strikes, demonstrations and civil disobedience. (**Mark McKinney**)

Further reading

See Cissé (2000) for a description of the 1996 occupation of the Saint-Bernard church in Paris.

CMF *Conférence Ministérielle de la Francophonie* (Ministerial Conference of the Francophone Countries). The CMF is normally constituted by the ministers of foreign or francophone affairs of the member countries. It ensures political continuity between the FRANCOPHONE SUMMITS and, in particular, has the task of ensuring that Summit decisions are implemented. See also FRANCOPHONE INSTITUTIONS.

Further reading

Consult the OIF website: http://www.*Francophonie*.org

Code de la nationalité (CNF) A legal code defining the conditions of access to French nationality and CITIZENSHIP, carrying with them a combination of rights and duties, such as the right to live in France and participate in elections as well as (until recently) compulsory national service for males. The CNF became a major political battleground during the 1980s and 1990s amid the debate over immigration (see MIGRATION) and the settlement of minorities originating in former French colonies.

Compared with countries such as Germany, France has for most of the last century operated relatively liberal nationality laws. After a period of residence in France, immigrants can apply fairly readily to become 'naturalised' French citizens. Most of their children and grandchildren have been automatically given French citizenship. This automaticity was thrown into question during the 1980s by the extreme right-wing *FRONT NATIONAL* and the centre-right RPR and UDF parties, which doubted the cultural assimilation (see *ASSIMILATION/INTÉGRATION/INSERTION*) and loyalty to France of immigrant minorities from former colonies, especially ALGERIA. In government between 1986 and 1988, the RPR and UDF attempted unsuccessfully to reform the CNF in such a way as to require the children of immigrants to request French citizenship, instead of receiving it automatically. This reform (from which second-generation Algerians were largely exempted for technical reasons) was eventually enacted when the centre-right parties returned to power in 1993 as part of a raft of changes known as the PASQUA laws designed to tighten immigration controls and make it easier to deport members of minority groups who, if they lacked citizenship, had weaker residence rights in France. The Left reversed most of these changes on taking office in 1997. (**Alec G. Hargreaves**)

Further reading

Revealing insights into the debate over the CNF are offered by the hearings of a special commission set up under the chairmanship of Long (1988).

Codes de la famille See FAMILY CODES, MAGHREB.

CODOFIL *Conseil pour le développement du français en Louisiane* (Council for the Development of French in LOUISIANA). Created in July 1968 by a unanimous vote of the Louisiana state legislature, CODOFIL's mission is 'to do any and all things necessary to accomplish the development, utilization and preservation of the FRENCH LANGUAGE as found in Louisiana for the cultural, economic and tourist benefit of the State'. To this end it has launched actions to improve the cultural status of French by restoring its legal status, to create competence in the French language through educational programmes, and to promote a positive image of CAJUN culture through the media. CODOFIL's *Comité du français Louisianais* also seeks to formulate a policy for the standardisation of Louisiana French and the establishment of orthographic norms. (**Marie-Anne Hintze**)

Colonial policy French colonial policy has generally been characterised as assimilationist (see *ASSIMILATION/INTÉGRATION/INSERTION*). From the end of the nineteenth century, the French stressed the 'civilising mission' that they claimed was at the heart of their colonial conquests, highlighting the 'superiority' of the French empire over its 'mercenary' English counterpart. The French proclaimed that colonisation would 'civilise' the 'primitive' peoples of their colonies, assimilating them into French culture. This process of creating 'black/brown/yellow Frenchmen' has been central to discussion of French colonialism, and it forms the heart of many texts written by colonised writers. For the Senegalese author Bakary Diallo, writing in the 1920s, assimilation is presented as an ideal to be obtained but, in later works such as C. H. Kane's *L'Aventure ambiguë* (1961; *Ambiguous Adventure*, 1963) and Chraïbi's *Le Passé simple* (1954; *The Simple Past*, 1990), assimilation is seen as a painful and alienating process.

However, historians have increasingly challenged the notion that French colonialism was based on assimilation, arguing that French policies were, in fact, far more pragmatic and similar to the British policy of indirect rule. Only a small percentage of colonised peoples received a French education, while the vast majority of the population were subject to the exigencies of *l'indigénat*, the repressive system under which the colonised paid a levy to the French and could also be made to work free of charge on behalf of the colonial regime. African novels such as Oyono's *Une Vie de boy* (1956; *Houseboy*, 1966) and Sembene's *Les Bouts de bois de Dieu* (1960; *God's Bits of Wood*, 1962) reveal the brutality underpinning French colonial authority – from summary imprisonment to savage beatings with the infamous *chicotte*. Reforms to this repressive system were gradually introduced, gathering pace after World War II. (**David Murphy**)

Further reading

Miller (1998) – excellent analysis of culture and colonialism.

Communauté Economique des Etats de l'Afrique de l'Ouest   See CEDEAO.

Communauté Financière Africaine   See CFA.

Communauté Financière du Pacifique   See CFP.

Communauté française   1958–60. The name given to the short-lived colonial constitutional structures created by France from 1958 to 1960 to prepare France's African colonies for independence. These were accepted by the territories involved by a plebiscite called by General DE GAULLE following the dissolution of the Fourth Republic.

Foreign affairs, defence, economic policy, higher education, the judiciary, interstate transport and telecommunications were implemented as Community policies. Constitutionally, the President of France (de Gaulle) was also President of the Community and was served by an Executive Council made up of the French Prime Minister and the leaders of the assemblies of the 12 heads of the African states, with the French ministers assigned to oversee Community policies. (**Antony Walsh**)

Comoros   The Islamic Republic of the Comoros (population 530,820; capital: Moroni) is made up of three volcanic islands, Anjouan, Mohéli and Grande Comore (also called Ngazidja), situated at the northern entrance to the Mozambique channel, between Mozambique and MADAGASCAR. The fourth island of the archipelago, MAYOTTE, chose to remain French at independence in 1976. As a former French colony, the Comoros islands are nominally Francophone, but in practice Arabic and a range of local African and Malagasy dialects are spoken. The population is predominantly Muslim, with a small minority of Catholics. The country is politically very unstable – the island of Anjouan attempted to secede in 1997–2000 – and extremely poor: a succession of corrupt and dictatorial regimes were cynically maintained in power by the support of French mercenaries and the former apartheid regime in South Africa. Its principal agricultural exports are vanilla and cloves, and the essence of ylang-ylang used in perfume manufacturing, but its subsistence farming and fishing are inadequate to feed the population and the country is dependent on imported rice and other basic foodstuffs. The nascent tourist industry has been blighted by political problems. The country has a very low level of literacy and its one internationally recognised writer, the novelist Mohamed Toihiri, author of *Le Kéfir du Karthala* (Paris: L'Harmattan, 1992), lives in exile in France. (**Peter Hawkins**)

Compaoré, Blaise Born 1950. Soldier and President of BURKINA FASO, served under Thomas SANKARA, as Minister of State, before usurping and executing him, with his prominent supporters, in 1987. Despite his reputed left-wing leanings, Compaoré embarked on a programme of privitisation and austerity measures sponsored by the IMF. After officially eschewing Socialism, he was elected president unopposed in 1991 and 1998. Compaoré faces criticism over corruption, press censorship, nepotism, and the state of the economy. The National Assembly has little power to provide the checks and balances to Compaoré's autocratic rule. (**Susan Fox**)

Further reading

Englebert (1996).

Condé, Maryse Born GUADELOUPE, 1937. Leading woman writer of the French Caribbean today. Prolific author and academic who has lived in Guadeloupe, Africa, Europe, the US. This nomadic trajectory is reflected in a diversity of geographical and historical settings: *Ségou* (1984; *The Children of Segu*, 1989), her first novel, centres on the Bambara kingdom, now part of MALI; *Moi, Tituba, sorcière…* (1986; *I, Tituba, Black Witch of Salem*, 1992) is the story of a forgotten Barbadian witch of the Salem trials. Condé is critical both of the essentialism of NÉGRITUDE, and of the programmatic tendencies of CRÉOLITÉ, although her writing has become more creolised (cf. *Traversée de la mangrove*, 1989; *Crossing the Mangrove*, 1995). Permeating her work is a wry, humorous and often bleak perspective, particularly on GENDER ISSUES. (**Maeve McCusker**)

Further reading

Callaloo (1995); Pfaff (1995).

CONFEJES *Conférence des Ministres de la Jeunesse et des Sports de la Francophonie* (Standing Conference of Francophone Youth and Sports

Ministers) was created in 1969 as a forum for ministers with responsibility for youth and sport, as well as to promote projects favourable to the social integration of young people and the development of opportunities and facilities for sport and sports training, including the *Jeux de la Francophonie*. Its headquarters are in Dakar, Senegal. See website: http://www.confejes.org.

CONFEMEN *Conférence des ministères de l'Education nationale* (Standing Conference for National Education Ministries) was created in 1960 as an interministerial forum for Education Ministers in Francophone countries to discuss and develop education policies, particularly in Francophone Africa.

Annual conferences on educational issues are held to allow the exchange of information on a wide range of pedagogical issues from formal to informal education amongst the organisation's 35 members. Recently it has been involved in researching means to apply the consequences of structural adjustment programmes (see Education, Sub-Saharan Africa) to education policies and investigating how African languages could be incorporated into school education.

The CONFEMEN has its headquarters in Dakar, Senegal. (**Antony Walsh**)

Conférence des Ministères de l'Education nationale See CONFEMEN.

Conférence des Ministres de la Jeunesse et des Sports de la Francophonie See CONFEJES.

Conférence Ministérielle de la Francophonie See CMF.

Confiant, Raphaël Born Martinique, 1951. Martinican writer. He is not only a prolific novelist but also a militant defender of the Creole language and co-signatory of the *Eloge de la créolité* (1989; *In Praise of Creoleness*, 1993). Although his early novels were written in Creole and published locally, Confiant has moved into the mainstream of French publishing (*Le Nègre et l'Amiral* was published by Grasset, 1988; his autobiography, *Ravines du devant-jour*, by Gallimard, 1993). His fiction, which focuses mainly on post-emancipation urban Martinique, is characterised by a playful, irreverent tone and by the incorporation of Creole into French. He is notorious for his virulent attacks on Césaire and *négritude*, and for the eroticised portrayal of women in his work. (**Maeve McCusker**)

Congo (*République du Congo*) Central African state, formerly known as Congo-Brazzaville, crossed by the Equator and the River Congo, bordering on Gabon, Cameroon, Central African Republic, Democratic Republic of Congo, Angolan enclave of Cabinda, Atlantic Ocean. Population approx. 2.6 million, mainly Bantu, with a small Pygmy minority. Three-quarters of the inhabitants live in urban areas. Capital: Brazzaville. Official language: French. Religions: Christianity (Catholics 54 per cent, Protestants 25 per cent), independent churches (14 per cent); traditional (5 per cent). Main resources: off-shore oil (45 per cent GNP; 90 per cent of exports) and timber. Main agricultural crop: cassava. Importer of basic foodstuffs.

The French colony of Congo was created on the right bank of the Congo river in 1891, with brutal exploitation by concessionary companies (rubber, ivory). Brazzaville became capital of AEF in 1910. The experience of many Congolese soldiers recruited for the French army in World War I was a potent factor in the creation of the nationalist, anticolonialist movement from the 1920s, as was the construction of the Congo–Océan railway, which claimed the lives of many thousand forced labourers. The 1940 Brazzaville revolt led to the town's establishment as the Free French capital. With Félix Eboué, DE GAULLE called together colonial administrators in 1944 at the BRAZZAVILLE CONFERENCE to discuss the future of the French colonies.

The first Congolese député, Félix Tchicaya, was elected to the French Constituent Assembly in 1945. After the 1958 referendum, Congo became an autonomous republic and independent in 1960, with Fulbert Youlou as President. In 1968, Captain Marien Ngouabi took power, establishing the PCT (*Parti congolais du travail*) and a Marxist–Leninist inspired regime. After his assassination (1977), he was succeeded by Colonel Joachim Yhombi-Opango, followed in 1979 by Colonel Denis Sassou-Nguesso. A popular revolt in 1990 provoked a National Conference, which produced a new constitution and Pascal Lissouba's election in 1992, although, after a brief civil war, Sassou-Nguesso was restored to power in 1997.

Congo has produced a number of intellectuals and writers, including: Jean Malonga, Guy Menga, Sylvain Bemba, TCHICAYA U TAM'SI, Jean-Baptiste TATI-LOUTARD, Maxime N'Debeka, Emmanuel DONGALA, Henri LOPÈS, Tchichellé Tchivela, SONY LAB'OU TANSI, Jean-Pierre Makouta-Mboukou, Théophile Obenga. It has a vital musical scene and a burgeoning theatre and cinema.

See also DEMOCRATIC REPUBLIC OF CONGO.

Conseil International de la langue française   See CILF.

Conseil Permanent de la Francophonie   See CPF.

Coopération   The French term for foreign aid, refers essentially to grants, 'soft' loans and technical assistance. The earliest forms of *coopération* date back to the 1920s and to the Sarraut Plan for the economic development of the French empire. A more concerted effort at colonial development began in the mid-1940s with the creation of the *Fonds d'Investissement pour le Développement Economique et Social*. This investment and development fund (later renamed the *Fonds d'Aide et de Coopération*) drew up modernisation plans and channelled subsidies to most parts of the French Union.

It was not, however, until the early 1960s that France established an international development aid programme and began directing the bulk of her assistance to her former Black African colonies. Paris signed bilateral *coopération* agreements with these newly independent states and established a Co-operation Ministry to deal exclusively with them.

The French *coopération* programme soon became one of the largest in the world but it was geared more towards maintaining French influence in Africa than it was towards tackling poverty. It was driven, above all, by cultural, political and commercial considerations, with aid being used to finance French-language schools, grandiose projects and over-priced exports.

French *coopération* remained virtually unchanged over the next three decades, despite growing criticism from French politicians (Cot, 1984) and NGOs (Brunel, 1993). It has, however, undergone important changes since the start of the 1990s, as aid has been subject to cutbacks and tied to democratic reforms in developing countries. It has also been focused on a wider range of issues (e.g. population control, AIDS) as well as on a larger group of privileged recipients (the *Zone de Solidarité Prioritaire*). Significantly, these recipients now include a number of ex-British colonies like South Africa, Nigeria and Tanzania as well as former French dependencies like VIETNAM, LEBANON and ALGERIA. (**Gordon Cumming**)

Further reading

Brunel (1993); Cot (1984); Cumming (2001) – comparative survey of French and British aid programmes, with emphasis on policy changes in the 1990s.

Côte d'Ivoire (Ivory Coast). French traders established trading posts along the coast of present-day Côte d'Ivoire from the mid-nineteenth century. The territory became a French colony in 1893, but French occupation was met with determined resistance, not completely suppressed until 1917. During this period, France established its colonial administration, including a head tax and widespread conscription of forced labour for public works and for French-owned cocoa plantations. Cocoa was introduced to Côte d'Ivoire during the First World War and became the territory's major export by the 1930s. Banana and coffee plantations were also established during the 1930s. By this time, African planters were playing an increasingly important role in coffee and cocoa production and becoming increasingly resentful of privileged treatment given to European planters, who received better prices for their crops and had access to forced labour, including that of the African farmers themselves. As a result, African planters organised themselves into a union, the *Syndicat Agricole Africain*, in 1944. Led by Félix HOUPHOUËT-BOIGNY, both a traditional chief and a French-trained medical assistant, the SAA was to form the basis of the territory's first political party, the *Parti Démocratique de la Côte d'Ivoire*, founded in 1946 when Africans outside the Four Communes were first granted political rights. Houphouët-Boigny was elected to the French Constituent Assembly in 1945; he was a *député* in the National Assembly from 1946 to 1958 and several times appointed as a French government minister under the Fourth Republic. Believing that it was premature for an underdeveloped territory such as Côte d'Ivoire, he reluctantly took independence from France in 1960, remaining its president until his death in 1993. Houphouët-Boigny was a key French ally in the region in the postcolonial era and France maintains a military base at Abidjan. By the time of his death, the country had gone through an economic boom and bust, with the result that it is today one of the world's most heavily indebted countries (calculated on a per capita basis). Its export earnings remain highly dependent on cocoa and coffee, the price of which has fallen dramatically in recent years. It has also gone through a period of political instability since Houphouët-Boigny's death. His successor, Henri Konan Bédié, was overthrown in a military *coup* in 1999 by General Guei, who was himself expelled from power by Laurent Gbagbo in 2000, following a bitterly contested presidential election. Gbagbo faces the difficult task of rebuilding the country's economy and reuniting what has become a politically and ethnically divided nation. (**Tony Chafer**)

Cotonou Agreement   See LOMÉ CONVENTION.

CPF   *Conseil Permanent de la Francophonie* (Permanent Council of *Francophonie*). The CPF is constituted by the personal representatives of the Francophone heads of state and governments, and presided over by the Secretary-General. Its remit includes the preparation of FRANCOPHONE SUMMITS and the monitoring of the implementation of CMF and Summit decisions, as well as the programmes of the operating agencies. See also FRANCOPHONE INSTITUTIONS.

Further reading

Consult the OIF website: http://www.*Francophonie*.org

Creoles, Caribbean   Creole languages emerge from prolonged contact between two language communities, in this case the encounter between European master and African slave on the plantation. Two historical factors account for the particularly intense and accelerated linguistic cross-fertilisation in the Caribbean: first, slaves with a common language had been segregated in order to discourage rebellion, and secondly, at the start of the colonial enterprise French was not yet a unified language, but accommodated a range of dialects. Thus, at the establishment of the plantation system there was virtually no shared language, and Creole (a fusion of African syntax and French vocabulary, and essentially an oral language) quickly emerged. Today, it is spoken mainly in HAITI (where it is the only language for the majority), MARTINIQUE and GUADELOUPE, each island having its own variations. Because of the extent of ASSIMILATION in Martinique and Guadeloupe, where French has been upheld as the prestige language of social advancement, attitudes towards Creole are often polarised. It has been long denigrated due to its association with slavery, but since the 1980s there have been attempts to counter decreolisation (e.g. the attempts to impose a standard orthographic system, and the inauguration of the French state exam, the CAPES, in Creole in 2001). (**Maeve McCusker**)

Further reading

Chaudenson (1995) – useful introduction by a leading Creole specialist which deals with the genesis and evolution of Creoles; the remit of the study extends beyond the Caribbean perspective to other creolophone regions, such as the Indian Ocean. Brooks (1999) – an accessible and up-to-date overview of the current status of Creole in the islands, which deals with issues that go beyond the strictly literary.

Creoles/*créolité*, Indian Ocean   Varieties of Creole language developed in those islands of the region where a large number of slaves were brought in by the colonial authorities in the eighteenth and nineteenth centuries, to work on the plantations: MAURITIUS, REUNION and the SEYCHELLES. Creole grew out of the need for a common language among the slave population, coming from many different parts of Africa, and their slave masters, who often spoke a regional variety of French. This produced slightly different Creoles in each of the islands, but they are mutually understandable for the local populations, for whom Creole is usually their mother tongue. The status of the language at the present time varies from one island to another. In the Seychelles it is the official language, although English and French are also widely spoken. In Mauritius, Creole has no official status, although it is the effective vehicular language common to all sectors of the population; English is the official language of administration and French is widely used in the media and journalism. In Reunion Creole is in the process of being officially recognised in accordance with the European charter of minority languages, and there are plans to incorporate it into the school curriculum; but French remains the official language of administration and instruction. In Mauritius and Reunion there is a growing body of LITERATURE written in Creole, and it has always been the language of popular song and also of popular forms of drama. The Mauritian dramatist Dev VIRAHSAWMY has written a considerable number of plays in Creole, while in Reunion local theatre companies such as the Théâtre Vollard (see THEATRE, INDIAN OCEAN) make extensive use of it. Poetry in Creole has been published by Carpanin MARIMOUTOU and Axel GAUVIN has written Creole versions of many of his novels. The 1977 convention for the phonetic transcription of Creole has not always been widely accepted, however, and the audience for such writing remains small. (**Peter Hawkins**)

Créolité, Caribbean   *Créolité* is a cultural and aesthetic initiative elaborated and enthusiastically promoted by a group of Martinican intellectuals (the novelists Patrick CHAMOISEAU and Raphaël CONFIANT, along with the Creole linguist Jean BERNABÉ). Their co-authored manifesto *Éloge de la créolité* (1989; *In Praise of Creoleness*, 1993) along with Chamoiseau and Confiant's *Lettres créoles* (1991), heralded a new and controversial departure in an already rich tradition of Martinican reflections on identity. The *Éloge* promised to surpass the essentialism of NÉGRITUDE (by valorising the values of plurality and multiplicity, rather than a mythical 'blackness') and the geographic specificity of GLISSANT's ANTILLANITÉ (by looking to Creole societies beyond the Caribbean, such as LOUISIANA). The *créolistes* celebrate the unpredictable, mosaic identity engendered in the plantation. They declare the need for an 'interior vision' which is not dictated by France, and for the reconstruction of history from the point of view of the ex-slave population. Crucial to their programme is the Creole language and its associated oral tradition, which is seen as the repository for a more authentic identity. The *Éloge* was a highly controversial intervention, particularly in the Antillean context. It has been heavily criticised for its didactic and programmatic stance, for its nostalgic glorification of a bygone age, for its lack of a political vision, and not least for the fact that despite the emphasis on the Creole language, the *Éloge* is written in French, and published with the prestigious metropolitan publisher Gallimard. (**Maeve McCusker**)

Further reading

Gallagher (1994) – a thorough and lucid exposé of the background to, and main limitations of, the *créolité* agenda; Condé and Cottenet-Hage (1995) – a highly critical collection of essays, which focuses particularly on issues of gender and sexuality.

Cultural identity   Forged in nationalist ideologies of the colonial period, the concept of cultural identity has found expression in both sociological and artistic forms, relating to the history, languages (see LANGUAGE POLICY) and sometimes RELIGIONS of the colonised peoples. The Francophone literatures of Africa began with a response to the French assimilationist policy (see *ASSIMILATION/INTÉGRATION/INSERTION*). However, if the FRENCH LANGUAGE appeared initially as an instrument of domination of indigenous cultures, inspiring intellectuals to revolt against it, the publication of these first works showed it not just as an essential tool for social advancement, but also as the means for articulating demands for political autonomy.

The *NÉGRITUDE* movement first affected Afro-Caribbean literature at the end of the nineteenth century, with the emergence of the RACE question and the affirmation of 'the Negro soul' and 'values of negritude'. This totalising project was soon confronted after World War II by differences between Caribbean and African values. In the Caribbean, the oral, CREOLE dimension came to the fore, with a new type of writing, following Creole syntax and tenses, while rejecting the rationalism of the French language. In HAITI, this produced the concept of *oraliture*.

Maghrebian cultural identity was first defined through notions such as *Algérianité*, based on geographical and historical factors, in opposition to French colonial identity. Algerian identity included all those, regardless of race, religion or language, who considered themselves Algerian and identified with Algerian independence. Following independence, this paradigm has undergone a fundamental shift. Using COLONIAL POLICY towards Arabic and ISLAM as a pretext, the new national governments sought to impose uniformity – one people, one language, one religion, thereby denying the Maghreb's original language, *TAMAZIGHT*. At the same time, progressive, open-minded intellectuals continued to campaign for cultural and religious DIVERSITY. Self-definition in the postcolonial period is seen not just in terms of an opposition to the former colonial power but also in relation to traditional values which may seem an outdated, inadequate response to the questions posed to Maghrebian societies by MODERNITY and new technology. In the 1980s and 1990s, younger writers and intellectuals seek inspiration in a hybrid vision, reflecting real or imaginary movements between the homeland of origin, the country of residence and the world at large. Favoured concepts are those of *métissage*, heterogeneity, mixing of genres, transculturality and dual genealogy (see HYBRIDITY).

Questions of cultural identity also figure large in QUEBEC, where writers caught between two dominant languages, French and English, seek out ways to express their own singularity, in relation to both their French origins, as well as the predominant American influence. (**Beïda Chikhi**)

Cultural imperialism   Terms like 'cultural imperialism' are used to define the new form of international domination, where uni-directional (top-down) cultural flows are, it is argued, coming exclusively from the rich centre (the West) to the periphery (less developed countries). (see CENTRE–PERIPHERY.) Hesmondhalgh suggests that this new form of imperialism is different from direct political and economic domination by colonial powers. It is based on more indirect forms of power, mainly cultural. One noticeable example of cultural imperialism is 'McDonaldisation' – the process by which principles of the fast food restaurant (along with Marlboro man, Coca-Cola, Hollywood, rock and rap music, NBA and American football) are coming to dominate more and more of the rest of the world. The burger is not only consumed physically, but also culturally as image and icon of a particular 'American' way of life.

This new form of international domination can also be found in modern sport. Guttman claims that, in spite of efforts at internationalism, all but one of the six presidents of the IOC have been European, and the sixth was American; African and Asian athletes compete on Western terms, in sports that either originated in or have taken their modern form in the West.

Others argue that the concept of GLOBALISATION is too complex to be reduced to a uni-directional process. Guttman also points out that cultural interaction is more complex than the domination by the totally powerful of the entirely powerless. Major critics of cultural imperialism have been concerned, firstly with the concept itself – Hall prefers speaking about cultural 'manipulation'. Secondly, cultural imperialism accounts have been accused of paying insufficient attention to the ability of audiences to negotiate the meaning of images or texts and make them to some extent their own. This kind of response to globalisation was named by Shelling as 'deterritorialisation', or the migration of cultural forms and identities from their original place and their reconstitution in their new contexts as 'diasporic forms'.

Examples of local response/resistance to globalisation, a response also referred to as '*créolisation*' and 'corrupt metaphor' (Hannerz, 1991), can be found in the music of Youssou N'Dour (West Africa), Mami and Khaled (Algeria) and Kassav (Caribbean, Zouk). All have adapted to new technological developments, but their domestic, original rhythm has not been totally transformed. Abu-Lughod (1991: 133) goes a step further, pointing to 'the orientalisation of western music', with the import and influence of music from the 'periphery' to the 'centre'. (**Mahfoud Amara**)

Further reading

Abu-Lughod (1991) – deals with issues linked to world system theory and global culture, as well as local response to global challenges in the domain of music, art, literature; Guttman (1993) – contains several examples of the diffusion of Western sports models and values in different parts of the world, which did not always happen through negotiation, particularly in colonised nations; Hannerz (1991) – deals with issues linked to world system theory and global culture, as well as notions of localisation or local response to global challenges (e.g. American culture) in the domain of music, art and literature; Hesmondhalgh (1998) – helpful coverage of major topics, particularly political, economic and cultural relations between developed and developing countries, defined also as core and periphery; Houlihan (1994) – raises the problem of the ability of non-Western cultures to challenge the imposed Western sporting model; Hall (1990); Shelling (1998).

Dadié, Bernard   Born 1916. Ivorian writer, dramatist and poet. Famed for his traditional oral '*contes*' written as lively short stories – *Légendes africaines* (1953), *Le Pagne*

noir (1955; *The Black Cloth: A Collection of African Folktales*, 1987) – this Catholic writer also published an autobiographical novel, *Climbié* (1956; *Climbié*, 1971), and a celebrated collection of poetry (1955). He went on to write 'reverse ethnography', with novels on travelling to Paris, then New York and Rome, which expose stereotypes of West Africans – *Un Nègre à Paris* (1959; *An African in Paris*, 1994), *Patron de New York* (1964; *One Way: Bernard Dadié Observes America*, 1994). In the 1970s plays appeared in quick succession, on African corruption (1970, 1971) and on Toussaint L'Ouverture (1973). (**Andy Stafford**)

Dahomey   Former colonial name of Bénin, a country in West Africa. One of its ancient capitals was Abomey, from where the kings of Dahomey, immortalised by Bruce Chatwin in *The Viceroy of Ouidah* (London, 1980), ruled and traded in slaves, until the arrival of a Brazilian slave-trader (hence the name of the official capital, Porto Novo) and then the French. Between 1863 and 1892, France slowly incorporated the area into its colonial empire, Dahomey becoming part of AOF in 1904, and a wide network of 'mission schools' was set up. Though independent from 1960, the country suffered fifteen years of political turmoil, until the *coup* by Mathieu Kérékou in 1972. (**Andy Stafford**)

Daily life, Indian Ocean   The texture of everyday life varies according to the contrasted economic situation of the region's islands. Reunion, administered as a French overseas department, has a standard of living in all ways comparable to western Europe, with the same levels of educational provision, health care, infrastructure, etc. It also undergoes the negative effects of its prosperity: traffic jams, the creation of an urban underclass and a wide gap betweeen the rich and the poor, a tension only partly alleviated by the French social security provision. Mauritius also enjoys a hard-earned prosperity, with low levels of unemployment, a high standard of living and an impressive record of educational achievement. The shift towards a sophisticated technological, industrial and service economy has led to an increasingly urban lifestyle for the majority of the population, concentrated in the towns in the centre of the island. Tensions subsist, however, between the different ethnic and religious communities, which occasionally break out into violent confrontation. The Seychelles remain a small, developing economy dependent on tourism and fishing for their prosperity, but enjoying a good standard of living. The shift from an agricultural to a service economy has led to a concentration of the population in urban areas such as the capital, Victoria. Madagascar is still struggling to develop from its 'third world' economic status: most of its population still live in rural areas, dependent on subsistence farming and cut off from the material benefits of modern technology by the lack of infrastructure: roads, rail and telecommunications are still inadequate or non-existent in many parts of the country. The urban areas around major cities such as the capital, Antananarivo, enjoy some of the benefits of a Western lifestyle, but the education system, health care and other basic services remain chronically underfunded. The development of mining, fisheries, tourism and specialised agriculture will help to create more wealth, but the rural areas have suffered considerably in recent times from damage by tropical storms, which have played havoc with the traditional subsistence agriculture, based on rice and cattle-herding. Madagascar remains dependent on international aid from the World Bank and technical support from developed nations such as France, whose influence remains strong. (**Peter Hawkins**)

Daily life, Pacific Ocean Pre-contact Polynesians and Melanesians lived in small villages, characterised by a subsistence economy, a chiefly political system (in POLYNESIA) or more egalitarian political organisation (in Melanesia) and a complex indigenous cosmology of cultural and religious beliefs. These structures changed with colonialism. Missionaries converted islanders to Protestant or Catholic Christianity. Economic projects – plantation agriculture, mining and, at a later stage, government employment and tourism – created a capitalist economy increasingly dependent on state investment and transfers. French colonial administration was put in place but, eventually, all inhabitants were granted CITIZENSHIP and representation in local assemblies as well as the French parliament (though nationalists campaigned for greater autonomy or independence). Meanwhile, IMMIGRATION of Europeans – free settlers, temporary residents and, in the case of NEW CALEDONIA, transported convicts – as well as Asian labourers, accompanied by inter-island migration, completely changed demographic and social structures. After a drop in population during the first decades of colonialism, numbers have increased rapidly (to 215,200 in New Caledonia, 241,600 in French Polynesia and 14,900 in WALLIS & FUTUNA). Papeete and Noumea, with populations of 96,100 and 83,400, respectively, are bustling cities whose inhabitants live a Europeanised-style life, complete with problems of shantytowns, alcohol and crime. Those living in outer islands or hinterlands, and those of Melanesian and Polynesian ancestry, remained disadvantaged, a situation leading to political tension and ethnic conflict. Efforts at cultural renewal (including recognition of Tahitian as an official language in French Polynesia), political negotiations and regional economic development have attempted to redress grievances. Most islanders, comfortably or not, combine indigenous cultural beliefs and practices with a consumerist and Gallicised daily life, far removed from the mythified Edenic visions of earlier travellers and writers, and contemporary tourist promoters. Paris remains the focus of political and economic authority and, for many, cultural values and aspirations. (**Robert Aldrich**)

Further reading

Barbadzan (1982) – interesting case study of cultural syncretism in French Polynesia; Marchal, Boulay and Kasarhérou (1990) – catalogue of exhibition also containing essays on Melanesian culture.

Damas, Léon Gontran 1912–78. Guianese poet. He was educated in MARTINIQUE and in France, where he studied law and ethnology and encountered NÉGRITUDE. His first collection of poems, *Pigments* (1937), is imbued with the values of *négritude* and articulates a particularly trenchant criticism of cultural ASSIMILATION. On his return to GUIANA, he became very involved in politics, serving a three-year term as parliamentary deputy. He then worked for UNESCO, before being appointed to a post at Howard University in Washington DC, where he died. Among his best-known works are two other poetry collections, *Black-Label* (1956) and *Névralgies* (1966). One of his most anthologised poems is 'Hoquet', a convulsive attack on the internalised RACISM of the mixed-race Caribbean bourgeoisie. (**Mary Gallagher**)

Debbouze, Jamel   Born MOROCCO, 1975. Comedian and actor. Shares with ANELKA a love of fast cars and a childhood in Trappes, a North Parisian *BANLIEUE*. Hit by a train aged 13, he lost the use of his right arm. His *tchatch* (backchat) was encouraged by the director of a local theatre company, and eventually earned him a daily spot on Radio Nova and sketches for Canal Plus television. 1995 saw his first one-man show and he has subsequently starred in the sitcom 'H' (for hospital) on Canal Plus, appeared in films, and had sell-out runs in stand-up. Films include *Le Ciel, les oiseaux et... ta mere!* by Djamel Bensalah (1998); *Astérix et Obélix: mission Cléopatre* by Alain Chabat (2001). (**Samantha Neath**)

Decolonisation   Unlike Britain, which decolonised its former white dominions by transferring power to local political leaders, France had no such tradition. As a result, when pressures for decolonisation grew after the Second World War, there was no precedent in French history to which France's governing élites could turn. Thus, at a conference organised in BRAZZAVILLE in 1944 to discuss the future of France's African empire, any possibility of self-government for the colonies was specifically ruled out, and the term 'decolonisation' itself only began to be used in French in the 1950s. The other key factor that framed the French approach to decolonisation after the war was the perception of France's post-war governing élites, of both right and left, of the key importance of the empire for France. Its preservation was seen as essential if France was to retain its great-power status in a new world order dominated by the two new superpowers, US and USSR. As a result, the French approach to decolonisation was framed by a mindset that saw decolonisation taking place through closer INTEGRATION with France rather than secession from it. The French Union, the new name given to the empire, was established in 1946 to enable this to happen. However, under pressure from external events and an increasingly active nationalist movement, the French Union rapidly began to disintegrate. Indochina never fully joined and other parts of the empire, increasingly frustrated with the slowness of the reform process, rapidly began to demand greater autonomy and eventually independence. The mindset described above led France into two wars of decolonisation, first in Indochina, from which France was expelled following its defeat at DIEN BIEN PHU in 1954, and then in ALGERIA, which became independent following a war which lasted from 1954 to 1962. In other parts of the world, however, notably TUNISIA and MOROCCO (which became independent in 1956), and Black Africa (1960), the transition to independence took place largely without violence and bloodshed and France was able to transfer power to local ÉLITES that were friendly to France. (**Tony Chafer**)

De Gaulle, Charles   1890–1970. French general and statesman who headed the Free French government in exile during World War II, founder and the first President of the Fifth Republic. Born in Lille to a conservative and strongly Catholic family, he graduated from the Saint-Cyr military academy (1912) and served with distinction under Pétain in World War I. Between the two wars, he taught military history at Saint-Cyr and acquired a reputation for his new ideas about the deployment of mobile armoured divisions instead of relying on static defensive fortifications (Maginot Line). After the fall of France, he escaped to London and on 18 June 1940 broadcast his historic appeal, inviting his compatriots to join him in a Free French resistance movement against the enemy. This June broadcast was the founding moment of the de Gaulle legend and gave him a sense of mission to represent and defend the 'greatness of France'. After the liberation of France, he returned to Paris and headed the Provisional Government. After twelve weeks in office, he resigned in 1946 because his proposals for a strong presidential government were rejected by the Constituent Assembly. He remained in a solitary self-imposed exile awaiting the call back to power. This occurred in 1958 when, following a military rebellion in Algeria, the National Assembly elected him Prime Minister and granted him emergency powers to solve the Algerian problem and restore political stability. He drafted a new constitution based on the principle of executive authority, had it approved by referendum, and was elected President of the Fifth Republic in 1959. Once in office, he disowned the defenders of *Algérie Française* when he realised the Algerian FLN could not be militarily defeated, and agreed to Algerian independence in the Evian Agreements (1962). Re-elected in 1965, he resigned in 1969 and worked on his memoirs until his death in 1970. (**Naaman Kessous**)

Further reading

Lacouture (1986) – a magisterial biography by the best authority on De Gaulle; Letwidge (1982) – an excellent biography in English.

Délégation générale à la langue française   The existence of bodies such as the *Délégation générale à la langue française*, which flourished in France from the 1960s onwards, reflects the long-standing tradition in Francophone culture of attempts by the public authorities to influence linguistic developments by direct intervention. In response to an upsurge of concern about the future of the French language, de Gaulle set up the *Haut comité pour la défense et l'expansion de la langue française* (1966). Successive reorganisations gave rise first to the *Commissariat général de la langue française* (1983), replaced in 1989 by the *Délégation générale à la langue française*. Since 1996 this committee of approximately 30 members is attached to the Ministry for Culture.

The *Délégation* plays a central role in devising, implementing, co-ordinating and monitoring governmental language policy. As part of its mission to promote the use of French within France, it oversees the implementation of the *Loi Toubon*. It also co-ordinates the proposals of the ministerial *Commissions de terminologie* responsible for devising new terminology in specialised fields such as electronics, finance or medicine or suggesting appropriate alternatives to borrowings from other languages. The *Délégation* periodically brings together the lists of new terms, after they have been approved by act of Parliament, in dictionaries of official terms (*Dictionnaire des termes officiels*).

Since the mid-1990s the promotion of French as an international language has gone together with the recognition of the role of other languages within FRANCOPHONIE. In conjunction with the Ministry for Foreign Affairs, the *Délégation* continues to monitor developments in language use in institutions such as the European Union or international organisations. It further seeks to devise policies supporting the use of French in the context of cultural and linguistic diversity and to promote multilingualism, for instance through innovative language teaching and translation practices, and the production of multilingual documents by the public services. (**Marie-Anne Hintze**)

Further reading

Judge (1993) – provides a lively discussion of the tradition of language planning in France. Ager (1996) provides further discussion of language planning in respect of *Francophonie*.

Democracy/democratisation   The term 'democracy' comes from the Greek *demos* (the people) and *kratos* (strength) and means 'rule by the people' or by the majority. Democracy may be either direct, with the people governing themselves; or indirect, with the electorate voting for representatives who rule in the name of the people, usually within the framework of political parties and an elected assembly. Indirect democracy is the form of government enjoyed by France and most Western countries. It is associated with freedom of expression, open government and competitive elections.

But while democratic freedoms were accorded to France's male CITIZENS after the 1848 Revolution, they were not generally extended to the French empire until after the Second World War. It was only then that colonial 'subjects' were allowed to elect representatives to local assemblies and the French National Assembly.

These democratic practices had not taken root by the time that France's colonies gained independence. It was not long therefore before newly independent states had moved from multi-party democracy to single-party, military or Marxist rule. These forms of dictatorship were tolerated during the Cold War when there was a danger that former French dependencies might be lured into the Soviet camp. But after the fall of the Berlin Wall in 1989, Paris adopted a policy of suspending aid to developing countries which refused to democratise. France initially adopted a tough policy line but soon grew wary of calling for democratisation, particularly in contexts where it might increase ethnic tension (RWANDA), enable anti-democratic groups to come to power (ALGERIA) or alienate strategically important countries (GABON). France's policy is now more reflective and hemmed in by debates about the legitimacy of imposing democracy on sovereign states, the effectiveness of democracy as a stimulus for development and the form of democracy that should be promoted. (**Gordon Cumming**)

Further reading

Cumming (2001) – see Chapters 5–9 for a critique of France's (and Britain's) attempts to use aid to promote democratisation in Africa; Lefort (1988) – collection of translated essays covering key questions of democracy and politics in modern societies.

Democratic Republic of Congo   The Democratic Republic of the Congo is a huge populous Francophone country in Central Africa. Originally known as the Congo

Free State, it became the Belgian Congo in 1908. It celebrated independence in 1960 but soon became the setting for civil war, political assassinations (see LUMUMBA), Marxist rebellions and Western military interventions.

In 1965, the country was taken over by General Joseph MOBUTU and became a one-party state under the control of Mobutu's 'Popular Revolutionary Movement'. In the 1970s, an 'Africanisation' programme was carried out under which the country was renamed Zaïre; the wearing of African dress was encouraged; and foreign-owned industries were nationalised and plundered by Mobutu and his supporters.

Despite its excesses, Mobutu's regime was widely regarded as a bulwark against Soviet expansion in southern Africa. It was, as such, supported by Western powers like America, Belgium and, above all, France, which signed COOPÉRATION agreements with Zaïre in the mid-1970s and provided military support in 1977 and 1978.

Mobutu's anti-Communist credentials were, however, less important in the post-Cold War period, and he came under pressure to DEMOCRATISE. He promised reforms but failed to deliver, prompting France and other donors to suspend aid in 1991. He subsequently patched up relations with France by allowing Zaïrean territory to be used for French military operations in RWANDA. However, his involvement in the Rwandan crisis generated discontent at home and led to the creation of an anti-Mobutu coalition, the 'Alliance'. This movement toppled Mobutu in 1997 and redesignated the country the Democratic Republic of the Congo. Its leader, Laurent KABILA, became President but soon dismayed Western donors by embroiling his country in a civil war and in a wider regional conflict. Kabila was assassinated in 2001 and replaced by his son Joseph, who has turned to France for help in securing peace. (**Gordon Cumming**)

Further reading

Africa South of the Sahara – the chapter on the Democratic Republic of Congo covers domestic politics and foreign relations; McNulty (1999) – analyses reasons for the collapse of Zaïre and provides useful insights into France's motives for supporting Mobutu.

Depestre, René   Born Jacmel, HAITI, 1926. Writer and intellectual. Founded the magazine *La Ruche* with ALEXIS and others. Exiled the first time in 1946. Studied in Paris until expelled in 1955 for political activities. Via Prague, Havana and Paris he returned to Haiti in 1957, but was put under house arrest for criticising DUVALIER. In 1959 he went to Cuba, was one of Che Guevara's close friends, and later taught at the University of Havana. From 1978 to 1986 he worked in Paris for UNESCO. Since then he has devoted himself to writing full-time in southern France, and has won many awards. Key texts: *Étincelles* (1945); *Journal d'un animal marin* (1964); *Un Arc-en-ciel pour l'Occident chrétien* (1967; *A Rainbow for the Christian West*, 1977); *Poète à Cuba* (1973); *Le Mât de cocagne* (1979; *The Festival of the Greasy Pole*, 1990); *Alleluia pour une femme-jardin* (1980); *Bonjour et adieu à la négritude* (1980); *Hadriana dans tous mes rêves* (1988; *Hadriana in My Dreams*, 1995); *Au matin de la négritude* (1990); *Éros dans un train chinois* (1990); *Anthologie personnelle* (1993); *Ainsi parle le fleuve noir* (1998); *Le Métier à métisser* (1998); *Comment appeler ma solitude* (1999). (**Susanne Heiler**)

Further reading

Leiner (1977) – places Depestre's writings in the Haitian cultural context.

Désir, Harlem   Born Paris, 1959. Co-founder of *SOS-Racisme*, France's best known antiracist youth movement. Son of a West Indian immigrant father and an Alsatian mother, he became a celebrity during the 1980s as President of *SOS-Racisme*, gaining wide media coverage for the organisation through his televisual charm. After vacating this position in 1992, he flirted with the French ecologist movement before joining the Socialist Party, under whose colours he became a Member of the European Parliament in 1999. (**Alec G. Hargreaves**)

Further reading

Hornblower (1990) focuses on Désir's role in *SOS-Racisme*.

Desjardins, Richard   Born Quebec, 1948. Singer–songwriter. Desjardins came to prominence in 1990 with the album and song 'Tu m'aimes-tu', which combines lyrical and poetic texts in a *chanson* style with ironical and satirical folk-blues in Quebec French, in a style reminiscent of Bob Dylan. (**Peter Hawkins**)

Destour   See Neo-Destour.

Devi, Ananda   Born 1960, Mauritian novelist. Ananda Devi is one of the most prolific and promising of the younger generation of Mauritian writers. She came to prominence with a collection of short stories, *Le Poids des êtres* (1987), and has followed these with a succession of mystical, poetic novels whose themes often reflect Hindu mythology and beliefs, such as *Le Voile de Draupadi* (1993). (**Peter Hawkins**)

Diabaté, Massa Makan   1938–88. Historian and one of Mali's foremost writers. He was of *griot* origin. His works include several editions of the famous Soundiata *epic*, of which *Janjon et autres chants populaires du Mali* (Grand Prix Littéraire de l'Afrique noire, 1971) contains the songs, and *Le Lion à l'arc* (1986), the most informative introduction; novels including a humorous trilogy on daily life: *Le Lieutenant de Kouta* (1979), *Le Coiffeur de Kouta* (1980), *Le Boucher de Kouta* (1982); and a limpid tale of a young boy's adolescence: *Comme une piqure de guêpe* (1980). (**Ingse Skattum**)

Further reading

Notre Librairie (1984) – articles by Diabaté, short reviews of several of his books.

Dib, Mohammed   Born Tlemcen, 1920. Algerian writer. He is a founder of Algerian literature in French, with over 35 major works. Dib raises questions regarding writing itself and the need to adapt poetic forms in line with the subject's desire for expression. His trilogy (*La Grande Maison*, 1952; *L'Incendie*, 1954; *Le Métier à tisser*, 1957), a historical fresco of the awakening of the Algerian people to national consciousness, has had wide appeal. It relates the tale of Omar, growing up in the women's quarters of *La Grande Maison*, then discovering rural life in a village, where, amidst rising political tension, a huge fire cannot be extinguished. Returning to Tlemcen, Omar finds the same explosive despair – *Le Métier à tisser*. The fire acts as a generator of metaphor, invading all levels of the text, and the writing blazes to destruction the colonial systems of economic exploitation and cultural alienation. Through its purifying flame, the fire sets free a long-stifled voice and draws on the tradition of legendary Algerian oral tales, with an unsettling effect on the novel's intended realism.

In *Cours sur la rive sauvage* (1964) Dib expresses a quest for self-identity, using metaphorical symbolism to express his dreams and ambitions. He returns to political themes, with a critique of independent ALGERIA's new leaders, in *La Danse du roi* (1968), *Le Maître de chasse* (1971), *Dieu en barbarie* (1973). With *Habel* (1977), Dib engages with the themes of exile, in the form of a labyrinthine, spiritual quest, imbued with nostalgia: *Les Terrasses d'Orsol* (1985), *Le Sommeil d'Eve* (1989), *Neiges de marbre* (1990), *L'Infante maure* (1994) – the last three set in the far north ('Nordic Trilogy'). *Le Sommeil d'Eve* illustrates his espousal of the theory of the subconscious as integral to the creative urge.

Le Désert du détour (1990) takes up the vast theme of the desert and its symbolism, showing that Dib had never completely left his homeland. This is confirmed by *La Nuit sauvage* (1995; *The Savage Night*, 2001), and *L'Arbre à dires* (1998), which explores the need to re-evaluate the meaning of words, expressing and motivating our being and histories. *Comme un bruit d'abeilles* (2001) is again a new departure, in which spatial boundaries are transcended to reach psychological and spiritual depths of universal impact. Prizes include the *Grand Prix de la Francophonie de l'Académie française*; Prix Mallarmé (*L'Enfant Jazz*, 1998). (**Beïda Chikhi**)

Further reading

Chikhi (1989, 1996, 1997).

Dibango, Manu Born CAMEROON, 1933. Saxophonist, singer and jazz musician. One of the best-known African musicians, he first developed his fusion of popular African dance rhythms and jazz in his native Cameroon, moving to the DEMOCRATIC REPUBLIC OF CONGO (then known as Zaïre) from 1961–6 and then to Paris. In 1973 his album *Soul Makossa* was a hit in the USA, and since then he has worked internationally, based in CÔTE D'IVOIRE and Paris, as an arranger and bandleader and providing film scores, notably for SEMBENE's film *Ceddo* (1977). (**Peter Hawkins**)

Diem, Ngo Dinh 1901–63. Anti-Communist Prime Minister (1954–5), then Head of State (1955–63) of South VIETNAM, overthrown by a US-backed *coup* in 1963.

Dien Bien Phu Town in the north-west of VIETNAM and site of an important battle which ended France's INDOCHINA WAR (1946–54). Following a disastrous decision to try and stop the Viet Minh forces entering neighbouring LAOS, 27 battalions of the French army, led by General Navarre, were besieged for 57 days by Viet Minh forces and then finally routed on 7 May 1954. Not only did this defeat mark the end of

France's involvement in Indochina, it sparked the ALGERIAN WAR OF INDEPENDENCE and encouraged other independence movements in France's colonies. (**Andy Stafford**)

Difference   See DIVERSITY.

Diglossia   This term was first used by the French linguist Marçais (1930–31) to depict the Arabic language. He defined it as '*La concurrence entre une langue savante écrite et une langue vulgaire, parfois exclusivement parlée.*' Ferguson (1959) states that the Arab world in general is characterised by diglossia: two varieties of Arabic co-exist – Classical and Dialectal Arabic. The first is a high variety because it is codified and standardised, it is associated with the Holy QUR'AN and embodies a great literary tradition. Dialectal (or Spoken) Arabic is the low variety – the language of everyday conversation, which is neither codified nor standardised.

In a diglossic context like that of North Africa, people take on a personality when they converse in Dialectal Arabic with family or friends, transferring to a different one to express their ideas in a formal situation requiring writing or speaking Classical Arabic. The spoken variety used varies considerably according to region, social class and gender. Ferguson's (1959) classification of Arabic varieties into High and Low does not correspond to the situation in North Africa, where three Arabic varieties are in a diglossic relation: Classical, Standard and Dialectal Arabic. Classical Arabic is used in the mosque, Ministries of Justice and Islamic Affairs, in official speeches, in classical poetry and literature. Instead of Classical Arabic, as Ferguson claims, it is Standard Arabic which is employed in writing a personal letter, in political or scientific discourse, in the media, education and administration. Linguistically, Standard Arabic is a simplified form of Classical Arabic.

Arabic-speaking children face the dilemma of speaking one Arabic variety at home with their parents, or in the street with their peers, but for writing, they turn to Classical or Standard Arabic. The latter is learned at school and does not equate with the native language ability. Dialectal Arabic, the mother tongue of the majority in North Africa, is used in informal settings, at home, in the street, with friends, etc. Conservatives view Dialectal Arabic as a corrupt form of Arabic with no prestige at all. (**Moha Ennaji**)

Further reading

Ennaji (2001); Ennaji and Sadiqi (1994); Youssi (1995).

Dion, Céline   Born Charlemagne, QUEBEC, 1968. Quebec pop singer of great international fame. Grew up in a musical family in rural Quebec as the youngest of 14 children. Her first album appeared in 1981. Breakthrough in France in 1983, and internationally in 1988, when she won the Eurovision Song Contest in Dublin. Dion has sold more than 10 million albums in French and 70 million in English, and her discography counts several international mega-hits, including *Céline Dion* (1992), *The Colour of My Love* (1993), *D'eux* (1995), *Falling Into You* (1996) and *Let's Talk About Love* (1997). She has received numerous international music awards. (**John Kristian Sanaker**)

Further reading

Demers (1999) – Dion as an incarnation of Quebec identity, between tradition and modern life.

Diop, Birago   Born Ouakem, SENEGAL, 1906; died 1989. Senegalese writer. Birago Diop is chiefly renowned for his collections of folk tales, *Les Contes d'Amadou Koumba* (1947) and *Les Nouveaux Contes d'Amadou Koumba* (1958) – tales from both collections are included in the English translation, *Tales of Amadou Koumba* (1966). He came to know SENGHOR when they were both students in Paris in the 1930s, and the influence of *NÉGRITUDE* on Diop's work can clearly be seen in his poetry collection, *Leurres et lueurs* (1960). Diop also wrote a highly acclaimed, five-volume autobiography (1978–89). (**David Murphy**)

Diop, Boubacar Boris   Born Dakar, SENEGAL, 1946. One of the most prominent Senegalese authors of the post-independence generation. A teacher by profession, his acclaimed first novel, *Le Temps de Tamango* (1981), deals with the disappointments and marginalisation of radical left-wing groups in Africa. The novel *Murambi, le livre des ossements* (2000) is Diop's contribution to Fest'Africa's 'Écrire par devoir de mémoire' project, which brought eight African authors together to visit RWANDA and write about the 1994 genocide. (**David Murphy**)

Diop, Cheikh Anta   Born Diourbel, SENEGAL, 1923; died 1986. Historian. Diop's ideas on the Black African origins of Egyptian civilisation have been both highly influential and deeply controversial. He studied physics and history in Paris but his doctoral thesis in history was rejected by the Sorbonne because of the startling connections he made between the culture of Sub-Saharan Africa and that of ancient EGYPT. Presenting Egypt as a 'Black' culture, Diop effectively argued that modern civilisation had emerged from south of the SAHARA, thus revealing the 'African roots' of rational thought, and challenging colonialist stereotypes of a primitive, irrational Africa. His general theory was later widely accepted even if doubts continue to be cast on his methodology.

His ideas were first published in *Nations nègres et culture* (1954) and developed in works such as *Antériorité des civilisations nègres* (1967; *The African Origin of Civilisation*, 1974) and *Civilisation ou barbarie* (1981; *Civilisation or Barbarism*, 1991). Diop also wrote a series of works, including *L'Unité culturelle de l'Afrique noire* (1959; *The Cultural Unity of Black Africa*, 1989) and *L'Afrique noire pré-coloniale* (1960; *Precolonial Black Africa*, 1987), on the socio-political history of Africa, demonstrating the advanced and complex nature of precolonial societies. Diop's theories constitute a major source of PAN-AFRICAN pride and CULTURAL IDENTITY for many Africans, and also African-Americans, as is shown in Martin Bernal's controversial *Black Athena* (1987).

From the 1960s, Diop worked as a researcher in the Institut Fondamental d'Afrique Noire (IFAN) in Dakar, after being refused a post in Dakar University because of his failed doctorate. A bitter critic of SENGHOR's regime, he led a number of opposition political parties. Ironically, after his death in 1986, Dakar University was renamed 'L'Université Cheikh Anta Diop de Dakar'. (**David Murphy**)

Further reading

Gray (1989) – interesting overview of Diop's ideas.

Diop, David Born Bordeaux, France, 1927; died 1960. Senegalese poet (raised in France), whose sole poetry volume, *Coups de pilon* (1956; *Hammer Blows*, 1973) has been hailed as a classic of African literature. Often categorised as a NÉGRITUDE poet, his poems are considered by many critics to be far more aggressive in their criticism of colonialism than those of other *négritude* writers. His radical reputation grew when he moved to newly independent GUINEA in 1958, siding with Sékou TOURÉ in his stand against French colonialism. He died tragically in a plane crash with his wife and two children. (**David Murphy**)

Diop, Ousmane Socé See SOCÉ, OUSMANE.

Diori, Hamani Born Sadouré, NIGER, 1916; died Rabat, MOROCCO, 1989. Politician. Hamani Diori was one of the first generation of Francophone African politicians to enter French political life after the Second World War. As co-founder of the *Rassemblement démocratique africain* with HOUPHOUËT BOIGNY he was elected to the French National Assembly in 1946 and was appointed deputy speaker in 1957. In 1960, as Niger's first President, he became an influential member of regional African organisations. Through the 1960s, with Léopold SENGHOR of SENEGAL and Habib BOURGUIBA of TUNISIA, he campaigned to promote the idea of a formal international Francophone organisation and to gain its acceptance by France. Hamani Diori was ousted by a *coup d'état* in 1974 and lived in exile in Morocco until his death in 1989. (**Antony Walsh**)

Diouf, Abdou Born Louga, SENEGAL, 1935. President of Senegal from 1981 to 2000, replacing Léopold Sédar SENGHOR. Diouf rose to power as Senghor's Prime Minister from 1970 to 1980. Although a skilled administrator, he lacked Senghor's political vision, and is often considered a mere 'technocrat'. However, he received widespread praise when he oversaw a peaceful handover of power to Abdoulaye WADE, who won presidential elections in March 2000, ending 40 years of unbroken rule by the *Parti Socialiste*. (**David Murphy**)

Further reading

Diop and Diouf (1990) – excellent overview of the first decade of Diouf's rule.

Diversity/difference These are key concepts for understanding France's contact with other cultures both at home and abroad. The terms, central to much POSTCOLONIAL thought, are often used interchangeably, but there is a need to distinguish between them. The notion of diversity acknowledges that cultures are characterised by a range of distinctive attitudes and values. Diversity can disrupt processes of colonial ASSIMILATION or GLOBALISATION by protecting the specificity of individual cultures from absorption into more dominant ones. The EUROCENTRIC notion of *EXCEPTION CULTURELLE* has recently been transformed into one of *diversité culturelle*, in an effort to suggest that France's protection of its own cultural and linguistic heritage is part of a wider struggle against Anglophone hegemony. However, unless such a defence of specificity is linked to a degree of cultural relativism, the recognition of diversity can become part of a process of EXOTICISM, whereby divergences from metropolitan cultural norms are seen as aberrant.

Although central to any understanding of diversity, the notion of difference does not necessarily focus on a fixed range of distinct cultures, but permits instead an understanding of the processes whereby cultures interrelate with and understand one another. Whereas diversity often implies distinctiveness, difference allows exploration of the new configurations that result when different cultures interact. In postwar France, the most striking illustration of this process can be seen in attitudes towards IMMIGRATION. In theory, French republican ideology resists cultural diversity and depends on the assimilation of different cultures into a uniform national identity. In reality, the attitude towards difference is more complex, and the heterophobic/mixophilic attitude (fearing difference and desiring integration) of assimilation co-exists with heterophilic/mixophobic attitudes (perpetuating difference and resisting integration). This belief that difference is an essential characteristic of humanity is not the ideological preserve of the Left or Right, for the *droit à la différence* (right to difference) has been central to the arguments of both antiracists and the National Front (see FRONT NATIONAL). (**Charles Forsdick**)

Further reading

Silverman (1999) contains a concise chapter outlining the complex debates in contemporary France over racism and difference (pp. 40–65); Todorov (1993) offers a comprehensive historical account of French attitudes towards cultural diversity.

Djabali, Hawa   Born Créteil, France, 1949. Algerian writer. She returned to ALGERIA as a teenager – living between Algiers and Lakhdaria. She trained in the Conservatoire, then worked in radio and theatre, writing and producing plays. Her work emphasises the oral tradition, largely transmitted by women. She left Algeria in 1989 and now works at the Arab Cultural Centre in Brussels. Her most recent novel, *Glaise Rouge* (*Algérie Littérature Action* (26), 1998), combines the tradition of oral heritage with hope in a series of utopian visions of the future. Other works include *Agave* (1983), and 'Entre urgence et création', *Algérie Littérature Action*, 15–16 (1997). (**Cathie Lloyd**)

Djaout, Tahar   Born Oulkhou, KABYLIA, 1954; assassinated Algiers, 1993. Algerian writer. In 1987, BENHADJ issued a *fatwa* condemning Tahar Djaout for his fiction and fervent critical journalism. An intellectual with popular esteem, Djaout's dedication to exposing the truth about ALGERIA's political and sociocultural realities led him to collaborate in the creation in January 1993 of *Ruptures*, an independent weekly. He published four novels – *L'Exproprié* (1981), *Les Chercheurs d'os* (1984), *L'Invention du désert* (1987), *Les Vigiles* (1981; *The Watchers*, 2002); poetry – *Solstice barbelé* (1975), *L'Arche-à-vau-l'eau* (1978), *L'Oiseau minéral* (1980), *Insulaire et Cie* (1980), *L'Etreinte du sablier* (1983); and short stories – *Les Rets de l'oiseleur* (1984). Ironically, his assassination increased his popularity and stature as a significant literary figure. His work has since become a reference for young Algerian writers.

Djaout's fiction was marked by his uncompromising stance towards corruption and what he considered a betrayal of the ALGERIAN REVOLUTION. The posthumously published novel, *Le Dernier été* (1993; *The Last Summer of Reason*, 2001) is an appropriate introduction to his work and life. It tells the story of a bookseller, Boualem Yekker, living in a country modelled on Algeria in the early 1990s with the rise of Islamic fundamentalism. Once a Republic, the country has now become a 'community in the faith'. His fiction is characterised by an insistence on universal values and truths. At first it appears deceptively simple: plots involve journeys and narrators debit political tirades. However, Djaout's work stands out within recent Francophone literary production for its originality and humanist values. His idealisation of the 'mother country' was stressed in a recent novel, *Un Algérien au paradis* by Rachid Messaoudi, in which Tahar Djaout is the main character. The novel details his time in hospital after the fatal attack, his memories running through his mind as he sinks into a coma. No longer a real person, Djaout is a fictional character, whose life is romanticised. (**Kamal Salhi**)

Further reading

Merahi (1998); Geesey (1996); Naudin (1996).

Djebar, Assia (Fatima-Zohra Imalayen) Born Cherchell, ALGERIA, 1936. Algerian writer, film-maker and university professor. Her career began early with the publication of her first novel, *La Soif* (1957; *The Mischief*, 1958). Three more novels followed, a shared theme being the generation of the ALGERIAN WAR OF INDEPENDENCE. Finding her writing becoming increasingly 'autobiographical', she retreated from novels during the 1970s to make two acclaimed films (see CINEMA, ALGERIA). This experience also allowed her to work in her oral mother tongue as she collected the wartime testimonies of women from her native region. With the publication of a collection of short stories, *Femmes d'Alger dans leur appartement* (1980; *Women of Algiers in their Apartment*, 1992), Djebar returned to prose writing with a new, more experimental style, melding together a single individual narrative voice with the voices of the multitude of Algerian women, past and contemporary, denied the opportunity to express themselves. Her major project from the 1980s onwards is the 'Algerian Quartet': *L'Amour, la fantasia* (1985; *Fantasia: An Algerian Cavalcade*, 1989); *Ombre Sultane* (1987; *A Sister to Scheherazade*, 1988); *Vaste est la Prison* (1995; *So Vast the Prison*, 1999), continuing the themes explored in *Femmes d'Alger* to build a vast panorama of Algerian female experience. Using historical research, she not only rewrites the history of the colonisation of Algeria by the French, but also rereads the history of the region, its legends and its symbolic figures. The metaphor of the palimpsest is often used by critics to describe this vast work of uncovering and rewriting. In addition, there are a number of works, such as *Le Blanc d'Algérie* (1995; *Algerian White*, 2001), a book of mourning for Algerian writers and intellectuals, from Albert CAMUS to an anonymous female schoolteacher executed in the violence of the early 1990s. An extremely powerful writer and prominent intellectual, she deserves to be seen as one of the major figures writing in French in the late twentieth century. (**Debra Kelly**)

Further reading

Clerc (1997) – excellent overview of the work since the 1980s, and especially on the links between the films and novels; Hornug and Ruhe (1998) – useful section in a more general volume on postcolonialism and autobiography.

Djemaï, Abdelkader   Born Oran, ALGERIA, 1948. Algerian novelist and journalist. He worked first in Oran, then moved to Paris, where he also organises cultural events, particularly in the suburbs. Novels include: *Saison de pierres* (Algiers: ENAL, 1986); *Mémoires de nègre* (Algiers: ENAL, 1991); *Un Eté de cendres* (Paris: Michalon/Les Temps Modernes, 1995); *Sable rouge* (Paris: Michalon, 1996); *31, rue de l'Aigle* (Paris: Michalon, 1998).

Further reading

Dib (1996) presents *Sable rouge* as a new departure for the Algerian novel; Boualit (1999) sets Djemaï's work in the wider context of Algerian writing in the 1990s.

Djibouti   An independent republic, since 1977, with a democratic government, situated in the Horn of Africa. Its ancient history is recorded in the poetry and songs of its nomadic peoples. The capital and only urban centre, Djibouti, where two-thirds of the population live, is linked by rail to Addis Ababa and is a natural harbour. It has a strategic location near the world's busiest shipping lanes. Environmentally, there are adverse effects of ship pollution and increasing signs of desertification. There is inadequate potable water for the needs of the population.

The population of 624,116 is mainly divided into two groups, both Muslim: the Afars, who are associated with Ethiopia, and the Somali-speaking Issas, who are associated with Somalia. Both groups, who are pastoral nomads, ignore political boundaries and frequently engage in fierce civil wars. However, interethnic governments have been in power since independence. There is also a 6 per cent Christian (Greek Orthodox, Protestant, Roman Catholic) minority. Djibouti's official languages are Arabic and French. The literacy rate is 46.2 per cent. The CITIZENSHIP laws, which favoured the Afar minority, were changed in 1977 to reflect demographic changes in the rest of the population.

Scanty rainfall limits crop production to fruit, including dates grown for export, and vegetables, so most food has to be imported. Oil is a key element in the country's open economy. Djibouti is a regional supplier of petroleum products. Fishing is a small industry and sea salt is a major resource. There are unexploited limited reserves of copper, gypsum and iron ore, but considerable exploited geothermal resources. An unemployment rate of 45 per cent, the effects of recession and civil war, and a high population growth rate swelled by immigrants and refugees are causing major economic difficulties. (**Susan Fox**)

Further reading

Coubba (1995).

DOM-TOM   When the French empire was rapidly dismantled in the two decades following the Second World War, not all of the former colonies opted to achieve inde-

83

pendence. The DOM-TOMs (*Départements et territoires d'outre-mer* - Overseas Departments and Territories) voted to adopt different statutes (first recognised under the 1946 constitution) that allowed them to maintain dependency on metropolitan France in a postcolonial era, whilst achieving a degree of autonomy. ALGERIA was divided into three DOMs until its independence in 1962. The current DOMs (GUADELOUPE, MARTINIQUE and French GUIANA in the Caribbean, REUNION in the Indian Ocean) are closely linked to mainland France, and have the same status as metropolitan departments. Although each has also been a region in its own right since 1982, Paris remains the ultimate source of legislation. Under the constitution, the TOMs are also part of the French Republic. Although they have greater political autonomy than the DOMs and their statutes are tailored to their individual needs, they too benefit from French economic and institutional support. Two of the current TOMs are in the South Pacific (French POLYNESIA and WALLIS & FUTUNA), and to these are added the TAAF (*Terres Australes et Antarctiques Françaises* – French possessions in Antarctica and four additional islands in the INDIAN OCEAN). NEW CALEDONIA, officially a TOM until 1999, now has a unique status that will allow progressive transfer of political power from France to indigenous institutions. The TOMs remain, therefore, at an institutional junction that allows either greater autonomy (such as the independence ultimately likely in New Caledonia) or closer ties to France (departmentalisation). Of a similar status to the TOMs are two *collectivités territoriales* (CTs), SAINT-PIERRE-ET-MIQUELON (two islands off Newfoundland, a DOM until 1985) and MAYOTTE (an island in the Indian Ocean). One critic has described the DOM-TOMs as the 'confetti of Empire', and French eagerness to maintain close links with these former colonial outposts perhaps reflects their strategic centrality to France's current foreign policy. (**Charles Forsdick**)

Further reading

Aldrich and Connell (1992) is the most comprehensive account in English of the DOM-TOMs; Belorgey and Bertrand (1994) and Mathieu (1993) provide concise introductory guides in French. There is a well-maintained site of the *Secrétariat d'État à l'Outre-mer*, with comprehensive information on the history, economy and culture of each DOM, TOM and CT (http://www.outre-mer.gouv.fr/domtom).

Dongala, Emmanuel-Boundzeki   Born CENTRAL AFRICAN REPUBLIC, 1941. Congolese novelist, poet and academic. He was raised in Brazzaville where he witnessed the 'Red Revolution', after CONGO's independence from France in 1958. This experience provided him with material for his renowned collection of acerbic and tender short stories, *Jazz et vin de palme* (1982). He was the sharpest critic of the country's turn in the 1960s towards Moscow and African socialism. The stories also arise from his exile in New York, where he is inspired by jazz saxophonist John Coltrane. His other novels have explored political commitment (*Un Fusil dans la main, un poème dans la poche*, 1973), pre- and POSTCOLONIALISM (*Le Feu des origines*, 1987; *Fire of Origins*, 2001) and ethnic and political division (*Les petits garçons naissent aussi des étoiles*, 1998; *Little Boys Come from the Stars*, 2001). (**Andy Stafford**)

Ducharme, Réjean   Born 1942. QUEBEC writer. His secret and reclusive life, despite his great literary successes, has made him something of a legendary figure. The characters of all his works, recalcitrant adolescents or disillusioned adults, similarly withdraw from life into their own eccentric marginality, but their experience is recounted in a literary style full of bewildering word-play, ironic quips, puns and literary allusions. His major texts are poetic novels, from *L'Avalée des avalés* (1966; *The Swallower Swallowed*, 1968) to *Dévalé* (1990), but he has also brought his unique style and vision to the stage (*HA, ha!* 1982; *Ha! Ha!*, 1986) and even to the cinema (see MANKIEWICZ). (**Ian Lockerbie**)

Duplessis, Maurice le Noblet   Born Trois-Rivières, 1890; died Schefferville, 1959. Founder of the right-wing, nationalist party *L'Union Nationale* in 1927. Duplessis was the Prime Minister of QUEBEC 1936–39, and from 1944 till his death in 1959. He was a strong defender of Quebec as a traditional French-Canadian society (Catholic and agricultural), but he did little to help the province adapt to the modern post-war model of society developing elsewhere in the Western world. Thus his negative reputation is due to his being the last traditionalist political leader before Quebec's 'silent revolution' (see RÉVOLUTION TRANQUILLE). (**John Kristian Sanaker**)

Duvalier, François   1907-1971. A doctor by training, Duvalier became President of HAITI in 1957, subsequently declaring himself 'President for life'. He ruled Haiti until his death with the aid of terror and his thugs, the *TONTON MACOUTES*. Known as 'Papa Doc'.

Duvalier, Jean-Claude   Born Port-au-Prince, 1951. Known as 'Baby Doc'. He came to power in HAITI upon the death of his father, François DUVALIER, in 1971. His rule was marked by crimes of repression and self-enrichment, until he was exiled to France in 1986.

Economic relations   Economic relations are best understood in terms of trade, investment, aid, loans and debt payments between two or more countries.

In the Francophone context, the main economic relationship is between France, which has the world's fourth largest economy, and her former colonies, which are nearly all developing countries. Paris's exchanges with her empire began with the slave trade and the sugar plantations of the French West Indies. With the abolition of slavery in 1848, France began to develop trade with ALGERIA, SUB-SAHARAN AFRICA and Indochina. But the economic relationship (the 'colonial pact') remained exploitative, as Paris used forced labour and cash crop production to secure raw materials needed by French industry.

After the Second World War, economic ties with Indochina and Algeria were damaged by colonial wars. But France's links with Sub-Saharan Africa remained exclusive thanks to French colonial assistance, price subsidies (*surprix*) and the workings of the FRANC ZONE (a largely Francophone African trading bloc whose currency, the CFA franc, is underwritten by the French Treasury).

At the time of DECOLONISATION in 1960, Paris maintained good relations with Sub-Saharan Africa through a series of economic COOPÉRATION agreements and through generous transfers of development aid. In the 1970s, relations were disrupted by falling commodity prices and rising oil costs, but they remained close thanks to France's rhetorical support for a New International Economic Order. In the 1980s, however, economic exchanges declined as the debt crisis deepened and aid was tied to painful economic reforms.

More recently, the end of the Cold War, GLOBALISATION and European economic integration have helped to make Paris's relations with her ex-colonies less protectionist. In this context, France has allowed competitors to break into Franc zone markets while intensifying trade with developing countries outside her former empire (e.g. South Africa, Nigeria) and with left-leaning states like VIETNAM and CAMBODIA. (**Gordon Cumming**)

Further reading

Adda and Smouts (1989) – critical survey of France's postcolonial economic relations with the Third World; Chipman (1989) – Chapter 7 gives a concise overview of French commercial, monetary and aid relations with African economies.

Economy, Indian Ocean   The principal economic resources of the Francophone Indian Ocean are tourism, fishing, large-scale agricultural produce such as sugar cane, but also specialised local output such as vanilla, cloves and other spices, and perfume essences such as ylang-ylang. Industrial development is very limited, with the possible exception of MAURITIUS, which has established a considerable textile industry oriented towards the export of finished clothing and is attempting to break into the domain of computer hardware and software. REUNION also has potential in this and other high-level technical areas but as an overseas department remains heavily dependent on mainland France. The only island with extensive mineral resources is MADAGASCAR, but these have been very little exploited, with the exception of precious stones. Local subsistence agriculture centres on rice production and cattle farming in Madagascar, and to a lesser extent in Reunion and Mauritius. There is a growing production of tropical fruit and fresh vegetables for the airfreight market as well as for local consumption. Tourism represents a major source of income for the whole region, with the SEYCHELLES and Mauritius leading the field as well-established exotic destinations. The other islands are developing the attraction of more specialised tourism: water sports in MAYOTTE, adventure and natural beauty in Reunion and Madagascar. In general the islands of the region all depend directly for their economic prosperity on the markets of the urbanised, Western world, and their level of development reflects their ability to exploit these to good effect. Mauritius probably represents the most successful independent economy, although the standard of living is probably higher in the French-supported territory of Reunion. At the other end of the scale Madagascar and the COMOROS struggle to feed their indigenous populations and seem trapped in a vicious circle of under-development and dependency on international aid. (**Peter Hawkins**)

Economy, Maghreb   There is no single Maghreb economy despite ALGERIA, MOROCCO and TUNISIA all being former French colonies. This reflects historical and political differences between them, and the continuing importance of France and the European Union as a market both for their products and as a destination for migrants. This means that attempts to create a regional economic union have been unsuccessful. Despite the emphasis on industrialisation during the BOUMEDIENNE era, the Algerian economy has remained the least diversified and remains heavily dependent upon exports of oil and gas, which account for 95 per cent of export revenues. Although Morocco and Tunisia were both significant exporters of phosphates during the colonial era, the importance of this sector has declined in favour of manufacturing and tourism. Clothing products make up some 60 per cent of manufacturing exports in Morocco and 65 per cent in Tunisia whilst agricultural exports are also important for both. All three countries have been hampered since the 1980s by the size of their debts (Algeria's debt at the beginning of 2000 was $30 billion) and have had to implement IMF and World Bank reform programmes. Privatisation policies have been pursued, most extensively in Morocco where the French multinational Vivendi took a 30 per cent stake in Maroc Telecom in December 2000 and where regulators have also been introduced in the telecommunications sectors as a means towards ending the central role of government in the economy. In 2000, structural adjustments introduced by Algeria led to 400,000 civil servants losing their jobs. Unemployment is high (30 per cent in Algeria and 20 per cent in urban areas in Morocco) whilst salaries are often low – some 40 per cent of Morocco's workforce earn less than £105 per month and 6.4m Algerians live below the official poverty line of $1 a day. Despite a dramatic fall in the birth-rate, rapidly rising populations mean that MIGRATION has become an important factor in the transfer of revenues, with an estimated two million Moroccan migrant workers in the European Union. See also EUROMED POLICY. (**Kay Adamson**)

Further reading

Aghrout (2000).

Economy, Pacific   Polynesians and Melanesians lived in a subsistence economy, based on agriculture, fishing and limited trading, before European contact. Foreign traders introduced new commodities (such as metal instruments), which they bargained for local products like sandalwood. Colonial control from the mid-1800s engendered projects, mostly unsuccessful, to create plantations of coffee, rice, indigo and (in TAHITI) cotton. The discovery of nickel in NEW CALEDONIA, the world's second richest source of the metal, revolutionised the island's economy in the late 1800s, leading to international investment, MIGRATION and shipping. Nickel quickly became, and remains, New Caledonia's most important product, accounting for nine-tenths of exports. Phosphate, mined on the island of Makatéa, provided the major export from French POLYNESIA from 1908 until reserves were depleted in the 1960s, by which time activities connected with NUCLEAR TESTING were becoming the motor for Tahiti's economy, as they were until testing ceased in the mid-1990s. In parallel, both New Caledonia and, especially, French Polynesia developed a tourist industry, and sought other exports (notably pearls from Polynesia). Exports, however, cover only a small proportion of French Polynesia's imports. WALLIS & FUTUNA failed to develop an export economy and rely on remittances from migrants to New Caledonia and French government transfers. The French state, in all three territories, is the largest single employer. Per capita income in New Caledonia and French Polynesia is high, but wealth is very unequally distributed, concentrated in the hands of the urban and European ÉLITE, leading to criticism that the territories have an unproductive and artificial economy dependent on French subsidies. The closing of the nuclear testing centre in French Polynesia, the volatile international market for New Caledonian nickel, lack of exploitable resources in Wallis & Futuna and the fickle nature of international tourism represent challenges for future economic growth and development. (**Robert Aldrich**)

Further reading

Freyss (1995) – comprehensive study of local economy; Poirine (1992) – contemporary economic history and future prospects for French Polynesia.

ECOWAS   See CEDEAO.

Eddy-Njock   See WEREWERE LIKING.

Education, Caribbean   The organisation of the educational system in GUADELOUPE and Martinique is identical to that of metropolitan France. Schools have a similar programme and observe the same academic calendar. The high number of people repeating the year at primary and secondary levels led to various debates on the adequacy of the school curriculum in these DOM – a well-established issue which is found in much Caribbean LITERATURE.

Although Guadeloupe and Martinique have had their own individual education authorities since 1997, all directives come from the Ministry of Education in France. In October 2000, the Minister, Jack Lang, raised the issue of regional identities as a way to reduce the failure rate in the DOM. His solution was twofold: adaptation of a programme for teaching history and geography; and development of the teaching of regional languages, notably with the creation of a CAPES (secondary school teaching qualification) in CREOLE from 2002. These, however, are recommendations; the decision to put them into practice lies with the Chief Education Officer and the schools. Conservative views among the various school representatives and parents together with the historical attitudes towards Creole create a concern that its inclusion will lower the educational standard. However, there are some institutions that are experimenting with the use of Creole as a language of instruction and as a subject in its own right.

With an adult literacy rate of 45 per cent and only 65 per cent attending primary schools, HAITI presents a much bleaker picture. Despite its early independence (1804) and the fact that Creole is the language spoken by 90 per cent of the population, French remains the administrative language and the one used in schools. The inability to master the FRENCH LANGUAGE has a greater impact in Haiti. Because of a high failure and drop-out rate, many parents choose to send their children to schools run by private or religious organisations. These constitute almost 90 per cent of Haitian schools and the only possible passport to social advancement. (**Marie-Annick Gournet**)

Education, Indian Ocean   The education systems of the Francophone Indian Ocean islands present a surprisingly diverse picture. In REUNION, the French model dominates without exception, and schooling is universal and free of charge, from the nursery to the 'lycée'. The syllabuses are essentially the same as in metropolitan France and very little concession has been made to local cultural specificities, such as the CREOLE language. Reunion also has its own well-endowed university, on a modern campus near the capital Saint-Denis.

MAURITIUS, on the other hand, still reflects the British influence. English is the medium of teaching, and, even in primary school, French and oriental languages, such as Hindi, are taught. A competitive 'eleven-plus' examination grades students according to ability and regulates access to secondary schools of more or less academic prestige. Thanks to a system of widespread private tutoring, the level of secondary education is generally high, the standards of the Higher School Certificate are demanding, and there are many more candidates for higher education than there are places available at the University of Mauritius, which operates a selective entry on the British model. A new technological university has just been opened, but many Mauritian students study abroad, in the UK, Australia, Singapore, France and India.

In MADAGASCAR, the education system is structured on the French model, but despite French aid suffers from a severe lack of resources, and primary education is far from universally available. There is an extensive network of mission schools sponsored by the Catholic and Anglican Churches, and a fee paying private sector in the urban centres. For an extended period, from the mid-1970s to the early 1990s, there was an attempt to impose the Malagasy language as a means of instruction, but French was reintroduced in 1992. The country has a federal university structure, with university institutions in most of the major urban centres, from Toliara in the south to Antsiranana in the North, as well as in the capital Antananarivo. (**Peter Hawkins**)

Education, Sub-Saharan Africa   After DECOLONISATION, increasing educational opportunities was one of the most significant challenges facing Sub-Saharan African governments and it continues to be the case today. Prior to the Second World War, France's colonial education policies were motivated by educating an African ÉLITE to assist territorial administration. After 1944, France started slowly expanding educational opportunities but these fell short of the expectations of a rapidly growing African urban class who were gaining political rights. At independence in 1960, all of France's former colonies (with the help of French COOPÉRATION and funding from many international sources) committed themselves to large investment in all forms of education from literacy classes and primary schools up to secondary schools and universities.

The results have been contrasting, but overall ultimately disappointing compared with the high ambitions held in the early 1960s. High investment in the 1960s and particularly in the 1970s saw the building of a large number of schools and colleges. The 1980s, however, saw a stagnation in the improvement in numbers of children receiving education and general literacy rates fell, as the former consensus that European-style educational systems would bring economic growth to Africa started to become discredited.

From the end of the 1980s, the introduction of structural adjustment programmes (policies designed to reduce government spending in the public sector and therefore create greater economic stability) at the insistence of international funding organisations, has brought a view that greatest investment should go to 'Basic Education' programmes concentrating on teaching vocational and basic literacy and numeracy skills that have the greatest impact on economic growth.

Since the early 1960s, France has invested heavily in African education in French-speaking countries, both sending teachers from France and part-financing many African students to be educated in France. Whilst this has been a part of the close ties that France has maintained with her colonies, this has also helped to maintain a core bloc of African countries in FRANCOPHONE INSTITUTIONS. The low literacy rates in French (both spoken and written) in these countries, however, expose the ambiguities of the notion of a Francophone community and reveal one of its greatest challenges for the future. (**Antony Walsh**)

Further reading

To understand the wide variety of problems in Francophone education and how they have evolved since 1960 see *Afrique contemporaine* (1994).

Egypt   Napoleon's occupation of Egypt (1798–1801) initiated an enduring French presence, resulting in, for example, Champollion's translation of hieroglyphic script (published 1824), and French involvement in the Suez Canal construction (opened 1869). During the nineteenth century, however, Britain became the leading colonial power in Egypt. French–Egyptian relations reached their nadir in 1956, when French forces co-operated with British and Israeli forces in a failed attempt to prevent Nasser's nationalisation of the Suez Canal.

In the 1960s DE GAULLE directed a renewal in French–Egyptian contacts. While MIGRATION between the two countries remains negligible, there are approximately half a million French-speakers in Egypt, and two daily French-language papers. A French University will shortly be established in Cairo. Each year, 100,000–200,000 French tourists travel to Egypt. Economic exchanges are increasing, with French investment in the Cairo metro and hospitals, and French co-operation in the launching of the 'Nile Sat' telecommunications satellite. In recent years, diplomatic contacts have been aided by the personal friendship of President CHIRAC and President Moubarak. The election of the Egyptian Boutros BOUTROS-GHALI as the first Secretary-General of FRANCOPHONIE in 1997 is further evidence of this renewal. (**Sharif Gemie**)

Elections   See ALGERIAN ELECTIONS 1991.

Élites   This term is used, primarily in relation to postcolonial Francophone states, to characterise the dominant social groups produced by the processes of social and economic development after DECOLONISATION. The postcolonial state plays a central role in the creation and maintenance of unity among the various factions of this élite. This unity is produced through the operation of patronage networks in which positions within state institutions and state revenue are utilised to gain the loyalty of this élite. The capacity to maintain this loyalty is an important element in the reproduction of political stability within a particular postcolonial state. (**Peter Langford**)

Further reading

Bottomore (1993); Nafziger (1988); Zartman (1982).

Emigration   See MIGRATION.

ENA *Etoile Nord Africaine*   Founded in Paris in 1924 by Abdelkader Hadj-Ali, a member of the Central Committee of the PCF (French Communist Party), the ENA was the first modern expression of Algerian nationalism. Originally allied to the PCF and appealing entirely to Algerian workers in France, it gradually fell under the control of Hadj-Ali's deputy, Messali HADJ. By 1935, the ENA had broken away from the PCF and become a purely Arab nationalist movement calling for full independence for ALGERIA, MOROCCO and TUNISIA. Uncompromisingly anticolonial and nationalist, it combined Marxist organisation with PAN-ARABIC and Pan-Islamic ideology. Constantly under attack by successive French governments, it was finally dissolved in January 1937. A few months later, it reappeared as the PPA. (**Naaman Kessous**)

Ennahda   The Ennahda or 'Revival' party of ALGERIA was founded in the 1970s and is led by Abdullah Djaballah. It attracted various people who later became senior figures in the Islamist movement, and was originally a cultural and social organisation based on religious teachings. Ennahda believes in the reintroduction of Islamic values into Algerian society. Although intolerant of SECULARISM, Ennahda has consistently denounced the use of violence and stresses the importance of political pluralism and the rule of law. It remained legally active after the FIS was banned in 1992. (**Susan Fox**)

Further reading

Labat (1995).

Ethnicity   See RACE.

Ethnocentrism   See EUROCENTRISM.

Ethnography   Ethnography is the field of anthropology that involves (i) direct contact with a culture and people through fieldwork, and (ii) the subsequent production of recorded data. The impartiality of the ethnographic method of 'participant observation' was called into question by early twentieth-century authors such as Michel

Leiris, whose involvement in the Dakar–Djibouti expedition of 1931 led him subsequently to explore the colonial foundations of his discipline (1950). Initially, Western ethnographers focused on cultures different from their own. However, following the Second World War, Francophone authors cast an ethnographic gaze on France itself, e.g. Bernard DADIÉ (1959), and French authors such as François Maspero (1990), have written more self-conscious ethnographic accounts of contemporary France, highlighting recently the country's ethnic and cultural DIVERSITY. (**Charles Forsdick**)

Further reading

Clifford (1988) outlines the evolution of twentieth-century French ethnography in a series of influential essays. See also Dadié (1959); Leiris (1950); Maspero (1990).

Etienne, Gérard   See FRANKÉTIENNE.

Etoile Nord Africaine   See ENA.

Ettahaddi   (Challenge), whose leader is a veteran Communist, Sherif El Hashemi, replaced the Algerian Communist Party, then known as *Le Parti Avant-Garde Sociale* (PAGS), in 1993. The party had joined the underground opposition to the 1965 BOUMEDIENNE *coup*, although Boumedienne sought its support subsequently, for his nationalisation programme. The government became uneasy at PAGS's powerful influence over the trade union movement and hounded out all its members from the unions after the 1988 riots. *Ettahaddi* proposes a break both with Islamic fundamentalism, to which it is adamantly opposed, and with the system of FLN 'rentier' bureaucracy. (**Susan Fox**)

Further reading

Stora (2001).

Eurocentrism   A European ethnocentrism. Ethnocentrism is the belief that the values and traditions of one's own culture are a universal norm – a phenomenon common to most world cultures. It is most commonly illustrated in cartography, a field in which mapmakers tend to place their own location at the centre of the world (see CENTRE–PERIPHERY). Eurocentrism is a regional version of this more general tendency, ignoring the specific aspects of non-European cultures and assuming that Western standards are not only superior but also universal. However, what distinguishes this European ethnocentrism from the self-centredness of other cultures is its role in the establishment of major empires that, by 1914, occupied about 85 per cent of the earth's surface. As Johannes Fabian has suggested (1983), European anthropologists have tended to see their own cultures as 'modern', and to relegate less technologically advanced cultures to a pre-modern period. In this process, known as the 'denial of coevalness', Europe provides a chronological norm whereby others are relegated to a state of primitivism and deemed to be in need of civilisation through colonisation.

Key aspects of French COLONIAL POLICY were justified by Eurocentric arguments. The ideology of the *mission civilisatrice* brought to non-Western peoples the 'benefits' of European civilisation (such as education and language), yet ignored the *status quo* in the colonised culture. The policy of ASSIMILATION absorbed individual colonies into the Greater France, erasing cultural differences and imposing a Eurocentric view of the world. A celebrated example of these ideas can be seen in Hergé (1982), in which Tintin teaches a group of Congolese children about 'Votre patrie: la Belgique' ('Your homeland: Belgium'). Postcolonial explorations of colonial culture have allowed a greater understanding of the workings of Eurocentrism, which persists in a variety of forms. DOM-TOMs have been seen, for example, as the perpetuation of a Eurocentric understanding of geography, in which metropolitan France forms the centre and these departments and territories the periphery. (**Charles Forsdick**)

Further reading

Shohat and Stam (1994) provide a comprehensive introduction to Eurocentrism, with a range of practical illustrations; Warnier (1999) offers a concise introduction to French attitudes to globalisation. See also Fabian (1983); Hergé (1982).

EuroMed policy   The Euro-Mediterranean partnership which forms the basis of the European Union's MEDITERRANEAN policy emerged from a conference held on 27–28 November 1995 between foreign ministers of the EU and twelve Mediterranean countries (ALGERIA, EGYPT, JORDAN, LEBANON, MOROCCO, SYRIA, TUNISIA, Turkey and the Palestinian Authority plus Israel, Cyprus and Malta with Libya having observer status). It has three main aims: to establish a common Euro-Mediterranean area of peace and stability; to create an area of shared prosperity through the progressive establishment of a free trade area which is to be accompanied by substantial EU financial support for economic transition; to develop human resources, promote understanding between cultures and rapprochement between its peoples as well as develop civil societies in the region. An important aspect of the subsequent policy framework has been the MEDA programme, which aims to provide bilateral financial assistance for structural adjustment programmes, as well as infrastructural and technological development in the countries of the region as a means to the establishment of a free trade area by 2010. Through this programme some €4685 million was set aside for the period 1995–99 although only €3437 million has actually been allocated. In practice, EU policy in the region has known several phases, the earliest of which was the Global Mediterranean Policy, launched by the European Economic Community in 1972. It was a first response by the EEC to the political and economic effects of the DECOLONISATION process of the 1960s and was primarily an economic policy, which aimed to promote industrial ouput and co-operation in the industrial, scientific and technical fields, and to encourage private investment (see COOPÉRATION). A concern about wider issues led to the setting up of a forum called the Euro-Arab Dialogue in Tunis in 1976 but the Camp David Accords of 1978 effectively suspended all further activity. (See also BARCELONA AGREEMENT.) (**Kay Adamson**)

Further reading

Xenakis and Chryssochoou (2001) – provides a comprehensive introduction to the background and current status of the European Union's Mediterranean policy.

Evian Agreements   Agreements signed between the FLN and France in March 1962 at Evian, establishing a cease-fire in the ALGERIAN WAR and defining the conditions of French withdrawal from ALGERIA and Algerian independence. As early as 1959, secret negotiations had taken place between France and the Algerian nationalists but agreement could not be reached on the status of French citizens residing in Algeria after independence and the country's partition (France wanted to retain the SAHARA with its newly discovered oil and gas, and atomic testing site). To break the deadlock, both sides made concessions, adopting 'declarations of principle' on economic and financial co-operation (see COOPÉRATION), the rights of French citizens in independent Algeria, and the French army's presence in the Sahara and the naval base of Mers-El-Kebir for a five-year period. The Evian Agreements were approved by referendum in April 1962. (**Naaman Kessous**)

Exception culturelle   The notion of *exception française* is the widely held and long-standing belief amongst the French that their position in a variety of fields – such as foreign/defence policy, women's rights – has a distinctively national flavour, and is under no obligation to adapt to more generally accepted norms (especially those of the Americans and British, often known collectively and dismissively as 'les Anglo-Saxons'). As France's influence as a world power waned during the twentieth century, this privileging of national specificity has seemed increasingly anachronistic. The *exception française* remains, however, an essential element in the formation of French identity and is a notion used regularly in the media to explain or justify a variety of phenomena. This is perhaps most apparent in cultural matters, where state interventions and subsidies are part of an official reaction against GLOBALISATION, Americanisation and the pervasiveness of the English language. The Ministry of Culture has a high profile, and the government attempts strenuously to promote French outside France (particularly through the agencies of *la FRANCOPHONIE*) whilst preventing the spread of Anglicisms at home. The specific notion of the *exception culturelle* (which emerged from the 1993 Uruguay round of the GATT – General Agreement on Tariffs and Trade – negotiations) has strengthened the French cultural presence abroad. It ensures that cultural products (especially cinema) are not treated in the same way as other goods by permitting continued state subsidy. There are quotas on French television/radio ensuring that at least 40 per cent of films/records broadcast are homemade. More recently, the exclusive overtones of the *exception culturelle* have been replaced by the more inclusive and more widely applicable idea of *diversité culturelle*. There is a need to rethink the notion of French exceptionalism in the light of the globalised and multi-ethnic make-up of contemporary France, where McDonald's and Disneyland are now firmly established and the rich contributions of several generations of immigrants have radically changed political and cultural life. (**Charles Forsdick**)

Further reading

For a general account of French post-war cultural policy, see Looseley (1995); for a range of approaches to the *exception culturelle* in a variety of contexts, see Kidd and Reynolds (2000).

Exclusion   Many inter-locking forms of exclusion – socio-economic, political, and cultural – exist in the French-speaking world and result from historical and structural inequalities of power, both at the micro and macro levels. These are partially the product of modern French colonialism and imperialism, and of the global spread of capitalism and more archaic exclusionary forces, such as sexism.

Socio-economic exclusion is basic and widespread, though often obscured by neo-liberal ideology of the free market. Working-class immigrants from regions colonized by France (e.g. ALGERIA, Indochina, MARTINIQUE, SENEGAL) provided a reserve army of cheap labour to France throughout the twentieth century, working in heavy industry (auto construction, mining), helping to build infrastructure (e.g. the Paris metro), fighting in the French army in all major wars until 1962, and performing service labour (house- and street-cleaning). The originating countries of these labourers were simultaneously incorporated into the margins of the French economy, tapped for natural resources but excluded from real economic control or benefits. In modified form, this exclusionary imperialist practice continues today, with beneficiaries including local ÉLITES (but not the general populations) of Third World countries and the peoples of over-developed countries, such as France and the United States.

Political exclusion meant the French refusal to allow colonised peoples any significant role in the governance of their countries, so that the majority indigenous population had only token political representation. The French government's continuing refusal to grant voting rights to non-EU resident aliens – often from former colonies – could be seen as a partial extension of this COLONIAL POLICY.

Contemporary cultural exclusion too has colonial roots. For example, under colonial rule, neither Arabic nor BERBER were used to any significant extent in French schools in Algeria, despite being the maternal languages of the Algerian people. (**Mark McKinney**)

Exoticism   The 'exotic' is a category to describe what is radically different from individual or collective experience. Exoticism is the process whereby such radical DIFFER-ENCE is translated from its original culture and represented in a domesticated, non-threatening way. Although there is evidence of exoticism in all cultures, it is predominantly associated with colonialism. Exoticism was central to French representations of its colonies, and has persisted in various forms in postcolonial French advertising and popular culture. One of the principal tasks of Francophone authors has been to counter exoticised metropolitan versions of their cultures and to present alternative indigenous representations. (**Charles Forsdick**)

Further reading

Segalen's essay (1986) has become a central point of reference in discussions of exoticism; see also Célestin (1995).

Eyadéma, Gnassingbé   See TOGO.

F

FAC *Fonds d'Aide et de Coopération*   See COOPÉRATION.

Fall, Malick   Born Saint-Louis, SENEGAL, 1920; died 1978. Senegalese poet (*Reliefs*, 1964) and novelist (*La Plaie*, 1967; *The Wound*, 1973).

Family, Algeria   Under colonialism, the family inevitably came under strain as the head of the household could no longer guarantee the family's wellbeing and security. MIGRATION to towns and later to France put further pressure on the extended, patriarchal structures. It also meant important support for families from overseas remittances. Following independence, the agrarian revolution failed to stem urban migration, and ALGERIA faced enormous housing problems with serious overcrowding. Marriages had to be postponed and the average age of marriage was driven up.

The FAMILY CODE has disrupted power relations within the household. Every year thousands of women rendered homeless following divorce risk exploitation. There are also on average 5000 births outside marriage every year, many the result of rapes during recent terrorism. Algerians' life expectancy is 66 (men), 69 (women), compared with Morrocans' 63/67, and Tunisians' 67/69. Since the National Programme for the Control of Demographic Growth was launched in 1983, contraception has been gradually accepted in Algeria. However, fertility rates of 4.1 are higher than in MOROCCO (3.5) and TUNISIA (3) (UNDP, 1998) – although more recent figures suggest Algerian figures now nearer to 3 (Oufreha, 1998). Maternal mortality rates in 1994, 160 per 100,000, compared favourably with 170 in Tunisia and the astronomical 610 in Morocco (UNDP). More recent figures cited in the national press (2002) found 120 in 100,000 women dying in childbirth, mainly because of a shortage of midwives.

Recent studies (Kateb, 2001) suggest basic changes in patterns of marriage, which remains a near-universal institution in Algeria (almost 97 per cent of adults have been married at some time). The average age of women at marriage is increasing – from 18 (1966) to 25 (1992). Research suggests that growing numbers of women are rejecting the idea of marriage before the age of 18 (Oufreha, 1998). Age-difference between spouses is also falling, possibly related to other factors, e.g. difficulties of finding suitable housing, or of associating freely with members of the opposite sex, but also signals one way in which social control over women has relaxed. Oufreha finds a growing preference for girl children: 92 per cent of Algerian women told a recent survey they would prefer girls to boys. This suggests important changes in women's self-perception and the way they negotiate patriarchal family structures forcing women to have large numbers of children in order to have boys (Lacoste-Dujardin 1986). (**Cathie Lloyd**)

Further reading

Kateb (2001); Lacoste-Dujardin (1986); Oufreha (1998).

Family codes, Maghreb (*Codes de la famille*) Following independence, countries of the Maghreb sought to re-establish Islam in their socio-legal institutions, most importantly through the family or personal status code, based on the *shari'a*. Tunisia has the most progressive such code; in Morocco and Algeria the codes are more restrictive and are currently under review following pressure from Women's move-ments backed by international agreements such as CEDAW, which are in turn opposed by religious conservatives/fundamentalists.

The Algerian Family Code (1984) established men's dominance over women: the husband is legally head of the household, he can repudiate his wives and there is insti-tutionalised sexual inequality in inheritance. A woman's consent to her first marriage is mediated by a male guardian who can deny her choice of husband, and the code legalises polygamy. It has become the most contested legal text in Algeria, underpin-ning repressive social practices, rooted in a conservative interpretation of Islam and backed by patriarchal society. Women's associations and political parties have been at the forefront of agitation for its abolition or fundamental reform. Some claim that the code is itself unconstitutional because it goes against the provisions for equality between the sexes in the constitution, not to speak of Algeria's international obliga-tions. International bodies such as the UN Committee on the Elimination of Discrimination Against Women have stressed that it violates women's rights.

The personal status code or *Moudawana* has a special significance in Morocco as the unique preserve of the king under colonialism. It was regarded as sacrosanct, so that recent campaigns for its reform in the 1990s had to confront the Moroccan establishment and risked violence from Islamic fundamentalists. King Hassan II recognised the need for change and proposed reforms of the right to divorce and the woman's right to child custody. A further attempt at reform in April 2001 through a *Plan d'action national pour l'intégration de la femme au développement* is currently stalled in consultations.

The Tunisian Personal Status Code of 1956, amended in 1965, 1966 and 1981, is the most progressive in the Arab world. The *Code du Statut Personnel* (CSP) secu-larised civil law and granted women legal majority and all subsequent rights and duties. It reformed marital law, prohibiting polygamy, ended repudiation, required that both parties consent to the union and established a minimum age of marriage (Brand, 1998). Similarly, educational rights were given to women in the early days of independence. Reforms in employment law entitled them to enter into contracts and work outside the home. They were given the right to vote and run for public office, in 1957. (**Cathie Lloyd**)

Further reading

Brand (1998).

Family issues, diaspora In France, *familles mixtes* ('mixed families') raise issues of citizenship and gender, and less directly of race. Marriages between French citizens and foreigners peaked at 10.7 per cent of all marriages in 1993, with Moroccans and Algerians at the forefront. This triggered diverse interpretations. The National Front (see Front National) demanded '*des Françaises pour les Français*' ('Frenchwomen for

Frenchmen'), while others perceived 'mixed families' as vulnerable, lacking the (mythical) unity of 'normal' families. Some researchers offer more positive accounts, in which '*mixité*' accelerates assimilation (see ASSIMILATION/INTÉGRATION/INSERTION) of foreigners and their children (faster naturalisation and secularisation etc.).

Much depends on precise circumstances (gender of immigrant, matrimonial practices, individual strategies, etc.), and on the law. All *mariages mixtes* were particularly vulnerable to restrictive legislation (1993 PASQUA Laws, 1997 Debré Law) on residency permits, naturalisation, visa controls and the nationality of children born in France to resident foreign parents (whose children lost their automatic right at birth to French nationality). Although marriages of convenience are rare, all marriages with foreigners were suspect and parents of French children could face deportation. After vigorous campaigns and hunger strikes, children born in France to a foreign couple and brought up in France gain French nationality at 18 (1997 Guigou Law), and foreign spouses automatically obtain a one-year residency permit (1998 Chevènement Law) – a real but limited progress.

The increasing complexity of family types affects definitions of what constitutes a 'family' when welfare/legal claims are made. What are the rights of partners married outside French law? Which jurisdiction should settle disputes over access to children? Although polygamy is illegal, there are about 8000 men living in polygamous marriages in France, mostly from Sub-Saharan countries. What are the rights of their additional families? As long as the law structures rights around marriage and citizenship, such issues will remain. (**Yvette Rocheron**)

Further reading

Barbara (1993) – a persuasive overview of couples seen as pioneers of a pluralist culture; Tribalat (1996) – Chapters 1–4, most useful on traditional matrimonial practices, including polygamy, and '*familles mixtes*'.

Fanon, Frantz Born Fort-de-France, MARTINIQUE, 1925; died Bethesda, USA, 1962. Psychiatrist, writer and revolutionary political activist, Fanon denounced the racial, social and political injustices of colonialism from the perspective of a black Martinican man. Fanon's first text, *Peau noire, masques blancs* (1952; *Black Skin, White Masks*, 1967), drew on his own experiences growing up in Martinique, his time in the Free French army during World War II (MOROCCO, ALGERIA and France) and as a student in post-war Lyons. He blends psychiatry, literature, social anthropology, psychoanalysis and philosophy (phenomenology and Sartrian existentialism in particular) to describe the alienating self-hatred black people in Martinique experience as they aspire to be culturally (and even epidermically) 'white', due to their own black identities being inferiorised by the colonisers. Yet for Fanon, RACISM prevents the metropolitan French from considering Antilleans as full equals: ASSIMILATION is therefore a mirage.

Fanon's subsequent writing details how this colonial oppression can be overthrown. Whilst the celebration of indigenous, precolonial cultures (as in, for example, *négritude*) might instil necessary pride, for Fanon, the coloniseds' seizing of agency could only take place within a political project focused on the future rather than one 'over-determined' by colonialism. Furthermore, this political project had to be collective, on the level of the nation. Fanon argued (1959/2001, 1961/1991, 1964/2001) that political violence was both justified and necessary: violence helped integrate a national (here Algerian) community around a common project (independence), and freed Algerians of their feelings of inferiority (Macey, 2001). As an innovative psychiatrist in Blida (1953–56) Fanon had witnessed the outbreak of the ALGERIAN WAR OF INDEPENDENCE (1954–1962). He sided with the FLN, going into exile in 1956, working as spokesman for the Provisional Algerian Government in Tunis and as its ambassador to Ghana until his death. Fanon's exhortations to radical, violent anticolonial struggle (e.g. Fanon 1961/1991), and his message that freedom had to be won, inspired Third Worldism in the 1960s and 1970s (see ANTICOLONIALISM). His legacy remains strong within Anglophone cultural studies, postcolonial historiography, and studies of racism, although many feminist analyses have been critical (see Sharpley-Whiting, 1998). (**Jim House**)

Further reading

Macey (2001) – the most thorough biography with excellent analyses of Fanon's texts; Gordon, Sharpley-Whiting and White (1996) – wide-ranging, multi-disciplinary collection of articles on Fanon's thought.

Fantouré, Alioume   Born GUINEA, 1938. Economist and novelist. Living and working in Europe for African economic development, he seeks to give a global, non-realist dimension to the dictatorships which afflicted African states after independence. His novels include *Le Cercle des Tropiques* (1972; *Tropical Circle*, 1981), *Le Récit du Cirque ... de la vallée des Morts* (1975); and a trilogy: *L'Homme du troupeau du Sahel* (1979); *Le Voile ténébreux* (1985); *Le Gouverneur du territoire* (1995). (**Denise Ganderton**)

Fares, Abderrahmane   1911–91. Algerian lawyer and politician. Member of the 1946 French Constituent Assembly, President of the Algerian Assembly in 1953. Moved from a position favourable to integration as part of the French nation, to support for the FLN. Head of the provisional Algerian government in 1962, before handing power to BEN BELLA, after independence. After arrest in 1964, he withdrew from politics upon his release.

Farès, Nabile   Born Collo, ALGERIA, 1940. Academic, psychoanalyst and writer. He sees himself as a political writer, inspired by the work of Jean AMROUCHE and KATEB YACINE. He has made a major contribution to a modern, forward-looking Algerian literature. He favours a mixture of genres and a militant stance, as illustrated by *Yahia pas de chance* (1970), a homage to the character, Hassan pas de chance, in Kateb Yacine's *Polygone étoilé*. His collections of poetry, *L'Exil et le désarroi* (1974) and *L'Exil au féminin* (1986), proclaim the distress of the immigrant. Farès's work argues for the Algerian people to take on board all the languages and cultures which have contributed to their history and culture. Other notable works include *Un Passager de l'Occident* (1971), *Le Champ des oliviers* (1966), in which tales involving a variety of mythical and historical figures from Algeria's history, along with literary allusions, are grafted on to an account of a train journey from Paris to Barcelona, and *L'Etat* *perdu* (1982), a text that defies genre categorisation and expresses the writer's revolt against systems of segregation which paralyse the development of societies and stifle MEMORY. (**Beïda Chikhi**)

Further reading

For a more detailed study of Farès's work, see Chikhi (1996, 1997).

FCFP   The Pacific franc. See CFP.

Fédération internationale des professeurs de français   See FIPF.

Feraoun, Mouloud   Tizi-Hibel, 1913; died El-Biar, 1962. Algerian writer, translator, teacher. He is the author of a founding text of North African writing in French, *Le Fils du pauvre* (1950, begun in 1939), describing the peasant life of KABYLIA. Other novels: *La Terre et le sang* (1953); *Les Chemins qui montent* (1957); *L'Anniversaire* (unfinished text; 1972). His published correspondence, *Lettres à ses amis* (1969), including letters to Emmanuel ROBLÈS and Albert CAMUS, is an important document of the period of the ALGERIAN WAR OF INDEPENDENCE, as is his published diary, *Journal 1955–1962* (1962; *Journal 1955–1962: Reflections on the French–Algerian War*, 2000). He was assassinated by a unit of the OAS on 15 March 1962. (**Debra Kelly**)

Ferron, Jacques   1921–85. QUEBEC author who combined prolific writing and political polemics with a full-time career as a doctor. He is best known for his short stories, collected as *Contes* (1968; selections in translation: *Tales from the Uncertain Country*, 1972; *Selected Tales of Jacques Ferron*, 1984) which, like most of his work, are marked by humour, irony and fantasy. Beneath the playful surface, however, there is a serious concern with social and political issues, including abuses in his own profession. Thus the charming Alice in Wonderland story of *L'Amélanchier* (1970; *The Juneberry Tree*, 1975) reveals the shocking neglect of mentally ill children. The state of Quebec (which he dubbed '*un pays incertain*') was his abiding concern. (**Ian Lockerbie**)

FFA Forum Francophone des Affaires   Network of Francophone businesses, with the objective of providing information and promoting commercial, industrial and technological interests within the Francophone world. Created in 1987 during the QUEBEC FRANCOPHONE SUMMIT, it is now closely associated with the new institutional framework of the OIF. (**Béatrice Le Bihan**)

Further reading

See website: http://www.ffa-i.org

FFS Front des Forces Socialistes   Political party founded in ALGERIA in 1963 by the exiled nationalist politician of Kabyle origin, Hocine AÏT AHMED. The Front contested the December 1991 elections, coming third by winning twenty-five seats in its Kabyle heartland (see ALGERIAN ELECTIONS, 1991). Although a secular party it nevertheless opposed the suspension of the election process in 1992. It was a signatory of the 1995

Rome agreement with the FIS and in 1997 it attacked President ZEROUAL's government for vote rigging and human rights abuse in the run-up to the municipal elections. However, the demonstrations by disaffected youth in Kabylia that began in March 2001 and Aït Ahmed's ill-health have seen the Front lose influence. (**Kay Adamson**)

FIPF *Fédération internationale des professeurs de français* (International Federation of French Teachers). A non-governmental organisation, bringing together associations from all over the world. Its aims are to facilitate discussion and collaboration, as well as to provide support for the teaching of the FRENCH LANGUAGE. See website: http://www.fipf.com

FIS *Front Islamique du Salut* (Islamic Salvation Front). The original Islamist party in ALGERIA, it was legalised in 1989 as part of President BENJEDID's political and economic reform programme and gained considerable success in the 1990 municipal and communal elections. In the first round of national elections in December 1991, it gained a majority in a low turnout vote of 41 per cent. The second round of elections due in January 1992 was annulled, setting in motion the present cycle of violence (see ALGERIAN ELECTIONS, 1991). In July 1992, its leaders – Abassi MADANI and Ali BENHADJ – were imprisoned, but released under house arrest in 1994. There were meetings between the FIS and representatives of President ZEROUAL in Rome in 1995 where they signed up to a national peace contract. The fighting has continued even though FIS abandoned support for the armed struggle in 1999. (**Kay Adamson**)

FLN *Front de Libération Nationale* Political party founded in 1954 by a group of nationalists trying to reconcile the warring factions of the independence movement against French colonial power in ALGERIA. From 1956 to 1962, the FLN played a dominant role in the ALGERIAN WAR OF INDEPENDENCE. In 1963, Algeria's first constitution established it as the sole political party. Its political authority was undermined by factional rivalries in the party, BOUMEDIENNE's militarily orientated presidency during the 1970s and political and social turmoil during the 1980s. With the legalisation of all political parties in 1989, the influence of the FLN declined. (**Susan Fox**)

Note: the FLN was also the name of the Vietnamese National Liberation Front, in its anticolonial struggle.

Further reading

Harbi (1980).

FLNKS *Front National de Libération Nationale Kanak et Socialiste* FLNKS is the major KANAK (Melanesian) and pro-independence force in the politics of the French overseas territory of NEW CALEDONIA. Formed in 1984 as a coalition of several parties – the *Union Calédonienne* the largest and oldest – and a trade union and women's organisation, the FLNKS draws on indigenous culture, anticolonialist and Third World ideas and French constitutionalism for its ideology. Membership includes some Europeans and Polynesians, but its focus and recruitment lies overwhelmingly among native Melanesians, four-fifths of whom support the Front. The FLNKS advocated the rapid achievement of a *Kanak*-based and communitarian independence, but recognised that other residents of the territory, including descendants of transported convicts and immigrant Asian and Polynesian workers, were 'victims of history' entitled to a place in a '*Kanaky*'. The Front used both extra-parliamentary and electoralist strategies (though sometimes boycotting elections), setting up local organising committees of militants, promoting '*Kanak* people's schools' and establishing ties with overseas trade unions and support groups. Some activists favoured more muscular tactics, and critics alleged that the FLNKS was responsible for attacks on European property, hostage-taking and assassinations during the mid-1980s as pro- and anti-independence groups clashed in virtual civil war. The so-called 'events' led in 1988 to the Matignon Accord, mandating a ten-year 'cooling-off' period. A Melanesian who was discontented with the FLNKS' seeming willingness to postpone independence assassinated the Front's charismatic founder and leader, Jean-Marie Tjibaou, the following year. Factional disputes and uncertainty about tactics have subsequently weakened the FLNKS, while changing conditions moderated its rhetoric (with increasingly talk about 'interdependence' between France and the territory), but the FLNKS remains the key Melanesian player in local politics. In 1998, a further accord foreshadowed New Caledonia gaining a somewhat vague 'sovereignty' between 2013 and 2018. (**Robert Aldrich**)

Further reading

Aldrich (1993) – an overview containing much material on New Caledonia; Henningham (1992) – another perspective on recent history.

Flosse, Gaston   Born Rikiea, Iles Gambier, 1931. President of the Polynesian government, leader of the *Tahoeraa Huiraatira* party, associated with the French RPR (Rally of the French People, a centre-right party). He has dominated Polynesian politics for many years, occupying a variety of elected and governmental positions in Polynesia and in France.

Foccart, Jacques   Born Ambrières, Mayenne, France, 1913; died 1997. French politician. He joined the Resistance during the Second World War and first met de Gaulle in June 1944. This was the beginning of a long association that only came to an end with de Gaulle's death in 1970. A founder member of the Gaullist *Rassemblement du Peuple Français* (RPF) in 1947, he sat on its National Council from the outset, becoming the party's general secretary in 1954. He was also a member of France's secret services. In 1953 he organised de Gaulle's visit to eighteen African countries, with the result that, when de Gaulle returned to power in 1958, Foccart was perfectly placed to become the president's special adviser on African affairs. He remained in this post until President Pompidou's death in April 1974. A leading figure in France's semi-clandestine African 'networks', he was associated with several actual or attempted *coup*s in Africa. However, he had the confidence of many Francophone African leaders and was an important intermediary between them and the French President. Following the March 1986 parliamentary elections, he was appointed by Prime

Minister Jacques CHIRAC as his personal adviser on African affairs, a post to which he returned in an unofficial capacity when Chirac won the presidential election of 1995 and in which he remained until his death in 1997. (**Tony Chafer**)

Food, Caribbean   Food in the CARIBBEAN reflects the diverse origins of its people. The origins of accras (fish, vegetable or seafood fritters) are a perfect illustration of the composition of Caribbean food. They are based on apple doughnuts (French), the apple replaced by dry salt fish (African approach) and seasoned with Indian spices. Some of the most famous Caribbean dishes combine Arawak, African, Indian and European styles successfully. The most commonly eaten meals include: fish blaff (poached white fish or shellfish); dumpling soup (Dutch inspired); crab *matété* (crab, prawn and vegetable, mixed with rice: a version of the Spanish paella); Congo bean and yam (from Africa); chicken, fish or goat colombo (mixture of spices similar to curry, an Indian legacy); cooked beans and tripe (France).

A typical two-course meal would start with some accras, Creole black or white pudding, or a local soup. This might be followed by bean and rice or some local vegetables (yam, bread-fruit, plantain, green bananas, sweet potatoes), accompanied by a blaff, court-bouillon (red fish poached in a sauce made with tomatoes with chilli) and chicken, pork, crab, goat or fish colombo. All these dishes would usually be flavoured with spices.

Breakfast tends to be very simple: milk for children, coffee for adults. People would normally take a sweet or savoury snack between ten and eleven as a supplement.

Cooking in the Caribbean requires time. Preparations normally start at least two hours before eating time. Meat and fish are usually left to marinate for the minimum of an hour prior to cooking. Vegetable dishes made with beans, dumplings or similar ingredients also require long simmering at low temperature. However, as social customs change, cooking and eating habits, too, are changing.

Cooking tends to be a field dominated by women. In GUADELOUPE, there is the *Association des cuisinières* (organisation for female cooks), with its own entry exam. Caribbean cooking is celebrated every year on 10 August in Point-à-Pître (Guadeloupe) with *la fête des cuisinières*, commemorating St Laurent, patron saint of cooks. (**Marie-Annick Gournet**)

Food, Maghreb   The food of the MAGHREB is a wonderful blending and mingling of cultural, geographical and religious influences (Arabic, BERBER, JEWISH, European). Although it may appear an exotic cuisine to an outsider, it is mostly simply prepared and well suited to family and social occasions, a favourite pastime in these countries, where hospitality is an obligation as well as a pleasure. The offering of food or a glass of mint tea, at least, dignifies every meeting or transaction. Shopping in the Maghreb is done mostly in bazaars and *souks*, where the foodstuffs give one an idea about the cuisine: the meat is mainly lamb, the poultry mainly chicken and pigeon. Aubergines, citrus fruits, courgettes, fresh herbs, green beans, onions, tomatoes are piled high in the various stalls. Dried fruit and spices are also popular, either used in fruit salads or cooked with meat. Couscous, whole wheat, cracked wheat, dried beans, chickpeas and lentils are used as the basis of dishes.

Moroccans use a huge range of spices, including saffron, turmeric and *harissa*, which is made out of chili and red pimento.

Couscous (a fine semolina), which is of Berber origin, is often eaten without cutlery, using the right hand (never the left). In ALGERIA, it is eaten as a dessert, as well as a main course. Meat-based savoury pastries, the Moroccan *bstilla* and the Tunisian *tagine malsouka*, are a traditional choice for party dishes. In TUNISIA fish is believed to have beneficial properties for health and happiness. Shad is a popular fish found in North African rivers, and stuffing it with dates is the traditional method to prepare it in MOROCCO and Tunisia. In Algeria a traditional dish is spiced sardines with garlic, served as *mezze* (hors d'oeuvre). (**Susan Fox**)

Forum Francophone des Affaires   See FFA.

Franc zone   One of the pillars of the Franco-African relationship in the post-independence era, the Franc zone comprises fourteen countries, all of which, with the exception of Equatorial Guinea, were former French colonies in Black Africa. The currency, the CFA (*Communauté Financière Africaine*) franc, was tied to the French franc at a fixed parity of 50CFA = 1 franc from 1948 until January 1994, when it was devalued by 50 per cent. The new parity of 100CFA = 1 franc applied to all zone members apart from the COMOROS islands, where the new parity was fixed at 75CFA = 1 franc. Member countries are required to hold two-thirds of their foreign currency reserves with the Bank of France in Paris. The CFA franc is currently pegged to the Euro, with a review planned for 2002–3. (**Tony Chafer**)

France-Plus   A pressure group rooted in France's Maghrebi (North African) immigrant minority, whose interests it sought to advance primarily by means of the CITIZENSHIP rights enjoyed by second-generation members of minority ethnic groups. Founded in 1985 with support from the French Socialist Party and led by Arezki Dahmani, the organisation enjoyed its high-water mark in 1989, when it claimed to have secured the election of several hundred Maghrebis as municipal (town) councillors. Disputes over its representativeness and financial irregularities led to its collapse in 1997. (**Alec G. Hargreaves**)

Further reading

Wihtol de Wenden and Leveau (2001), a general study of minority ethnic mobilisation, includes coverage of France-Plus.

Franco (François Luambo Makiadi)   Born Kinshasa, CONGO; died 1989. Musician. A legendary figure in African popular music, he gained an international reputation under the name of 'Franco'. After the formation of his band, *O.K. Jazz*, in the 1950s, Franco became a leading proponent of 'Congolese rumba', blending Latin and African elements in a style which soon became popular across Africa. In particular, Franco's guitar style was hugely influential, spawning many imitators. In the course of his thirty-year career, he recorded over 150 albums. His death in 1989 was marked by four days of national mourning. (**David Murphy**)

Franco-African summits   The first annual Franco-African summit took place in 1973 and involved presidents or ministers from France and ten Francophone African countries. It is now (since 1988) held biannually and attracts 50 African leaders plus the Secretary-Generals of the UN and the Organisation for African Unity (see OAU). The size of these informal gatherings reflects France's growing influence in Africa and the importance of the themes discussed (e.g., DEMOCRATISATION, debt). Yet while these meetings make valuable recommendations (e.g., an inter-African peacekeeping force, an AIDS fund), they also perpetuate France's neo-colonial relations with Africa and give respectability to despotic African leaders. (**Gordon Cumming**)

Francophone Black Atlantic   An area of study that analyses the dialogue between Africa and the Americas, especially the CARIBBEAN, initially bracketing metropolitan France. Acknowledging the deep similarities between African and Caribbean Francophone cultural forms, it also questions the relationship between history and MEMORY. Slavery is therefore the key historical category, whose status in determining 'identity' and cultural forms is deemed difficult to quantify.

The NÉGRITUDE movement is one of the earliest and best examples of a Black Atlantic phenomenon, affirming the fundamental importance of the African diaspora, and positing the 'return to Africa' as a metaphorical (and in some cases, real) route to finding Black identity and dignity under colonial control. The Atlantic triangular circuit of Africa–Americas–France can be seen as redolent of the triangular slave trade. Caribbean Francophone writers such as Aimé CÉSAIRE, Edouard GLISSANT, René DEPESTRE, Maryse CONDÉ remodel and retrace the Atlantic circuit. Frantz FANON was the archetypal Black Atlantic theorist writing in French: a Martinican who devoted himself to Algerian liberation in the 1950s, and whose theories made the return trip across the Atlantic in the 1960s, to influence the Black Power movement in the United States. Ironically, Fanon is barely appreciated in his native Caribbean.

If Caribbeans are seen as having experienced a double exile – forced removal from Africa and then discrimination under colonial control – then a third exile – that of Caribbeans having to move to France to find work – is in evidence. The exile of Haitians to North America, especially to Canada, has added a fourth dimension to the Atlantic circuit. Other aspects of the circuit are those found in *voyage à l'envers* ('reverse ETHNOGRAPHY'), whereby African writers (such as Ousmane SOCÉ, Bernard DADIÉ, NGANDU NKASHAMA, Alain Mabanckou) visit France and turn the tables on France and its ethnographic tradition. The movement of American Black intellectuals and writers to France during the twentieth century is another important dimension (Fabre, 1985). (**Andy Stafford**)

Further reading

Gilroy (1993) – classic text of definition of this area of study; Pettinger (1998) – impressive anthology of key texts, but almost entirely Anglophone.

Francophone discourse   At the heart of all Francophone discourse is an insistence on the 'universality' of the FRENCH LANGUAGE and culture, seen as the shared heritage of all Francophone nations/regions (see UNIVERSALISM). The egalitarian nature of this discourse is underlined by the fact that many of the strongest supporters of *la Francophonie* come from outside of France. In the 1960s, Africans and French Canadians were instrumental in the creation of FRANCOPHONE INSTITUTIONS, seeking to unite the far-flung regions of the Francophone world. The French saw *la Francophonie* as a means of defence against the spread of English around the world, stressing France's global presence. In this linguistic combat, French is often characterised as the language of *liberté, égalité, fraternité*, while English is associated with capitalism and GLOBALISATION. This process intensified in the 1990s when *la Francophonie* positioned itself as a defender of cultural pluralism, promoting the rights of all minority cultures/languages, in the era of globalisation.

However, critics argue that this idealistic Francophone discourse that speaks of a worldwide 'family' of French speakers ignores political and economic differences within the Francophone world. Indeed, the unity and brotherhood of Francophone discourse finds little reflection in the realities of French neo-colonial policies in Africa (see NEO-COLONIALISM) or the living conditions of many Francophone Africans in France. The establishment of the *Organisation Internationale de la Francophonie* (OIF) in the 1990s was an attempt to bridge this gap between rhetoric and reality, forging closer economic and political ties between Francophone nations. One of the major challenges for the OIF is to make Francophone discourse seem relevant to a much wider public in all Francophone countries. (**David Murphy**)

Further reading

Maugey (1993) – an enthusiastic supporter of *la Francophonie*; Parker (1996) – excellent critique of Francophone discourse in relation to Africa.

Francophone institutions   The term 'Francophone institution' covers a vast array of pressure groups, semi-public and private associations and non-governmental organisations. The most significant is the *Organisation Internationale de la Francophonie* (OIF), which brings together heads of state, prime ministers and government ministers from around the French-speaking world to co-ordinate common policies to promote and share a common cultural heritage as defined by bi-annual summits. The first of these summits was held in Versailles in 1986 some quarter of a century after France's DECOLONISATION of Sub-Saharan Africa.

The bi-annual summit serves to shape the general principles and priorities of the Francophone movement. Summits are defined and elaborated after diplomatic preparation by two main preparatory bodies: the *Conseil Permanent de la Francophonie* (CPF), which consists of personal representatives of heads of state and government, and the *Conférence Ministérielle de la Francophonie* (CMF), which brings together ministers of foreign (and/or Francophone) affairs of member states, who oversee the implementation of summit decisions. The main figurehead for the OIF is the Secretary-General (who since 1997 has been Boutros BOUTROS-GHALI), who promotes the OIF on the world stage, notably in major international organisations such as the United Nations or UNESCO.

Once formulated, policies are implemented by five agencies. The *AGENCE INTER-GOUVERNEMENTALE DE LA FRANCOPHONIE* (formerly the ACCT) is the principal directing agency, concentrating on projects in education, culture and development and giving support to smaller, more specialist Francophone associations. The five specialised agencies are the AUF, promoting inter-university co-operation and training; the UNIVERSITÉ SENGHOR in Alexandria, EGYPT, specialising in training civil servants the international Francophone television channel TV5; and finally AIMF (*Association Internationale des Maires et responsables de capitales et métropoles partiellement ou entièrement Francophones*), which oversees shared projects between cities and towns in the industrialised and developing world. (See also Appendix.) (**Antony Walsh**)

Further reading

For an introductory overview of Francophone institutions see Barrat (1997).

Francophone summits   Bi-annual gatherings of French-speaking presidents, prime ministers and heads of cultural communities that meet to discuss cultural, political and economic issues in an effort to maintain and strengthen Francophone co-operation and to present a common Francophone front on the world stage. There have been nine summits in total: Versailles in 1986, Quebec in 1987, Dakar (Senegal) in 1989, Paris in 1991, Mauritius in 1993, Cotonou (Bénin) in 1995, Hanoï (Vietnam) in 1997, and Moncton (Canada) in 1999. A ninth summit was planned in Beirut (Lebanon) for September 2001, but has been postponed until 2002, because of the events of 11 September.

The participants of the summits are 51 countries, states and French-speaking communities from throughout the world. Whilst the participation of many representatives can be explained by the continued importance of the FRENCH LANGUAGE after colonial rule, the presence of such countries as Albania, Bulgaria, Macedonia and Romania reflects the ambitions of some states to associate themselves with other cultures than English and is recognition that Francophone co-operation offers a potential for creating links and exchanges of a nature that is very different from other international groupings.

The preparation and follow-through of summit decisions is carried out by two organisations, the *Conseil Permanent de la Francophonie* and the *Conférence ministérielle de la Francophonie*, respectively (see FRANCOPHONE INSTITUTIONS). At the conclusion of each summit, which is held in camera, resolutions are issued reflecting the consensus of decisions made at the summit.

Each summit is given a general theme that reflects an issue of importance to the community. In Dakar in 1989, for example, the theme was North–South co-operation and in Mauritius in 1993, the two major themes were human rights and unity in DIVERSITY. Most recently for Beirut in 2001/2, the chosen theme was cultural dialogue. Such themes have, on occasions, brought significant actions from participants. In Dakar, France used the summit to cancel development aid debts owing from its African partners (replying to a similar gesture by Canada to do the same, in the summit two years previously). In Mauritius, the final resolution saw all states backing France's decision to refuse the USA's attempt to remove the cultural exception clause (*EXCEPTION CULTURELLE*) in the GATT talks of the same year. (**Antony Walsh**)

Further reading

For a relatively recent summary of recent Francophone summits and how they fit into overall structures see Ager (1996).

***Francophonie*, birth and development**   As an institutional concept, the creation of institutions to assemble Francophone states regularly has been problematic and, at times, diplomatically delicate in the light of French foreign policy priorities and given the politically sensitive nature of the minority status of FRENCH LANGUAGE speakers in countries such as Canada or Belgium.

After France's DECOLONISATION of Sub-Saharan Africa, the pressures for an international Francophone organisation came from two main sources. Firstly they emerged from the newly independent African states who sought a culturally based diplomatic forum and, secondly, they came from the newfound confidence of the French-speaking Canadian province of QUEBEC pressing for greater cultural and political autonomy. Although backed by the inter-African organisation OCAM (*Organisation commune africaine et malgache*) in 1965 and supported by presidents Léopold SENGHOR of SENEGAL and Habib BOURGUIBA of TUNISIA, France expressed no interest in a proposed Francophone community with relations based on concentric circles, with the closest ties binding France with her former African colonies and the loosest with Canada, Belgium and Switzerland.

In this same period, however, despite the failure of proposals for gatherings of heads of state, a number of non-governmental groups, such as CILF, appeared, supported financially by the French and Canadian governments. Partly due to the activities of these organisations, France and Canada came to a diplomatic understanding in 1969 to allow the creation of the ACCT, which would permit the first officially sanctioned international Francophone organisation to initiate projects in a wide range of cultural areas for its 28 members.

Léopold Senghor attempted both in 1977 and in 1979 to resurrect the idea of FRANCOPHONE SUMMITS but made little progress when faced with the diplomatic complexities of how the Canadian federal government could accept Quebec's participation.

Agreement came in 1986 when the first Francophone summit was held in Versailles, followed by a second in Quebec a year later. Building on projects already instigated by the ACCT, these summits increased the number of FRANCOPHONE INSTITUTIONS and the scope of their activities and ambitions. By the turn of the twentieth century, some 51 member states and governments attended Francophone summits with four observer states. (**Antony Walsh**)

Further reading

See Whiteman (1987) – a well-researched broad overview of the birth of *Francophonie* as an institutional grouping, stressing the importance of African countries in bringing it about.

Frankétienne (aka Gérard Etienne)   Born 1936. Haitian writer, poet, painter, dramatist, academic. Unlike many of his dissident compatriots, he still lives in HAITI. Critical of Haiti's dictatorial regimes, he avoids sanctions by his innovative writing style, known as 'spiralism'. *Dezafi* (1975) was at the time only the second published novel in CREOLE and the first in Haitian. Republished in French as *Les Affres d'un défi* (2000), it mixes narrative decentring with Creole oral tradition and indigenous words. Thus it is hard to describe his pieces as 'novels'. *L'Oiseau schizophone* (1998), using many typographic and narrative styles, shows further his radical experimentation. (**Andy Stafford**)

French language   French belongs to the Romance group of languages, that share Latin as a common ancestor. It emerged as an independent language around the ninth century. From the twelfth to the eighteenth centuries, the dialect of the Paris region established itself as the most prestigious, displaced Latin as the language of government and scholarship, and acquired a standardised form based on the usage of the Parisian élites. However, it was not until the mid-nineteenth century with the development of an industrial economy and compulsory education that the use of the French language extended throughout France.

French is thus the historic language of parts of Europe settled by the Romans in the first two centuries BC: France, parts of Belgium, Luxemburg, Switzerland and Italy. As a result of emigration and settlement, mostly before the eighteenth century, French also spread to regions of North America, the Caribbean and the Indian Ocean where distinct forms of French have developed. In a third group of countries, mostly in Africa, the presence of French is linked to the colonial expansion of the nineteenth and twentieth centuries.

Across the world, there are today approximately 100 million regular speakers of French as a first or second language, a further 60 million occasional users, and 100 million learners of French as a foreign language. The perception that French fulfils a special role as a world language, second only to English, therefore rests not on the absolute number of speakers but, rather, on its presence in every continent and its cultural prestige.

Much of the discourse surrounding French in the twentieth century has been marked by anxiety and the feeling that the language was under threat: internally through the laxity of French speakers, and externally, due to the all-pervasive international presence of the English language and Anglo-American culture. One response to these threats has been renewed direct state intervention in LANGUAGE POLICY and the development of the idea of partnership within *FRANCOPHONIE*, focusing on the defence of linguistic and cultural DIVERSITY. (**Marie-Anne Hintze**)

Further reading

See Rickard (1989) and Lodge (1993) for historical accounts of the development of the French language, Ager (1996) for an overview of linguistic, economic and political issues facing *Francophonie*, and Rossillon (1995) for maps and statistics about language use in the Francophone world.

Front des Forces Socialistes   See FFS.

Front National   French political party, founded in 1972. The *Front National* (FN) evolved from a tiny group to gain significant national success beginning in the 1980s.

Under Jean-Marie Lᴇ Pᴇɴ, the FN united several far-right factions, eventually replacing the PCF as the largest working-class party. It resurrected a French political current that had great notoriety during the 1930s, had dominated the collaborationist French Vichy regime, but was defeated and marginalised in 1944. The FN reworked colonialist ʀᴀᴄɪsᴍ and anti-semitism, and disseminated its virulent strain of xenophobia throughout French society, gathering as much as 17.85 per cent of the vote in a presidential election.

The FN argues that newly immigrated communities of colour, especially North Africans, are responsible for the economic crisis that France entered beginning in 1974, when oil prices rose dramatically. Although erroneous, this thesis gained wide currency in slogans such as 'One [two, three] million immigrants, one [two, three] million unemployed [French persons].' Mainly by scapegoating immigrants of colour, the party split the working class along racial lines, diverting energy away from needed urban renewal, acceptance of cultural ᴅɪᴠᴇʀsɪᴛʏ and multi-ethnic, working-class unity.

During his pre-FN career, Le Pen was a far-right deputy who supported French colonialism in Aʟɢᴇʀɪᴀ, and fought in French colonial wars in Indochina and in Algeria, leading to accusations that he was involved in the torture of captured enemy soldiers. More recently, he has repeatedly been judged guilty of racist statements and was temporarily disbarred from electoral activity because he had roughed up a Socialist Party candidate. Le Pen's heavy-handed leadership and reluctance to ally the FN with the moderate right helped create support for Bruno Mᴇ́ɢʀᴇᴛ, his second-in-command, and led to a power struggle that split the party in 1999, causing a significant loss of influence for a few years. However, in the first round of the 2002 presidential election, Le Pen caused a major upset by coming second, after out-going president Cʜɪʀᴀᴄ, and thereby eliminating Prime Minister Jᴏsᴘɪɴ, the Socialist Party candidate, from the run-off election. Some of the largest street demonstrations in French history were quickly organised against Le Pen. In the run-off, left-leaning voters closed ranks with the moderate right to hand the scandal-plagued Chirac a landslide victory. Two months later the FN was unable to win any seats in the new National Assembly. (**Mark McKinney**)

Further reading

Marcus (1995) provides a useful survey of the FN.

Gabon   An equatorial country on Africa's Atlantic coast, bounded inland by Equatorial Guinea, Cᴀᴍᴇʀᴏᴏɴ and Cᴏɴɢᴏ. The capital is Libreville, which is named after a settlement begun by liberated slaves in the mid-nineteenth century. The population of 1,208,436 comprises several ethnic groups, namely 30 per cent Fang; 20 per cent Eshura; 15 per cent Mbete; 15 per cent Omyene and 10 per cent Kota with a 63 per cent literacy rate. Population estimates for Gabon take into account the effects of excess mortality due to AIDS. Life expectancy is 52 years. Religion: 62.5 per cent of the population is Roman Catholic; 18.8 per cent Protestant; 12.1 per cent Indigenous Christian. Traditional religions comprise 2.9 per cent and Muslims 0.8 per cent. The official language is French with Fang and Eshura local languages.

Little is known of Gabon's tribal life before European contact, namely Portuguese traders in the fifteenth century, but tribal art suggests rich cultural heritages. Bantu ethnic groups settled in the area from the thirteenth century onwards. The coast became the centre of the slave trade in the sixteenth century. France assumed the status of protector by signing treaties with coastal chiefs in 1841. From 1910 to 1959, Gabon formed part of the French Equatorial Africa federation, and it became independent in 1960. It has been ruled by an autocratic president, Omar BONGO, since 1967, but the introduction of a new constitution with a multi-party system in the early 1990s allowed for a more transparent electoral process and reform of governmental institutions. A small population, abundant natural resources and foreign private investment have made Gabon one of the more prosperous African countries, although a large proportion of the population remains poor because of the great disparity between high and low-income earners. Natural resources are oil, iron ore, diamonds, gold, manganese, uranium, timber and hydropower. The chief agricultural crops are cassava, plantains and sugar cane. (**Susan Fox**)

Further reading

Rossatanga-Rignault (2000).

Gallaire, Fatima   Born El Arrouch, ALGERIA, 1944. Algerian playwright and novelist. Best known for her play *Princesses* (1988), which has been performed in Paris, New York and London and deals with the tragic clash of modern and traditional values which takes place when a young woman returns to her native village after living in France and marrying a Frenchman. Other plays deal with such themes as circumcision, *La Fête virile* (1992), and polygamy, *Les Co-épouses* (1990). Disillusioned by the difficulty in getting her work staged, she is currently working on short stories and novels. (**Debra Kelly**)

Gamaleya, Boris   Born 1930. Reunionese poet and dramatist. A militant member of the Communist Party of REUNION, Gamaleya defended the distinctive identity of his island in a long epic poem, *Vali pour une reine morte* (1973), which celebrates the achievements of runaway slaves who established themselves in the inaccessible mountain interior of the island during the first century of colonial occupation from the late seventeenth century onwards. Gamaleya's more recent poems, such as *Le Volcan à l'envers* (1983), often take the form of dramatic dialogues, but have rarely been performed in the theatre. (**Peter Hawkins**)

Garneau, Hector de Saint-Denys   Born Montreal, 1912; died Sainte-Catherine-de-Fossambault, QUEBEC, 1943. Poet. Garneau is considered one of Quebec's first modern poets. He published only one book of 28 poems, *Regards et jeux dans l'espace* (1937), which he finally withdrew from public circulation. He continued to write, but not to publish (the critical edition of his complete works published in 1971 contains 1300 pages). For Garneau, writing is a salvation and a mystery at the same time. From the themes of games, children and landscapes, he explores the darkest of shadows, as well as the unnamed. The moral quest of the poet seems to be annihilated by the stagnation of social values. The writing experience brings the poet to discoveries and, ultimately, to the deepness of silence and death. (**François-Emmanuël Boucher**)

Further reading

Brochu (1999); see also the documentary film, *Saint-Denys Garneau* (1960).

GATT General Agreement on Tariffs and Trade   1947–95. A multilateral international treaty signed in Geneva (Switzerland) by the world's major trading countries. GATT emerged from wartime and post-war negotiations (Bretton Woods and Havana) to expand international trade and promote economic development by the removal or reduction of import quotas and tariffs (taxes on imported goods). As early as 1941, the United States and Europe decided that a prosperous and lasting peace depended not only on the creation of a stable international political order based on principles laid down in the United Nations Charter but also on the creation of a stable, liberal international economic system. Originally designed to serve as an interim agreement for the more comprehensive International Trade Organisation (ITO), GATT became, by default, the only multilateral agreement covering the issue area of world trade when, in 1950, the US Congress refused to ratify the Havana charter and the proposed ITO collapsed. Yet, participating states considered trade issues important enough to continue, through a series of negotiations ('trade rounds'), the process of reducing trade barriers. After six rounds of negotiations, with tariffs on most goods substantially reduced, GATT members began implementing other non-tariff policies in such areas as customs valuation, subsidies, antidumping, and services. However, by the late 1980s, contracting parties became convinced that the increasing complexity of the global economy and the protracted disputes it caused, notably over the sensitive issues of agricultural and textile tariffs, needed a more formal, powerful, international trade organisation. During the final GATT round, the Uruguay Round, member states completed negotiations and agreed to replace GATT by the creation, in January 1995, of the World Trade Organisation (WTO), a global trade institution with a legally binding dispute-resolution mechanism. (**Naaman Kessous**)

Further reading

Zeiler (1999) – a comprehensive study of GATT and its complicated evolution; Isaak (2000) – a critical analysis of the global economy.

Gauvin, Axel   Born 1950. Reunionese writer. His main output is novels but he has also written some poetry and plays. A militant defender of the use of CREOLE, he has many of his novels published in two complementary versions: in creolised French and Reunionese Creole. In his novels, for example in *L'Aimé* (1990), he writes of the personal and social conflicts of modest REUNION islanders, often framed in experimental narratives. Some of his early Creole poems, such as 'Bato fou', have become

anthems of Reunionese cultural independence, as sung by the group Ziskakan. (**Peter Hawkins**)

Gbagbo, Laurent   See CÔTE D'IVOIRE.

Gender issues   It is only since 1945 that women have had political rights in France itself. Under colonialism, no significant progress was made in respect of the social and political position of colonised women, who played an important role in the liberation movements, particularly in ALGERIA. Although independence brought with it a formal recognition of women's equality in constitutional terms, gender-based discrimination and oppression in employment, education, social and family issues remain the norm in the postcolonial Francophone world at large, although it takes different forms in the various countries and regions.

While all women are concerned with issues concerning the control of their own bodies, their sexuality and fertility, these take various forms, depending on the particular social practices that operate in their different situations. This also applies to the degree of control they have in respect of their relationship to their children. Parental rights, skewed heavily in favour of fathers, are the norm in countries, which have incorporated a patriarchal interpretation of Islamic law, and the legacy of the Napoleonic Family Code (see FAMILY CODES). Caribbean women face rather different problems and issues, some of which arise from the dislocation of the family as a result of centuries of slavery and its aftermath.

Although gender-based issues are sometimes presented as a conflict between tradition and MODERNITY, this is rarely a clear cut distinction. As with the question of the VEIL, the reality is far more complex. What is clear is that economic, social and political progress in postcolonial societies will not be achieved in any real sense without women's involvement in the process. See also WOMEN'S MOVEMENTS; FAMILY ISSUES, DIASPORA; FAMILY, ALGERIA; NGOS; SECULARISM.

Further reading

Ahmed (1992), Mernissi (1985) – on the debates around gender and Islam; Amrane (1991) – for an account of women's role in the Algerian War; see also Gadant (1995) on women's position within Algerian political ideology; *Nouvelles questions féministes* (1985) – a special issue on French Caribbean women; Oyeronke (1997) – for an African perspective on gender issues; Scott (1995), Gordon (1996) – on women's role in the development process.

Geneva Accords, Geneva Agreement   See INDOCHINA WAR.

Ghachem, Moncef   Born Mahdia, 1946. Tunisian poet. Publications include *Car vivre est un pays* (Editions Caractères, 1978), *Cap Africa* (L'Harmattan, 1989), *Orphie* (MEET, Saint Nazaire, 1997). His collection of short stories, *L'Epervier: nouvelles de Mahdia* (SPM, 1994) is a celebration of the characters who touched upon his life in his home town.

GIA *Groupe Islamique Armé*   First of several armed groupings which emerged in ALGERIA, following the army's annulment of the final round of voting in the elections

1991–92 (see ALGERIAN ELECTIONS, 1991). Its foundation is attributed to Mansouri Meliani. Its cell-based structure has caused difficulty identifying and containing its members. This structure has also encouraged splinter movements, including the AIS (Islamic Salvation Army), and MIA (Armed Islamic Movement). The GIA claimed responsibility for the murder in August 1993 of Kasdi Merbah, a former security chief, and it is also considered to have been principally responsible for many of the civilian murders. Periodically weakened by arrests, it nevertheless continues to play a role in the violence in Algeria. (**Kay Adamson**)

Giap   See VO NGUYEN GIAP.

Glissant, Edouard   Born Lamentin, MARTINIQUE, 1928. Martinican writer, poet, and academic. Director: *Le Courrier de l'Unesco*, 1982–88. Professor of French, City University of New York. Vice-President, International Writers Parliament. Glissant developed the notion of ANTILLANITÉ, or the specific *Caribbean* identity of Martinique, (*Le Discours antillais*, 1981; *Caribbean Discourse: Selected Essays*, 1989), challenging an identity assimilated to Frenchness, as well as CÉSAIRE's NÉGRITUDE, which looked towards African ROOTS. *Antillanité* was not a plea for narrow cultural specificity; it rather advocated links with Caribbean neighbours, as well as an opening-up to the world at large, seeing the process of *créolisation* as the key factor in this identity.

The hybrid, shifting, unpredictable Martinican identity was being eroded by what Glissant claimed was 'cultural genocide' and needed to be reclaimed, not necessarily by proclaiming it loud and clear, but also through silence, and what he terms the 'right to opacity', in which the transparent universalising gaze of European culture was rejected – variants on the MARRONNAGE theme. New importance was also given to redefining the relationship to the land, from one of exile from the ancestral soil into a symbiotic ecological unity, in which people and land existed as interdependent elements. The favoured image to express this new organic connectedness is the RHIZOME, which, unlike roots, representing the nostalgic search for origins, signifies the present characteristics of Martinican identity, running shoots into a web of relationships, rather than an essence transmitted from the past.

Glissant is an important novelist, notable for works such as *La Lézarde* (1958; *The Ripening*, 1959), which won the Prix Renaudot, *Malemort* (1975), *La Case du commandeur* (1981), *Tout-Monde*, (1995), *Sartorius* (1999). His collected poems were published by Gallimard in 1994. He has also developed new perspectives in aesthetic theory (*Poétique de la Relation*, 1990; *Poetics of Relation*, 1997), which transcend the expression of the fixed individual particularity of the self or the other, to articulate, as part of a collective voice, what he terms the 'relation', including the interaction between what passes as the norms of universalist Western thought and the 'DIVERSITY' of emerging peoples.

Further reading

For a clear and concise introduction to Glissant's thought, as well as the concepts of *négritude*, *antillanité* and *créolité*, see Burton and Reno (1995) – Chapter 10; see also Majumdar (2001); and the introduction to Glissant (1989); and for detailed studies, see Britton (1999), Dash (1995).

Globalisation   The belief that the world is becoming rapidly more integrated, in both economic and cultural terms. Linguistically, the term predicts the world triumph of English, at the expense of French (and of other languages). The phenomenon, not entirely new in the history of capitalism, has its negative and positive aspects. The unholy alliance of the IMF, the World Bank, the World Trade Organisation and the OECD, not to mention transnational corporations, is seen by many anti-capitalists to have inflicted inestimable damage on (so-called) 'developing' countries. The French-speaking world is no exception. AFROPESSIMISME is one result; a significant exodus of peoples from the French Caribbean, South-east Asia and North Africa towards France is another. Globalisation and immigration of French-speaking people to France are thus intimately connected.

There is also the pessimistic view that the DIVERSITY of world cultures is being slowly but surely eroded by the spread of Western (especially North American) culture. Smaller, less 'advanced' cultures are threatened by a process of 'entropy', whereby Western models and language(s) impose themselves upon indigenous cultures, whilst ransacking these cultures for the art markets and museums back in the West. France plays a highly ambivalent role in this. On the one hand, it tries to stem the 'McDonaldisation/Coca-Colaisation' of the world via protectionism (blocking Anglophone, and especially Hollywood cinema, for example); on the other hand, it imposes its own cultural hegemony on French-speaking countries (French cinema is a good example here).

A number of Francophone Caribbean writers have recently tried to challenge this cultural entropy, by positing the HYBRIDITY of CREOLE culture as the positive future. 'Diversality', coined by CHAMOISEAU and CONFIANT, is the neologism for this possibility of cultural diversity in a universalised and globalised world. (**Andy Stafford**)

Further reading

Marfleet (1998) – an informative and readable, if partisan and highly political account, with a good bibliography; Bauman (1998) – useful and general overview of globalisation's effects.

Godbout, Jacques   Born Montreal, 1933. QUEBEC writer and film-maker. First known in the 1960s as a radical partisan of Quebec independence and a strong opponent of the traditional clerical power. Since then, he has had a prominent position in the cultural establishment in Quebec. His best novels, *Salut Galarneau!* (1967; *Hail Galarneau!* 1970), *Une Histoire américaine* (1986; *An American Story*, 1988), show Godbout as an excellent observer of the transformations of Quebec society in his time.

Godbout has worked on the National Film Board staff since 1960, and has made a solid career as a documentary film-maker – *Le Mouton noir* (1992), *Anne Hébert 1916–2000* (2001). (**John Kristian Sanaker**)

Further reading

Smith (1995) – a presentation of Godbout's double career as a writer and a film-maker.

Gorodé, Déwé   Born NEW CALEDONIA, 1949. KANAK writer and politician who was jailed for her pro-independence activities during the 1970s. Her work ranges from the politically engaged lyric poetry of *Sous les cendres des conques* (1985) to the short stories of *Utê Mûrûnû* (1994) and *L'Agenda* (1996). She uses various techniques, including an intense realism and a form of 'magic realism', to address the central issues of *Kanak* life in New Caledonia. Her first play, *Kanaké 2000*, which is about the life of Jean-Marie Tjibaou, was premiered at the 8th Pacific Arts Festival in Noumea in October 2000. (**Kamal Salhi**)

Gouvernement provisionnel de la république algérienne   See GPRA.

GPRA *Gouvernement provisionnel de la république algérienne*   Provisional government set up by the Algerian leaders in exile in Tunis in 1958 to prepare the way for post-independence government. Its first President was the veteran nationalist, Ferhat Abbas, with Krim Belkacem as vice-president and head of the armed forces. In the 1961 reorganisation in Tripoli, Abbas was replaced as President by Ben Youssef Ben Khedda, with Krim retaining his post of vice-president and becoming Minister of the Interior. However, in September 1961, Ben Khedda sought to disband the army General Staff. As a result, he lost the support of Boumedienne, who then teamed up with Ben Bella, tipping the political balance in Ben Bella's favour. (**Kay Adamson**)

Grandbois, Alain   Born Saint-Casimir-de-Portneuf, Quebec, 1900; died Quebec, 1975. Poet and novelist. He completely transformed artistic values in Quebec in the 1940s. His most significant publication is *Les Îles de la nuit* (1941), an audacious book of poems deploring the literature of commitment rooted in prejudices and resentment. As the Second World War ended, he expressed the loss of youth, aspirations and beliefs in short stories – *Avant le chaos* (1945; *Champagne and Opium*, 1984) – which deal with life in exile on the margins of French Canadian society. Wavering between a rejection of traditional certainties, the absence of a new trueness to life and his personal instability, Grandbois finds the only possible hope in poetry, the sole way to express certainties about humanity, love and spirituality, as in the poems in *L'Étoile pourpre* (1957). (**François-Emmanuël Boucher**)

Further reading

Bolduc (1994); Gallays and Laliberté (1997); Pérusse (1994).

Grande Mosquée de Paris   See Paris Mosque.

Gratiant, Gilbert   Born Saint-Pierre, Martinique, 1895; died 1985. Martinican writer. He was a founding father of modern literature in Martinique, and a politically committed poet. From a young age he studied in France, became *agrégé* in English, then taught in Fort-de-France (Césaire was a student), Montpellier, and Paris. Founder of the journal *Lucioles* (1926–28). He published poetry in French (*Poèmes en vers faux*, 1931), some in *La Revue du monde noir*, but after 1935, he wrote his poetry in Creole (beginning with 'Joseph lévé!'), collected in successive editions of *Fab 'Compè Zicaque*. He is seen as a precursor of the *créolité* movement. A member of the Communist Party from 1945, he took part in the first International Congress of Black Writers and Artists in 1956. In 1965 he was awarded the Grand Prix Littéraire des Antilles.

Green March The 'Green March' was organised in October 1975, but planned long before, by HASSAN II of MOROCCO, after the International Court of Justice (ICJ) rejected Morocco's and MAURITANIA's claim to the former Spanish SAHARA, maintaining the right of the Saharawi people to self-determination. About 50,000 Moroccans were transported by bus to the region to join troops who had already crossed the border. Hassan's refusal to withdraw the marchers unless Spain entered into direct negotiation, deflected Spain from holding a referendum and culminated in the Madrid agreement between Spain, Mauritania and Morocco. (**Susan Fox**)

Griot The *griot* is the traditional guardian of the history and values of the community in West Africa, and it is widely claimed that the contemporary African artist is the rightful heir to this tradition. Although often considered a universal phenomenon in Africa, the *griot* is to be found only in those West African societies which were once part of the thirteenth-century MALI empire. These societies are made up of a complex structure of castes and orders, and it is to the lower, 'inferior' caste that the *griot* belongs. Each *griot* is attached to a corresponding noble family, whose praises the *griot* is paid to sing. Consequently, the *griot*, although charged with preserving the myths and values of society, is looked down upon as a deceitful flatterer. With the decline of the noble families, many contemporary *griots* now sing the praises of the new political ÉLITE. Others attempt to earn a living through music – e.g. the Senegalese singer, Youssou N'DOUR is from a *griot* family.

It is commonplace to link the contemporary African artist with the tradition of the *griot*. The Senegalese writer and film-maker Ousmane SEMBENE has described the filmmaker as the closest figure to the *griot*, as film combines music, gesture and storytelling, in a communal gathering. However, in many African films and novels, *griots* are portrayed as hypocrites who simply sing the praises of the highest bidder. Essentially, the modern representation of the *griot* revolves around the tension between the image of a professional manipulator of language who speaks in praise of the rich and powerful, but who is also permitted to speak painful truths. (**David Murphy**)

Further reading

Diop (1981) – explains role of *griot* within a West African community; Laye (1980) – fascinating study of *griot's* art.

Groupe Islamique Armé See GIA.

GSPC Groupe salafiste pour la predication et le combat (Salafist Group for Call and Combat) was a faction of the Algerian Islamic terrorist group, the GIA, until 1988. Under its leader Hassan Hattab, GSPC reputedly has links with the al-Qaeda network. GSPC concentrates its operations mainly on the security forces and high-profile civilian targets and is often behind ambushes and the murder of soldiers in mountainous areas. It finances its operations by racketeering, cross-border smuggling, money laundering activities and support networks outside ALGERIA. GSPC rejected the 1998 amnesty and continues its attacks. (**Susan Fox**)

Further reading

Labat (1995).

Guadeloupe A French DOM (Overseas Department), made up of a group of islands in the eastern CARIBBEAN, off the north-western coast of South America. The two principal islands, separated by a channel known as the Rivière, are Basse-Terre, with the capital of the same name, to the west and Grande-Terre to the east. The main town on Grande-Terre, and principal port of the department, is Pointe-à-Pitre.

The nearby island dependencies are Marie-Galante, La Désirade and Les Saintes. Guadaloupe's other dependencies, Saint-Barthélemy and Saint Martin, are located 160 miles to the north-west. Basse-Terre is the most mountainous of the islands and includes the department's highest peak, Soufrière (4900 ft/1500 m), an active volcano. The population is composed mainly of blacks and mulattoes with a small European minority, primarily descendants of Breton and Norman colonists. Guadaloupe's currency is the Euro. A popularly elected general council and regional council administer the department, with a high-ranking civil servant, appointed by the French government. Four deputies and two senators represent the islands in the French parliament.

Guadeloupe's history is of great interest. Following the failure of four chartered companies to colonise the island permanently, it was annexed by France in 1674 and made a dependency of MARTINIQUE. During the second half of the seventeenth century, the French colonists resisted attacks by the British, who finally captured the island in 1759, retaining it until 1763, when it again passed to France. In 1775 Guadeloupe and Martinique became separate colonies, but the British regained Guadeloupe briefly in 1794 and again in 1810, when their occupation lasted six years. Slavery was abolished in 1848. Guadeloupe was made an overseas department of France in 1946. There was an active independence movement during the 1980s and, following a series of bombings in 1984, the French authorities outlawed the Caribbean Revolutionary Alliance, a militant pro-independence organisation. Although Guadeloupe retained its status as a department, in 1982 it became a 'mono-departmental region'. Guadeloupe's cultural mix, history and traditions make it an attractive, welcoming place. (**Kamal Salhi**)

Further reading

Abenon (1992).

Guèye, Lamine Born Saint-Louis, SENEGAL, 1891; died 1968. Senegalese lawyer and politician. Guèye was a highly influential figure in Senegalese politics, founding the Senegalese socialist party in 1929. Elected a deputy after World War II, his finest political achievement came in 1946 when he introduced the law which brought an end to the distinction between 'subjects' and 'CITIZENS' (see CITIZENSHIP) in France's colonies. His party's dominance of Senegalese politics was short-lived, however, as

SENGHOR split from the socialists in 1948 to form the *Bloc Démocratique sénégalais*, which became the major political force in the 1950s. Upon Senegalese independence in 1960, Guèye became President of the National Assembly. (**David Murphy**)

Guiana, French   A large country, dominated by rainforest, north of Brazil and east of Surinam. Capital: Cayenne. Today, it is the only non-independent territory on the South American continent and France's last remaining mainland overseas territory. Carib and Arawak Indians first began trading with the Dutch, who then established riverside sugar plantations worked by slaves from Africa. It was first settled by the French in 1604. Historically, French Guiana experienced several periods marked by a different set of identities. After the abolition of slavery, a labour force from India, China and South-east Asia arrived. In the period of the penal colony, from 1854 to the early 1950s, political and criminal prisoners were deported to the Guianese islands (notably Devil's Island) – one famous prisoner being Dreyfus. This period coincided with its gold rush, the lucrative exploitation of gold having started in 1855. In 1946, Guiana became a French DOM and, in 1982, with GUADELOUPE and MARTINIQUE, a member of the 'French region' known as Antilles-Guyane. From 1968, it has hosted the French/European space-rocket launching site at Kourou. This is a pole for attracting new immigrants into the territory, along with the high standard of living, maintained through French subsidy, in spite of high levels of unemployment. Diverse cultures and racial groups blend together in a complex brew. However, its mixed population seems to resist the unlikely geo-political myth of its French identity. Like ANTILLANITÉ and NÉGRITUDE, Guiana has defined its own multi-ethnic identity, phrased in the concept of *Guyanité*, based on a consistent ethno-historical multilingual culture. This multiplicity is often reflected in the make-up of Guiana's oral literature and performing arts. Although CREOLE is a current language, Guiana's mainstream twentieth-century literature is produced in French, with some Creole exceptions. This literature expresses concerns ranging from adventure, search for identity, to more political commitment. (**Kamal Salhi**)

Further reading

Adelaïde-Merlande (1994); Ndagano (1994) – see 'La Guyanité ou la question de l'avenir guyanais', pp. 17–39.

Guinea   West African state on Atlantic coast, sharing borders with Guinea-Bissau, SENEGAL, MALI, CÔTE D'IVOIRE, Liberia, Sierra Leone. Capital: Conakry. Population approx. 8 million, composed of Peuls (40 per cent), Malinke (26–30 per cent), Soussous (11–20 per cent) and other smaller ethnic groups. Official language: French; 85 per cent of population are Muslims. Guinea ranks second in the world, in producing and exporting bauxite (75 per cent of its exports in 1999 were of minerals) and also has rich resources in iron-ore, gold, diamonds, lead, zinc, uranium, hydro-electric power, and timber. There is some production of aluminium, but the economic potential of the country has not as yet been realised.

French colonisation of Guinea at the end of the nineteenth century met considerable resistance until 1912. Guinean soldiers fought in the French army in both world wars. The first Guinean député, Yacine Diallo, was elected to the French Assembly in 1945 and the nationalist struggle was taken forward, especially by the PDG (*Parti démocratique de Guinée*), led from 1952 by Sékou Touré. Under his leadership, Guinea was the only colony to vote No to association within the French Community (see COMMUNAUTÉ FRANÇAISE) in the referendum of 1958, when it took its independence. France immediately suspended all aid and support. See the entry on Sékou Touré for details of the period between 1958 and his death in 1984.

A military *coup* brought Colonel Lansana Conté to power in 1984 and a series of economic, financial and political reforms was set in train to dismantle the system established by Sékou Touré. Elections took place in 1993, confirming Conté as President, and he was re-elected in 1998. However, the political situation remains volatile, with interethnic unrest and conflicts in neighbouring Sierra Leone and Liberia threatening stability.

There is a rich artistic and oral tradition, some of it based on the epic of SOUNDIATA. There is also a lively and innovative musical scene. Notable figures, writing in French and some from exile, include Camara LAYE, Alioume FANTOURÉ, Williams SASSINE, Tierno MONÉNEMBO. Newer writers include Nadine Bari, Cheikh Oumar Kanté, Lamine Kamara, and Boubacar Diallo.

Haddad, Malek   Born Constantine, 1927; died Algiers, 1978. Algerian novelist, poet and journalist. He abandoned his studies at Aix-en-Provence in 1954. After meeting and working with KATEB YACINE, his novels, written in a lyrical prose, were produced between 1958 and 1961, most notably *Je t'offrirai une gazelle* (1959). After independence, he abandoned writing in French, seeing the FRENCH LANGUAGE as a form of exile, and published no more fiction. He returned to cultural journalism in Constantine in 1962, became Director of Culture at the Ministry of Information and Culture, 1965–68, and Secretary of the *Nouvelle Union des écrivains algériens*, from 1974.

Further reading

Bekri (1986); Bonn (1990).

Hadj, Messali   Born Tlemcen, 1898; died Paris, 1974. Algerian political activist. The son of a shoemaker and a member of the Derkawa brotherhood, a *sufi* sub-order, Messali Hadj was drafted into the French army during the First World War. Afterwards he stayed in France as a labourer and joined the PCF (French Communist Party). President of the ENA in 1926, he was the first Algerian nationalist to call for the independence of ALGERIA in 1927. As a result, he spent many years in prison or in exile. In 1935, he fled arrest to Geneva where he was influenced by Chekib Arslan, advocate of PAN-ARABISM and Pan-Islamism. Returning to France, he broke all ties with Communists following the dissolution of the ENA in 1937 by the Popular Front government. All the parties Messali founded afterwards (PPA in 1937, MTLD in 1946, MNA in 1954) combined Marxist organisation with Pan-Islamic ideology. By 1956, he had faded into political oblivion and lived on in Paris. (**Naaman Kessous**)

Haine   See *LA HAINE*.

Haiti   Haiti (capital: Port-au-Prince) is the independent republic occupying the western third of the island situated between Cuba and Puerto Rico in the Greater Antilles. (The eastern part of the island consists of the Dominican Republic.) The country's official languages are now French and CREOLE, although only 30 per cent of the population understand the former; 80 per cent of Haitians are officially Catholic, most of whom are also followers of voodoo.

In the late eighteenth century, the plantation economy of Haiti, known then as Saint Domingue, made this CARIBBEAN island colony France's richest overseas possession. Revolution broke out, however, in 1791, and the declaration of Haitian independence on 1 January 1804 made this the first successful slave revolt in world history. Although Haiti was widely celebrated as the first Black republic, its two centuries of post-independence history have been blighted by often-violent conflict over ethnicity and class. As a result, the Haitian experience has served not only as an inspiration for colonised peoples, but also as a warning for those who have achieved independence. Haiti remains the poorest country in the western hemisphere, although it is rich in artistic and literary terms.

After the Second World War, the country was led by a series of rapidly replaced presidents until François DUVALIER ('Papa Doc') came to power in 1957. His violent regime was supported by an armed militia (the *TONTONS MACOUTES*). Thirty years of the Duvalier dictatorship came to an end in 1986, when François's son, Jean-Claude ('Baby Doc'), went into exile. Elections in 1987 and 1988 were either abortive or fraudulent, but a former priest, Jean-Bertrand ARISTIDE ('Titide'), won a landslide victory in 1990. The victim of a *coup* the following year, he returned from exile in 1994 shortly after the landing of 21,000 American troops whose aim was to disarm the militia. As Haiti prepares to celebrate its bicentenary in 2004, the political and economic future remains highly unstable. (**Charles Forsdick**)

Further reading

Nicholls (1996) provides the best introduction in English to post-independence Haiti. For a full account of the Haitian Revolution, see James (1980).

Hammam   The word means 'spreader of warmth' in Arabic and refers to a public bath, comprising steam baths and pools. The custom of using the *hammam*, which became very popular throughout Islamic countries, was adapted from Greek and Roman methods of hot air bathing. The *hammam* gained religious significance and was used to comply with Islamic laws of hygiene and purification. It became an essential part of local social life, but was also a quiet retreat. The *hammam* is associated with health cures for many ailments, including gout and rheumatism. (**Susan Fox**)

Hampâté Bâ, Amadou   See Bâ, Amadou Hampâté.

Hanoune, Louisa   Born 1954. Algerian trade union leader and socialist, leader of the *Parti des travailleurs* (Workers' Party). Not only is she a prominent woman activist, both emancipated and an intransigent opponent of Islamic fundamentalism, she is also an important critic of the Algerian government. Imprisoned in 1983 and in 1988, she opposed the cancellation of the legislative elections in 1991 (see Algerian elections, 1991). Her staunch belief in democracy is supported by a Trotskyist version of Marxism, a political tradition seemingly smothered by the FLN in the 1950s. (**Andy Stafford**)

Harbi, Mohammed   Born El-Arrouch, 1933. Historian of the FLN and the Algerian revolution, although he himself was a young militant and member of the Messaliste party, MTLD. One of the authors of the Tripoli Programme and editor of *Révolution africaine*, he was imprisoned by both Presidents Ben Bella and Boumedienne. He was finally allowed to leave Algeria in 1973 and has since lived in France. He has published the first volume of his *Mémoires* (2001), covering the period 1945–62. His family, of originally poor peasants, was one that took advantage of the 1863 Senatus-Consulte and the limited access to property for native Algerians it provided. (**Kay Adamson**)

Further reading

Harbi (2001) – Chapter 1 provides an understanding of what it was like growing up in Algeria in the 1930s and 1940s.

Harem   Meaning 'forbidden', 'secluded', this term was applied to the women's quarters in a Muslim household. It has its origins in pre-Islamic times, when women enjoyed a certain amount of freedom in this enclosed society. However, the seclusion of women became more common with the advent of Islam. Only very rich households were able to support harems, in which the women, neither wives nor prostitutes, were at the disposal of the male owner. Close male relations often forced women into harems, to forge political alliances. Although harem women were technically all slaves, rank was jealously guarded and depended on degree of relationship with the owner. The harem owner's mother, called the *valide sultana* in royal circles, had her own household, wielding power over the other women and often selecting others for the harem. The next highest rank, called *kadin* belonged to those who had children, and the highest-ranking *kadin* was the mother of the eldest son. Jealousy among the *kadins* and concubines led to intrigue, attempted and actual murder. The harems of Ottoman Empire sultans were under the supervision of the *kislar aga* or Chief Black Eunuch, who was the highest ranking official after the Sultan and Grand Vizier. The *kislar* often became very wealthy from bribes and wielded considerable power. He executed a woman if she displeased the sultan, who had absolute power of life and death over the harem. The eunuchs were chosen for their supposed ugliness. There are still harems in existence in remote areas of the Muslim world and the conservative societies of the Arabian Gulf. (**Susan Fox**)

Further reading

Croutier (1989).

Harkis   Name given to Algerians who fought in the ALGERIAN WAR OF INDEPENDENCE on the side of France, believed to number 200,000. The name also covers, by association, those Algerian Muslims who worked for the French colonial administration and believed in France's continued ownership of ALGERIA (Hamoumou, 1993). The name derives from a battalion (the *Harka*, or mobile auxiliaries) which was incorporated into the French army to fight against the FLN. The *Harkis* were notorious for the brutality of their military operations, both in Algeria, and in Paris against the exiled FLN and their supporters (Péju, 2000). After the war, French defeat and the gaining of independence, the *Harkis* were, not surprisingly, considered traitors and forced to leave Algeria after 1962. Many *Harkis* and their families perished in FLN reprisals (up to 150,000), and a colonel in the *Harkis* has since accused the French army and government of doing nothing to protect them (Méliani, 1993). Those promised CITIZEN-SHIP in France were unceremoniously dumped in transit camps and old concentration camps in southern France, and were then ignored for many years. Despised by their compatriots and segregated from them, and also suffering discrimination by the French State, they became a lost generation, until the second generation, sons and daughters of the *Harkis*, began in the late 1980s and early 1990s to demand social justice alongside the burgeoning BEUR and ANTIRACIST movements. Ferdi has produced an autobiographical account (*Un Enfant dans la guerre*, 1981) of a boy press-ganged into the *Harkis* during the War, and CHAREF a fictional account (1989) set within a *Harki*-descendants' community. (**Andy Stafford**)

Further reading

Méliani (1993) – insider view of the plight of the *Harkis*, from their mobilisation up to the 1990s; Hamoumou (1993) – accessible account by the son of a *Harki*.

Hassan II   Born Rabat, MOROCCO, 1929; died 1999. King Hassan Ben Mohammed Ben Youssef was the eighth sultan of the Alaoui dynasty, which has ruled Morocco since the seventeenth century. Educated in the royal palace of Rabat under the tutorship of BEN BARKA, then in Bordeaux, where he obtained in 1952 a Masters degree in Public Law. In 1956, he was appointed by his father, King MOHAMMED V, as Chief-of-Staff of the Royal Armed Forces. In 1958, as Crown Prince, Hassan II crushed the Rif and the Tafilalt rebellions, strengthening the power of the palace. In 1962, Hassan II was proclaimed King of Morocco following his father's unexpected death. He proclaimed a constitutional monarchy with the king holding both religious and political authority. The 1970s were marked by serious political unrest. In consecutive years – July 1971 and August 1972 – the king survived two attempted military *coups*, the first at his Skhirat Palace during his birthday celebrations and the second when air force jets attacked his plane as he was returning to Morocco from France. A number of officers, among them Mohammed OUFKIR, were either killed or executed. The cadets who took part in the putsch were held prisoner in secret jails (where many perished) such as the infamous Tazmamart, whose existence has only became public knowledge in more recent years.

In 1974, King Hassan II called for 350,000 Moroccans to take part in the Green March to liberate the Sahara territories from Spain. Since then, Morocco and the Polisario have been engaged in a war over the legitimacy of Western Sahara. From the mid-1990s to his death, the King promoted the gradual democratisation of the country and appointed, in a symbolic gesture, the leader of the opposition as Prime Minister.

On the international level, King Hassan II maintained good relations with the US and Europe both of which appreciated the moderate state of Morocco amidst the general unrest in Arab Middle-Eastern politics. Throughout the 1970s and 1980s, the king played a major role in peace negotiations between Palestine and Israel. King Hassan II was succeeded by his son Mohammed VI. (**Laïla Ibnlfassi**)

Further reading

Hassan II (1976).

Haut Conseil de la Francophonie   Committee set up in 1984 by President François Mitterrand under the aegis of the Ministry for Foreign Affairs to oversee all policies relating to Francophonie. The committee is chaired by the President of the Republic. Its official function is to define the roles to be played by *Francophonie* and the French language in the modern world; to collect data and compare experiences, especially in the fields of teaching, communication, science and technological advances; to identify issues and matters of urgency and suggest appropriate action. The *Haut Conseil* also has a consultative role in preparing the summit meetings of Francophone heads of state. (**Marie-Anne Hintze**)

Further reading

See website: http://www.diplomatie.fr/Francophonie/hcf

Hazaël-Massieux, Marie-Christine   Born Paris, 1947. Sociolinguist, grammarian, leading specialist in Creole languages and literatures, director of the *Institut d'études créoles et francophones* since 1995, Professor at the University of Provence. Has published widely on linguistic descriptions of French Creoles and literatures in Creole, particularly from the Caribbean (*Chansons des Antilles, comptines, formulettes*, 1987). Her book *Ecrire en créole* (1993) is groundbreaking in both its theoretical and practical insight into the transition of French Creoles from spoken to written languages. Main editor of *Etudes créoles*, she has also devised her own website on the French Caribbean Creoles. (**Roshni Mooneram**)

Further reading

See http://creoles.free.fr

Hazoume, Paul   1890–1980. Writer from the former French colony of Dahomey (now Bénin). His pioneering historical fresco *Doguicimi* (1935; *Doguicimi: The First Dahomean Novel*, 1989), which can claim to be one of the earliest African novels in French, is based on extensive research into local folklore and customs, and depicts the fate of the eponymous heroine in the elaborately described court of Ghêzo, one of the traditional kings of Abomey. He was also the author of ethnological, political and religious studies, such as *Le Pacte du sang au Dahomey* (1937). (**Peter Hawkins**)

Headscarf Affair (*Affaire du foulard*)   In October 1989, three young Muslim women from Creil near Paris were excluded by their headteacher (Ernest Chenière) from attending school classes on account of their Islamic headscarves (*hijab*). The headscarves, Chenière alleged, constituted a form of religious proselytism and there-fore infringed rules governing France's secular state education system – a supposedly 'neutral' space devoid of 'conspicuous' religious insignia. An immense political and media debate ensued. The wearing of Islamic headscarves – a complex religious and cultural practice (Gaspard and Khosrokhavar, 1995) – had previously attracted little attention. However, long-term suspicion of the headscarf from colonial times (con-sidered a sign of cultural resistance to French imperialism) (Blank, 1999), combined with developments specific to the decade immediately preceding 1989 to nationalise this 'Affair': increasingly negative media images of Islam had flourished as FRONT NATIONAL successes made 'immigration' and 'French identity' central political issues. Furthermore, many republicans considered the assimilatory role of the education system to be in crisis.

Those supporting exclusion argued that allowing Islamic headscarves in school tol-erated women's oppression and Islamic 'fundamentalism'. Yet those against exclu-sion nonetheless shared their opponents' ideological framework that viewed secular education as neutral, Islam as radically 'different', and the school as the way to 'eman-cipate' young Muslims (Silverman, 1992, pp. 111–13). Socialist Education Minister Lionel JOSPIN overturned Chenière's exclusion order, referring the case to the Council of State, which supported Jospin's position, ruling (27 November 1989) that Islamic headscarves did not constitute 'conspicuous' religious signs *per se*. In September 1994 the question returned, as the then Education Minister, right-winger François Bayrou, issued a circular to headteachers in an attempt to support the exclusion of women wearing headscarves (see CIRCULAIRE BAYROU). The juridical position in relation to the 1989 Council of State's (advisory) ruling remains uncertain, as does the ability of French SECULARISM to adapt to religious and cultural DIVERSITY. (**Jim House**)

Further reading

Silverman (1992) – pp. 111–18 give an excellent overview of the wider themes behind this debate; Blank (1999) – fully contextualised discussion of the 'Affair' within a postcolonial, feminist framework.

Hébert, Anne   Born Sainte-Catherine-de-la-Jacques-Cartier, QUEBEC, 1916; died Montreal, 2000. The leading lady of Quebec literature and the evident first choice of students and academics in this field, though she lived most of her life in Paris. Hébert is the author of a great number of poems, short stories, plays and novels, but she mainly owes her success to a series of novels published from 1970 onwards, particu-larly *Kamouraska* (1970; translated into English under the same title, 1973), *Les Fous de Bassan* (1982; *In the Shadow of the Wind*, 1984) and *Le premier jardin* (1988; *The First Garden*, 1990). These formally accomplished works describe tragic, solitary destinies in a closed, oppressive society ruled by TRADITION. Hébert has won several prizes, and a film has been made about her life by Jacques GODBOUT: *Anne Hébert 1916–2000* (2001). (**John Kristian Sanaker**)

Further reading

Ducrocq-Poirier *et al.* (1996) – papers from Sorbonne conference, with contributions by leading Hébert specialists.

Henry, Thierry   Born Chatillon, Paris, 1977. Soon after France's football World Cup victory in 1998, Henry joined Juventus in Italy, a transfer full of promises. He hardly had any impact though, spending most of his time on the bench – his career destined, despite his young age, to a premature end. Arsene Wenger, manager at Arsenal, brought him to the London club to fill the void legated by Nicolas ANELKA's departure for Real Madrid. Henry soon blossomed – his pace bewildering defenders, his accuracy deadly and goals raining, one of which, scored early in the 2000–2001 season against Manchester United, was a challenger for goal of the decade. Now, Henry is the undisputed centre forward of the French national team and possibly one of the best in the world. (**Salah Zaimeche**)

Hiawatha   A legendary sixteenth-century Native American chieftain, and subject of Longfellow's narrative poem, *The Song of Hiawatha*. This is based on legends and stories compiled and authenticated by Henry Schoolcraft, superintendent of Indian Affairs, and his Native American wife Jane. Hiawatha was said to have been chief of the Mohawk tribe, and founder of the five-tribe League of the Iroquois, which was allied with the British against the French, and, in the eighteenth century, with the British against the colonists in the American War of Independence. (**Susan Fox**)

Further reading

Henry, T.R. (1955).

Hijab   See HEADSCARF AFFAIR.

Hiro, Henri   Born Moorea, 1944; died Huahine, 1990. Leading Polynesian cultural activist in the 1970s and 1980s. Hiro was educated in his native language before taking a theology degree in Montpellier and returning to POLYNESIA to run the *Maison de la Culture* at Tipaerui. A poet, film producer, theatre director and actor, he also translated novels from French into *reo ma'ohi* (Tahitian) and worked tirelessly as a Tahitian language activist. He was instrumental in the Polynesian antinuclear movement and involved in the creation of *La Mana Te Nunaa*, a socialist, independentist political party. Resisting nostalgic or reactionary appeals to cultural essentialism, his work challenged French and American CULTURAL IMPERIALISM and was committed to the rehabilitation of a contemporary Polynesian culture founded on self-awareness and a more carefully negotiated approach to outside influences. (**Charles Forsdick**)

Hizb al IstiqLal   'Independence' party founded in MOROCCO in 1943 by Allal El Fassi. It provided much of the inspiration for the independence movement. In 1958, the leader of the party's radical faction, Abdullah Ibrahim, became Prime Minister. In subsequent coalition governments, ISTIQLAL secured ministerial posts, but its political influence fluctuated between 1960 and 1992, attributable to unsuccessful attempts to curb the power of the monarchy. According to its manifesto, *IstiqLal*'s aims are to raise living standards and confer equal rights on all, but the claim to the WESTERN SAHARA is stressed. (**Susan Fox**)

Further reading

Hughes (2000).

Ho Chi Minh   1890–1969. Charismatic Communist leader of VIETNAM independence, and minor Francophone poet. Born Nguyen Sinh Cung, became Nguyen Ai Quoc whilst in Paris after World War I. After witnessing the launch of the French Communist Party in 1920, he returned to colonised Indochina to lead the long struggle for independence, and founded the Vietnamese Communist Party, whilst suffering long bouts of illness and imprisonment. Briefly courted by the French after World War II, he was soon a sworn enemy, launching the (First) INDOCHINA WAR against colonial control in 1946. The next twenty years saw him lead the Viet Minh and then the Viet Cong against French and American forces. (**Andy Stafford**)

Hondo, Med   Born MAURITANIA, 1936. Mauritanian film-maker, actor and theatre director. Med Hondo settled in France at the beginning of the 1960s, working as a cook and docker but also enrolling for drama classes. Hondo has acted in films and the theatre in France, and set up the theatre company *Griotshango*, for which he also directs plays. In 1971 Med Hondo filmed his feature *Soleil O*, an innovative work denouncing the injustices to which immigrants to France were subjected. This work has since become one of the seminal pieces of Francophone African cinema, for its combative tone and visual style. Other feature films by Med Hondo are *Les Bicots-nègres, vos voisins* (1973), *West Indies ou les nègres marrons de la liberté* (1979), *Sarraounia* (1986), *Lumière noire* (1994) and *Watani, un monde sans mal* (1997). (**Rachael Langford**)

Further reading

Signaté (1994).

Houari, Leïla   Born Casablanca, 1959. Moroccan writer, stage director, video pro-ducer. Her family emigrated to Belgium, where she grew up. Her texts explore the lives of second-generation Maghrebian immigrants (*BEURS*). She works as a French teacher in Lissabon. Works include *Zeïda de nulle part* (1985); *Quand tu verras la mer: Recueil de récits* (1988); *Les Cases basses: Théâtre* (1993); *Poème fleuve pour noyer le temps présent* (1995). (**Susanne Heiler**)

Further reading

Gontard (1993) – pp. 179–89, for an analysis of *Zeïda de nulle part* in the context of the writing of Moroccan women novelists; Segarra (1997).

Houphouët-Boigny, Félix Born Côte d'Ivoire, 1905; died 1993. Francophone African leader. Born into the royal family of Yamoussoukro, he served as an 'African doctor' until he inherited his father's plantations in 1940.

In 1944, he became president of the African Planters' Union and protested against French colonial labour practices. He then formed a political party, the *Parti Démocratique de la Côte d'Ivoire*, and became president of a wider African movement, the *Rassemblement Démocratique Africain* (RDA). He was elected to the French National Assembly in 1946 and forged an alliance with the French Communist Party. He broke with the Communists in 1951 and subsequently served in several French cabinets (1956–59). He used his ministerial office to secure greater autonomy for individual African territories and to ensure the break up ('balkanisation') of the West Africa Federation (*Afrique Occidentale Française*, AOF). He led his country to independence in 1960.

Houphouët became President and remained in power for over three decades. He instituted a one-party regime that was sustained through mild coercion, political astuteness and charismatic leadership. His early years brought rapid growth and were marked by his anti-Communist rhetoric, liberal economic policies and strong ties with France. His later years were marred by a downturn in the economy, criticism over his construction of an expensive Catholic basilica and complaints about his handling of the 1990 presidential elections.

Despite these criticisms, Houphouët was still known affectionately to Ivorians as 'The Old Man' and he remained France's favoured link with black Africa. Having befriended every French president since DE GAULLE, he retained an effective veto on moves to reduce French financial support for Africa. It was no coincidence therefore that the devaluation of the main Francophone African currency, the CFA franc, occurred only weeks after Houphouët's death in December 1993. (**Gordon Cumming**)

Further reading

Amondji (1984) – study of Houphouët's life and politics; Nandjui (1995) – survey of Houphouët's close relations with France.

Humbert, Marie-Thérèse Born 1940. Mauritian novelist. Humbert made her reputation with *A l'autre bout de moi* (1979), a novel about the social tensions of family life affecting women of mixed-race origin in Mauritius. Most of her literary career has been spent in France, and occasionally she returns to Mauritian subject-matter, as in *La Montagne des Signaux* (1994). (**Peter Hawkins**)

Huston, Nancy Born Calgary, Alberta, 1953. Canadian author, originally Anglophone, now writing in French. Since 1973 she has lived in Paris, where she completed her doctoral thesis under Roland Barthes. Huston considers her distance from the French language and the co-existence of two languages beneficial in finding forms of literary expression. Her texts, both fictional and non-fictional, often deal with identity problems and women's roles in society. Novels: *Les Variations Goldberg* (1981); *Histoire d'Omaya* (1985; *Story of Omaya*, 1987); *Trois fois septembre* (1989);

Cantique des plaines (1994; *Plainsong*, 2001); *La Virevolte* (1994; *Slow Emergencies*, 2001); *Instruments des ténèbres* (1996; *Instruments of Darkness*, 1997); *L'Empreinte de l'ange* (1998; *Mark of the Angel*, 1999); *Dolce agonia* (2001; published simultaneously in translation under same title). Essays include: *Dire et interdire: éléments de jurologie* (1980); *Mosaïque de la pornographie* (1982); *Pour un patriotisme de l'ambiguïté* (1995); *Limbes* (2000; bilingual). Correspondence: *À l'amour comme à la guerre* (1984); with Leïla SEBBAR: *Lettres parisiennes* (1986). Has also written children's books. (**Susanne Heiler**)

Hybridity   Hybridity (*métissage*) describes a mixing and inter-penetration of different cultures. In racial theory – for example, that of the Comte de Gobineau of the mid-nineteenth century – this form of mixing is stigmatised as a bastardised and impure form of identity. Immigration must therefore be opposed as it dilutes the RACE or nation and leads to the creation of a 'mongrel breed'. After the horror of the Holocaust, the notion of racial purity has been disproved, even though it still has the power to motivate those intent on 'ethnic cleansing'. In contemporary societies, in which the fusion of peoples and cultures is becoming more and more the norm, hybrid identities are more commonly accepted as a fundamental part of postcolonial and postmodern life. (**Max Silverman**)

Further reading

Bhabha (1994) – essays on the formation of hybrid identities in contemporary culture; Glissant (1989) – essays on the hybrid nature of French Caribbean societies and literature during and after colonisation by France.

Hyvrard, Jeanne   Born 1945. French economist and writer. She worked for a time in MARTINIQUE, and is sometimes mistakenly held to be a CARIBBEAN writer. She is currently a teacher in a *lycée technique* in the Paris suburbs. The history of the Caribbean, and its legacy, mark much of her work, but especially *Les Prunes de Cythère* (1975). Her writing is published by Des Femmes and is a highly poetic and idiosyncratic exploration of identity, motherhood, madness and language. Her fusional thinking and passionately held views on poetic language and thought, when brought to bear on elements of Caribbean landscape, culture and society, create a mutually illuminating effect. (**Mary Gallagher**)

IAM   Rap group from Marseilles. Their name ('Invasion Arriving from Mars', 'Independent Autonomous Marseillais') hints at the recurrent themes in their work: each of the six members, of diverse origins, has a persona reflecting an identification obsession with Egyptian, African or Far Eastern cultures. The first album, *De la*

planète Mars, was released in 1991, expressing youngsters' growing sense of EXCLUSION and their resistance to the FRONT NATIONAL. Named best group in 1995, they are now big business, but remain faithful to Marseilles, investing in young talent whilst pursuing solo careers. (**Samantha Neath**)

Identity   See CULTURAL IDENTITY; NATIONHOOD/NATIONALISM.

Ieng Sary   Cambodian KHMER ROUGE leader, related to POL POT by marriage.

Imalayen, Fatima-Zohra   See DJEBAR, ASSIA.

Imazighen   See BERBERS.

Immigration   See MIGRATION.

Indian Ocean   See thematic index.

Indochina War   1946–54. Known as the First Indochina War or the Franco-Viet Minh War, and fought predominantly in VIETNAM, this war of independence between France and the colonised peoples of the south-east Asian peninsula, was lost by the French after the battle of DIEN BIEN PHU in 1954. American support for the French army and fears of Communism spreading led to the 'American war' in Vietnam (1965–75). The 1946 uprising, led by the Communist HO CHI MINH, was sparked by a minor incident in Haiphong bay and was initially a guerrilla war. The Chinese Revolution of 1949 then encouraged the Viet Minh forces to recruit more widely. American aid now flowed to France, to the tune of US$3 billion by 1954. The Geneva Conference, trying to find peace in Korea and Indochina, started just weeks before the Dien Bien Phu defeat. This defeat, and Mendès-France becoming French Prime Minister, forced France to talk directly to the Vietnamese leadership. The Geneva Accords divided Vietnam in two along the 17th parallel, the North controlled by Ho Chi Minh's Communists and the South by Ngo DIEM's anti-Communist puppet government. This parallel became the dividing line for the American war. Though led by the astute Nguyen Van GIAP, the Viet Minh forces nevertheless had lost by 1954 an estimated 200,000 troops, France 93,000. Testimonies of the war are found in the photojournalism of Robert Capa, Pierre Schoendoerffer – who subsequently made a film of the war, *Dien Bien Phu*, considered problematic for its point of view (Cooper, 2001, 212–16) – and other photographers, who disappeared in combat. Opposition in France to the war was slow to emerge, but crystallised by the *affaire Henri Martin*. Martin was a sailor who was jailed in 1950 for refusing to fight, and, defended by Sartre, released in 1953. (**Andy Stafford**)

Further reading

Ruscio (1987) – good overview, which sees the Franco-Indochina War in its relationship to French decolonisation.

Insertion   See ASSIMILATION.

Intégration   See ASSIMILATION.

Islam, France   France's second religion, Islam is largely the result of (post)colonial MIGRATION. French colonialism saw Islam as its radical 'other', and constructed French identity and CITIZENSHIP in opposition to it. The noun *Musulman(e)* ('Muslim') has always operated as an ethnic and/or racial rather than purely religious marker. Accordingly, estimates of the numbers of 'Muslims' in France (most of whom are Sunnite) vary greatly from 1.75 million to 4 million. The widest definitions include all those in France from majority Muslim countries (ALGERIA, MOROCCO, Pakistan, TUNISIA, Turkey), Africa (especially MALI, MAURITANIA, SENEGAL) and the COMOROS, plus their descendants. More succinct assessments define 'Muslims' by regular religious worship and/or cultural or ethnic identification (Césari, 1994). There are also size-able Francophone Muslim minorities in Belgium.

Whilst Islam in France has a long history, only since the 1970s has it gained greater social and political visibility. Firstly, Muslims themselves have demanded more rights (prayer space in factories and hostels, planning permission for mosques), following the decision by most Muslim migrants to stay in France permanently: temporary migration had previously largely dispensed with formal religious practice. The transnational, diasporic *Umma* (community of Islam) has provided symbolic support for its followers (of whatever generation) against widespread RACISM. Secondly, this greater visibility has also been imposed from the outside: metropolitan French public perceptions of Islam have generally been hostile, equating usually apolitical French Islam with radical 'political' Islam, political violence, conflict in Algeria, and essentialised 'racial' and 'cultural' 'DIFFERENCE' (see HEADSCARF AFFAIR, *FRONT NATIONAL*, RACISM, ANTIRACISM). The absence of a single, institutionally recognised Muslim representative body – notably due to French Islam's great national and ethnic diversity has also delayed the obtaining of greater religious rights. However, following ratification of an agreement (2000–01) between the state and the main Muslim organisations in France, Islam is very slowly integrating a similar, more equitable legal framework alongside Catholicism, Protestantism and Judaism (see *LAÏCITÉ*). (**Jim House**)

Further reading

House (1996) – an overview of the main contemporary themes set within an historical perspective; Césari (1998) – an accessible guide to how young Muslims in contemporary France view their religion.

Islam, Maghreb   Islam spread to the MAGHREB very quickly after the death of the Prophet Muhammad in AD 632. The early conversion of the BERBER population gener-ated an energy which saw a Muslim army led by a Berber general begin the conquest of Spain in AD 711. Political change in the eastern part of the Muslim world and the establishment of a new dynasty enabled the Maghreb and Spain under the Umayyads to create an independent and dynamic cultural and economic centre in the western MEDITERRANEAN that became a conduit for scientific and artistic ideas into Europe. The early establishment of an independent Muslim power in the Maghreb was accompa-nied by a cultural synchronism in which different traditions within Islam were typi-fied by the region's adhesion to Malikism. Of particular importance were the emergence of *tariqa* with their charismatic leaders and the development of local reli-gious centres or *zawiya*. These offered alternative routes to spirituality to that of the mosque and the ULAMA. French colonial rule severely disrupted the relations between these different traditions and by favouring the *tariqa* leaders at the expense of the *ulama* unbalanced power between them. The early twentieth-century nationalist movements were inspired by the Salafiyyist movement – Allal el-Fassi and the Hızʙ AL IsᴛɪǫLᴀʟ in Morocco, Ben Badis and the Association of Algerian Ulama in Algeria, al-Thalaabi and the Dᴇsᴛᴏᴜʀ party in Tᴜɴɪsɪᴀ. Whilst authenticity could be claimed by the sultan in Morocco and Tunisia's Zitouna mosque, no equivalent institutions survived colonial rule in Algeria. The resultant religious vacuum after independence led Algeria's rulers to encourage an Islamic revival whose inspiration was drawn from outside the region. Political events in the Muslim world also helped the shift towards Islamist movements that has characterised the region during the 1990s. Whilst the ensuing struggle has been particularly fierce in Algeria, both the late Hᴀssᴀɴ II of Morocco and the Tunisian president, Bᴇɴ Aʟɪ, have used force to limit the influence of similar movements in their countries. Thus the belief in the moral power of the regeneration of Islam by the region's leaders has not been fulfilled in practice. See also FIS. (**Kay Adamson**)

Further reading

Bulliet (1994); Joffé (1997); Mernissi (1993).

IstiqLal   See Hızʙ ᴀʟ IsᴛɪǫLᴀʟ.

Ivory Coast   See Côᴛᴇ ᴅ'Ivoɪʀᴇ.

Jeune Afrique   A weekly news magazine, born in 1961 to replace its previous, short-lived incarnation, *Afrique Action*. The prime mover behind the magazine was Béchir Ben Yamed, who continues to write a weekly column. His aim was to provide a forum for debate for the newly independent African nations. Based in Paris, but distributed throughout Francophone Africa, the magazine soon became one of the main sources of criticism of neo-colonial politics (see Nᴇᴏ-ᴄᴏʟᴏɴɪᴀʟɪsᴍ, and of corrupt African regimes, leading to periodic censorship in numerous African countries. In the 1960s, the magazine was given the sub-title *L'Intelligent*, as a declaration of 'young' Africa's growing maturity. (**David Murphy**)

Jeux de la Francophonie   This cultural and sporting event brings together Francophone athletes and performers every four years in the spirit of the original Olympic Games. It also aims to reinforce tenuous French-speaking traditions by inviting representatives from less obvious countries. The idea emerged from the 1987 Conference of Francophone Heads of State and Governments. The games have been staged in Morocco (1989), Paris (1994), Madagascar (1997), and Ottawa-Hull (2001), where 3000 participants took part in various visual and performing arts, such as painting, traditional dance, story telling, poetry, photography, and paralympic and able-bodied sports from boxing to beach volleyball. Niger will host the event in 2005. (**Geoff Hare**)

Jewish culture   See North African Jewish culture.

Jospin, Lionel (Robert)   Born Paris, 1937. Leading French socialist. He won a scholarship in 1956 and became a student activist, campaigning against France's part in the Algerian War of Independence. He joined the Union of the Socialist Left in 1956 then the United Socialist Party two years later. He graduated from the *Ecole Nationale d'Administration* in 1965 and began a career in the Foreign Ministry. He left in 1970 to teach economics and resume his political activism.

Jospin joined the Socialist Party in 1971 and was initially a protégé of François Mitterrand. He became party spokesman on Third World affairs (1975–79) and International Relations (1979 81). He was chosen as party Secretary in 1981 and elected to parliament the same year. He served as Education Minister (1988–92) and presided over the Headscarf Affair. He lost his parliamentary seat in 1993 but, with grassroots support, became the presidential candidate of the Left in 1995. He lost to Jacques Chirac but did win the 1997 parliamentary elections to become Prime Minister.

As Premier, Jospin has concentrated on domestic unemployment and international issues which impact directly on the French economy (e.g. European economic integration). He has travelled extensively (e.g. Morocco, Senegal) but has done so – except in the case of his trip to the Middle East in March 2000– to reinforce President Chirac's message on foreign policy. The one area where he has given the lead in foreign affairs has been Sub-Saharan Africa. As a former Trotskyist, Jospin has condemned France's neo-colonial practice of supporting Francophone African dictators and has pressed for a greater emphasis on democracy in French African policy. He has slashed military assistance to Africa and reformed development aid policies and structures. Although he sought to build on these achievements and enhance his international stature ahead of the 2002 presidential elections, he was eliminated after the first round of the ballot and immediately announced his intention to withdraw from politics. (**Gordon Cumming**)

Further reading

Agir ici et Survie (1996) – compilation of critical surveys of French African policy, see pages 325–36 for Jospin's reformism; Leclerc (2001) – study of Jospin's life and politics.

Josselin, Charles   Born 1938. Minister for *Coopération* and *Francophonie*, 1997–2002.

Joual   *Le joual* is the derogatory name (coming from the slurred pronunciation of the word *cheval*) given to the popular form of French spoken in Quebec, often denounced for its allegedly slovenly articulation, deviant grammar and use of numerous

Anglicisms. During the Révolution tranquille, however, it was adopted by many writers (e.g., Tremblay, Renaud), who saw it as a genuine vernacular that had significance for Quebec identity. Conflicting attitudes to *joual* still exist, but, now that Quebec enjoys greater linguistic security (see Language/Language policies in Quebec), they are no longer held so passionately. (**Ian Lockerbie**)

Jouhaud, Edmond Born Bou-Sfer, Oranie, 1905; died 1995. Former French airforce chief (1958–60) and a central figure in the April 1961 generals' putsch. With Generals Challe and Zeller, he made the declaration on Radio France on 22 April 1961 that the military were taking charge of Algiers in the name of a French Algeria. He relied on the 1st REP (*Régiment étranger de parachutistes* – the Legionnaires) to provide the key military support for the putsch. With Salan, he attempted to persuade Challe not to capitulate and continued the fight in Oran until his arrest on 25 March 1962. Condemned to death on 13 April 1962 for his part in the putsch, he was pardoned and released in 1967. (**Kay Adamson**)

Jugurtha 154–104 bc. Military commander of east Numidia or Mazyssile, now eastern Algeria. He was descended from a local ruling dynasty based in Aurès. Thanks to his high intelligence and charismatic personality his fellow citizens placed great trust in him and he was able to make his mark on the history of Ancient Numidia (North Africa) with his fierce and tenacious resistance to the Roman occupying forces, 111–105 bc. After several years of warfare, 105 bc saw many meetings called to discuss a peace settlement, in the course of which a trap was set to capture Jugurtha, who was imprisoned and starved to death. He died on 7 January 104 bc, but is still very present in the memory of North Africans. (**Kamal Salhi**)

Further reading

Gaid (1995).

Julien, Pauline 1928–99. Quebec singer. Her charm, liveliness and beauty were put at the service of her passionate Quebec nationalism. Her partner was the nationalist poet Gérald Godin, who became a minister in the first *Parti Québécois* (PQ) government (see René Lévesque). It was the ability of the PQ to attract such gifted artists which helped to give it its progressive image. Her talent as a singer is preserved in many recordings. Her life with Godin and involvement with the PQ is the subject of an attractive documentary: Dorothy Todd Hénaut's *A Song for Quebec* (1988). (**Ian Lockerbie**)

Juminer, Bertène Born Cayenne, Guiana, 1927. Guianese doctor, academic, writer. A long-time supporter of independence for the French Caribbean territories, he was a friend of Frantz Fanon and taught medicine in Tunisia, Morocco, Iran, Senegal and France, before returning to the Caribbean, where he was rector of the Antilles-Guyane Academy. His novels express an ironic reflection on questions of black identity and postcolonial Africa: *Les Bâtards* (1961; *The Bastards*, 1989); *Au Editions du Seuil d'un nouveau cri* (1963); *La Revanche de Bozambo* (1968; *Bozambo's Revenge:*

or, Colonialism Inside Out, 1976), *Les Héritiers de la Presqu'île* (1979); *La Fraction de seconde* (1990). Joining with those who seek to develop a particularly CREOLE vision of the Caribbean's global prospects, he co-signed a 'Manifesto' for a new future for the *départments d'outre-mer* (DOM) in 2000.

Further reading

Chamoiseau, Delver, Glissant and Juminer (2000).

Jutra, Claude 1930–86. QUEBEC film-maker of high repute. His early, semi-autobiographical *A tout prendre* (1963) was one of the first expressions of a new artistic spirit in Quebec and *Mon Oncle Antoine* (1971) has regularly been voted the best Canadian film. His later career was dogged with difficulties. *Kamouraska* (1973) was drastically cut by the producers and only restored much later. He left Quebec for a time and made several films in English in Toronto. *La Dame en couleurs* (1984) transposed his own artistic difficulties, which were compounded by the early onset of Alzheimer's disease, provoking his death by suicide in 1986. (**Ian Lockerbie**)

Kabila, Laurent Désiré 1940–2001. Self-proclaimed former President of the DEMOCRATIC REPUBLIC OF CONGO. He began as a leader of the failed 1964–65 rebellion in the eastern Congo. He regained prominence in 1995, organising the *Alliance des Forces Démocratiques pour la Libération du Congo* (AFDL), supported by RWANDA, Uganda and Angola. The AFDL captured the capital, Kinshasa, in May 1997 and Kabila then appointed himself President. In 1998, Kabila, supported by Angola, CHAD, Namibia, Sudan and Zimbabwe, broke with Rwanda and Uganda, starting a new conflict in the Congo. With his assassination in 2001, his son Joseph then proclaimed himself President. (**Peter Langford**)

Further reading

Willame (1999).

Kaboré, Gaston Born 1951. Film-maker from BURKINA FASO. Kaboré studied history then film-making in Paris, and returned to Burkina Faso as a government advisér on cinema from 1977 to 1981, and director of the national Cinema Centre until 1988. Kaboré is a distinguished screenwriter, director, producer and teacher, and was secretary-general of the *Fédération pan-africaine des cinéastes* (FEPACI). His major feature films to date are *Wend Kuuni* (1982), *Zan Boko* (1989), *Rabi* (1992) and *Buud Yam* (1997). They focus on themes of social and political relevance in modern Africa, often depicting the lives of ordinary people with an allegorical intention. (**Rachael Langford**)

Further reading

Givanni (2000); Malkmus and Armes (1991); Ukadike (1994).

Kabylia (*Kabylie*) A region in north-eastern ALGERIA that extends for over 150 miles along the MEDITERRANEAN coast between Algiers and Bgayet (Bejaïa) and about 100 miles inland. It is divided notionally into two main areas: *Grande Kabylie* in the west, centred around the mountains of Djurdjura that reach heights of 6000 feet (1830 metres); and *Petite Kabylie* to the east, where the mountains rise to about 3500 feet (1067 metres). Kabylia is a largely untamed landscape of rugged mountains and isolated valleys. Many areas are inaccessible for much of the year due to snow and rain. This apparent isolation has given local people a strong sense of cultural independence, and Kabyles do not like to admit speaking languages other than Kabyle, a variant of TAMAZIGHT or BERBER. French is often used as a second language rather than Arabic. Although Kabylia appears to be a thoroughly secular society, most of the population is Muslim, with a minority of Christians, who are not particularly prominent. A small proportion of the Kabyle population is also believed to have Jewish ancestors. Women enjoy great liberty and independence in Kabylia. (**Kamal Salhi**)

Kagamé, Paul Born 1957. President of RWANDA, 2000–. After the Rwandan 'social revolution' of 1959, Paul Kagamé left Rwanda as a refugee, aged two, for Uganda. He later served, together with many of the Rwandan diaspora, in the Ugandan guerrilla army of Yoweri Museveni in its successful war against Milton Obote. After the war, the attention of the Rwandan diaspora in Uganda focused upon returning to Rwanda. Kagamé joined the Rwanda Patriotic Front and became its leader after the failure of its first attack into Rwanda in October 1990. After four years of conflict, the RPF installed a government in July 1994. (**Peter Langford**)

Kahina, Dihya (Al) 660–703. A legendary BERBER queen, born in the Aurès mountains. In the middle of the seventh century, Arab armies appeared in North Africa, determined to conquer the area and introduce ISLAM to the local people. The Berber tribes fiercely resisted invasion and decades of war ensued. Al Kahina emerged as a resistance leader and fighter and proved amazingly successful at uniting the Christian, Jewish and pagan Berbers against their common enemy. Her reputation as a strategist and prophetess spread throughout North Africa until her final defeat in battle. (**Naaman Kessous**)

Kanak Word derived from the Polynesian word *Kanaka*, which means 'man'. It was adopted by missionaries and other Europeans during the nineteenth century. The settlers began to use it, gallicised as *Canaques*, in a pejorative sense. The term was re-adopted in the 1970s as the invariant *Kanak* by Melanesians as a gesture of cultural re-appropriation and political affirmation associated with local independence movements. It should be compared with the word 'Melanesian', which was coined by the French navigator Dumont d'Urville in the 1830s to designate the indigenous population of NEW CALEDONIA and other islands in Melanesia (Papua New Guinea, Fiji,

Vanuatu, the Solomons). New Caledonia was first populated by Austronesian MIGRA-TIONS from South-east Asia *c.* 3000 BC. (**Kamal Salhi**)

Kane, Cheikh Hamidou   Born Matam, SENEGAL, 1928. Senegalese writer. His first novel, *L'Aventure ambiguë* (1961; *Ambiguous Aventure*, 1963) has been heralded as a classic of African literature. Its story of an educated African torn between his African and European identities, has served as a model for many subsequent authors. Generally associated with the *NÉGRITUDE* movement, he was also a close political ally of SENGHOR, serving as a minister in his government. His only other novel is *Les Gardiens du Temple* (1995). (**David Murphy**)

Further reading

Little, J. P. (2000) – excellent analysis of cultural context of Kane's masterpiece.

Karembeu, Christian   Born Lifou, 1970. Neo-Caledonian footballer. He was the first Neo-Caledonian to become a national sporting hero – with the 1998 World-Cup-winning French football team, who came to symbolise a new multi-racial French identity. Fiercely proud of his *KANAK* roots and culture, he was criticised by J.-M. LE PEN for not singing the national anthem before international matches. Emerging from the youth academy at Nantes, with whom he won the French championship, he joined Sampdoria, moving on to Real Madrid, winning the Champions League, before going to Middlesborough then to Greece. In December 1998, he married Slovakian top model Adriana in a highly mediatised wedding. (Geoff Hare)

Further reading

Dauncey and Hare (1999).

Karone, Yodi   Born 1954. Cameroonian writer, living in Paris, whose works include: *Nègre de paille* (Grand Prix de Littérature africaine, 1982); *Le Bal des Caïmans* (1980); *A la recherche du cannibale amour* (1988); *Les beaux gosses* (1991).

Kassovitz, Mathieu   See *LA HAINE*.

Kateb Yacine   Born Constantine, 1929; died 1989. Algerian writer. As a child he lived in various places, depending on where his father, a civil servant in the Algerian judicial administration, was posted. After completing his basic schooling, he continued his studies at a French college. On 8 May 1945 he took part in riots in Setif, discovering the intoxication of the popular spirit and the brutality of the repressive measures taken against it. He was excluded from college but enrolled in a school in Bône (now Anaba). He fell hopelessly in love with a cousin, older than himself and already married, whom he later immortalised in his writing as the character Nedjma. Kateb began to write, publishing a collection of poems, *Soliloques* (1946). Between 1946 and 1947 he was active in the ranks of the PPA. In 1947 he made his first trip to Paris, where he met Albert Béguin and André Chamson. From 1948 to 1950 he was a journalist for *Alger Républicain*. He joined the PCA. Living in difficult material and familial conditions, he began a wandering existence that continued until his death. His great novel *Nedjma* (1956; English translation under the same title, 1991) won him an international reputation, and he went to live abroad. His plays, most notably *Le Cercle des représailles* (1959), were staged in France and Belgium. He worked with highly regarded directors, such as Jean-Marie Serreau, noted for empowering dramatists from African colonial territories. Many liberal French intellectuals were eager to champion Kateb's precocious literary talent, including Jean-Paul Sartre, an opponent of the ALGERIAN WAR. In the post-independence period Kateb Yacine was seen as the most important literary voice of the young generation of Africans. During the 1960s, in particular following the publication of his novel *Le Polygone étoilé* (1966), Kateb found himself frustrated by political realities. In 1971 he gave up writing in French to work in Algerian Arabic and BERBER, committing himself to a radically new form of popular political theatre. All his plays are collected in French translation in *Boucherie de l'espérance* (Editions du Seuil, 1999). For anyone interested in a theatre of empowerment that is able to communicate with popular audiences, his oeuvre constitutes some of the most important work of its time anywhere in the world. (**Kamal Salhi**)

Further reading

Salhi K. (1999); Arnaud (1986).

Keita, Modibo   See MALI.

Keïta, Salif   Born Djoliba, MALI, 1949. Malian singer. He is renowned for his distinctive, soaring voice which has made him one of Africa's most successful singers. This albino vocalist began his career with the Malian pop groups the Rail Band and the Ambassadeurs. The major breakthrough for this latter group came in 1978 when they moved to Abidjan (IVORY COAST) and recorded their groundbreaking album, *Mandjou*. Keïta then launched a solo career, moving to Paris in the early 1980s. His Western-recorded albums, the best known of which is *Soro* (1987), have enjoyed considerable success in the World Music charts. See also MUSIC, SUB-SAHARAN AFRICA. (**David Murphy**)

Kelkal, Khaled   1971–95. Political activist, infamous to mainstream society for involvement in political terrorism, but a hero for some *BANLIEUE* youths. When he was two his family left ALGERIA for France, and Kelkal grew up in Lyons, where at the *lycée* he felt excluded as an Arab. In 1990, despite claiming innocence, he was sentenced to prison for three burglaries. While imprisoned he learnt Arabic and renewed his faith in ISLAM. His participation in a deadly series of Islamist bombings in France led to a massive manhunt, ending in a shootout with police on 29 September 1995. M6 censored the injunction to '*Finis-le!*' from its televised video of his death. (**Mark McKinney**)

Ken Bugul   (Pseudonym of Mariétou Mbaye.) Born SENEGAL, 1948. Senegalese writer. She has published four novels, the first of which, *Le Baobab fou* (1982; *The Abandoned Baobab: The Autobiography of a Senegalese Woman*, 1991) is a semi-autobiographical novel. After a twelve-year gap she began to publish again, producing *Cendres et braises* (1994), *Riwan ou le chemin de sable* and *La Folie et la mort* (2000). (**Nicki Hitchcott**)

Kessas, Ferrudja Born Paris, 1961. Writer of Algerian descent, whose parents were immigrants. After entering an arranged marriage with a cousin in ALGERIA at the age of 19 she became anorexic and persuaded him that she needed to return to France, where she wrote her semi-autobiographical novel *Beur's Story* (Paris: L'Harmattan, 1990). In it, fictionalised versions of Kessas's experiences are divided between two main characters: Farida, who refuses to accept the straitjacket forced upon her by her parents, and Malika, who takes a more conciliatory approach. (**Alec G. Hargreaves**)

Further reading

Derderian (1993) focuses on gendered aspects of Kessas's novel.

Kettane, Nacer Born 1953. Writer and minority rights activist, who trained as a doctor. In 1986 he published *Droit de réponse à la démocratie française*, a cogent analysis of France's treatment of the Maghrebi-French. His semi-autobiographical novel, *Le Sourire de Brahim*, spans the period from the OCTOBER 1961 massacre of Algerian immigrants during the ALGERIAN WAR OF INDEPENDENCE to the electoral victory of François MITTERRAND in 1981, which initially gave much hope to the Maghrebi-French. In 1981, Kettane also helped found *RADIO BEUR*, of which he became station president. (**Mark McKinney**)

Further reading

Hargreaves (1992 and 1997) provides essential information on Kettane and his work.

Khadda, Mohamed Born Mostaganem, 1930; died Algiers, 1991. Algerian artist. From a modest family, he was apprenticed as a printer. He went to work as a typographer in Paris (1953), plunging himself into the world of galleries and museums and, despite his legendary shyness, associating with the Algerian intellectual milieu. He absorbed contemporary art, also discovering the Arabic graphic tradition, African sculpture, Japanese and Chinese watercolours. From 1956 his paintings linked geometric structures, Arabic and BERBER letters with an impressionist palette. He returned to Algiers in 1963, until 1973, working as a printer by day and painting at night. He was criticised by the ruling FLN for his lack of concessions towards socialist realism and his uncompromising attitude towards his non-figurative painting. He was politically engaged and painted frescoes and debated with the non-specialist, arguing that all painting was abstract and that it was all around, in carpets, fabrics and other designs. (**Cathie Lloyd**)

Khaïr-Eddine, Mohammed Born 1941. Moroccan novelist and poet. He is of BERBER origins, and was closely involved with *SOUFFLES*. His writing is emblematic of what Marc Gontard (1981) has called 'the violence of the text' in Moroccan Francophone literature. *Agadir* (1967) is the best-known novel by this (self-styled) 'linguistic guerrilla' and anti-authoritarian, who, as a civil servant in Casablanca, was deeply affected by having to establish survivors' names after a massive earthquake. The late 1970s saw him promote the theme and practice of *errance* (1978) – in which language and creativity are plundered to source an identity of movement and dissolution – and then publish a novel on French colonialism: *Légende et vie d'Agoun'Chich* (1984). (**Andy Stafford**)

Khaled (Khaled Hadj-Brahim)   Born Oran, 1960. Algerian musician. He moved to France in 1986 and is credited with bringing RAÏ to an international audience. Married with two daughters, his predilection for 'wine, women and song' have earned him appearances in court and a mention by IAM as the Arabic Public Enemy. Has been criticised, like CHEB MAMI, with whom he appears in the 1997 film *100 per cent Arabica*, for introducing 'Western' musical influences to *raï* (notably in his collaboration on 'Aicha' with Jewish singer-songwriter Jean-Jacques Goldman). His 1998 charity concert: *1,2,3, Soleils* with Faudel and Rachid Taha, was highly acclaimed. (**Samantha Neath**)

Further reading

Khaled (1998).

Khatibi, Abdelkebir   Born El Jadida, 1938. Moroccan writer, literary/art critic, and academic. He co-edited an early anthology of North African writers of French expression (Memmi, 1964); published his thesis as *Le Roman maghrébin* (1968) and has written other works on literature. In addition to sociological studies, he is best known for three novels: *La Mémoire tatouée: Autobiographie d'un décolonisé* (1971); *Le Livre du sang* (1979), *Amour bilingue* (1983; *Love in Two Languages*, 1990). All show a powerful use of the FRENCH LANGUAGE and a concern with postcolonial identity. He has also written poetry, plays and essays. (**Debra Kelly**)

Khider, Mohammed   Born Algiers, 1912; assassinated Madrid, 1969. He served, along with Ahmed BEN BELLA and Hocine AÏT AHMED, as one of the three external representatives of the CRUA (see ALGERIAN WAR OF INDEPENDENCE). He was the oldest member of the key group of FLN organisers and the only one to have been a member of the Algerian nationalists' earliest organisation, the *Etoile Nord-Africaine*, founded in the 1920s by Messali HADJ amongst Algerian workers in Paris. Like BOUDIAF and Ben Bella, he spent much of the actual struggle in a French prison. He supported Ben Bella but they disagreed over the relationship between party and state, with the result that Khider resigned his post of Secretary-General of the FLN but kept the party's funds. (**Kay Adamson**)

Khieu Samphan   Cambodian KHMER ROUGE leader.

Khmer Rouge   (Red Khmers). The name attached in the 1970s to members of the Communist Party of Kampuchea (CPK), later known as the Party of Democratic Kampuchea. The Khmer Rouge came to power in 1975, after a fierce civil war against the forces of Lon Nol. During their time in power they pursued a policy of purification of the Khmer race and the establishment of a classless society, through brutal repression and coercion and the mass evacuation of town-dwellers into the countryside. It is estimated that several million Cambodians lost their lives under these policies. Ousted from power by the Vietnamese invasion of 1978–79, they continued to wage a guerrilla struggle for the next ten years. The main Khmer Rouge leaders include Pol Pot, Ieng Sary, Khieu Samphan, Son Sen, Mok (Chhit Choeun). See also Cambodia; Sihanouk.

Konaré, Alpha Oumar   Born Kayes, Mali, 1946. Malian statesman and politician. He was elected President of Mali at the first democratic elections in May 1992 and re-elected in 1997. His second and last five-year term expired in May 2002. Of international stature, he is President of ECOWAS (Economic Community of West African States). PhD in history and archaeology, Poland, 1975; minister under President Moussa Traoré, 1978–79; founder member of the Cultural Co-operative Jamana, a pioneer of independent press, private radios and local languages; also founding member of the leading political party, ADEMA (Alliance for Democracy in Mali) and a vanguard figure in the fight for democracy. (**Ingse Skattum**)

Konaté, Moussa   Born Mali, 1951. Malian novelist, playwright, theatre director, publisher. In 1997, inspired by a mission to make Malian literature more accessible, he created a publishing house, Editions du Figuier, which began by publishing children's books, before moving to books for a wider audience. His works include: *Le Prix de l'âme* (1981); *L'Or du diable* (1985); *Le Cercle féminin* (1985); *Fils du chaos* (1986); *Chronique d'une journée de répression* (1988); *Mali: ils ont assassiné l'espoir* (1990); *Un appel de nuit* (1995); *Goorgi* (1997).

Koran/Qur'an   The Qur'an is known as the word of Allah revealed to his Prophet Mohammed during the early part of the seventh century CE. The text of the Qur'an remains in its original form as it was known to the Prophet Mohammed, and stands as an eternal miracle of eloquence.

The Qur'an is made of 114 chapters, called *surahs*. Each *surah* contains a number of statements, called *Ayahs*. With the exception of one *surah*, 'Repentance', all the *surahs* of the Qur'an are preceded by the expression 'In the Name of Allah, Most Gracious, Most Merciful'. The *surahs* are divided into two categories known as Meccan and Medinan *surahs*, according to the place of revelation: the first being revealed to the Prophet Mohammed by the angel Gabriel (*Jibril*) in Mecca and the second being revealed to him in Medina, to which he migrated in 622CE, seeking refuge from the persecution he and his companions faced at the hands of the Meccan pagans.

There are eighty-six Meccan *surahs* and twenty-eight Medinan *surahs*. The first *surah* to be revealed to the Prophet is *surah* 96 and the last revelation was *surah* 110. Therefore these *surahs* are not arranged by order of revelation, but rather according to the knowledge the Prophet's companions preserved of the divine command to His Prophet. The final order of arrangement of the text was codified by the companion

Zayd Ibn Thabit at the command of the Caliph 'Uthman Ibn 'Affan, who ordered and oversaw the collection of the Qur'an into one book. This arrangement is unanimously believed to be unique in coherence.

As to the themes of the Qur'an, there is one major theme, which is the relationship between God and His creatures, and it deals with all issues that concern Muslims, such as wisdom, worship, law and doctrine. It represents the prime source of the Muslim's faith and practice, as well as providing guidelines for proper human conduct. (**Zahia Smail Salhi**)

Further reading

Abdel Haleem (2001).

Kourouma, Ahmadou Born CÔTE D'IVOIRE, 1927. One of Africa's foremost writers with stylistically innovating novels, marked by humour, humanism and political satire, inspired by oral literature: *Les Soleils des indépendances* (1968; *Suns of Independence*, 1981), a classic; *En attendant le vote des bêtes sauvages* (1998; *Waiting for the Vote of the Wild Animals*, 2001), a key novel of present-day dictatorship; *Allah n'est pas obligé* (2000; Prix Renaudot 2000), a black humour story of a child-soldier in the tribal wars of Liberia and Sierra Leone. (**Ingse Skattum**)

Further reading

Derive (1979–80) – excellent explanation of the integration of oral literature in his first novel; Borgomano (2000) – good explanations of the cultural and political background of his 'dictatorship' novel.

Laâbi, Abdellatif Born 1942. Moroccan poet, translator and dissident political activist. In 1972 he was tortured and imprisoned for eight years by the Moroccan regime on account of his socialist ideas. Editor of *SOUFFLES* alongside Abraham SERFATY, he became a *cause célèbre* for human rights groups and opponents of MOROCCO's repressive political system. As well as producing a lyrical but violently experimental poetry, both before going into and whilst inside prison (1969, 1976, 1981, 1986), he has published a selection of his prison correspondence (*Chroniques de la citadelle d'exil: lettres de prison*, 1983), turned into a prose poem (*Sous le baillon, le poème: écrits de prison*, 1982), both providing an account of his time as an internee. (**Andy Stafford**)

Lacoste, Robert Born Azerat, France, 1898; died Dordogne, 1989. French Politician. He was an active CGT (Socialist) militant syndicalist, highly decorated for distinguished service in the world wars. He was DE GAULLE's minister (industry) in 1944, mayor of Azerat (1945–89), served in two constituent assemblies (1945/46), was elected parliamentary deputy (1946–68) and minister several times during the Fourth Republic. Premier MOLLET appointed him Resident-Minister in ALGERIA in 1956. A strong supporter of French Algeria, Lacoste used the special powers, granted to the Mollet government by parliament, to pursue policies of ruthless repression and reform. He was later elected senator (1971–80). (**Marianne Durand**)

Further reading

Horne (1987) – useful coverage of the history of the Algerian War. Read from page 154 for a detailed account of Robert Lacoste's reforms and his repression of Algerian nationalists.

Lafleur, Jacques   See RPCR.

La Haine   Mathieu Kassovitz's second full-length film, after *Métisse* (1993); a box-office hit and critical success when it was released in 1995. Dedicated to the memory of Makome M'Bowole, a young Zairean killed in a Parisian police station in 1993, *La Haine* narrates a series of confrontations between police and BANLIEUE youths: the police shooting of an Arab youth, who subsequently dies; the violent uprising to protest over this event; and the final confrontation, probably fatal. Inspired by Spike Lee's *Do the Right Thing* (1989), *La Haine* differs by its depiction of a multi-ethnic friendship (a black, an Arab and a Jew). (**Mark McKinney**)

Laïcité   A term referring to the French understanding of SECULARISM, or separation of church and state, and to the neutrality of the state regarding religious affairs. The 1905 legislation instituting *laïcité* abolished the Napoleonic Concordat (1801–02), under which the French state had previously officially recognised Roman Catholicism, Protestantism and (later) Judaism. *Laïcité* sealed the triumph of republican over anti-republican forces allied to the Catholic Church. Republicans sought to relegate religion to the private sphere, thereby making the public, political sphere autonomous. Based on Enlightenment rationalism, republicanism is suspicious of religion, which is viewed as 'backward'. The secular state school system, conceived during the Third Republic (1871–1940), transmitted a secular morality to rival Catholic values, and is still considered by many republicans today as a 'neutral', tolerant space (see HEADSCARF AFFAIR). After 1945, the 1905 secular settlement became relatively consensual and well established. However, since the early 1980s, *laïcité* has once again attracted heightened political interest. Whilst the 1905 settlement addressed the three main religions of the time (see above), large-scale MIGRATION from majority Muslim countries (e.g. ALGERIA, Morocco, Turkey) during the twentieth century has seen ISLAM become France's second religion. Muslims, as part of a more general revival of interest in religion in French society, and as a re-affirmation of religion as a component of ethnicity, have pushed for greater rights since the 1970s. However, the benefits of *laïcité* (in particular in relation to religious associations) only started to be extended to Islam in 2001. The apparent neutrality of French secularism has also been questioned. For example, the secular state school calendar none the less remains based around Catholicism. Whilst Article Two of the Fifth Republic's constitution (laid down in 1958) stipulates that the state theoretically respects 'all religious beliefs', there have been calls (Baubérot, 1990) for *laïcité* to accept a greater degree of religious DIVERSITY. (**Jim House**)

Further reading

Baubérot (1996) – accessible collection of key constitutional texts accompanied by expert analyses that assess both the historical and contemporary significance of *laïcité*; Baubérot (1990) – an attempt to provide a new theoretical grounding for secularism in a more diverse society.

Lake Meech Accord   The protracted negotiations among the Canadian provinces at Lake Meech sought to satisfy five constitutional demands by QUEBEC, which had prevented it from agreeing to the repatriation of the constitution by TRUDEAU in 1982 (see LÉVESQUE). Agreement was reached among the eleven provincial premiers in 1987, but the Accord foundered later, when two provincial legislatures failed to ratify it. A second attempt in 1991, known as the Charlottetown Accord, also failed. Ironically, the Quebec premier who found himself rebuffed by Canada was Robert BOURASSA, a convinced federalist. (**Ian Lockerbie**)

Lakhdar Hamina, Mohammed   Born 1934. Algerian film-maker, known for his portrayal of the human element in his depictions of the ALGERIAN WAR OF INDEPENDENCE. Films include *Le Vent des Aurès* (1967; Prix du premier film, Cannes); *Chronique des années de braise* (1975; Palme d'Or, Cannes); *Vent de Sable* (1982); *La Dernière image* (1986). See also CINEMA, ALGERIA.

Lamizana, Abubakar Sangoulé   Born Touga, UPPER VOLTA (since 1984 BURKINA FASO), 1916. Soldier and president. Lamizana came to power in a military *coup* in 1966. After a new constitution was approved in 1970, with Gerard Ouedraogo appointed as Prime Minister, Lamizana ousted him in 1974, in order to retain power. He was himself ousted in a *coup* in 1980 led by Saye Zerbo.

Langevin, André   Born Montreal, 1927. QUEBEC journalist, novelist and dramatist. He is especially known for his first two novels where he relates the destiny of people faced with the absurd. *Évadé de la nuit* (1951), his first novel, was notable in the 1950s for its critique of French Canadian society repressed under harsh moral rules. *Poussière sur la ville* (1953; *Dust over the City*, 1955) relates the story of a man, unable to take charge of his own destiny, who encloses himself into an interior world of despair. Alienation, failure and restricted spaces characterise his aesthetic. His last novel, *Une Chaîne dans le parc* (1974; *Orphan Street*, 1976) expressed suffering and violence in the most simple and bare style. (**François-Emmanuël Boucher**)

Further reading

Brochu (1985).

Language/Language policies in Quebec   French has been the language of QUEBEC since the foundation of New France as a French colony in 1608. Not surprisingly, however, the history of the language in this distant continent has been significantly different from that in its original European setting. Two forces have particularly influenced its evolution: the environment and politics. In North America, French (like English) naturally developed many new words, expressions, language habits and pronunciation patterns that did not occur in Europe, and also *retained* features that disappeared from European usage. This process in itself has made Quebec French as distinctive a language variety as American English, in both spoken and written forms, but the character of the language was further affected by the impact of history in 1763 when New France became a British colony. This led to the overwhelming domination of French by English for the next two centuries, and an Anglicisation of the language (at its most extreme in *JOUAL*) that provoked feelings of alienation and dispossession in French Canada.

The aim of the *RÉVOLUTION TRANQUILLE* of the 1960s was to restore French to its proper place as the language of a modern national community. This was accomplished principally by legislation (the CHARTER OF THE FRENCH LANGUAGE) making French the one official language of Quebec. In addition Quebec governments have, in different ways, encouraged the promotion of European French as the preferred norm, and discouraged recognition of the distinctiveness of Quebec French.

Although mild contention still surrounds both the language legislation and the question of the preferred norm, there is no doubt that these language policies have been extremely successful in restoring French and returning Quebec to the position of a leading Francophone nation. (**Ian Lockerbie**)

Further reading

Plourde (2000) gives a comprehensive overview of all the issues. Bouchard (1998) is a detailed account of the fears of Anglicisation.

Language policy   A major characteristic of most Francophone societies that have emerged as independent entities since the 1950s and 1960s is that, although they constitute states, they have not become unified nations with single languages. For various reasons, it is rare for these states to have a shared political culture common to all ethnic groups. Many different cultural and linguistic groups have been brought together through force or diplomacy under common rulers. In situations of this kind, language is vital as a means of communication between different groups, becoming a significant factor in political cohesion and social learning. In the past, common languages have emerged as a result of increased contact between different language groups. The Francophone states, on the other hand, have seen large-scale governmental programmes of language planning or language policy intended to equip their populations for internal communication. Any language that becomes an official language, regardless of any direct intervention in the educational system, comes to occupy an important part in school and college curricula. Given the large number of new independent states that have emerged in the postcolonial Francophone world, there are variations in the actual policies undertaken. However, whatever the differences in details, these policies are distinguished by the extent to which they are based on one of two general approaches: integration or assimilation (see *ASSIMILATION/ INTÉGRATION/INSERTION*. The integrationist approach accepts a situation of linguistic pluralism, and provides for the preservation and use of the major languages of the country. The assimilationist approach seeks to use official and unofficial measures to eliminate linguistic diversity in favour of a single language. This policy often proceeds on the assumption that a sense of NATIONHOOD depends on the adoption of a single language. Whatever the strategy employed, decisions about the specific language or languages to be used for national purposes confront policy-makers in the new postcolonial states with difficult choices. A fundamental element of the French heritage is the position of pre-eminence accorded to the language of the former colonial power. (**Kamal Salhi**)

Further reading

Kibbee (1998).

Language policy, Indian Ocean   The language policies of the Indian Ocean islands are quite varied, despite their general adherence to the Francophone community. French is the official language of REUNION, as it is an overseas department (DOM) of the French Republic, although there have recently been some moves to recognise CREOLE, the vehicular language of most native Reunionese, as a result of the European charter of minority languages. This is confined for the moment to the education system, with the creation of teaching diplomas in Creole.

In MAURITIUS, English is the language of instruction in the education system, but French is widely taught from primary school onwards, as are Asian languages such as Hindi, Tamil and Mandarin Chinese. French is widely used in journalism and the media, and is the predominant language of literary expression. On the other hand, Creole is the effective vehicular language of most Mauritians, yet it is has no official status, in spite of its widespread use in the theatre and popular music.

The SEYCHELLES is the only state to have adopted Creole as its official language, but English and French are widely taught and spoken.

In MADAGASCAR, the Malagasy language was imposed as the medium of instruction in the education system during the revolutionary years from the mid-1970s to 1991, but after a change of political regime French was re-introduced. Malagasy is, even so, widely used as an official language of administration and is still common in schools; it remains the vehicular language of most of the island's population.

In the tiny archipelago of the Islamic Republic of the COMOROS, French is still the official language, but Arabic and local Comorian dialects are widely spoken. (**Peter Hawkins**)

Laos   South-east Asian country, bordering China, Thailand, VIETNAM, CAMBODIA and Burma. Main resources: timber, hydroelectric power. Main agricultural crop: rice. Estimated to be ranked third in the world as a producer of opium. Capital: Vientiane. Population: 5.5 million. Official language: Lao. French is fairly widely spoken. Religion: Buddhist (60 per cent); animist and other traditional (40 per cent).

Laos was a French protectorate from 1899, as part of the Indochina Union. The nationalist movement, led by Princes Souvanna Phouma and Souphanouvong, fought in vain to prevent the return of the French, after Japanese occupation during World

War II. Souphanouvong went on to form the Communist Pathet Lao, which pursued an anticolonial struggle (see ANTICOLONIALISM), with the support of the Viet Minh, until independence in 1953. Souvanna Phouma led the country through the difficult period of the Vietnam War, until elections in 1973 brought the Patriotic Front (ex-Pathet Lao) to power, followed by the abolition of the monarchy in 1975 and the establishment of a socialist republic. After a period of collectivisation, there were some moves to economic liberalism. Laos joined ASEAN in 1997 and is a member of the OIF.

Larifla, Dominique   Born 1936. Guadeloupean senator and former President of the *Conseil général*.

Laroui, Abdallah   Born Azemmour, 1933. Moroccan historian. A highly esteemed scholar, who taught at the University of Rabat. His area of specialisation is Maghrebian history and Arab affairs in the postcolonial period. In his view, the nature of Islamic or Arabic societies with a common colonial heritage can only be understood if their historical differences are taken into account. Liberalism alone can pave the way to MODERNITY for these societies, whereas NATIONALISM and ORIENTALISM are unsuitable ideologies. Key texts: *L'Histoire du Maghreb: Un essai de synthèse* (1970; *The History of the Maghrib: An Interpretive Essay*, 1977); *Crise des intellectuels arabes: traditionalismes ou historicisme?* (1974; *The Crisis of the Arab Intellectual: Traditionalism or Historicism*, 1976); *L'Idéologie arabe contemporaine* (1982); *Islam et modernité* (1987); *Islamisme, modernisme, libéralisme: esquisses critiques* (1997); *Islam et Histoire* (1999). (**Susanne Heiler**)

Law 101   Law 101 (1977), also called *La Charte de la langue française* (CHARTER OF THE FRENCH LANGUAGE), is the definite recognition of French as QUEBEC's official language (first stated by Law 22 in 1974). It aims at strengthening the position of French versus English as a school language, a working language and a *surface* language (publicity, official signs). The impact of the Law has been most important in bilingual Montreal. One of its main effects has been to give immigrant children education in French instead of English. Amended several times, Law 101 has been a great source of conflict between French nationalists and the English minority of Quebec. (**John Kristian Sanaker**)

Further reading

Levine (1990) – excellent documentation of the effects of the Law, especially in the Montreal area.

Laye, Camara   Born Kouroussa, GUINEA; 1928; died Dakar, SENEGAL, 1980. Guinean writer. His French colonial education and his gradual withdrawal from the culture of his birth exemplify the experience of many young African intellectuals. His first novel, *L'Enfant noir* (1953; *The African Child*, 1980), was written in France and describes a boy growing up in a rapidly changing Guinea. The novel was attacked for its apparent lack of ANTICOLONIAL commitment and its focus on the mystical elements of West African culture, but it remains a powerful exploration of cultural transformation and the experience of dwelling between cultures. After publishing a second novel, *Le Regard du roi* (1954; *The Radiance of the King*, 2001), Laye returned briefly to the newly independent Guinea in 1958 but fell foul of its leader, Sékou Touré. His third and final novel, *Dramouss* (1966; *Dream of Africa*, 1968), is a fictional account of his exile in Senegal. (**Charles Forsdick**)

Further reading

See King (1980) for a general account of the author's work and career, and Azodo (1993) for a detailed study of his fiction.

La Zone   Originally a name for the space of military fortifications surrounding Paris, *la zone* now refers to areas of post-industrial decay and desolation, sometimes inhabited, on the margins of French cities. The term retains earlier connotations of violence and of limits between self/other, inside/outside. *La zone* is an operating concept in popular culture (song, detective novels, comics, speech). The term is relevant to Francophone studies insofar as many working-class postcolonial immigrants settled in these areas, in BIDONVILLES, *cités de transit* and *zones d'urbanisation prioritaire* (ZUPs), partially duplicating the territorial divisions of colonial space. (**Mark McKinney**)

Lê, Linda   Born Dalat, 1963. Writer of Vietnamese origin, but who has lived in France since her early teens. The experimental style of her novels challenges previous Vietnamese literature in French, a category which she resists. Work includes *Un si tendre vampire* (1987), *Les Evangiles du crime* (1992), *Calumnies* (1993; *Slander*, 1996), *Les Dits d'un idiot* (1995), *Les Trois Parques* (1997).

Further reading

Roberts (2000) – a discussion of the work of two writers of Vietnamese origin, Lê and Kim Lefèvre.

Lebanon   Middle Eastern country, bordering the MEDITERRANEAN Sea, between Israel and Syria, with a population of about 3.5 million (70 per cent Muslim, 30 per cent Christian) and an adult literacy rate of 86 per cent. Achieved independence from League of Nations mandate, under French administration, in 1943. The 'National Pact' established proportionate representation for the main religious groups, e.g. Maronite Christians, Sunni Muslims, Shia Muslims. The stability this provided was shattered in the civil war (1975–91). The official language is Arabic, although French is widely used. Writers who have chosen to write in French include Amin Maalouf, Charles Corm, Fouad Gabriel Naffah, Farjallah Haik, Georges Schehadé and Andrée Chedid (of Lebanese extraction, living in France). Member of OIF.

Le Chevallier, Jean-Marie   Politician. He was elected mayor of the southern French city of Toulon under the colours of the extreme right-wing *Front National* (FN) in 1995. Toulon was the largest city to fall under FN control. Elected to parliament in 1997, Le Chevallier left the FN in 1999 and failed in his bid for re-election as mayor in 2001. His authority had been weakened by in-fighting within the local party and by charges of malpractice concerning his administration of the city. (**Alec G. Hargreaves**)

Further reading

Martin (1996) examines Le Chevallier's electoral success in Toulon.

Leclerc, Félix   Born La Tuque (Mauricie) 1914; died Île d'Orléans, Quebec, 1988. Storyteller, poet, dramatist, and radio animator and from 1950 cabaret-artist, he is mainly known as the pioneer of Quebec French songs. His publications and performances were committed to political issues, such as the dependency of the colonies on the colonisers (*Petit livre bleu de Félix*, a book of maxims, 1978); national consciousness (two famous songs: 'L'Alouette en colère', 1970, and 'Le Tour de l'Isle', 1980); and humanitarian sensibility (*Adagio*, a book of tales, 1943). His work emphasises the civic responsibility of journalists and artists to denounce exploitation of the poor and encourage humanity to fight for their rights. Love, death, life of simple people, wonder, solitude and nature are characteristic themes in his writing. (**François-Emmanuël Boucher**)

Further reading

Bertin (1987); Brouillard (1994); Paulin (1998).

Léger, Alexis Saint-Léger   See Saint-John Perse.

Lepage, Robert   Born 1957. Quebec dramatist and theatre director. He has achieved a worldwide reputation for his innovative style of 'image theatre', mixing spoken text, sound, movement and visual effects in a cinematic way. His own plays include large-scale collaborative works (*La Trilogie des dragons*, 1985; *Les Plaques tectoniques*, 1988) and many one-man shows, which he both writes and performs (*Vinci*, 1986, *Aiguilles et opium*, 1991). He is also in great demand internationally as a guest producer of classic texts by Shakespeare, Strindberg and others, and has directed striking films from his own scripts, especially *Le Confessional* (1995). (**Ian Lockerbie**)

Le Pen, Jean-Marie   Born La Trinité-sur-Mer, Brittany, 1928. French politician. He is leader of the extreme right-wing Front National, which gained a high public profile during the 1980s and 1990s. Le Pen served as an army officer and member of parliament during the Algerian War of Independence, gaining a reputation as a brutally uncompromising French nationalist. The *Front National*, which he founded in 1972, built its electoral fortunes by exploiting French fears of immigration, mingling anti-Arab rhetoric with anti-semitism. In the 2002 presidential elections, le Pen caused a major upset by gaining 17 per cent of the first round vote, robbing the Left of a place in the second round, in which he was defeated by Jacques Chirac. (**Alec G. Hargreaves**)

Further reading

Souchard *et al.* (1997) – analyses Le Pen's political rhetoric while Perrineau (1997) examines his sources of electoral support.

Lévesque, René   1922–1987. Quebec politician. He is famous as the founder of the separatist *Parti Québécois* (PQ) in 1968, and Prime Minister in the first PQ government of 1976–80, which enacted the Charter of the French Language and held the first referendum on the possible separation of Quebec from Canada. It was under Lévesque's leadership that Quebec nationalism shed the reactionary stance it had had under Maurice Duplessis (1890–1959) and adopted socially progressive policies. As a former TV journalist and Liberal Party minister, he combined nationalism with political moderation, not least, paradoxically, in the compromise version of separatism which he elaborated. Under his 'Sovereignty-Association', an independent Quebec would have retained ties with Canada in important fields such as defence and financial policy. Some commentators attributed his marked defeat in the 1980 referendum to this ambiguity. But the evidence is rather that his hesitations concerning independence mirrored those of public opinion, which has always wanted maximum autonomy for Quebec, without severing all ties with Canada (see Bourassa). Despite nearly achieving victory in the second referendum in 1995, the PQ has not abandoned Lévesque's compromise position, even today.

It was in part the public's faith in Lévesque which ensured the re-election of the PQ in 1981, despite the referendum defeat. Yet in this second term in office, Lévesque's career went into decline. He was out-manoeuvred by his arch-opponent Trudeau in the process of the repatriation of the Canadian constitution in 1982, thereby failing to secure the constitutional guarantees that Quebec demanded (see Lake Meech Accord). He also compromised his progressive image through clashes with the trades unions. But his resignation as Premier in 1985 and his death in 1987 were greeted with a public sadness which showed the special place he had in the affections of the nation. (**Ian Lockerbie**)

Further reading

The two-volume biography by Godin (1995/8) is exhaustive on the man and his ideals. See McRoberts (1997) for the constitutional issues.

Lini, Walter   1942–99. Vanuatan politician and Anglican priest. As leader of the VP (*Vanuaaku Pati*), he led the country as Prime Minister, from independence in 1980 until 1991.

Literature, Berber   There is an increasing modern production of poems, novels, songs, films and theatre pieces in Berber regional variations such as Taqbaylit (Kabylia, Algeria), Tarifit (Rif area in Morocco), Tašlhiyt (Chleuh area in Morocco), and Tamasheq (spoken by the Tuaregs in Mali and Niger). A general characteristic is its social engagement, although love and suffering in emigration are also inspiring themes. Written, recorded, and diffused through the Internet, this modern production is inscribed in a variegated context, featuring a lively output of oral material and the interaction of literary traditions in different languages (see Orality in Moroccan culture).

Alongside the production in Tamazight/Berber, Berber writers also compose poems and novels in European languages. This literary production, often characterised by the authors' attention to languages and regions of origin, is innovative in language, style and themes. The use of French (and far less extended use of Dutch and English) is clearly linked to past and present conditions (colonisation and emigration).

The oral genres are an important source of inspiration for written production. Until the nineteenth century, most literary genres were orally produced and known only locally. This explains why denominations, characterisations and use of oral genres vary between the different areas. However, comparative approaches show important parallels among the locally based genres. Analysis has revealed the general apposition of two broad poetic genres (Bounfour, 1999: 19): on the one hand, poetry more or less influenced by written Arabic models and presenting religious themes; on the other, the sung poetry further diversified in long and short poetic forms and in masculine and feminine genres. Similarly, there are narrative genres more or less influenced by the Arabic written tradition, as well as more local narratives about heroes such as Mqidec or Amerolqis and tales about local tribes, towns and saints. Ancient and recent collections of tales and poems, from almost two centuries, allow readers to enjoy elaborate literary traditions and get a glimpse of still vigorous oral productions. (**Daniela Merolla**)

Further reading

Bougchiche (1997); Bounfour (1999); Galand-Pernette (1998).

Literature, Caribbean   The name given to the writing from France's South American *département* of GUIANA, from independent HAITI, and from the islands of GUADELOUPE and MARTINIQUE, both *départements* of France in the CARIBBEAN. Though all have produced a highly variable literature, there is perceived now to be a *littérature antillaise*. Caribbean identity is deemed to be 'hybrid' – the meeting of pre-Colombian indigenous peoples, African slaves, European and *métis* elements and Indian indentured labour. This HYBRIDITY has given rise to an innovative use of language and a generic adventurism in its Francophone literature.

The question of CREOLE language, its status and relationship to French, appears both as a medium and as a crucial theme, especially in Haiti where the majority speaks Creole. The ambivalence towards French leads to playful and lively, baroque style. *CRÉOLITÉ* tends to divide Caribbean literature into two camps. It is seen by some writers as a way of getting beyond the crude (but nonetheless real) determinants in Caribbean life: slavery and its legacy, colonialism and NEO-COLONIALISM, *ASSIMILATION*, discrimination, exploitation and (near) forced exile by metropolitan France. Aimé CÉSAIRE is by far the most famous writer in French from this region; the theorist of *NÉGRITUDE*, his *oeuvre* dwells on these themes. Many Caribbean writers declare their indebtedness to him: Maryse CONDÉ, Daniel MAXIMIN, Edouard GLISSANT, Raphaël CONFIANT, Patrick CHAMOISEAU, René DEPESTRE. However, many have since 'swerved away' from Césaire's influence, to embrace *créolité* and ANTILLANITÉ, rejecting (what they deem to be) Césaire's assimilation into French metropolitan letters, and rewriting Caribbean history from the point of view of its subjects. Thus history – telling stories, usually in an oral fashion – is a regular feature of the Caribbean novel in French, of which Chamoiseau's *Texaco*, winner of the prestigious Prix Goncourt in 1992, is a good example. (**Andy Stafford**)

Further reading

Chamoiseau and Confiant (1991) – lively, unconventional, stimulating, historical overview, with illustrations, index and chronology.

Literature, diaspora   Literature produced by writers scattered across spaces beyond the territories in which they have their ethnic origins. The concept of a diaspora (denoting the dispersal of a people) tends to be applied mainly to ethnic groups whose settlement outside their countries of origin was driven by forced MIGRATION (e.g. the slave trade) or by economic or political necessity (e.g. poverty or political oppression). It is less commonly applied to migrants and their descendants when they hold positions of economic and/or political strength (e.g. white settlers during the colonial period). The extent to which writers may be classified as diasporic also depends in part on the strength or weakness of their links with the country from which they or their ancestors migrated.

Through shared memories and cultural traits, Francophone writing in the Caribbean, where a large part of the population is descended from slaves of African origin, displays many diasporic features, though direct contacts with Africa are now relatively weak. Since DECOLONISATION, the settlement within France of immigrant minorities originating in former colonies has brought the emergence of new diasporic groups and associated bodies of writing. Conscious links with their countries of origin tend to be strongest among writers who were born and raised overseas before migrating temporarily or permanently to France. Tahar BEN JELLOUN, Calixthe BEYALA and Gisèle PINEAU are typical of migrant writers originating respectively in North Africa, West Africa and the Caribbean. A growing body of work with less pronounced but still visible connections with those regions is being produced by second-generation members of minority ethnic groups raised in France by immigrant parents. The largest corpus of work of this kind is by second-generation Maghrebis, popularly known as BEURS, typical of whom are Azouz BEGAG, Mehdi CHAREF and Farida BELGHOUL. (**Alec G. Hargreaves**)

Further reading

The essays in Ireland and Proulx (2001) cover writers of diverse origins; Hargreaves (1997) focuses on writing by second-generation Maghrebis.

Literature, Indian Ocean   The Francophone islands of the Indian Ocean have been extraordinarily productive in the literary field, particularly in poetry. REUNION has a poetic heritage going back to the late eighteenth century, when figures such as Evariste de Parny and Antoine Bertin achieved notoriety in the pre-Romantic and Revolutionary period in France. MAURITIUS, too, produced some notable poets in the nineteenth century, such as Léoville L'Homme, but the most celebrated is surely the leading French Parnassian poet Leconte de Lisle, a native of Reunion. In the early years of the twentieth century the Mauritian poet Robert-Edward Hart achieved a high level of international recognition, as did the visionary and aphoristic writings of Malcolm de CHAZAL, admired by French literary figures such as Jean Paulhan and André Breton. The latter part of the twentieth century saw a growth of interest in the literary potential of CREOLE, with the early poems of the Reunionese poet Jean ALBANY, the novels of Axel GAUVIN and the plays of the Mauritian Dev VIRAHSAWMY. The strong literary and poetic tradition of the Malagasy language was adapted into French in the early years of the twentieth century by Jean-Joseph RABÉARIVELO, and the nationalist struggle for independence was reflected in the poetry of Jacques RABÉMANANJARA. Recently both Mauritius and MADAGASCAR have seen the emergence of successful women novelists, such as Marie-Thérèse HUMBERT, Ananda DEVI and Michèle RAKOTOSON; and the French writer Jean-Marie Le Clézio, having assumed his Mauritian origins, has championed the recognition of the Hindi novelist Abhimanyu Unnuth. Even the tiny COMOROS archipelago has seen the publication of its first novels, those of Mohamed Toihiri. The literary output of the region remains singularly rich, with publishing houses in Reunion and Mauritius complementing the recognition of Indian Ocean writers in France. (**Peter Hawkins**)

Further reading

Jack (1996).

Literature, Maghreb   Francophone literature in the Maghreb is a product of the Maghrebian contact with the FRENCH LANGUAGE. France occupied the three countries of the Maghreb, beginning with ALGERIA in 1830. In TUNISIA and MOROCCO, French rule was implemented in 1881 and 1912 respectively. The French presence and the institution of French, through the policy of ASSIMILATION, produced a literature written in the language of colonisation by Arab and BERBER writers. This literature flourished especially in the 1950s with such writers as Albert MEMMI, Driss CHRAÏBI and KATEB YACINE, who published the following novels repectively: *La Statue de sel* (1953; *The Pillar of Salt*, 1956), *Le Passé simple* (1954; *The Simple Past*, 1990) and *Nedjma* (1956; *Nedjma*, 1991). These were to become canonical texts in Maghrebian literature and their authors acknowledged as trailblazers of a flourishing literary tradition. The 1950s generation was concerned with protest themes: its writing was an expression of revolt against colonial rule and a manifesto for the war of liberation, especially in Algeria where the ALGERIAN WAR OF INDEPENDENCE was the lengthiest and bloodiest in the history of French colonisation. Post-independence generations of Maghrebian writers – those of the 1970s and 1980s – produced a literature that challenged religious and sexual taboos, but most significantly, they voiced people's concerns with political unfairness and abuse of human rights by the ruling ÉLITES. Consequently, a number of writers and intellectuals who criticised their country's leaders and their abuse of power saw their voices muted. In some cases, their defiance resulted in imprisonment, as in the case of the Moroccan poet Abdellatif LAÂBI, who lost his freedom for upholding the rights of expression in his literary magazine *SOUFFLES*, a magazine with Marxist–Leninist tendencies which was subsequently censored and then banned. The 1990s saw the emergence of a writing that defied the surge of Islamic fundamentalism in North Africa. For Islamist movements, especially in Algeria, writers and intellectuals were perceived as the enemy within – a perception which gave way to summary murders and executions. Women authors writing in French have been engaged in voicing women's concerns from as early as 1947 with the publication of *Jacinthe noire* by Marguerite Taos AMROUCHE. However, it was with writers like Assia DJEBAR that women's literature established a presence on the literary scene. Though Francophone literature was predicted to vanish with the implementation of the policy of ARABISATION throughout North Africa in the 1970s, a number of new names and new work continue to contribute and add to the wealth of this literary tradition. (**Laïla Ibnlfassi**)

Further reading

Arnaud (1986); Khatibi (1968).

Literature, Quebec   The small subordinated society of French Canada (see QUEBEC) did not enjoy conditions favourable to significant literary development until the nineteenth century. What then emerged was a patriotic literature, chronicling the distinctive history and life of French Canadians, as in de Gaspé's engaging *Les Anciens Canadiens* (1863; *The Canadians of Old*, 1864). The rural novel became the major genre, inspiring Louis Hémon's *Maria Chapdelaine* (1913; English transl., 1921), the supreme patriotic text, as well as RINGUET's *Trente Arpents* (1938; *Thirty Acres*, 1940) and Germaine Guèvremont's *Le Survenant* (1945; *The Outlander*, 1978). An underlying melancholy, partly reflecting an alienated consciousness in French Canada, found expression in poetry, notably that of NELLIGAN and Saint-Denys GARNEAU. The twentieth century saw steady growth in literature, with poets such as Alain GRANDBOIS and novelists like Albert Laberge and Claude-Henri Grignon, reaching its climax in an explosion of creativity after the Second World War. Sustained by the national self-confidence stemming from the RÉVOLUTION TRANQUILLE, Quebec writing now has a wide-ranging diversity. One important strand is literature in JOUAL (TREMBLAY, BEAULIEU), demonstrating the expressive power of the popular language. Another is the increasing number of writers from other cultures (Naïm Kattan, Dany Laferrière, Sergio Kokis, among others) whose work enriches the national canon. The first postwar generations of ROY (Gabrielle), HÉBERT, POULIN, Tremblay, GODBOUT, DUCHARME, MIRON and others are now being followed by younger generations of equally significant writers, such as Monique Proulx, Gaétan Soucy, and Louis Hamelin.

Burgeoning literary activity is also occurring in Francophone communities elsewhere in Canada, not only in ACADIE, but equally in ONTARIO and the West – proof that these communities have a vitality that belies demographic trends. (**Ian Lockerbie**)

Further reading

In the plethora of critical studies that exist, no single book will meet all needs. The best approach may be through overviews as in Tétu de Labsade (2000) and selective bibliographies, as in Hamel (1997), to find suitable texts for personal further reading.

Literature, Sub-Saharan Africa   Literature in French from Sub-Saharan Africa first emerged in the early decades of the twentieth century (earlier texts by Africans were largely historical or ethnographic). In the 1920s, Ahmadou Mapaté Diagne and Bakary Diallo wrote admiringly of France's 'civilising mission' in Africa. From the 1930s, *NÉGRITUDE* writers turned towards the African past, celebrating traditional

African culture: the poetry of Léopold Sédar Senghor and novels such as Camara Laye's *L'Enfant noir* (1953; *The African Child*, 1980) and Cheikh Hamidou Kane's *L'Aventure ambiguë* (1961; *Ambiguous Adventure*, 1963), all provide brilliant, if deeply contrasting, examples of *négritude*'s vision of Africa.

In the 1950s, the anticolonial novel was born: Ferdinand Oyono, Mongo Beti and Ousmane Sembene all wrote of the violence and hypocrisy that underpinned French colonialism. However, within several years of independence, African writers turned their criticism towards the new African regimes. Two works have come to represent this disillusionment with decolonisation: Yambo Ouologuem's *Le Devoir de violence* (1968; *Bound to Violence*, 1971) and Ahmadou Kourouma's *Les Soleils des indépendances* (1968; *Suns of Independence*, 1981). These novels challenged both political and literary assumptions, adopting a playful and experimental style that departed from the social realism and political commitment of many previous African writers. The works of Sony Labou Tansi and V. Y. Mudimbe built on this approach in the 1970s and 1980s, and Kourouma re-established himself as an important novelist in the 1990s. Women writers emerged in the 1980s with Mariama Bâ's *Une si longue lettre* (1980; *So Long a Letter*, 1981). She has been followed by important writers such as Werewere Liking, Calixthe Beyala and Véronique Tadjo. Publishing houses have been established in Africa (NEA, CEDA) but most African texts are still published in France, either by African specialists, *Présence Africaine* and L'Harmattan, or by mainstream publishers such as Editions du Seuil. (**David Murphy**)

Further reading

Mortimer (1990) – good overview of the Francophone African novel.

Lomé Convention   The Lomé Convention was a collective aid and trade agreement between the European Community (EC) and the former colonies of EC member states. It was the direct successor to the Yaoundé Convention but differed from it in a number of respects. Firstly, it did not concentrate so exclusively on Francophone Africa but involved agreement with African, Caribbean and Pacific (ACP) countries (some 71 by the late 1990s). Secondly, it was more generous, with the number of European donors rising to 15 and with ACP states enjoying free access to European markets on a non-reciprocal basis. Thirdly, it was more elaborate, with export support mechanisms like Stabex and Sysmin as well as new institutions like the EC–ACP Joint Council and the Joint Consultative Assembly. Finally, it was more ambitious and sought to promote political, alongside economic, reforms in recipient states.

First signed in the Togolese capital in 1975, the Lomé Convention was hailed as a model for economic partnership between North and South and was regularly renewed (1979, 1984, 1989). It was, however, openly criticised by some (northern) European states for being over-bureaucratic and ineffective in promoting development. It was also attacked by the World Trade Organisation for flouting international rules on free trade and for privileging some developing countries over others. It was, moreover, condemned by independent analysts for perpetuating neo-colonial practices (Ravenhill, 1985) and for serving the interests not so much of ACP states as of

Lomé's contributors, notably France, which used the Convention to share her aid burden and to secure contracts for uncompetitive French businesses.

The fourth Lomé Convention expired in 2000 and was replaced by the more streamlined Cotonou Agreement. Cotonou guarantees collective aid and trade privileges until 2008 but will then be phased out in favour of individual agreements with ACP countries and regions. (**Gordon Cumming**)

Further reading

Lecomte (1999) – brief study of implications of Lomé for Francophone countries; Mailafia (1997) – helpful overview of EC–African economic relations, with Chapters 3–4 focusing on Lomé; Ravenhill (1985).

Lopes, Henri   Born Kinshasa, 1937. Congolese writer, politician and diplomat. Lopes was educated in France, first in Nantes and then in Paris, where he graduated from the Sorbonne. He returned to the Congo in 1965 to take up a teaching post at the *Ecole normale supérieure d'Afrique centrale* in Brazzaville but following the arrival in power of Marien Ngouabi in 1968 Lopes pursued a political career. He was appointed to a number of ministerial posts, including Education and Foreign Affairs, and from 1973 to 1975 he was Prime Minister of his country. Lopes resigned from his post as Minister of Finance in 1980 to take up a position as Deputy Director-General at UNESCO in Paris. In 1998 he was appointed Congolese ambassador to France, Spain, Portugal, the United Kingdom and the Vatican. For the last two decades he has been a member of the Haut Conseil de la Francophonie and the *Conseil supérieur de la langue française*, has served on numerous panels of judges for cinematographic and literary prizes and is currently a candidate for the post of *Secrétaire Général* of the *Organisation Internationale de la Francophonie*. Lopes has managed to combine a successful political and diplomatic career with an equally successful career as a writer. Although his early work is rather didactic in tone, the evident political commitment does not swamp the human interest of his fiction. His first major publication was a collection of short stories, *Tribaliques* (1971; *Tribaliks*, 1987), which was followed by two novels in which he denounces a range of abuses hindering African development. His finest novel to date is undoubtedly *Le Pleurer-Rire* (1982; *The Laughing Cry*, 1987), a complex portrayal of an African dictator. His more recent work up to and including *Dossier Classé* (2002) has been technically more innovative and thematically more ambitious, tending to focus on questions of personal and cultural identity. (**Patrick Corcoran**)

Further reading

For an interesting discussion of *Le Pleurer-Rire*, see Corcoran (2002); Daninos (1987).

Louisiana   The French connection with Louisiana goes back to 1682 when Cavelier de la Salle explored the Mississippi basin and named the territory in honour of Louis XIV. A French colony from 1731 until 1763, it was then ceded to Spain, briefly returned to France in 1800 and sold by Napoleon I to the United States in 1803.

Initial settlement of the territory by the French was slow and colonisation did not really start until around 1717, by which time the first African slaves had been introduced. In 1750, the population numbered 4000 whites and 2000 blacks. Colonisation increased rapidly in the 1760s with the arrival of French-speaking ACADIANS (or CAJUNS) from eastern Canada following forcible deportation by the British. In the early nineteenth century came refugees from HAITI and Cuba. This period witnessed the establishment of a prosperous plantation economy, supported by slave labour, on the cotton and sugarcane plantations. Later waves of immigrants were mostly Anglophone whites. In the early twentieth century, improved communications, industrialisation and a law passed in 1921 to forbid French-language education, all contributed to a substantial decrease in the number of French speakers throughout the state.

From 1803 until 1865 French remained an official language in Louisiana. Today, the most widely used spoken variety is Cajun French, which has similarities with the variety spoken in Canada, while some descendants of the earliest colonists use a more or less standard variety of French and a smaller number still speak a French-lexicon CREOLE, similar to Haitian Creole. In the 1990 US census, over a million inhabitants of Louisiana claimed French ancestry with 261,678 reporting that they spoke French, Cajun French or Creole at home.

Actions launched since 1968 for the preservation of the FRENCH LANGUAGE and culture in Louisiana (the French movement) include designating French as the officially recognised second language of the state, and the founding of the Council for the Development of French in Louisiana (CODOFIL), which supports French-language educational programmes. (**Marie-Anne Hintze**)

Further reading

Valdman (1997) provides a comprehensive treatment of the overall linguistic situation of Francophone Louisiana. See also Rossillon (1995) for maps and figures concerning numbers of speakers and institutions, and Henry (1993) for a discussion of the CODOFIL's role in the French movement.

Lounès, Matoub   Born 1956; assassinated 1998. Algerian musician. A self-taught performer, Lounès acquired popularity for his interpretations of traditional TAMAZIGHT material, before composing his own. Often confused with RAÏ, his music shared its irreverent stance towards religious and political authorities (cf. his *Tamazight* interpretation of the Algerian National Anthem in 1998). However, unlike *raï*, Lounès's arrangements were almost entirely acoustic, centred on his lute-playing. He sang simple lyrics, in *Tamazight*.

Lounès's politicisation began with his military service, when he saw how KABYLE recruits were insulted. He participated in the 1980 Kabyle revolt. His music grew popular with Kabyle youth, and among migrants in France, with two sell-out concerts at the prestigious Paris venue, Zenith, in 1995. Wounded by gunmen in 1988, kidnapped by Islamists in 1994, he went into four-year exile in France. In the fatal attack of June 1998, blamed on GIA Islamists, three bullets were fired into his head.

Never openly a party-member, his stubborn defence of SECULARISM and demand for *Tamazight*/Arabic linguistic parity were close to the politics of the Kabyle-based RCD (Rally for Culture and Democracy) in the mid-1990s. (**Sharif Gemie**)

Lumumba, Patrice   Born Onalua, Congo, 1925; died 1961. First Prime Minister of independent Congo in 1960. Almost immediately, the provinces of Katanga and Kasai attempted to secede, backed by Belgian force, leading Lumumba to turn to the Soviet Union for assistance. In late 1960, General MOBUTU seized power and Lumumba was imprisoned, then executed in January 1961 (CIA and Belgian involvement in his death is widely suspected). Lumumba's death was seen by many as an illustration of the failure of DECOLONISATION, and he has been heralded as a martyr by later generations of African radicals. (**David Murphy**)

Ly, Ibrahima   1935–89. Malian writer. He studied in Dakar and France, and was President of FEANF (Federation of African Students in France). Returned to MALI in 1973 but was imprisoned in Bamako for four years in 1974 by the Moussa Traoré regime. Due to resulting ill-health he completed only one novel, *Toiles d'araignées* (1982), and left a second incomplete at his death – *Les Noctuelles vivent de larmes* (1990; published in the collection *Paroles pour un continent*). His pessimistic view of Africa's present ills is that they go back to precolonial roots, and are due to the persistence of traditional attitudes. (**Denise Ganderton**)

Maalouf, Amin   Born Beirut, 1949. Lebanese writer. Maalouf studied sociology. He began working for the weekly *An-Nahar* in 1971. The quality of his reporting allowed him to make many journeys in Africa and Asia. Maalouf settled in Paris in 1976, working as a journalist, and in 1983 published his first book, *Les Croisades vues par les Arabes* (*The Crusades through Arab Eyes*, 1984). In 1986 he published his historical novel *Léon l'Africain* (*Leo the African*, 1988), which was marked by its great narrative drive. His interest in the great Persian poet Omar Khayyam resulted in the writing of another novel, *Samarcande* (1988; *Samarkand*, 1992). This was followed in 1991 by a fictionalised autobiography, *Les Jardins de lumière* (*The Gardens of Light*, 1996), and by *Le Premier siècle après Béatrice* in 1992 (*The First Century after Beatrice*, 1993). Moving between fiction and history, he displayed his great narrative gift in his fifth novel, *Le Rocher de Tanios* (1993; *The Rock of Tanios*, 1994), which won the Prix Goncourt. He then turned to the question of exile in *Les Echelles du Levant* (1996; *Ports of Call*, 1998). This panoramic narrative describes the life of a man and his family who move between the Middle East and France in the form of a therapeutic conversation between the two main protagonists, Ossyane and his interlocutor. (**Kamal Salhi**)

Machoro, Eloi   New Caledonian KANAK independence leader. He was killed by gendarmes in 1985.

Madagascar   An island republic off the south-east coast of Africa. Population 14,592,380 The population of the 'Grande Ile' is made up of peoples of African extraction, living mainly around the coasts, and others of Melanesian origin, who came originally from South-east Asia to settle in the central highlands, bringing with them the distinctive Malagasy language. The island was politically unified under a monarchy only in the late eighteenth century, but soon became the object of Franco-British colonial rivalry, with the French finally imposing their military presence in 1896. Traces of British missionary influence survive, however, in the large Protestant community. Catholicism is widely practised, as are the strong local animist traditions; there is also a small Islamic minority. Resistance to the French colonial presence grew after the Second World War, with a brutally suppressed uprising in 1947. The country finally achieved independence in 1960, under a republican constitution. This was ousted in 1972 by a military *coup*, which brought in a Marxist regime, subsequently headed by Didier Ratsiraka, who remained in power until overthrown in 1991. Under a new and democratic republican regime Ratsiraka was re-elected as President in 1996. The impoverishment of the country, a legacy of the Marxist years, has still not been reversed, aggravated by a series of tropical storms which devastated the east of the country in 2000. The French presence has re-asserted itself, and the policy of 'Malgachisation' of the education system under the Marxist regime has been abandoned since 1992. With French help, the tourist industry is beginning to grow, the national university network is being restored, and the enormous mineral resources of the island are beginning to be exploited. The unique island heritage of flora and fauna is being preserved from the encroachment of agriculture and forestry, and the impoverished urban environment of the capital Antananarivo gradually improved. Although there exists a strong literary tradition using the Malagasy language, publishing outlets are limited, and many writers use French to reach a wider audience, through prize-winning plays, novels and poetry, widely appreciated in Francophone literary circles. Malagasy popular music has found an appreciative audience in international World Music festivals, and the island's distinctive flora and fauna are often celebrated in natural history programmes for television. (**Peter Hawkins**)

Madani, Abassi   Born 1936. Algerian politician. He is leader of the Algerian FIS party (*Front Islamique du Salut*). In 1954, he was imprisoned for the duration of the ALGERIAN WAR OF INDEPENDENCE following an attack on a radio station. He came into prominence during the 1988 riots against one-party rule by the FLN. Although the FIS technically won the 1991 legislative elections (see ALGERIAN ELECTIONS, 1991). Madani was imprisoned for threatening state security after riots and a strike preceded them. He was released in 1997 when the military wing of the FIS declared an unconditional cease-fire. (**Susan Fox**)

Further reading

Labat (1995).

Maghreb   See ECONOMY; FOOD; LITERATURE; MUSIC; SPORT.

Maillet, Antonine   Born in the Acadian community of Bouctouche, New Brunswick, 1929. Canadian writer. She studied in Moncton and Montreal, taught literature and worked for Radio Canada in Moncton. She has also worked in the theatre and as a translator. Her socio-critical novels usually describe the Acadian region and its culture by depicting the life of simple, energetic characters in a language resembling sixteenth-century French. In 1979, *Pélagie-la-Charrette* was the first novel written by a non-French author to receive the Prix Goncourt. Key texts: *Pointe-aux-Coques* (1958); *On a mangé la dune* (1962); *La Sagouine* (1971); *Pélagie-la-Charrette* (1972; *Pélagie*, 1982); *Par derrière chez mon père* (1972); *Don l'Orignal* (1972; *The Tale of Don l'Orignal*, 1978); *Gapi et Sullivan* (1973); *Mariaagélas* (1973; *Mariaagélas: Maria, Daughter of Gélas*, 1986); *Évangéline Deusse* (1975; *Evangeline the Second*, 1987); *La Veuve enragée* (1977); *Cent ans dans les bois* (1981); *La Contrebandière* (1981); *La Gribouille* (1982); *Crache à pic* (1984; *The Devil is Loose*, 1986); *Le Huitième jour* (1986; *On the Eighth Day*, 1989); *L'Oursiade* (1990); *Les Confessions de Jeanne Valois* (1992); *Le Chemin Saint-Jacques* (1996); *Chronique d'une sorcière de vent* (1999). (**Susanne Heiler**)

Further reading

Maillet and Hamel (1990).

Makiadi, François Luambo   See Franco.

Malek, Redha   Born 1939. Algerian politician and diplomat. Member of the delegation which signed the Evian Agreement in March 1962, he also helped to draw up the 1962 Tripoli Programme. Afterwards a diplomat, he was a key figure in the negotiations to free the US hostages in the Teheran embassy siege. In 1992, after Boudiaf's death, he was co-opted on to the High State Council (HCE) and served first as Minister of Foreign Affairs under Belaïd Abdesselam and then as Prime Minister from August 1993 to April 1994. Anti-Islamist, he saw Algeria's first priority to be economic reform and was central to the negotiations in 1993 with the IMF. (**Kay Adamson**)

Mali   Landlocked, desert or semi-desert country (1,241,231 sq. km), bounded by Algeria, Burkina Faso, Guinea, Côte d'Ivoire, Mauritania, Niger and Senegal. Highest temperatures occur from April to July; the rainy season is June–September. There are two main rivers, the Senegal and the Niger. Of the 11 million inhabitants, approximately 1 million live in the capital, Bamako; 47 per cent of the population is below 15 years of age, 3 per cent over 65 years, with life expectancy at 46.66 years and the fertility rate: 6.89 children per woman. On the HDI (Human development indicator) Mali comes 165th of 174 countries. It is a poor country, with 80 per cent of the people engaged in farming and fishing. Most of the population are Muslim (90 per cent), with 9 per cent holding indigenous beliefs and 1 per cent being Christian.

French, the official language, is spoken by *c.* 10 per cent. There are thirteen 'national' languages: Bambara is widely spoken (80 per cent), and there are regional languages – Fulfulde (Peul), Tamasheq, Songhai, Soninke (Marka, Sarakole) – and local languages – Bobo (Bomu), Bozo, Dogon, Khassonke, Malinke, Miniyanka (Mamara), Moor (Arabic, Hassaniya), Senoufo (Shenara). Many people speak more than one language.

The currency of Mali is the CFA FRANC. GNP: 2.6 billion dollars, $250 per capita (1998). The main exports are cotton, gold and livestock; 2.2 per cent of GNP was spent on education in 1998, with a gross enrolment rate of 48 per cent, and 60 per cent or more of the population being illiterate. Since 1992, AEEM (*Association des Elèves et Etudiants Maliens*) has led violent student strikes that hamper schooling.

Mali has a rich cultural and historic heritage. Its long history dates from the medieval empires of Ghana (eighth to twelfth centuries), Mali (thirteenth to fifteenth centuries – founded by SOUNDIATA), and Songhai (fifteenth to sixteenth centuries), with its capital at Gao and Koranic centres of learning at Djenne and Tombouctou. These empires were followed by the Bambara kingdom of Segou (seventeenth to nineteenth centuries) and the Fulani kingdom of Macina (nineteenth century) up to the French colonisation, which took place in 1880–95. As a French colony the country was known as the French Sudan until 1960, when the independent republic of Mali was proclaimed on 22 September (now a national holiday). In 1968 the first president, Modibo Keita, was overthrown in a military *coup*, led by Moussa Traoré – himself overthrown in 1991. Amadou Toumani Touré led a transitional government until the democratic elections in 1992, which were won by Alpha Oumar KONARÉ. The ending of the Tuareg rebellion of 1990–96 was marked by the burning of weapons in the 1996 'Flame of Peace'. (**Ingse Skattum**)

Further reading

Konaré (2001); http://www.odci.gov/cia/publications/factbook/geos/ml/html – wealth of facts, updated statistics.

Mambety, Djibril Diop   Born Dakar, SENEGAL, 1945; died 1998. Senegalese film director. Generally considered to be Africa's first avant-garde director, Mambety came to film via the theatre. His best known work, *Touki-Bouki* (The hyena's voyage, 1973) is a visually stunning film that borrows from Western experimental cinema but is also heavily influenced by oral narrative traditions from his native Senegal. After a long break, Mambety directed another celebrated, but less experimental, film, *Hyènes* (Hyenas, 1992), based on a Friedrich Dürrenmatt play. In the 1990s, he began but did not complete a trilogy of short films about Dakar before his untimely death. (**David Murphy**)

Mami   See CHEB MAMI.

Mammeri, Mouloud   Born in ALGERIA (KABYLIA), 1917; died 1989. Algerian scholar and writer. After primary schooling in his home village, he studied at the Lycée Gouraud in Rabat (MOROCCO), and the Lycée Bugeaud in Algiers, after which he went to France to study at Louis-le-Grand Lycée. After the Second World War, he was employed as a teacher of literature. In 1952 he made himself widely known with his controversial novel *La Colline oubliée*. In the post-independence period he was

Professor of Anthropology at Algiers University, and pioneered the teaching of the BERBER language. Mammeri safeguarded Berber cultural heritage, including popular poetry and folk-tales. He died in a car accident in 1989. (**Zahia Smail Salhi**)

Further reading

Salhi, Z. S. (1999).

Mangrove   Swampy forest found in tropical climates, which produces ariel ROOTS that form a dense, tangled network. For contemporary Caribbean writers, the mangrove provides a powerful metaphor for identity. In Maryse CONDÉ's best-known novel, *Traversée de la Mangrove*, it figures primarily as a stagnant, foreboding and impenetrable space, reflecting perhaps the condition of contemporary GUADELOUPE. The CRÉOLITÉ writers see the mangrove's proliferation of interlacing roots in more positive terms, declaring that 'La créolité est [...] notre mangrove de virtualités' (*Eloge de la créolité*, p. 28). CHAMOISEAU evokes the threatened (but ecologically essential) mangrove extensively in *Texaco* to elaborate the precarious state of CREOLE culture. (**Maeve McCusker**)

Manifeste du peuple algérien   Composed by moderate nationalist Ferhat ABBAS and published on 10 February 1943, the Manifesto was a charter of reforms calling for the abolition of colonialism, the right to Algerian self-government, and proposing a fully democratic constitution for ALGERIA. The Manifesto, breaking with the assimilationist perspective (see *ASSIMILATION/INTÉGRATION/INSERTION*), spoke of a sovereign Algerian nation and an Algerian state. The document, signed by both moderate and radical Algerian leaders, was presented to Governor-General Peyrouton on 31 March 1943 and to the Allies. Peyrouton formed a Franco-Algerian commission which produced the *Additif*, a specific set of reforms rejected after the Free French arrived in Algeria (1943). (**Marianne Durand**)

Further reading

Kaddache (1980) – Chapter 20 deals in detail with the Manifesto of the Algerian People and its significance in the history of Algerian nationalism.

Mankiewicz, Francis   1944–99. QUEBEC film-maker, best known for *Les Bons Débarras* (1980), from an original film script by the legendary Réjean DUCHARME, a touching and powerful depiction of a one-parent family, which also symbolises the social evolution of Quebec. The same themes of difficult family relationships occur in *Les Beaux Souvenirs* (1981), a less successful collaboration with Ducharme, *Le Temps d'une chasse* (1972) and *Les Portes Tournantes* (1988). (**Ian Lockerbie**)

Maran, René   Born Fort-de-France, MARTINIQUE, 1887; died 1960. Writer and colonial civil servant. He wrote novels, short stories and biographies of African explorers. His parents were Guianese, but he was born in Martinique and educated in Bordeaux. While an administrative officer in French Equatorial Africa, he began work on *Batouala, véritable roman nègre* (1921; *Batouala*, 1922), a novel combining detailed descriptions of African village life with an indictment of the French colonial system. Maran was the first Black author to win the Prix Goncourt with this polemical text. He published a sequel, *Djouma, chien de brousse* (1927), an account of colonial culture seen through the eyes of Batouala's dog. Maran continued to publish widely until his death. His subsequent work attracted little critical attention, undoubtedly because it was eclipsed by the more affirmative voices of authors associated with the NÉGRITUDE movement. (**Charles Forsdick**)

Marche des Beurs   See MARCHE POUR L'ÉGALITÉ ET CONTRE LE RACISME.

Marche pour l'égalité et contre le racisme   Also known as *La marche des Beurs* (the BEURS' March), this diverse ANTIRACIST social movement (comprising mostly young descendants of North African migrants from Lyons), left Marseilles on 15 October 1983, eventually reaching Paris on 3 December 1983 in a blaze of media attention, accompanied by 100,000 supporters. The march protested against the wide levels of racial attacks and institutionalised discrimination encountered by many young people from France's run-down public housing estates. The concrete gains of the protest were slim (a ten-year foreigners' residency card was introduced). Symbolically, however, the march affirmed how multicultural France had become, revealed high levels of everyday RACISM, and represented an important assertion of agency by socially marginalised groups. (**Jim House**)

Further reading

Bouamama (1994) – Chapter 2 describes the key events and themes of the March, whilst the book provides an excellent overview of 1980s antiracist movements.

Marimoutou, Jean-Claude Carpanin   Born 1956. Reunionese poet, lyricist and literary critic. Carpanin's collections of poetry, such as *Romans pou la ter ek la mer* (1995), are usually bilingual, with versions of the same poems in both CREOLE and French. The poems celebrate and explore his complex island identity, and several of his Creole texts, such as 'Saigon'. have become popular song lyrics for the group Ziskakan. Carpanin has regularly written for the group since their earliest years, and is also an eminent academic commentator and analyst of the literary heritage of REUNION. (**Peter Hawkins**)

Mariotti, Jean   Born Farino, NEW CALEDONIA, 1901; died 1975. A New Caledonian writer of European descent. Although he spent most of his adult life in Paris, much of his work is set in the Pacific, including what is considered his major novel, *A bord de l'Incertaine* (1942), which deals with conflicts between the European and Melanesian/KANAK communities and perspectives. Other works include: *Au Fil des jours. Tout est peut-être inutile* (1929), *Les Contes de Poindi* (1941; *Tales of Poindi, c.* 1941), *La Conquête du séjour paisible* (1952) and *Daphné* (1959).

Marronnage   (Marooning). Term used in the Caribbean, originally for the fleeing from the plantations of runaway slaves, who took refuge in the mountains and other isolated places. It is now used to refer to forms of resistance against oppression or cultural control, which may not involve outright confrontation, but rather a variety of tactics to escape from the oppressor's control, ranging from silent passive resistance to alternative economic, cultural and creative projects.

Martinique   There has been a French presence in this Caribbean DOM since the seventeenth century, when a sugar plantation economy was established with the use of African slave labourers, under the control of white settlers, or Békés. Although the French Revolution resonated in the islands, slavery was only abolished in 1848, with the establishment of universal manhood suffrage, allowing male Martinicans to participate in French elections from the time of the Third Republic, yet the island was still ruled by a colonial governor. The major political change came in 1946 with *départementalisation*, the integration of the territory into the new Fourth Republic to give equal status with other French *départements*. The measure was proposed, with a view to ending colonialism, by Aimé Césaire, newly elected *député* in the French Assembly, as well as mayor of Fort-de-France, Martinique's capital, who was to dominate the island's political life for the rest of the century. The contradictions of *départementalisation* soon emerged. Not only was decision-making centralised in Paris, it coincided with socio-economic changes, which saw the sugar-industry's rapid decline, faced with competition from European sugar beet. The once thriving economy was transformed into one with practically no significant production, or products (e.g. bananas, pineapples) made uncompetitive on the world market by European wage rates, which had been fought for as part of the logic of *départementalisation*. Consumption of imports from France, however, has boomed. The result has been endemic unemployment (approx. 30 per cent), particularly amongst young people (up to 50 per cent), with emigration to mainland France encouraged, and, at the same time, a high standard of living comparable with Europe, as a result of French grants, subsidies and social welfare. The paradoxes of this state of well-off dependency have created a sense of social dislocation and problems of identity. These have been clearly articulated by thinkers and writers, such as Glissant, Chamoiseau, Confiant and Bernabé, as part of a vibrant intellectual and literary culture on the island. (See also Creole, *créolité*, Education, Literature, Music.)

Further reading

Burton and Reno (1995) – a collection of essays which provides a good introduction to the key economic, social, political and cultural issues in Martinique today, in the context of the other French Caribbean territories.

Marzouki, Moncef   Born 1945. Tunisian doctor, writer and human rights activist.

Masson, Loys   1915–69. Mauritian poet, essayist, novelist, dramatist. As a young man he left his native island in 1939 for France, never to return, but many of his novels dramatise the social conflicts of Mauritian society, such as *L'Étoile et la clef* (1945) and *Le Notaire des Noirs* (1961; *Advocate of the Isle* or *The Whale's Tooth*, 1963). He enjoyed a long and successful literary career in France during the years following the Second World War. (**Peter Hawkins**)

Maunick, Edouard   Born 1931. Mauritian poet and diplomat. Maunick's first collection of poems *Ces Oiseaux du sang* (1954) was honoured by the Académie française, and in 1960 he left Mauritius for Paris, where he worked for the review PRÉSENCE AFRICAINE. His poetic style is reminiscent of that of Aimé Césaire, to whom he dedicated *Toi, laminaire* (1990) and with whom he shares a nostalgia for the imagery of African cultures and the theme of revolt against postcolonial alienation. He was until recently Mauritian ambassador to South Africa. (**Peter Hawkins**)

Mauritania   Country on the Atlantic coast of north-west Africa, bordered by WESTERN SAHARA and ALGERIA to the north, MALI to the east and SENEGAL to the south. The capital is Nouakchott, with a population of 2.4 million, 99 per cent of which is Muslim. The predominant ethnic group is the Arabic-speaking Moors, and the other five Black groups are French-speaking (with local languages), mostly for political reasons. The literacy rate is estimated at 30 per cent. Since independence from France in 1960, huge deposits of minerals and the fishing industry have brought Mauritania prosperity. The 1991 Referendum led to the introduction of a new constitution, which guaranteed certain rights and the protection of the pluralist democratic character of the multi-party electoral system. (**Susan Fox**)

Further reading

Hamody (1995).

Mauritius   Island in the south-west Indian Ocean with a population of 1,159,730. Capital: Port-Louis. A former British and previously French colony, independent since 1968, a republic since 1992 and a member of the Commonwealth. Mauritius has a prosperous and dynamic economy, originally based on sugar cane, which occupies a large proportion of the cultivable land, on textile manufacturing, on tourism and a growing electronic and computing industry. Uninhabited until occupied by the Dutch in 1598, the island has a population of varied origin: a majority from different parts of the Indian sub-continent, a sizeable minority from Sub-Saharan Africa and smaller numbers of Chinese and white Franco-Mauritians. The different communities tend to maintain a strong sense of CULTURAL IDENTITY: Hinduism is predominant, but balanced by a considerable presence of Catholicism and Islam. The official language of administration and government is English, which is also the language of the highly competitive state education system. Most Mauritians speak CREOLE, however, on a day-to-day basis and the media, journalism and literature predominantly use French. Indian languages are widely taught as an option at school, as is Mandarin Chinese. The high standard of living of the island is the result of astute management of its resources: agriculture, but also tourism, which has benefited from the discreet development of the island's seductive coral-reef coastline, and the rapid adaptation of a formerly agricultural workforce to new, technological industries. Even so, many educated Mauritians seek their fortune abroad, and the island maintains strong cultural links with Britain, France, India, South Africa, Australia and the major nations of the developed world. The island already boasts one major university and is about to launch a second, reflecting the strong demand for higher educational qualifications. It also has a distinguished literary and cultural heritage, its poets and novelists well known in Francophone literary circles since the mid-nineteenth century. It shares with REUNION the distinctive local musical and dance tradition of the Sega (see MUSIC, INDIAN OCEAN) and a growing literary and dramatic production in Creole. (**Peter Hawkins**)

Maximin, Daniel   Born 1947. Guadeloupean novelist and poet. He is best known for his triptych: *L'Isolé Soleil* (1981; *Lone Sun*, 1989), *Soufrières* (1987), and *L'Ile et une nuit* (1995). Having studied in France, where he has been based for some time, he writes of the CARIBBEAN in an open perspective. Although his novels are all marked by thematic and textual circulation, the French is not particularly inflected by CREOLE, and the underlying values resonate more with the historical obsession and pan-Caribbean sensibility of GLISSANT's work than with the inscapes of the CRÉOLITÉ movement. Popular or populist culture does not impinge much in this writing, which is underlaid by an extraordinarily dense intertextual network, and by a preoccupation with music. (**Mary Gallagher**)

Mayotte   An island overseas territory since 1841, Mayotte is geographically part of the COMOROS archipelago at the northern entrance to the Mozambique Channel, but attached to France as a result of the 1976 referendum. Population: 128,000; capital: Mamoudzou. The economy of the island is almost entirely dependent on French assistance, but it does export shellfish, essence of ylang-ylang and vanilla, and produces manioc and bananas for local consumption. There is a nascent tourist industry, which has yet to be developed fully. The local population, predominantly Muslim, speak some French and a variety of local Malagasy and African dialects. The island has benefited from the French education system, and its first accredited author, Abdou S. Bacou, in 1996 published a novel in REUNION. (**Peter Hawkins**)

M'Barali, Claude   See MC SOLAAR.

Mbaye, Mariétou   See KEN BUGUL.

MCB *Mouvement Culturel Berbère*   A cultural movement that seeks to defend the specificity of BERBER culture, language and history. Its aims include official recognition of the Berber language and restoration of rights to Berber-speakers by the Algerian authorities, full integration of the Berber language into the education system and the use of the language in public life. The MCB's social programme is opposed to the Arabic–Islamist agenda, most notably on language, culture, history, and its views on political power, MODERNITY and religion. The movement lays claim to territory that encompasses ALGERIA, MOROCCO, TUNISIA, Libya and MAURITANIA, extending into the northern regions of MALI and NIGER. Founded in Algeria in the 1940s, it has continued to exist until the present. It is particularly rooted in KABYLIA, Algiers, among the emigrant community in France and in regions with major concentrations of Kabyles; since the 1970s it has spread to Aurès (eastern Algeria) and M'zab (southern Algeria). Intellectuals supported it during the 1940s and the working classes, university teachers and students in the aftermath of independence. Since 1980 it has enjoyed the support of the entire Kabyle population. (**Kamal Salhi**)

Further reading

Ouerdane (1993).

MC Solaar Born Dakar, SENEGAL, 1969, as Claude M'Barali. French rapper. He was raised in Paris, and became one of the leading figures in the development of French rap music in the early 1990s, under the name of MC Solaar, with songs such as 'Caroline' and 'Le Nouveau Western' enjoying huge success. Composed by a graduate in French literature, Solaar's songs are renowned for their elaborate word play and literary references. This saw him cast by the media as the 'acceptable face' of French rap, capable of marrying 'French' and 'Black' culture. As more 'hardcore' rap acts, such as NTM, with their violent verbal attacks on the police and French society, became popular, Solaar came to be seen as outdated by many rap fans. (**David Murphy**)

Mechakra, Yamina Born Meskiana, Aurès, 1949. Algerian writer who trained and still practises as a doctor. She is most known for her novel on the ALGERIAN WAR OF INDEPENDENCE, *La Grotte éclatée* (1979).

Meddeb, Abdelwahab Born Tunis, 1946. Tunisian writer, broadcaster and editor. His work in many different genres marks a decisive turning-point in modern Maghrebian literature. In addition to his characteristic fragmentary and decentred writing, akin in some respects to that of KATEB YACINE, Meddeb is noted for his translations and adaptations of *soufi* poetry: *Le Tombeau d'Ibn Arabi* (1987), *Les Dits de Bistami* (1989). He is also acclaimed for his role in publishing major Maghrebian authors, as editor of *La Bibliothèque arabe* series, for Sindbad, his work as a presenter of *Cultures d'Islam* for France Culture, and as editor of the review *Dédales*, the theoretical foundations of which are subtly illustrated in his two novels, *Talismano* (1979, revised edition 1987) and *Phantasia* (1986). *Talismano* is the story of the poet's return to his native land, in which real and imaginary images of places visited abroad are interwoven with the new polycultural vision which he brings to bear on his old haunts, through a labyrinthine style, multi-layered with linguistic diversity and pulsating with bio-rhythmic dynamism. In *Phantasia*, the author–narrator wanders through Paris, seeking to grasp the symbolic and cultural interconnections of this 'foreign' city, through the endless quest for the female image, embodied by Aya and always out of reach. The reader is thrust into the fascinating world of the fusion of east and west, in which the writing, through its aesthetic of the fragment and wealth of cultural references, creates an effervescent poetic register, in which the musical and rhythmic variations evoke the theme of the passage and return, between self and other, poet-novelist and reader. Most recent publications: *Matière des oiseaux* (poems, 2001; Prix Max Jacob); *La Maladie de l'Islam* (2002). (**Beïda Chikhi**)

Further reading

Chikhi (1996) for a more comprehensive study of Meddeb's work.

Media, Indian Ocean   All the islands of the south-west Indian Ocean have access to the television channels of RFO, the French overseas television company, broadcasting from REUNION. The other islands also have their own national channels, which feature broadcasting in the local languages other than French: the Mauritian Broadcasting Corporation, for instance, broadcasts extensively in Hindi, with daily showings of Indian films, and regularly in English and Chinese. Reunion also has several privately owned television stations, such as Antenne Réunion and Canal Réunion, a local subsidiary of the French subscription channel Canal Plus. All the islands similarly have access to Radio France International, but local FM stations tend to dominate the airwaves, with a diet of popular music and local news. All the islands have their own local press, usually pluralist, with at least two dailies competing for the attention of the island's readers. In Reunion the two dailies, *Le Quotidien* and *Le Journal de l'Ile*, are respectively left-wing and right-wing in sympathy, corresponding to the political divisions of the island. In MAURITIUS, the two dailies *Le Mauricien* and *L'Express* are both published in French, with occasional features in other languages such as English or Hindi. In MADAGASCAR, one of the popular dailies, *Midi Madagasikara*, publishes extensive articles in Malagasy, although the headlines are usually in French. Reunion and Mauritius both possess a growing computer and software industry, and both islands have established a considerable number of local websites; Madagascar is following suit, but is hampered by lack of resources and poor communications. (**Peter Hawkins**)

Mediterranean   The idea of the Mediterranean as representing a distinct cultural, political, or economic space can be traced back to the time of the Roman Empire. The ending of the Roman Empire, despite the presence of Byzantium at its eastern end, meant that for the next thousand years, the only effective authority to create some kind of global Mediterranean presence was ISLAM. The Moors were established in Spain from the seventh century through to 1492, when the Muslim city of Granada fell to the Catholic monarchs, Ferdinand and Isabella, and the Ottoman Turkish Empire had its capital in Istanbul from the late fifteenth century. However, the modern image of the Mediterranean as a political, economic and cultural space owes its place firstly to the writings of the philosophers of the Enlightenment; and secondly, to the impetus provided by the French Revolutionary wars, and the scientific research expeditions which accompanied them. These incursions culminated in the conquest of ALGERIA, which began in 1830, through which means the French state began to create a new empire in the Mediterranean.

Subsequently, historians such as Fernand Braudel and Henri Pirenne have explored the idea of a Mediterranean unity. During the 1930s and the 1940s, French Algerian writers such as Albert CAMUS (*Le Mythe de Sisyphe*) used the theme of the Mediterranean as a means to explore their ambivalence to their own world of French Algeria, whilst others, such as the poet Paul Valéry, were inspired by a romanticism of a Mediterranean past dominated by images of the troubadours, the crusades and the Renaissance. The break-up of France's colonial empire meant that this idea of a Mediterranean community lost its political imperative. Nevertheless, the idea of the Mediterranean as 'the mother of peoples' is still employed today even if more mundanely expressed through the metaphor of car ferries running between the Maghrebine coastline and France. (**Kay Adamson**)

Further reading

Hordern and Purcell (2000) - provides a contemporary exploration of the meanings which have been attached to the idea of the Mediterranean. They also provide an introduction to the ideas of Braudel and Pirenne, among others.

Mégret, Bruno   Born Paris, 1949. French politician who served during the 1990s as second-in-command to Jean-Marie Le Pen, leader of the extreme right-wing Front National (FN). He had earlier been a member of the centre-right RPR party, which he quit to run as a FN parliamentary candidate, becoming a *député* in 1986. Rivalry between Le Pen and Mégret led to a split in the FN in 1998. Mégret's breakaway party, the *Mouvement National Républicain* (MNR), fared badly in subsequent elections and the FN also lost votes in spite of Le Pen's breakthrough to the second round of the 2002 presidential election. (**Alec G. Hargreaves**)

Further reading

Jarreau (1997) offers an incisive political profile.

Memmi, Albert   Born Tunis, 1920. Jewish writer and academic. A sociologist, he is interested also in psychoanalysis. His seminal text *Portrait du colonisé, précedé du portrait du colonisateur* (1957; *The Coloniser and the Colonised*, 1965) has a preface by Jean-Paul Sartre. His sociological studies include studies on Jewish identity, e.g. *Portrait d'un juif* (1962; *Portrait of a Jew*, 1962), and racism, e.g. *Le Racisme* (1982; *Racism*, 2000). He wrote introductions for early anthologies of Maghrebian literature in French (1964; 1969). His novels include: *La Statue de sel* (1953; *Pillar of Salt*, 1955) with a preface by Albert Camus; *Agar* (1955; *Strangers*, 1960); *Le Scorpion* (1969; *The Scorpion, or The Imaginary Confession*, 1971). Recently he has published his autobiography, *Le Nomade immobile* (2000). (**Debra Kelly**)

Memory   With a series of official commemorations celebrated towards the end of the twentieth century (bicentenary of the French Revolution, 1989; 150 years since the abolition of slavery, 1998), memory has become the subject of often controversial debates in France. Much attention has been focused on the Vichy period, with the result that an overabundance of collective memories has led to what historian Henry Rousso describes as the 'Vichy syndrome'. This willingness to recall the Occupation, especially in literature and film, has not triggered any similar interest in memories of the French empire. Some commentators have claimed that such near obsession with Vichy disguises a deep-felt anxiety about France's colonial legacy (and in particular about the defeats in the Indochinese and the Algerian Wars). As a result, major events such as the 1931 *Exposition coloniale* or the *Bataille de Paris* have slipped from collective memory.

Metropolitan memory and colonial memory remain, however, closely interrelated, and such a schematic division of the two is largely misleading. As Bertrand Tavernier makes clear in his 1989 film, *La Vie et rien d'autre*, official memories of the First World War have customarily excluded the (nevertheless considerable) contributions of colonial troops (*tirailleurs indigènes*). The bicentenary of the French Revolution forced historians to acknowledge the importance of the revolution in HAITI for the direction of events in France itself. Yet as OCTOBER 1961 revealed, French amnesia persists in relation to its colonial wars, and it is only recently that individual memories of the widespread use of torture in ALGERIA have led to official recognition of the practice. Moreover, works such as *La Guerre sans nom* (1992), Tavernier's documentary portrait of French conscripts in Algeria, and Yamina BENGUIGUI's *Mémoires d'immigrés* (1997) suggest that a consensus of commemoration, dependent on selective, 'official' versions of history, is being replaced by a more complex and searching form of postcolonial memory, in which the individual and collective intersect. (**Charles Forsdick**)

Further reading

Nicolaïdis (1994) contains useful essays on various aspects of colonial memory; Wood (1999) includes an introduction to debates about memory in contemporary France and chapters devoted to Algeria.

Menil, René Martinican philosopher. He was influenced by Surrealism and Marxism. As a student in Paris, he was associated with Etienne Lero and Jules Monnerot, in the production of the anticolonialist *Légitime Défense* (1932). Upon his return to Martinique, he co-founded with Aimé and Suzanne CÉSAIRE the literary review *Tropiques* in 1939. Remaining in the Martinican Communist Party, unlike Césaire, he wrote scathingly on some aspects of NÉGRITUDE and is credited with first formulating the notion of ANTILLANITÉ – or specific West Indian culture (Burton and Reno, 1995: 146). His essays were published in *Tracées* (1981).

Mernissi, Fatima Born Fez, MOROCCO, 1940/41. Moroccan sociologist. She was born only 500 metres away from the Qarawiyin University, one of the most ancient centres of learning in the Maghreb. Her schooling began in local nationalist schools in colonial Morocco, and continued at the Mohammed V University in the postcolonial period. She obtained her PhD in sociology at Brandeis University, Massachusetts, USA, in 1973. Her thesis was later published as *Beyond the Veil: Male–Female Dynamics in a Modern Muslim Society* (1975), a book that made her well known as a sociologist whose work focused on the issue of Muslim women. (**Zahia Smail Salhi**)

Further reading

Mernissi (1988; 1994; 1995).

Messaoudi, Khalida Born Sidi Ali Moussa, KABYLIA, 1958. Algerian feminist politician and anti-fundamentalist activist. Messaoudi, a mathematics teacher, became active in the WOMEN'S MOVEMENT, campaigning from 1981 against the introduction of the FAMILY CODE. Active in the AITDF (*Association pour le triomphe des droits des* *femmes*) from 1990, she failed to get the requisite number of signatures to stand in the 1991 elections, but was elected to the Algerian parliament in 1997 for the RCD, of which she became vice-president in 1993. Following disagreements with the RCD leader, Saad Saadi, and a hostile reception in Tizi Ouzou in May 2001, she decided to leave the RCD and concentrate on the feminist organisation *Rachda*. Her book, *Une Algérienne debout* (1995; *Unbowed: An Algerian Woman Confronts Islamic Fundamentalism*, 1998), written in conjunction with Elisabeth Schemla, is based on the accounts of women terrorised by armed fundamentalist groups.

Further reading

Messaoudi (1995).

Métissage See Hybridity.

M'Fouilou, Dominique Born 1942. Congolese writer, whose publications include *La Salve des innocents* (1979), *Les Corbeaux* (1980), *L'Inconnu de la rue Mongo* (1999), *Ondongo* (2000).

Michaux-Chevry, Lucette Born Guadeloupe, 1929. Lawyer and politician. She is a major political figure in the French-speaking Caribbean islands. Like many of her fellow citizens, she went to metropolitan France to pursue her higher education. She graduated from the Sorbonne and became a lawyer in 1954. Her political career started in 1957, following her election as town councillor for Saint-Claude. It took off after 1972 when she was elected President of the Council for Guadeloupe. She then occupied various political posts, including General-Secretary for Francophonie (1986), Deputy for Guadeloupe (1988, re-elected 1993), Minister for Humanitarian Action and Human Rights (1993), Mayor and Senator of Basse-Terre (1995), adviser to President Chirac (1995). She is currently town councillor for Basse-Terre and President of the Council for Guadeloupe. The 'Iron Lady' of Guadeloupe has been involved since 1995 in a controversy regarding the whereabouts of a large amount of money allocated for reconstruction projects following hurricane damage in Guadeloupe. Although there has not been sufficient proof to convict her, the accusation has, to some extent, tarnished her reputation. (**Marie-Annick Gournet**)

Micone, Marco Born Montelongo (Molise, Italy), 1945. Italian dramatist, writing in French. He emigrated from Italy to Montreal, Quebec, in 1958. After publishing a study of the plays of Marcel Dubé, he has taught at various institutions, among them the University of Montreal. Based on his observations of the importance of immigrant culture for Canadian society, Micone supports a policy of cultural hybridisation, which creates mutual, new benefits instead of keeping the multicultural society rigidly segregated. He has translated Italian writing into French. Key texts: *Gens du silence* (1982; '*Voiceless People*', 1984); *Addolorata* (1984; *Addolorata*, in *Two Plays*, 1988); *Déjà l'agonie* (1988; *Beyond the Ruins*, 1995); *Babele* (1989); *Le Figuier enchanté* (1992). (**Susanne Heiler**)

Further reading

Simon (1985).

Migration   People have always moved from one place to another. However, the modern meaning of migration dates from the development of modern capitalism in the West, industrialisation, and the fixing of frontiers between nation-states. Nineteenth-century colonialism established links between metropolitan France and other parts of the world which were largely instrumental in setting up patterns of migration in the Francophone world in the twentieth century. There was already an Algerian community in France in the inter-war period but it was during the post-war period of economic growth in the West that France opened its doors to large numbers of 'colonial' migrants. In the 1960s especially, many migrants came from the countries of North and Sub-Saharan Africa to seek employment in France and then to settle there permanently. With the economic recession of the 1970s, the question of immigration was perceived by some, not only as an economic problem but also as a problem of social integration of different peoples and cultures. At the same time, immigrant associations, antiracist organisations and various social and political commentators argued for a more considered approach to the place of migration (and its ramifications) in the construction of French internal and external relations. Today the question of migration is at centre stage for many countries. Ease of movement of culture, capital, communications and commodities, the construction of Europe, and the growing divide between the richer and poorer countries, have all had a bearing on the facility of and restrictions on movements of people in recent years. Although frontiers are porous when it comes to commodities and communications, authorities are not so hospitable when it comes to human traffic. The danger today is a new backlash by the West against refugees and economic migrants from the poorer countries. (**Max Silverman**)

Further reading

Silverman (1992) – overview of migration flows to France and immigration discourse and policy in the context of the construction and development of the modern nation-state; Wihtol de Wenden (1988) – comprehensive survey of migration flows and immigration policy in modern France.

Milla, Roger   Born 1952. Cameroonian footballer. CAMEROON is known to many because of footballer Milla's exploits in the 1990 World Cup, when the 38-year-old's stylish goals that took the *Lions indomptables* so close to the semi-finals were celebrated with sways of the hips around the corner flag in improvised *makossa* rhythm. Cameroon's flamboyant success forced FIFA to open the competition to more African nations. African player of the year (1975 and 1976) with Yaoundé's Tonnerre, he left for a decade with French clubs, where he felt exploited. He has been voted African player of the century, and Cameroon, African team of the century. (Geoff Hare)

Further reading

Rühn (2000).

Mimouni, Rachid   Born Boudouaou, ALGERIA, 1945; died 1995, when a wave of assassinations was claiming the lives of many of his friends – writers, poets, playwrights.

He is one of the most widely read Algerian writers. His work has links with the oral tradition of great mythical tales, yet he also made use of modern narrative techniques and cinematic writing. A prolific author, denouncing the evils of colonial and post-colonial society, Rachid Mimouni proved to be a great novelist and a master of the genre's conventions, producing texts which are highly readable. His works, *Le Fleuve détourné* (1982), *Tombéza* (1984), *L'Honneur de la tribu* (1989; *The Honour of the Tribe*, 1992) were honoured with several prestigious prizes. His pamphlets against Islamic fundamentalism, particularly *De la barbarie en général, de l'intégrisme en particulier* (1993), earned him the wrath of the terrorists. After death threats against his family, he became an exile in Tangiers, 'a city which rhymes with Algiers', where he hoped to find a home from home. However, to his great disappointment, he found his absence from Algeria unbearable. (**Beïda Chikhi**)

Further reading

Chikhi (1997).

Miron, Gaston   Born Sainte-Agathe-des-Monts, 1928; died Montreal, 1996. QUEBEC writer and politician. For almost half a century, Miron played an important part in Quebec's intellectual life. He co-founded the publishing house L'Hexagone (1953), and did much to promote Quebec literature. He owes his public fame to a single book, re-edited several times, the collection of poems, *L'Homme rapaillé* (1970; *Embers and Earth*, 1984, a bilingual edition). His poetry is close to spoken language (Miron was famous for his recitals) and dedicated to Quebec and the construction of national identity. Miron as *homo politicus* was a strong defender of the idea of Quebec independence. (**John Kristian Sanaker**)

Further reading

Etudes françaises (1999) – well-documented special issue.

Missionnaires d'Afrique   The *Missionnaires d'Afrique*, popularly known as the 'White Fathers' (*PÈRES BLANCS*), were founded in 1868 by the bishop of Algiers, the future Cardinal Lavigerie. He saw them as the means by which he would be able to proselytise the Catholic faith amongst ALGERIA's Muslims whilst at the same time responding to the failure of the Mac-Mahon goverment to deal with the 1868 famine in KABYLIA. In 1878, Pope Leo XIII allowed them to extend their missionary role to the Sudan and central Africa where their political importance gave them a leading role in the transfer of the Bemba kingdom to British rule. (**Kay Adamson**)

Mitterrand, François (Maurice Marie)   Born Jarnac, 1916; died Paris, 1996. French statesman. He grew up in a rural middle-class Catholic milieu. After studying law in Paris, he enlisted and was captured by the Germans in 1940. He escaped in 1941 and worked simultaneously for the Vichy regime and the Resistance.

He was elected to parliament in 1946 and led a centrist grouping, the *Union Démocratique et Socialiste de la Résistance*. He held numerous cabinet posts (e.g. Minister for France's Overseas Territories, Interior Minister) during the Fourth

Republic before becoming the presidential candidate of the Left. He was twice defeated (1965, 1974), twice elected (1981, 1988) and twice forced to share power with right-wing prime ministers (1986–88, 1993–95).

As the first left-wing President of the Fifth Republic, he introduced socialist economic policies and became a champion of the Third World. He called for a New International Economic Order, advocated debt relief and promised to re-direct aid away from Francophone black Africa towards left-leaning states in Latin America. By 1983, however, he was facing recession and had to abandon these reforms. He restored privileged relations with autocratic Francophone African presidents, resumed French military interventions in Africa and, in 1984, established an advisory council to organise the first FRANCOPHONE SUMMIT.

In his second septennat, Mitterrand adapted foreign policy to post-Cold War realities. He emphasised European integration, halted NUCLEAR TESTING in the South Pacific and extended French influence in Anglophone countries like South Africa and 'socialist' states like VIETNAM. He also took tentative steps towards 'normalising' Franco-African relations by linking COOPÉRATION to democratic reforms and by authorising the devaluation of the Francophone African (CFA) franc.

Mitterrand's later years were marred by allegations about his Vichyite past (Péan, 1994) and his support for RWANDA's genocidal regime (Krop, 1994). He died in 1996, having secured his place in history as France's longest-serving president. (**Gordon Cumming**)

Further reading

Giesbert (1996) – well-informed biography written in a journalistic style; Krop (1994); Péan (1994); Wauthier (1995) – Part IV gives a readable account of President Mitterrand's African policy.

Mixed families   See FAMILY ISSUES, DIASPORA.

Mobutu, Sese Seko (Marshal)   1930–97. Soldier and political leader. President of Zaire (now DEMOCRATIC REPUBLIC OF CONGO), 1965–97. He was an infamous dictator, renowned for brutal suppression of DEMOCRACY and for his lavish lifestyle. Rising to prominence during the anticolonial struggle against Belgium alongside Patrice LUMUMBA and involved in his assassination, this army colonel took power in 1965, created a one-party state and shifted allegiance between China and USA. Using Bantuisation and Africanisation as a smokescreen, Mobutu liquidated all opposition, and stole the country's considerable natural wealth, stowing away a sum estimated to be equivalent to Zaire's national debt. Opposition to him grew through the 1990s, and he was finally deposed in 1997. (**Andy Stafford**)

Modernity and tradition   Modernity is the term given to the age of Enlightenment in Europe, following the Renaissance, in which ideas of science, emancipation and progress were embraced as the means towards a reinvention of 'Man' and the creation of a more rational and civilised world. Modernity set itself against tradition, superstition and particular belief systems which maintained the privileges of the Church, enforced the divine right of kings and prevented individuals from attaining true freedom and self-expression. The ideas of modernity which underpinned movements of individual and national self-determination in the West were, ironically, often the same ideas which were employed to justify the nineteenth-century colonisation of non-Western countries. Western ideas of rationality, progress and civilisation were used as the yardstick by which to measure all peoples; those still steeped in tradition, myth and religion were deemed primitive in comparison with Western modernity (see UNIVERSALISM). Modernity's spirit of emancipation and enlightenment was therefore dependent on the classification of numerous others as backward and barbarous. Anticolonial movements exposed and challenged the assumptions of Western modernity vis-à-vis the rest of the world and called for a new respect for different traditions and cultures which had hitherto been devalued. A fundamental feature of the contemporary postcolonial world is therefore a profound questioning of the major tenets of Western modernity. Colonialism and the catastrophe of the Holocaust, both of which were planned and executed by those at the very heart of the 'civilised' West, have led many to reconsider, in a more sceptical and critical light, the absolute and abstract truths of Western modernity about progress and the construction of civilised 'Man'. (**Max Silverman**)

Further reading

Bauman (1991) – profound critique of the excesses of modernity and its inhospitable treatment of 'the other'; Touraine (1992) – one of the best overviews in French of the main features and major failings of modernity by the most celebrated contemporary French sociologist.

Mohammed V   1901–61. Member of the Alaowite dynasty, which ruled MOROCCO from 1664, and sultan from 1927 under the French Protectorate. During the period of Vichy domination, he refused to enforce the Nuremburg Laws against the Moroccan Jewish population. He was a persistent advocate for independence. Mohammed, who was a popular figure, ruled as an absolute monarch from 1956. In domestic policy, education, health, employment, energy policy and the tourist industry became top priorities. In foreign policy, Mohammed's claims for Malian and Mauritanian territory in the SAHARA were later dropped. (**Susan Fox**)

Further reading

Entelis (1989).

Mohammed VI   Born 1964. King of MOROCCO in succession to his father, HASSAN II, since 1999. He declared an amnesty for about 8000 convicted criminals, but this did not include political prisoners, among them WESTERN SAHARANS. Mohammed has failed to address alleged human rights abuses by Moroccan troops. On the domestic front, the king has presided over a general liberalisation with some lifting of press censorship, evidence of more open government and firm policies to address the disparity between the country's rich and poor. (**Susan Fox**)

Further reading

Bourqia and Miller (1999).

Mokeddem, Malika   Born southern Saharan region of ALGERIA, 1949. Algerian writer. She studied medicine and practised as a nephrologist before launching a second career as novelist in 1990 with *Les Hommes qui marchent*, a thinly disguised autobiographical account of a childhood spent in a remote desert village. Encouraged by her grandmother, a nomadic tribeswoman who becomes an inspirational icon, storyteller and folk-healer for her people, the young girl defies local tradition to go to school and university. Mokeddem has described her education as 'the first of many journeys into exile' (Franco-Irish Literary Festival, Dublin, April 2001). Other novels include *Le Siècle des sauterelles* (1992); *L'Interdite* (1993; *The Forbidden Woman*, 1998); *Des Rêves et des assassins* (1995; *Of Dreams and Assassins*, 2000); *La Nuit de la lézarde* (1998); and *N'zid* (2001), the title of which is an Arabic word meaning both 'to continue' and 'to be born'). Her novels reinforce the idea of exile as a positive space for women denied a voice in their own country, and *N'zid* raises the hypothetical question 'Supposing Ulysses had been a woman?' Mokeddem describes literature as her true homeland; of nomadic origin, she has no need of roots. Writing, she says, is 'an act of memory'. (**Christine O'Dowd-Smyth**)

Mollet, Guy   Born Flers, France, 1905; died Paris, 1975. Teacher and politician. Mollet joined the Resistance in 1941. He was mayor of Arras 1945–75, parliamentary deputy, and served in two constituent assemblies (1945/46). A SFIO (Socialist Party) activist, Mollet became secretary-general of the SFIO 1946–69. A minister in several Fourth Republic cabinets, he was Premier 1956–57. Noted for supporting a European federation, his commitment to Anglo-French intervention in Suez (1956) and his uncompromising defence of French ALGERIA, he resigned over parliament's refusal to raise taxes to support his policies in Algeria, later becoming senator (1959). (**Marianne Durand**)

Further reading

Lefebvre (2001) – a fascinating account of Guy Mollet's premiership in relation to his policies in Algeria, and in particular his reaction to use of torture by French forces during the Algerian War.

Monénembo, Tierno   Born 1947. Guinean novelist. Monénembo came to prominence with his first novel, *Les Crapauds-brousse* (1979; *The Bush Toads*, 1983), a dry and devastating satire of the socio-political climate of the post-independence dictatorship of Sékou TOURÉ in GUINEA. This forced him into exile, first in Africa and later in France, and many of his novels since then have reflected his nomadic existence, set in France, like *Cinéma* (1997), in Brazil, like *Pelourinho* (1995), or, as in the case of his recent fiction, *L'Aîné des orphelins* (2000), inspired by a visit to post-genocide RWANDA. (**Peter Hawkins**)

Mongo Beti   (Pseudonum of Alexandre Biyidi) 1932–2001. Cameroonian writer. Mongo Beti first came to prominence in the 1950s with a series of anticolonial satirical novels: *Ville cruelle* (published 1954, under the pseudonym of Eza Boto), *Le Pauvre Christ de Bomba* (1956; *The Poor Christ of Bomba*, 1971), *Mission terminée* (1957; *Mission Accomplished*, 1958) and *Le Roi miraculé* (1958; *King Lazarus*, 1960). In fundamental disagreement with the regime of newly independent CAMEROON, from

1960 onwards Mongo Beti remained in France as a political exile for most of his life, only returning in 1993. Apart from political novels such as *Remember Ruben* (1974; Eng. trans. 1980), he published several critical essays such as *Main basse sur le Cameroun* (1972) and *La France contre l'Afrique* (1994), before returning to more traditional novel writing with *Perpétue ou l'Habitude du malheur* (1974; *Perpetua and the Habit of Unhappiness*, 1978). In 1978, he founded a revue, *Peuples noirs, peuples africains*, a forum for criticism of NEO-COLONIALISM in Africa. His recent novels such as *L'Histoire du fou* (1994; *The Story of the Madman*, 2001) continue to present an uncompromising picture of the vicissitudes of everyday life in post-independence Cameroon, where he had recently set up a bookshop. (**Peter Hawkins**)

Morocco   A country of the Maghreb, approximately 446,500 sq. km and with a population of *c.* 30 million. It is bounded on the west by the Atlantic, in the north by the MEDITERRANEAN and to the east and south-east by ALGERIA. Capital: Rabat. Most Moroccans live in the western coastal plains, flanked by the Atlas Mountains (up to 4165m), the Rif mountains in the north (up to 2440m) and the SAHARA desert to the south. The economy is mainly agrarian but there are also rich phosphate resources, some phosphate-based and other industry, and a thriving handicrafts sector, producing textiles, leatherwork, ceramics and carpets. Revenues from expatriate Moroccans and tourism are also significant.

The indigenous people are the BERBERS. Phoenicians, Carthaginians, Romans, Vandals and Byzantines have all had a presence. The first Arab rulers invaded in the seventh century, bringing the conversion of the population to ISLAM. Arab and Berber dynasties succeeded, including Almoravid, Almohad and Sharifian dynasties. The present monarchy belongs to the Alaoui dynasty, which has ruled Morocco since the seventeenth century. In the early twentieth century, Morocco was divided into French and Spanish protectorates and, in spite of the successes of Abd-el-Krim's resistance, regained its independence only in 1956, though Spain continues to hold some territories, including the coastal enclaves of Ceuta and Melilla. Since independence, the country has seen the establishment of a constitutional monarchy and a multi-party system. However, in spite of reforms during the 1990s, the implementation of DEMOCRACY has remained problematical, under the autocratic rule of HASSAN II, from 1961 to his death in 1999, with a repressive regime characterised by disregard for human rights, especially following attempts on his life in 1971 and 1972. A campaign was launched in 1974 to gain control of the WESTERN SAHARA (see GREEN MARCH). Morocco continues to assert its sovereignty over the territory, in spite of international rulings and resistance from the Sahraoui movement, POLISARIO. The new king is MOHAMMED VI.

The official language is Arabic, but French is widely spoken in urban areas, and Spanish in the northern cities. There is a thriving production of literature in French by writers some of whom are of international renown, such as Tahar BEN JELLOUN, Driss CHRAÏBI, Abdelkebir KHATIBI. See also CINEMA; ORALITY; *TAMAZIGHT*.

Further reading

Entelis (1989); Hughes (2000).

Morsy, Zaghloul   Born 1934. Moroccan poet and academic. As well as setting up the first university department of literature in Morocco in the 1960s in Rabat and tutoring those who were to become the key players in Souffles, he has produced some rare and rich poetry. The success and dazzling debut of *D'un soleil réticent* (1969), welcomed by (amongst others) Alain Bosquet and Roland Barthes, was not followed up until *Gués du temps* (1985). He has since had a distinguished career with UNESCO in Paris. (**Andy Stafford**)

Moudjadihin   Muslim fighters engaged in *jihad*. From the Arabic root 'to strive', *jihad* connotes diverse meanings from an individual spiritual struggle towards perfect faith to a physical struggle to propagate Islam. Medieval Muslim law described *jihad* as a divinely endorsed struggle to establish Muslim hegemony over non-Muslims in order to spread Islam. This kind of *jihad* can be self-defence or an attack on un-Islamic regimes. Not every Muslim has a duty to perform offensive *jihad*. *Moudjahidin* are those able-bodied men who execute *jihad*. *Moudjahidin* who die in battle become martyrs and are guaranteed a place and special privileges in Paradise. (**Marianne Durand**)

Further reading

Derradji (1997) – Chapter 9 analyses the impact of *jihad* and the role of the Algerian *Moudjahidin* during the Algerian revolution.

Mouvement Culturel Berbère   See MCB.

MTLD *Mouvement pour le triomphe des libertés démocratiques*   (Movement for the Victory of Democratic Freedoms). See PPA; Belkacem; Ben Bella; Hadj; Harbi.

Mudimbe, V. Y. (Vumbi-Yoka or Valentin-Yves)   Born 1941. Congolese writer and philosopher, currently Professor of French at Stanford University, USA. An influential figure in African and Francophone studies in the USA, Mudimbe made his reputation with novels such as *Entre les eaux* (1973; *Between Tides*, 1991), about an African priest who becomes a resistance fighter, *Le Bel immonde* (1976; *Before the Birth of the Moon*, 1989), a reflection on political corruption depicting the relations between a government minister and a prostitute, and *L'Ecart* (1979; *The Rift*, 1993), an account of the mental breakdown of an African ethnographic researcher. These have been complemented by a series of ambitious philosophical and anthropological essays, such as *L'Autre Face du royaume* (1983), *L'Odeur du Père* (1982) and *The Invention of Africa* (1988), which mount a sustained critique of western Africanist discourse. (**Peter Hawkins**)

Mulroney, Brian   Born 1939. Conservative Prime Minister of Canada 1984–93. He was brought up and educated in Quebec as totally bilingual. His federal premiership was devoted to two causes which had great popular support in Quebec, the pursuit of the Lake Meech Accord (1987), and the North American Free Trade Agreement (1992). The former, like its successor, the Charlottetown Accord, was a failure (see also

BOURASSA), but the latter succeeded and still governs trade relations between Quebec and the rest of the continent. Mulroney left politics in 1993. (**Ian Lockerbie**)

Mururoa   See NUCLEAR TESTING.

Music, Caribbean   Seven main forms of music are associated with French-speaking Caribbean islands: Gwo Ka, Bel Air, Quadrille, Creole Mazurka, Creole Waltz, Biguine and Zouk. Their origins can be traced to the seventeenth century. The first music indigenous to these islands was Gwo Ka in GUADELOUPE and Bel Air in MARTINIQUE. Within both of these there are different rhythmic patterns that were traditionally performed for specific occasions: wakes, work, evening gatherings and other special events. Gwo Ka's roots lie in the slaves' conditions on the plantations; it is an all-embracing form of expression that combines singing, dancing, some percussion and drumming. While Bel Air is no longer widely practised, Gwo Ka is thriving and has become an integral part of Guadeloupean cultural identity. There is an annual Gwo Ka festival in July.

Quadrille, found in the Caribbean in the eighteenth century, is a mixture of music and dance of European and African origin. Unlike Gwo Ka, this music was first adopted by colonists. Major differences include rhythm and instruments. Gwo Ka's main (and sometimes only) instrument is the Ka (drum) while Quadrille has accordion, violin, guitar, bass drum, shaker and *guiro*.

Creole Mazurka is mostly of European origin and was adopted by Caribbean orchestras at the beginning of the twentieth century. Mainly played at balls, today it is almost non-existent. Creole Waltz, belonging to the same period, is very similar to Mazurka. Both can be called 'town music'.

Biguine was the product of a cross-fertilisation of styles but was also influenced by New Orleans jazz. It was played by big bands and was very popular in the twenties. Biguine's popularity spread outside the Caribbean and was played in Parisian nightclubs in the 1930s and 1940s. Zouk finally supplanted it in the 1980s. This new musical form, performed by such musicians as *Kassav*, brought the music of Guadeloupe and Martinique to a wider international audience.

Through its diverse rhythm and forms, Francophone Caribbean music reflects its diverse origins and influences – African, French, Spanish, English and Asian. (**Marie-Annick Gournet**)

Music, diaspora   Adapting Paul Gilroy's (1993) model of diaspora to the Francophone world, we can see that music facilitates the constitution of diasporic communities within France and their communication with other groups around the globe. This process can be oblique and strikingly multicultural: for example, Maghrebi-French rocker Mounsi has related his early interest in the music of James Brown. During the 1970s, young Maghrebi-French listened to African-American music in West African and Caribbean nightclubs in France and travelled to Britain to purchase hard-to-find records by Brown. To help express his minority consciousness, Mounsi incorporated references to Brown and to Chester Himes, an African-American expatriate novelist, into his music (Moreira, 1987).

Cachin (1996) describes rap's immense success in France today. Inspired by African-American and Latino hip-hop culture, musicians progressively infused rap music with Francophone references, synthesising a new product. A significant reason for the success of rap music in France is the similarity in oppressive conditions experienced by (post)colonial minority groups there and in the USA and the resistant, creative responses to them that American youths have made through rap.

Raï provides a third example of Francophone diasporic music. This hybrid, urban musical form combines Western and North African elements and was invented in its present form by Algerian artists in the 1970s and 1980s. Now repackaged by transnational capitalist enterprises for sale as a world music, raï nevertheless exists as diasporic music within North African communities in France, appealing to a sense of homeland. Played at concerts, wedding parties and on ethnic minority radio programmes, raï often circulates on cassettes made in Algeria, helping Maghrebi-French to maintain a sense of attachment to an ancestral homeland. (**Mark McKinney**)

Music, Indian Ocean　All the islands have distinctive local musical styles, which are often not known outside the region. The CREOLE-speaking islands of MAURITIUS, Rodrigues, REUNION and the SEYCHELLES share the tradition of the Sega, the song and dance form developed by the islands' African slave populations in the eighteenth century, and consisting originally of a simple chant and response form accompanied by percussion instruments such as the 'ravane', a kind of tambourine. The sensual dance form was initially regarded as indecent by the colonial authorities, but the style was gradually adopted in the nineteenth century by the white settler population, who added European instrumentation such as the violin. The distinctive 6/8 tempo is slightly disconcerting to Western ears, more used to variations of 4/4 time; the lyrics have often been poetic and sometimes subversive, and almost always in Creole. In recent times the style has been sanitised for tourist consumption, but there has also been a revival of its traditional forms. In Reunion a related form, the Maloya, after many years of repression because of its association with animist rituals, was rediscovered and developed in the 1970s as a vehicle for poetic and political expression by a generation of singers, poets and songwriters, who added the colouring of modern electronic instruments to produce a distinctive Reunionese style; it maintained the use of traditional percussion, however, such as the 'caiamb', a tray-shaped rattle, and the 'rouler', a large bass drum. MADAGASCAR's musical traditions are quite different, but well known throughout the region, and even worldwide. There are several local dance rhythms, such as the 'salegy', and local instruments such as the 'vali', a kind of bamboo harp, feature extensively. Local types of homemade guitar such as the 'kabosy' have led to a considerable expertise on that instrument, and there is also a strong local tradition of a cappella harmony singing. Groups from the region have toured extensively and performed in 'World Music' festivals, but their styles are not as internationally familiar as reggae, for instance, which has been assimilated by many groups from the islands. (**Peter Hawkins**)

Music, Maghreb　The classical ensembles of the Maghreb, which mainly perform ancient Andalusian suites, consist typically of a dozen musicians. The instrumentalists include a number of violin or viola players, a *rahab* player, lute players, drummers, flautists, cellists and a pianist. The ensemble is led by an *ud* (lute) player.

Drumming tradition in the Maghreb countries centres on small, portable drums, such as frame, goblet and kettledrums. The frame drum plays an important role as substitute for the human voice in Islamic religious music. It also lends rhythm for dancing. In Morocco, groups of women may sing to the accompaniment of a frame drum supplied with jingles, a spike fiddle, small cymbals, and kettledrums, each playing her own instrument.

The *Gnawa* brotherhood of Morocco preserves ancient spirit music with West African roots. The *Groupe Jajouka* taps into a deep, mysterious music stretching back into Berber history.

Raï (meaning 'an opinion') originates from western Algeria. Its emergence is generally associated with the migration from rural areas into the cities of western Algeria to escape economic depression, starting in the 1930s. It has simple but characteristic lyrics. *Raï* has incorporated Western instruments into the local repertoire. *Cheb* and *chaba* are the titles given to male and female singers, respectively, of the *Raï* style, e.g. Cheb Khaled. The fact that a great number of singers use the word in their artistic names is perceived as a self-conscious label expressing a rising youth identity in Algeria.

Tunisian music is characterised by the diversity of its modes (*Maqamat*) and variety of the rhythms. The *Nouba* is the oldest and most authentic form of Andalusian classical music. *Chghoul* and the *Bachraf* musical traditions originate from Turkey. Music of the Mashreq has also had an influence on Tunisian music. (**Susan Fox**)

Further reading

Guettat (1980).

Music, Sub-Saharan Africa Musical styles vary widely from one part of Sub-Saharan Africa to another but two basic forms predominate: folk music and pop music (or 'Afropop'). In general, folk music is considered to be the music of a specific community, passed from one generation to another, whereas popular music emerges in 'modern' societies where there is a clear distinction between producers and consumers of music. African folk music generally accompanies specific aspects of daily life – work, storytelling, initiation rites, weddings, funerals – and, in many societies, musicians belong to a specific caste (e.g. GRIOTS in West Africa). There exists a huge variety of percussion, string, wind and keyboard instruments throughout Africa, which form the basis of different folk musics.

Afropop is an extremely hybrid form of music. The first great pan-African popular music was the Congolese rumba of the 1950s (FRANCO, Tabu Ley ROCHEREAU), which borrowed heavily from Afro-Cuban music. From the 1970s, Afropop made increasing use of 'traditional' instruments. For example, MALI's Salif KEÏTA combined Afro-Cuban brass sections, jangling guitars imitating the sound of the *kora* (a 24-stringed West African harp), soaring vocals and often deeply traditional lyrics, expressing the values of Mande culture. Keïta's career also illustrates the changing status of music in Africa: born into a noble family, he was able to overcome his family's disdain for the 'ignoble' career of musician. Afropop reached Western audiences in the 1980s when 'World Music' became popular and many African musicians now base themselves in Paris. Leading Francophone African musicians include Youssou N'Dour (Senegal), Papa Wemba (Congo-Kinshasa), Manu Dibango (Cameroon). (**David Murphy**)

Further reading

Bebey (1975) – interesting overview of African folk music, but very dismissive of Afropop; Ewens (1991) – lively and informative introduction to Afropop.

NAFTA North American Free Trade Agreement   This established a free trade area between Canada, Mexico and the USA. The agreement was implemented in 1994.

Nanga, Bernard   Born Mbakomo, near Yaounde, 1934; died 1985. Cameroonian writer, whose publications include *Les Chauves-souris* (1980) and *La Trahison de Marianne* (1984).

Nationhood/nationalism   Nationalist movements played a major role in defining the shape of the new nation-states which emerged with DECOLONISATION. With independence, there was a shift to nation-building, when the problems of nationhood and national identity could no longer be subsumed in opposition to the colonial power alone. Some of these problems resulted from the artificial boundaries imposed by empire; others were more deep-seated ethnic, tribal, religious, linguistic and cultural divisions. Although the process of national construction was inspired in most cases by variants on the French political model of the nation-state, it has proved difficult to implement in practice, premised, as it is, on a strong national state, a solid democratic tradition and a unifying national culture, all of which have proved problematical in the former French colonies. Different countries have adopted various strategies: in Algeria, for instance, there has been an attempt to forge the unity of the nation through the construction of an Arab-Islamic Republic.

The continuing supremacy of France, in Franco-African relations in particular, has also led the sometimes struggling new nations to look to broader supra-national links, in wider PAN-AFRICAN or PAN-ARABIST entities, though hitherto without much concrete effect. The Francophone movement, in spite of its early idealistic inspiration, has played only a marginal role in reinforcing horizontal ties with other member states. Indeed, it has increasingly become a vehicle for reinforcing vertical relations with the former colonial power, notably through the reinforcement of French cultural influence, particularly on governing ÉLITES and middle classes, but also in the economic and political domains, where the recent reform of Francophone institutions will further strengthen this tendency.

Quebec nationalism has quite different roots, in which the search to maintain a homogeneous cultural and linguistic identity, separate from that of Anglophone Canada, has expressed itself through the formation of a political nationalist movement.

Further reading

On nationhood/nationalism in general – Anderson (1983), Balibar and Wallerstein (1997), Gellner (1983), Hobsbawm (1990); on French nation – Silverman (1992); on Algerian national identity – Majumdar (2000).

Ndadaye, Melchior   See Burundi.

Ndiaye, Marie   Born France, 1967. Writer whose mother is French, her father Senegalese. Published her first novel at the age of eighteen with the prestigious Parisian publishing house, Editions de Minuit. Her second novel, *Comédie classique* (1987), is composed in a single sentence. It was her fourth novel, *En famille* (1990; *Among Family*, 1997), which won her critical acclaim. To date she has published seven novels and one play, *Hilda* (1999; Eng. trans. 2002). (**Nicki Hitchcott**)

N'Dour, Youssou   Born Dakar, Senegal, 1959. One of Africa's most famous musicians and singers, N'Dour created *mbalax*, a dance music based on complex polyrhythms and abrupt changes of tempo. He began his career, in the 1970s, with Senegal's leading pop group, the Star Band, which played Cuban-style rumbas. N'Dour 'Africanised' their style, introducing instruments from local folk musics, before forming his own band. In 1994, he had a worldwide number one hit with 'Seven Seconds' (with Neneh Cherry). In 1998, he wrote and sang (with Axelle Red) the official world cup song, 'Do you mind if I play?' (**David Murphy**)

Néaoutyine, Paul   New Caledonian, pro-independence politician.

Négritude   Political and cultural movement, and theory of Black solidarity and anti-racism, first developed in the 1930s and 1940s, by Aimé Césaire, Léopold Senghor and Léon Damas. Though attempting to unite all Black peoples in the world subjugated by European colonialism and Western racism, it insisted on the centrality of Africa (and hence slavery) in determining Black pride. Launched in Paris in the 1930s, inspired by the Harlem Renaissance and theorised often via poetry, the movement led to the launch in 1947 of the bilingual journal *Présence Africaine*.

Renowned for its lack of a coherent and agreed definition, the movement has often been criticised (rather abstractly) as an antiracist form of 'racism', as it was perceived to promote Black culture as *superior* to White culture. However, a reading of key texts such as Césaire's 1950 speech *Discours sur le colonialisme* (1955) shows the character of the movement as merely a *stage* towards Black liberation and the end of racism, rather than an *end* in itself. Once the cultural imbalance foisted by European colonialism and slavery, whereby Africa and its diasporas were deemed 'inferior' to the advanced West, was challenged and redressed, the need for *négritude* would, argued Césaire, be '*dépassé*' (surpassed). This is the tone of Sartre's renowned 1947 essay 'Orphée noir', and of the writings of FANON. However, critics have rightly pointed out that many African rulers, since independence, have benefited politically from the concept, by twisting it to justify their autocratic regimes, such as that of SENGHOR in SENEGAL (Towa, 1971; Adotévi, 1971), not to mention that of MOBUTU whose 'bantuisation' of ZAIRE drew heavily on *négritude*. Other critics, such as the Nigerian winner of the Nobel Prize for Literature Wole Soyinka (1976), have wondered why, if the tiger does not need to proclaim its 'tigritude', Black people should need to vaunt their 'blackness'. (**Andy Stafford**)

Nelligan, Emile Born Montreal, 1879; died 1941. Most famous French Canadian poet and first to surpass the patriotic poetry encouraged by the authorities until the late nineteenth century. Symbolist, his opus is often compared to that of Baudelaire, Rimbaud and Verlaine. Before the age of 19, Nelligan wrote some 170 poems, published in 1904, after his internment in a mental health hospital. He is especially known for *Le Vaisseau d'or* and *Soir d'hiver*. His poetry is characterised by a high level of musicality in his incantatory style and in his themes (evocation of Saint Cecilia and many musical instruments). His preferred theme is death, explored through the symbols of coffin, corpse, cemetery, loss of childhood, snow, pain and agony. His lyricism still expresses today's concerns for the quest for life that is ultimately found, for Nelligan, in the awareness of death. (**François-Emmanuël Boucher**)

Further reading

Beaudoin (1996); Wyczynski (1999).

Neo-colonialism A political theory, first elaborated by the Ghanaian leader Kwame Nkrumah, which explains how colonial countries maintain their influence and control over ex-colonies, even after independence. Thus, though winning freedom from France, French-speaking countries in Africa seem to be still tightly tied to their old colonial master. With the French franc controlling the monetary system in many of the African ex-colonies, and French companies (especially in oil, gas, and minerals) exploiting Africa's riches, French politicians, and even the French army, pull the strings behind many regimes. Elsewhere, in the French-Caribbean and French-Pacific regions, officially part of France's *département* system, neo-colonialism is alive and well. (**Andy Stafford**)

Neo-Destour The Neo-Destour party, formed by Habib BOURGUIBA, Ahmed Mestiri, Mongi Slim and Saleh Ben Youssef in 1934, was a radical faction of the Destour, or Constitutional party, which led the Tunisian independence movement from 1920. Following independence from France and elections in 1956, Neo-Destour became the governing party, and continued as sole political party under Bourguiba's presidency. After adopting quasi-socialist policies in 1964, the party's name was changed to the Destourian Socialist Party (PSD). Neo-Destour was revamped by President BEN ALI in 1987 to become the Constitutional Democratic Rally (RCD). (**Susan Fox**)

Further reading

Toumi (1989).

New Brunswick   Province in eastern, maritime Canada. The only Canadian province which is officially bilingual (since 1975). The French-speaking population (about 30 per cent) are mostly descendants of the once deported Acadians (see ACADIA). Formerly disparaged, their culture is today most vital. The FRENCH LANGUAGE seems relatively well protected against *ASSIMILATION*, thanks to a complete educational system (from nursery school to university – Moncton has the only monolingual French-speaking university in Canada outside QUEBEC), and due to its geographical concentration: important regions in the north (the Acadian Peninsula), in the north-west (Madawaska, Gloucester, Kent) and north of Moncton are monolingual French-speaking. (**John Kristian Sanaker**)

Further reading

Peronnet (1993) – short historical introduction and useful analysis of the socio-linguistic complexity.

New Caledonia   Situated in the Melanesian area of the south-west Pacific, New Caledonia (*Nouvelle Calédonie*) is made up of a number of islands (the main one being Grande Terre). The archipelago is geographically and ethnically diverse; its capital is Nouméa, in whose district 60 per cent of the total population live. The principal natural resource in the islands is nickel. Agriculture, fishing and tourism are their major industries. In 1774, James Cook was the first European to visit New Caledonia, and he was followed the next year by the French admiral La Pérouse. The French annexed it in 1853, shortly after which a penal colony was opened there. Indigenous revolts following annexation were brutally suppressed. During the Second World War, New Caledonia provided 2000 troops for the Allies; 50,000 American servicemen were stationed there. The archipelago became a TOM (*territoire d'outre mer*) in 1946 and the indigenous population slowly began to win civil rights; disappointment after the inhabitants voted to retain the statute of TOM in 1958 led to growing unrest. Throughout the 1980s, the local independence movement – led by the FLNKS (*Front de Libération Nationale Kanak et Socialiste*) – grew in strength. Attempts to suppress it led to political crisis, hostage-taking and extreme violence, culminating in the massacre at the Gossanah cave on Ouvéa in May 1988. The Prime Minister, Michel Rocard, was forced to intervene directly, with the Matignon Accords (June 1988) both calming tensions in the region and leading to the subsequent Nouméa Accords (May 1998). These triggered a rolling programme of reforms, granting local institutions parity with the French state in governing the archipelago, and will eventually allow residents to vote on full independence. In a novella (1998), Didier Daeninckx has linked the insurrectionary events in New Caledonia of the 1980s to the *Kanak* experience in the colonial period. He suggests that contemporary, postcolonial dilemmas cannot be fully understood without a wider understanding of French imperialism. (**Charles Forsdick**)

Further reading

Aldrich (1993) and Belorgey and Bertrand (1994) give clear accounts of the independence movement of the 1980s, the background to it and its political aftermath. See also Daeninckx (1998).

Ngal, Georges   (Also known as **Ngal, Mbwill a Mpaang.**) Born Mayanda, 1933, in what is now the DEMOCRATIC REPUBLIC OF CONGO. Congolese writer. He has pursued an international career as an academic in Switzerland, Zaïre, USA, France, Belgium, Germany, and LEBANON. His substantial corpus consists of works of literary criticism, including a major study of Aimé CÉSAIRE (1975), as well as works of philosophy and literary theory. His novels include *Giambatista Viko ou le viol du discours africain* (1984), *L'Errance* (1975) (both of which tackle the issues facing the modern African writer, including the difficult balancing of African and European influences, tradition and MODERNITY), *Une Saison de symphonie* (1994), *Un Prétendant valeureux* (1991).

Further reading

Kazi-Tani (2001).

Nganang, Alain Patrice   Born Yaounde, CAMEROON, 1970. Cameroonian writer. He won the Marguerite Yourcenar Prize 2001 for his novel *Temps de chien*. Nganang is also an academic, specialising in the African cinema, who has lived and studied in Germany and taught French and German at Shippensburg State University, USA.

Ngandu Nkashama, Pius   Born Mbujimavi, Belgian Congo, 1946. Congolese writer. A prolific author of novels, poetry, plays and criticism, Ngandu Nkashama is central to the generation of writers who emerged from post-Independence Congo (ex-Zaire). A fierce critic of MOBUTU's regime, he has lived in exile since 1982, teaching in France and ALGERIA. His novels, marked by striking political realism, include *Le Pacte de sang* (1984) and *La Mort faite homme* (1986). The partially autobiographical *Vie et moeurs d'un primitif en Essonne quatre-vingt-onze* (1987) is an acerbic account of his experiences as an African *coopérant* in France in 1981–82. In 2000, he became the Executive Director of the Centre for French and Francophone Studies at LSU (Baton Rouge). He has published numerous critical works and an important bibliography of Francophone African literature. (**Charles Forsdick**)

Further reading

For an account of Ngandu's work, with some biographical details, see Tcheuyap (1998). Spleth (2000) studies Ngandu's account of his time in Essonne.

NGOs/non-governmental organisations   Non-profit making bodies, most of which are financed by private donations and are active in development work in the Third World. Most take the form of voluntary aid associations, charities, churches and pressure groups.

The French NGO community is several hundred strong and focuses heavily on Francophone Africa and war-torn states such as CAMBODIA and LEBANON. Some of the largest and most famous French NGOs work in the medical field and include Bernard Kouchner's *Médecins du Monde* and Nobel Peace Prize winners like *Médecins Sans Frontières* and *Handicap International*. Other well-known organisations include the famine relief agency *Action Contre la Faim*, the human rights group *Féderation Internationale des Droits de l'Homme* and the voluntary service *Volontaires du Progrès*.

But while a handful of French NGOs maintain a high profile internationally, the majority are little known, underfunded and geared towards tackling single issues like women's rights (*Femmes et Changements*) or child sponsorship (*Aide et Action*). In view of their small size and institutional weaknesses, most NGOs have banded together to form 'umbrella groups', like *Co-ordination Sud*. The aim has been to secure a greater share of the official aid programme for grassroots NGO activities. This strategy appears to be working as the French state, which has for years ignored NGOs, has now recognised the need for more official funding of NGO projects. The French government has also begun consulting NGOs systematically in official advisory bodies like the *Commission Coopération Développement* and the *Haut Conseil de la Coopération Internationale*.

Yet the prospect of closer co-operation with government brings its own dangers. NGOs may lose their reputation for independence, may alienate grassroots organisations in developing countries or may find themselves in the front line of diplomatic activities in countries (e.g. RWANDA) where an official French presence would exacerbate tensions. (**Gordon Cumming**)

Further reading

Burnell (1997) – Chapter 9 gives an overview of the challenges facing Western NGOs; www.ibiscus.fr – useful website which includes a comprehensive list (*répertoire*) of French NGOs involved in development work (*Organisations de Solidarité Internationale*).

Ngouabi, Marien   See CONGO; LOPES.

Ngoye, Achille   Born 1944, Belgian Congo (now DEMOCRATIC REPUBLIC OF CONGO). Congolese writer. From journalism and other interests based on the African musical scene in Paris, he has become a writer of crime and detective fiction, some of it based on the fictional African state of Kalina, headed by the Marshal-President Pupu Muntu. Titles include: *Kin-la-Joie Kin-la-Folie* (1993), *Agence Black Bafoussa* (1996), *Sorcellerie à bout portant* (1998), *Yaba Terminus* (1999), *Ballet noir à Château Rouge* (2000), *Big Balé* (2001).

Niger   Landlocked West African country, whose capital is Niamey. The population of 10,355,156 comprises several ethnic groups, namely, 54.1 per cent Hausa; 21.7 per cent Dendi, Songhai and Zerma; 10.1 per cent Fulani; 8.4 per cent Tuareg; 4.2 per cent Kanuri and 0.2 per cent Teda, with a literacy rate of 13.6 per cent; 80 per cent of the population is Sunni Muslim and 20 per cent have traditional beliefs. The official language is French with Hausa, Songhai and other local languages.

Archaeological evidence shows that the area was inhabited in the Palaeolithic period. Various ethnic groups – the Tuaregs, the Hausa, the Zerma and the Fulani – occupied parts of Niger over the centuries and established regional power bases from which to extend their territory. Niger was colonised by the French in 1914 and became a colony in 1922. In 1958, it became an autonomous republic within the French Community and fully independent in 1960.

Niger held its first free and open elections in 1993. A 1995 peace agreement ended a five-year Tuareg insurgency. The government was overthrown by a military *coup d'état* in 1996. Numerous violations of human rights subsequently ensued. Power was assumed in April 1999 by a military junta, which supervised a restoration to DEMOCRACY. A freely elected democratic government took office later that year. Despite legal protection within the Constitution, women, ethnic minorities and disabled persons suffer discrimination in education, employment and property rights. Niger is still recovering from devastating Sahel droughts in the 1970s. Agriculture is the principal economic activity, concentrating on the rearing and export of livestock and the cultivation of groundnuts, millet, and sorghum. Uranium is Niger's chief export. Other mineral reserves are coal, tin and phosphates and unexploited copper, gold, iron, and oil. It is an exceedingly poor country, with debt relief and economic aid covering operating expenses, public investment and fiscal reforms. (**Susan Fox**)

Further reading

Decalo (1997).

Nini, Soraya   Born Toulon, southern France, 1960. Writer of Algerian descent. Her semi-autobiographical novel *Ils disent que je suis une beurette…* (Paris: Fixot, 1993) explores the experiences of an adolescent girl torn between the conformist pressures of her immigrant parents and a desire for personal freedom similar to that enjoyed by her French peers. A film adaptation of the novel was released under the title *Samia* in 2001. (**Alec G. Hargreaves**)

Further reading

McIlvanney (1998) offers a feminist reading of Nini's novel.

Noah, Yannick   Born Sedan, France, 1960. Tennis player and singer. His father is Cameroonian and his mother French. Yannick Noah spent his early childhood in Africa. A successful tennis player in the 1980s and 1990s, he won the French Open at Roland Garros at the age of 23 and led the French team to victory in the Davis Cup in 1991. In 1993, he began his musical career with Urban Tribu and had some success with the song 'Saga Africa'. He has divided his time since between music, tennis and charity work, especially for the organisation *Les Enfants de la Terre*.

Non-Aligned Movement   First convened in Belgrade, in 1961, largely through the initiative of Yugoslavian President Tito. He had expressed concern that an accelerating arms race might result in war between the USSR and the USA. Twenty-five nations were represented at the first conference, with subsequent conferences involving ever increasing participation by developing countries. The administration of the movement is non-hierarchical and rotational, providing all member states with an opportunity to participate in global decision-making. The practice of the Movement is to make decisions by consensus. (**Susan Fox**)

North African Jewish culture   A dynamic interplay of diverse cultural traditions. The essence of North African Jewish culture lies in its diversity. Jewish communities lived within other societies, retaining their cultural and religious traditions from the outset, but at the same time, co-existing peacefully with other groups, whether they were Punic, BERBER or Arab, and sharing linguistic ties and similar customs and traditions. Communal cohesion and external pressures of intermittent discrimination and persecution have reinforced a strong cultural Jewish identity.

Jewish culture arrived in North Africa from Palestine and Phoenicia about 586 BCE, and was interwoven with Punic and Berber tradition and later modified by Arabic culture. Italian Jews, Sephardi refugees from Portugal and Spain in the fourteenth and fifteenth centuries and the French Jews in the nineteenth century brought powerful cultural influences.

Linguistic influences on North African Jewish culture are Sabir (an amalgamation of Italian, Provençal and Spanish), Berber dialects, Arabic, Judeo-Spanish (Ladino), and French. The Maghrebi Jews, particularly after the influx of the Sephardim, made significant contributions to the cultural advancement of Judaism and Jewish culture, with intellectual life thriving in Fez, Tlemcen and Kairouan. These centres of learning were of vital importance in transferring the Hebrew culture from East to West. The Sephardim enriched native Jewish cultural life, introducing Jewish thought of a European orientation, bringing about a resurgence in Jewish scholarship, and also introducing a theatrical tradition, attributable to cultural and religious links with Jews in Italy and the Netherlands. The Sephardim also introduced the esoteric traditions woven into Judaism – the Kabala. During the nineteenth century, the educational and cultural activities of the *Alliance Israélite Universelle*, gave a new impetus to Jewish cultural life in North Africa. (**Susan Fox**)

Further reading

Chouraqui (1998).

North American Free Trade Agreement   See NAFTA.

November 1st 1954   On this date the Algerian FLN began military action against the colonial regime. This revolt resulted in uniting Algerians in a fight against France. The FLN published a tract calling for Algerian independence through armed struggle. On the night of 31 October to 1 November, between midnight and 3 a.m., about seventy attacks of varying intensity and success took place in ALGERIA, ranging from fires, cut telephone wires and home-made bombs to destruction of cork and tobacco stocks and attacks on police barracks; 1 November, also known as *La Toussaint*, is National Day in Algeria, marking the anniversary of the start of the ALGERIAN WAR OF INDEPENDENCE. (**Marianne Durand**)

Further reading

Harbi (1981) – pp. 101–3 contains the unedited tract distributed by the FLN as a declaration of war, on 1 November 1954; Harbi (1984) – looks in detail at the historical context surrounding the start of the Algerian War of Independence.

NTM   *Nique ta mère* ('F**k your mother'). As their name indicates, a hardcore rap group from the Seine-Saint-Denis BANLIEUE. Like IAM, they released their first album in 1991. Their second was boycotted by radio stations because of the track 'Police'. They were sentenced to six months' imprisonment and banned from appearing live in 1996 (later reduced on appeal) because of their inflammatory remarks concerning the police during an anti-FRONT NATIONAL concert. The singer, Joey Starr, has subsequently been sentenced for assaulting a former girlfriend and for firearms' possession. Their fifth album, *Le Clash*, appeared in 2001. (**Samantha Neath**)

Nuclear testing   With the independence of ALGERIA, which deprived France of a nuclear testing site in the SAHARA, President DE GAULLE transferred the experiments to a remote and sparsely populated Pacific atoll, Mururoa, located in French POLYNESIA (with Fantataufa and Hao as back-up bases). Construction of the site began in 1963, and the first test took place in 1966. France carried out over forty atmospheric tests between that date and 1974, despite mounting protests in Polynesia and overseas about deadly nuclear radiation. France replied that pollution was minimal, but nevertheless switched to underground tests (exploding nuclear material in the boreholes of atolls); some 134 tests were conducted until 1992, when President MITTERRAND suspended testing. President CHIRAC resumed the explosions in 1995, which provoked an unparalleled protest by environmental groups, antinuclear political parties and foreign countries, particularly independent South Pacific states, Australia, New Zealand and Japan. The final test took place in early 1996, and the testing sites were then closed. France subsequently signed the Rarotonga Treaty establishing a nuclear-free zone in the South Pacific. The testing had provided substantial employment for French Polynesians (and French expatriates) and injected massive revenue into the territory, but severely tarnished France's regional reputation. Paris always claimed that the tests were necessary for French national security and caused negligible human and environmental damage, but opponents remained unconvinced about their safety or benefits. The RAINBOW WARRIOR incident (1985), in which the French sank the flagship of the ecology organisation Greenpeace in Auckland harbour, symbolised the conflict over nuclear testing. For more than thirty years nuclear testing formed the centrepiece of France's geo-political activities in the South Pacific, contributing a justification for retention of control over its territories and its claims to be a major international power. (**Robert Aldrich**)

Further reading

Aldrich (1993) – see Chapter 9: 'Nuclear testing, the 'New Pacific' and French international policy'; Alomes and Provis (1998) – essays on nuclear testing and the reactions to it.

OAS *Organisation Armée Secrète*   (Secret Armed Organisation). The story of the OAS parallels European settlers' stubborn resistance to equality for Muslim Algerians. The settlers fought bitterly against the granting of the most slender rights to the Muslim majority, even to Muslim élites willing to become French in status, custom and culture, whilst the OAS was to fight independence for Algeria, by all means available. The Algerian War of Independence (1954–62) was reaching its final stages as France, now led by General de Gaulle, exhausted by the heavy financial burden and human losses (eventually costing the lives of over 29,000 French soldiers), had begun negotiations with the Algerian FLN (National Liberation Front). An attempt by a quartet of generals to topple de Gaulle failed. The OAS, led by one such general, Salan, took over, aiming to thwart Algerian independence. Bands of armed settlers began to slaughter as many non-Europeans as they could, and destroy as much of Algeria as their bombs could manage – the aim being, at one and the same time, to derail the peace process and to unleash their own murderous despair. Civilians were murdered in their thousands, so much of Algeria's best went into ruins, the National Library and its rare archives one such loss; Mouloud Feraoun, a writer in French of the first order, another. Most often, the victims were just ordinary people going about their daily business. One day the OAS decided to murder all women servants in French homes, calling it '*Le Jour de la Fatma*'. Scores of women fell to their bullets that day. The OAS failed to derail the peace, though, and Algeria became independent. The losers were the hundreds of thousands of settlers who now had to leave a country they dearly loved. They could no longer remain after the needless bloody episode of the OAS. (**Salah Zaimeche**)

Further reading

Alleg (1981); Courrière (2001); Stora (1993).

OAU Organisation of African Unity   Founded in 1963, the organisation was based in Ethiopia and led by a secretary-general with a four-year mandate. Designed by its founders as a means of uniting the newly independent African nations, the OUA had great difficulty in imposing its will on the emerging states, being virtually powerless to prevent either internal strife within African nations or conflicts between countries. Demand for reform was led by Libya's Colonel Gaddafi, who promoted the idea of an African Union to replace the OAU. After years of negotiations, the African Union was finally agreed in 2001, with an Ivorian, Amara Essy, elected as Secretary-General. This new organisation will eventually have its own parliament with deputies elected in each of the constituent member states. (**David Murphy**)

OCAM *Organisation Commune Africaine et Malgache*   (Common Organisation of African Countries and Madagascar). See *Francophonie*, birth and development.

October 1961 French security forces killed between 150 and 250 Algerians on and around 17 October 1961 before, during and after a peaceful demonstration in Paris by 25,000 supporters of the Algerian nationalist *Front de libération nationale* (FLN) against the night curfew imposed by police chief Maurice Papon; 11,538 protestors were detained. Those killed were shot, beaten, tortured or drowned in the Seine or canals. This explosion of state violence had many causes. Violent repression in the colonies was commonplace, and had been transferred to metropolitan France from the 1930s onwards as the perceived danger of Algerian nationalism increased. In metropolitan France, long-standing public antipathy to Algerians had worsened during the course of the Algerian War of Independence, as had police hostility to Algerians, especially due to FLN armed attacks on security forces. The Gaullist state covered up the massacre, suppressing the limited protests organised by Algerians and their French support networks and deliberately misinforming parliament. The mainstream Left protested far more strongly after the Charonne massacre in February 1962, and the memory of Charonne subsumed that of October 1961. Furthermore, Algerian nationalist leaders, keen to continue peace negotiations with de Gaulle, did not publicise the massacre. However, the memory of October 1961 was kept alive throughout the 1960s and 1970s by Algerian migrant groups, and has resurfaced into the public domain since the 1980s as antiracist and counter-cultural associations have sought to establish a parallel between the October massacre and the high levels of physical and symbolic racism that Algerians and their descendants continue to face. These associations now commemorate the massacre annually and demand official recognition of the numbers killed and of state responsibility. October 1961 has thereby taken on a wider significance as emblematic of racial violence, official impunity, lack of accountability and of France's difficulties in coming to terms with its colonial past (see House, 2001). (**Jim House**)

Further reading

Einaudi (2001) – a vivid reconstruction of the lead-up to and events of 17 October, using FLN archives; Brunet (1999) – detailed but conservative historical examination of security force involvement, using police archives.

OIF *Organisation Internationale de la Francophonie* (International Francophone Organisation). The OIF encompasses the official institutions of *La Francophonie*. The name was adopted at the Ministerial Conference held in Bucharest in 1998, as part of the process of constituting a new political institutional framework for what had hitherto been a somewhat nebulous group of Francophone organisations. See also Francophone institutions; Appendix.

Further reading

See website: http://www.Francophonie.org/oif.cfm

Ontario Canadian province. Whereas Canada is officially bilingual on the federal level, the province of Ontario is officially English-speaking. Although the French-speaking minority is the most important Canadian French-speaking population outside QUEBEC (close to 500,000), it represents less than 5 per cent of the total population of the province and is subject to seemingly irreversible assimilation (see *ASSIMILATION/INTEGRATION/INSERTION*).

Important instruments in the struggle against assimilation are a complete school system in French (in certain areas of concentration), a university network, radio stations, newspapers and an active publishing sector defending a French-Ontarian literature. The defence of French-speaking hospital services has been of great symbolic value. (**John Kristian Sanaker**)

Further reading

Jaenen (1993) – an important contribution to the description of Franco-Ontarian economic, social and cultural characteristics.

Orality in Moroccan culture   Orality is a fundamental ingredient of Moroccan culture. Speech regulates everyday life, and communication is mainly channelled through two oral languages: Moroccan Arabic and BERBER. Orality constitutes a powerful system that deeply shapes the way visual and non-visual representations of cultural roles and values are constructed and perpetuated. Related to seeing and hearing, orality is central to the Moroccan speech community's sensory experience and a valuable source of 'authentic' information.

Orality is related to illiteracy and women, the vast majority of whom are illiterate, mastering only one or both mother tongues. Printed and electronic texts do not reach illiterate women. Monolingual, or even bilingual, Moroccans do not understand mainly French or Standard Arabic movies and television programmes.

Orality has a dual status in MOROCCO: both a 'degenerate', 'vulgar', 'low class' medium of expression, because it is vehicled by non-prestigious languages – Berber and Moroccan Arabic; at the same time, a symbol of identity and authenticity, because of its link with Moroccan cultural specificity.

The power of *lkelma* (the word) is attested in many deep aspects of Moroccan culture, such as marriage contracts, business contracts, and even legacies, until recently conducted exclusively through the oral medium.

Morocco is full of signs that oral literature is strong and alive: storytellers are seen in market places and cafés, as well as homes; the KORAN is still learned by rote; the call for prayers is publicly announced five times a day; and centuries-old poetry recited even among illiterate people.

Oral literature is the most authentic, un-Westernised literature in Morocco. Until recently, written literature was considered the only prestigious 'literary' form. Now, oral literature is receiving more attention. Including oral histories and folktales, it covers a broad range of social writings, revealing authentic symbolic formations and systems of representations. It is full of mysteries dismissed by Western modernism: demons and other supernatural agents intervening in the lives of humans, ecstatic dreams, miracle cures and superstition. Oral literature is continually presented, represented and exhibited in a recursive way as the images and symbols constituting the core system of cultural themes in a society tend to recur in an infinite number of distinct and original expressions, exhibitions and texts. (**Fatima Sadiqi**)

Further reading

Baker (1998); Berque (1978); Brett and Fentress (1996).

Organisation Commune Africaine et Malgache   See OCAM.

Organisation of African Unity   See OAU.

Orientalism   This term, originally describing the work of Orientalist scholars in various academic fields (such as history and philology), has been popularised in a POST-COLONIAL context since its use by the Palestinian-American critic Edward Said (1978). Said's influential text was translated into French (prefaced by Tzvetan Todorov) in 1982, but failed to have the same impact in a Francophone context, where the reaction to postcolonial criticism has been indifferent or even hostile. Said's work is nevertheless heavily dependent on the thought of Francophone authors such as FANON and Foucault, and his conclusions are echoed by North African critics such as Anouar Abdel-Malek and Abdelkebir KHATIBI. Orientalism takes as its illustrations a number of nineteenth-century French travellers (e.g. Flaubert, Nerval) in the hazily defined area known as the 'Orient', stretching from North Africa (and even Southern Spain) to the Far East. It examines the ways in which this geographical area was – and continues to be – constructed in European thought as a marked DIFFERENCE whereby the West defines itself. Said's principal contention is that knowledge and representation of other cultures become means of controlling elsewhere, and that generations of authors, travellers, politicians and commentators have (often unwittingly) been complicit in the perpetuation of assumptions and stereotypes on which such authority depends.

Orientalism continues in a number of forms, particularly in the West's attitudes to 'ISLAM', invariably linked (especially in the media) with fundamentalism, extremism and even terrorism. A number of contemporary Francophone North African authors have engaged with Orientalist stereotypes in their work (e.g. Assia DJEBAR and Leila SEBBAR), but Orientalism persists in contemporary culture, especially in the images of other cultures used in advertising and cinema. (**Charles Forsdick**)

Further reading

For a ground-breaking analysis of Orientalism, see Said (1978); McMurray (1997) provides a specific case study of Orientalist attitudes to North Africa in contemporary France, whilst Orlando (1997) explores the ways in which Francophone North African authors have subverted Orientalist imagery in their work.

Orville, Xavier   Born 1932; died Paris, 2001. Martinican writer. His vision of the Caribbean owes little to any particular school or movement. His language is not especially creolised, but his style does blend fantasy, surrealism, magic, humour and satire. His novels *L'Homme aux sept noms et des poussières* (1981) and *Moi, Trésilien-Théodore Augustin* (1996) exemplify his whimsical, inventive vision. The latter work, while painting a deeply satirical portrait of the irresponsibility at the heart of the French Caribbean political void, and demystifying the cult of the hero turned tyrant, has a lightness of touch that belies its philosophical grappling with notions of POST-COLONIAL time. (**Mary Gallagher**)

Ouédraogo, Idrissa   Born Burkina Faso, 1954. Film-maker. Ouédraogo studied film-making in Burkina Faso before completing his training in Paris. His early documentaries (1981–86) depict disappearing traditions in his native country. His feature films have won him international renown, receiving several prizes in Africa and Europe, although Ouédraogo feels that European audiences have often misunderstood them as poetic tales, when in fact they deal with the realities of African life. His feature film output to date consists of *Le choix/Yam Daabo* (1986), *Yaaba* (1988), *Tilaï* (1990), *Karim et Sala* (1991), *Samba Traoré* (1992), *Le Cri du coeur* (1994), and *Kini et Adams* (1997). (**Rachael Langford**)

Further reading

Givanni (2000); Malkmus and Armes (1991); Ukadike (1994).

Oufkir, Mohammed   1921–72. Soldier and head of security for Hassan II, often referred to as the latter's '*éminence grise*'. He became head of Moroccan state security when Morocco became independent, and increased his power by ruthless quelling of several attempted *coups* and the opposition to Hassan's rule throughout the 1960s. He was responsible for the murder of exiled opposition leader Mehdi Ben Barka in Paris. Oufkir's motives for staging the 1972 attempted *coup* to replace the monarchy by a republic, led by the Socialist Union of Popular Forces, have never become clear. (**Susan Fox**)

Further reading

Perrault (1990) – A critical account of the Oufkir case and Morocco's human rights record.

Oulema/'Ulama   A cultural, social and religious movement, founded in 1931 by Ibn Badis, which preached against drinking alcohol, smoking and gambling. Their main concern was a revival of Arabic language and culture, and a return to orthodox Islam. For this purpose they opened Arabic schools, where children were taught during the day and adults in the evenings, and a number of cultural clubs, such as *Nadi al-tarraqqi* (1926), and issued journals like *Al-Muntaqid* (1925), *Al-Basa'ir* (1936–56). The '*Ulama*'s efforts resulted in a great flow of Arabic poetry, which was used as an instrument of reform. (**Zahia Smail Salhi**)

Further reading

Ageron (1979).

Ouologuem, Yambo   Born 1940. Malian writer and poet. His only major novel, *Le Devoir de violence* (1968; *Bound to Violence*, 1971), won the Prix Renaudot, but was accused of extensive plagiarism, notably by the Jewish writer André Schwarz-Bart. Discredited and out of print, it remains even so one of the precursors of the disenchanted view of post-independence Africa subsequently developed by such influential figures as Ahmadou Kourouma and Sony Lab'ou Tansi, sharing with them a devastating and unflinching dry humour. The novel depicts the brutal abuse of power by the Saïfs, a dynasty of traditional African rulers, and as such served as an ironic antidote to the idealistic excesses of the *négritude* movement. (**Peter Hawkins**)

Oussekine, Malik   Born 1963; died 1986. A student, of Moroccan immigrant origin, who died after being beaten by police during demonstrations in Paris against government plans for reforming higher education. His death helped to strengthen opposition to the reforms, which were withdrawn by the government shortly afterwards. It was also seen by many as symptomatic of police RACISM, for Oussekine, visibly of foreign origin, was the only person to die during the demonstrations. (**Alec G. Hargreaves**)

Further reading

Prévost's (2001) investigation into Oussekine's death is highly critical of the police and other officials.

Oyono, Ferdinand   Born 1929. Cameroonian writer and diplomat. He was CAMEROON's ambassador to Liberia, had postings in Belgium and France; spent ten years as an attaché to the United Nations; and was appointed director of UNICEF in 1977. Oyono is the author of three novels: *Une Vie de boy* (1956; *Houseboy*, 1966), *Le Vieux Nègre et la médaille* (1956; *The Old Man and the Medal*, 1967) and *Chemin d'Europe* (1960; *Road to Europe*, 1989), which focus on the injustices of the colonial system still in place when they were published. The works have a unique comic tone, and criticise the injustices of colonial rule through the use of likeable, naïve protagonists who are awakened to its harsh realities. (**Rachael Langford**)

Further reading

Corcoran (2001).

Pacific Islands Forum   Formerly known as the South Pacific Forum (1971–2000), the Pacific Islands Forum provides a forum for debate and co-operation for independent Pacific Island countries, Australia and New Zealand. Its headquarters is based in Fiji. Heads of government hold an annual meeting, which is followed by a post-Forum dialogue meeting, involving ministers representing its dialogue partners, including France and the European Union. France was temporarily suspended from the dialogue from 1995 to 1996, following concerns about its NUCLEAR TESTING policy. NEW CALEDONIA has had observer status since 1999.

Pacific Ocean   See ART AND CULTURE; DAILY LIFE; ECONOMY.

PAGS   See *ETTAHADDI*; PCA.

Palcy, Euzhan   Born MARTINIQUE, 1958. Martinican film-maker. She is known as the first black woman film-maker to have directed a mainstream Hollywood feature-length film. Palcy began her career in Martinique as a television writer and director, with an ambition to make films in which black actors would have positive roles and the black population would be portrayed in a more accurate manner. Her first television drama, *The Messenger* (1975), resulted in her leaving to study film-making in Paris. She was fortunate to meet the famous film director François Truffaut, who gave her the encouragement to make her first feature-length film, *Sugar Cane Alley* (1983). The film is an adaptation of Martinican novelist Joseph ZOBEL's *Black Shack Alley* (*Rue Cases nègres*). With highly praised reviews and over 14 international prizes, *Sugar Cane Alley* was Palcy's passport to the film industry. Her determination to remain an ambassador of the black population who are often under- or misrepresented in films led her to refuse many proposals worth millions of dollars from Hollywood. Her film *A Dry White Season* (1989), for which Marlon Brando was nominated for an Oscar, further illustrated her ideology. Palcy has since made one film, *Simeon* (1992). Her filmography however includes a number of productions dealing with various themes: apartheid, music, political corruption, biography, police brutality etc.

Filmogaphy includes: *The Messenger* (1975; TV, producer); *The Devil's Workshop* (1982; producer); *Sugar Cane Alley/Rue Cases nègres* (1983; director/writer); *A Dry White Season* (1989; director/writer); *Simeon* (1992; producer); *In Darkest Hollywood: Cinema and Apartheid* (1993; actress); *Aimé Césaire: A Voice for History* (1994; director/writer/producer); *Ruby Bridges* (1998; TV, co-producer); *Acapulco Black Film Festival* (2000; TV, actress); *The Killing Yard* (2001; TV, director). (**Marie-Annick Gournet**)

Pan-Africanism   Political theory and belief in African unity, throughout Africa and its diasporic cultures. Based on a rich heritage stretching back through Garvey and Du Bois to the end of slavery, and having points in common with NÉGRITUDE, Pan-Africanist ideas came to the fore during and immediately after DECOLONISATION, especially through the Ghanaian Kwame Nkrumah. The desire for a pan-Africanist solution for the African countries throwing off French colonial control, whereby these French-speaking countries could unite in a loose, independent federation, was undermined in 1958 by their near-unanimous 'yes' (with the exception of GUINEA-Conakry) to DE GAULLE's proposal of continued ties to France. (**Andy Stafford**)

Pan-Arabism   One definition is: 'macro-nationalism, or the projection of micro-nationalism onto the larger geographical area, based on common interests (religion, culture and race) as the basis for aspiration for political entity, in more than one state' (Tibi, 1981: 44). Starting during the Ottoman period as a cultural movement, particularly in Iraq, SYRIA and Jordan, seeking recognition for Arab language and identity, this Arab NATIONALISM promoted religious toleration and separation of religion from politics. It was transformed after the First World War to a nationalism entirely in opposition to Western imperialism. In the 1950s and 1960s, its main aim was to combine Pan-Arab national considerations with those of sub-national identities, 'ensuring the separate independence of the Arab states, while at the same time keeping the doors open for gradual measures of co-operation, integration and unification' (Ibrahim, 1996). The establishment of the League of Arab States formalised this compromise.

The new world system, GLOBALISATION, multinational diversification and division of labour, as well as the generalisation of the Western model of nation-state, have together created contradictory imperatives for Third World and particularly Arab nations, resulting in disillusionment with a previous era of nationalism, that did not realise its 'populist hopes' (Buell, 1994: 116). The new geo-political and economic situation has had an impact on the fragmentation and localisation of Arab nationalism. The division of Arab nations with the Maghreb and Gulf unions and Middle East co-operation, the 'Islamisation' of Sudan, the 'Africanisation' of Libya, the crisis between WESTERN SAHARA and MOROCCO, the political division of the Arab League during the Gulf War, and at various points in the Palestinian–Israeli conflict, these are all evidence of the heterogenisation of Pan-Arab nationalism. For Tahar BEN JELLOUN (1997: 159) Arab ideology is confronted by universalist challenges and internal conflicts, underestimated in the past. These internal problems have been used as a veil by political regimes in the Arab world to resist DEMOCRACY. Arab nations, today, are hesitating between the options of political entity (the Western model of the nation-state), cultural identity shared with the rest of the Arab nations that constitute the Arab world, or the larger entity of the Islamic community. (**Mahfoud Amara**)

Further reading

Ben Jelloun (1997); Buell (1994) – helpful overview of major topics related to postmodernism approach, postcolonialism and liberalisation theory, e.g. Africanism, acculturation, and armed struggle; Hussein (1997); Ibrahim (1996) - includes issues related to contemporary problems that Pan-Arabism is facing due to globalisation and the emergence of Islamic movements; Tibi (1981) - contains a critical study of modern Arab nationalism, between Islamic solidarity and a Western secular model of nation-state.

Panneton, Philippe   See RINGUET.

Papon, Maurice   Born Gretz-Armainvilliers, France, 1910. French civil servant. In April 1998, by then long retired, Papon was convicted and sentenced to ten years' imprisonment for collusion in the deportation of Jews from south-west France (1942–44) to Nazi death camps. Papon's activities during Vichy (1940–44) were only widely publicised in 1981. At trial, his role as Paris police chief during the OCTOBER 1961 massacre was also highlighted. Interestingly, much of Papon's Interior Ministry career (1935–67) was within colonial administration, notably as prefect (1949–51) and then superprefect (1956–58) of Constantine: this latter period coincided with great repression against Algerian nationalists, a repression that was subsequently exported to France. (**Jim House**)

Further reading

Golsan (2000) – provides academic studies of Papon's biography, translations of key newspaper articles written during the 1997–98 trial, and usefully situates Papon's case within contemporary debates on memory.

Paris Mosque (*Grande Mosquée de Paris*)   France's oldest purpose-built mosque, constructed during the 1920s at the initiative of the French state in recognition of the role played by Muslim troops from French colonies in North and West Africa during the First World War. Following DECOLONISATION and the settlement in France of immigrant minorities originating in former colonies, the Paris Mosque passed under the control of ALGERIA and became an important player in rivalries over the representation of France's growing Muslim population. (**Alec G. Hargreaves**)

Further reading

Kepel (1987) includes a chapter detailing the history of the *Grande Mosquée de Paris*.

Parizeau, Jacques   Born 1930. QUEBEC politician and a leading member of the separatist *Parti Québécois* (PQ). He served as Finance Minister in the first two PQ governments (1976–84), but resigned in 1984 in protest at René LEVESQUE's compromise position on Quebec independence. On his election as Premier of Quebec in 1994, he launched a new referendum on independence (1995), but on a proposal which was in effect a new version of Lévesque's compromise. In this form the campaign almost achieved a historic victory, but Parizeau squandered his political triumph through an ill-judged speech blaming Anglophone and ethnic voters for the defeat. He immediately resigned as Premier, but the mishandled results of 1995 still cast a heavy shadow over Canada–Quebec relations even today. (**Ian Lockerbie**)

Parti du Peuple Algérien   See PPA.

Parti Québécois   See PQ.

Pasqua, Charles   Born Grasse, southern France, 1927. French Gaullist politician. In the mid-1980s and mid-1990s, he served as Interior Minister in centre-right governments, spearheading tough laws on immigration and related issues, such as the *CODE DE LA NATIONALITÉ*. The Pasqua laws led to increased deportations of immigrants and at the same time to a legal and humanitarian quagmire in which many illegal immigrants, known as *SANS-PAPIERS*, could be neither expelled from France nor granted legal residence there. (**Alec G. Hargreaves**)

Further reading

In contrast with Nair (1994), Carton (2001) presents a generally sympathetic picture of Pasqua.

Pathet Lao   See LAOS.

PCA *Parti Communiste Algérien*   (Algerian Communist Party). Established as the Algerian region of the *Parti communiste français* in 1923, it achieved independent status in 1936. Despite its name the *Parti communiste algérien* was primarily representative of radical elements of the European population. Muslim Algerian membership did increase after 1936, partly as a result of Maurice Thorez's speech of February 1939 declaring Algeria's peoples to be a nation in formation. However, the majority of its European members were ambivalent towards the Muslim population and even after the independence struggle began, favoured a French ALGERIA even though some members such as Henri ALLEG and Maurice Laban did support the FLN. (**Kay Adamson**)

Pélégri, Jean   Born Rovigo, 1920. Algerian writer of French descent (*PIED NOIR*) and film actor. Read philosophy in Algiers, fought in World War II. After graduating from university, he started working as a teacher in Paris. He has lived in France since 1960, his literary works, however, deal with Algerian subjects, such as the ALGERIAN WAR OF INDEPENDENCE. With Mourad Bourboune and Jean SÉNAC he founded the important cultural and literary review *Novembre*. Key texts: *L'Embarquement du lundi* (1952); *Les Oliviers de la justice* (1959; *The Olive Trees of Justice*, 1962); *Le Maboul* (1963); *Le Cheval dans la ville* (1972); *Les Monuments du déluge* (1967); *Ma Mère l'Algérie* (1989); *Les Étés perdus* (1999). Poetry: *L'Homme caillou* (1965); *La Rose de sable* (1970); *L'Homme-nénuphar* (1975). Theatre: *Slimane* (1968); *L'Homme mangé par la ville* (1970). Film: *The Olive Trees of Justice* by James Blue, Jean Pélégri and Sylvain Dhomme (1961). (**Susanne Heiler**)

Further reading

Le Boucher (2000) – for a well documented account of the life and work of Pélégri.

Pepin, Ernest   Born Lamentin, GUADELOUPE, 1950. Writer. He has had many occupations loosely linked to literature including: French teacher, literary critic and presenter of a literary TV programme. Since 1996 he has been Deputy Director of Guadeloupe's Council. His literary activities have earned him such titles as: *Chevalier de l'Ordre des Arts et des Lettres* and *Chevalier de l'Ordre National Mérite*. Key texts: poems – *Au verso du silence* (1984), *Salves et salive* (1986), *Boucan de mots libres* (1991), *Babil du Songer* (1997); novels – *L'Homme au Bâton* (1992), *Coulée d'or* (1995), *Tambour Babel* (1996), *L'Ecran rouge* (1998), *Le Tango de la haine* (1999). (**Marie-Annick Gournet**)

Pères Blancs   The Society of Missionaries of Africa, a Catholic missionary group, was formed in 1868 by Charles Lavigerie, Archbishop of Algiers. It consisted of two groups: the Order of White Fathers (*Pères Blancs*) and the Missionary Sisters of Our Lady of Africa (*Soeurs Blanches*). Their missionary work was pursued throughout ALGERIA, with the construction and administration of orphanages, schools and hospitals. Their activity was concentrated in particular upon the regions of KABYLIA and the SAHARA. In 1878, their first missionaries were sent to Sub-Saharan Africa. In 1898, their first mission was established in BURUNDI and in 1900 in RWANDA. (**Peter Langford**)

Further reading

Renault (1994); Linden (1977).

Periphery   See CENTRE–PERIPHERY.

Perrault, Pierre   1927–99. QUEBEC documentary film-maker who pioneered the techniques of Direct Cinema to make films of great ethnographic value, which are also fervent expressions of his Quebec nationalism. His early films, beginning with *Pour la suite du monde* (1963), describe the customs and traditions of a community on the lower St Lawrence as implicit symbols of a deep-rooted French-Canadian identity. Later themes include Quebec's ancestral links with France, the problems of the Amerindian peoples, and the remote areas of the North, whose magnificent landscapes and animals expressed for him the soul of Quebec. (**Ian Lockerbie**)

Further reading

See Coulombe and Jean (2000).

Pham Van Dong 1906–2000. Vietnamese elder statesman. He was one of the early revolutionaries who joined Ho Chi Minh to found the Viet Minh. Dong was fiercely opposed to the French colonial presence and later US intervention in Vietnam, and was a bitter critic of the division of Vietnam, supported by both China and the Soviet Union, following the Indo-Chinese War. Major policy errors include the 1950s land reform campaign in which 15,000 Vietnamese died, and the 1978 intervention in Cambodia, which left Vietnam isolated. Dong served as government adviser until 1996. (**Susan Fox**)

Further reading

Post (1989).

Pham Van Ky Born 1913. Vietnamese writer. Grand Prix du Roman de l'Académie Française, 1961. Novels include *Frères de sang* (1947; *Blood Brothers*, 1987), *Des Femmes assises ça et là* (1964), *Celui qui régnera* (1954) – dealing with issues of culture, identity, the relation to the homeland and the relationship between East and West.

Further reading

Yeager (1987) – a study of the Vietnamese novel in French.

Pieds noirs Term used to describe French and European settlers in Algeria, said to derive from the fact that they wore black, polished shoes. The first settlers were officers and soldiers of the French expeditionary force that invaded Algeria in 1830. Intensive settler colonisation began in the 1840s, reaching its height in the 1870s. Initially, settlers were criminals, political deportees of the 1848 revolution, refugees from Alsace-Lorraine after the 1870 Franco-Prussian war, and large numbers of unemployed peasants and workers. In the 1880s followed Italians, Spaniards and Maltese. There were also Jews who lived in Algeria well before colonisation. The settler population consisted of many who were not of French origin; European settlers were granted automatic French citizenship only in 1889. The fusion of these diverse European elements into one *pied-noir* community occurred between 1890 and 1914, thanks to schooling, military service, mixed marriages and the belief that they formed a new 'race'. A small group of about 10,000 were *gros colons*, large landowners, wine growers and industrialists, while about 30,000 unskilled labourers were as poor as the average Algerian. Between these two extremes of wealth and poverty lay the majority (school teachers, shopkeepers, office clerks, nurses, bus drivers, technicians). The presence of this large population of European settlers (1 million out of 10 million) made the ALGERIAN WAR a bitter and protracted conflict. Since the majority of the *pied-noir* population dominated economic and political life in Algeria, they had a large stake in the country and relentlessly blocked any reform in favour of granting Algerians equal voting rights and full French citizenship. When the EVIAN AGREEMENTS were signed in March 1962, the majority of the *pieds noirs* decided to oppose Algeria's independence by endorsing the OAS's scorched earth policy, which destroyed the future they might have had in an independent Algeria. In the summer of 1962, all the *pieds noirs* left Algeria in a mass exodus. (**Naaman Kessous**)

Further reading

Ageron (1979) – an indispensable work for the understanding of the origins of French colonisation and its implantation on Algerian soil; Julien (1979) – a thorough study of settler society from 1871 to 1954.

Pineau, Gisèle   Born Paris, 1956. Novelist and psychiatric nurse of Guadeloupean parentage. Pineau's creolised French and celebration of key aspects of CARIBBEAN culture (the supernatural, the oral tradition, the role of the elders) suggest affinities with the CRÉOLITÉ movement, though she is particularly interested in the condition of women. *La Grande Drive des esprits* (1994; *The Drifting of Spirits*, 1999) is the saga of a doomed Guadeloupean family, and won the 'Grand Prix des Lectrices de *Elle*'. The semi-autobiographical *L'Exil selon Julia* (1996) is the story of a young girl growing up in a profoundly racist Paris, and also explores the sense of exile experienced by the eponymous grandmother who comes to the metropole to escape an abusive husband. (**Maeve McCusker**)

Further reading

Pineau (1995).

Placoly, Vincent   1946–92. Martinican novelist, playwright, political activist. His first novel, *La Vie et la mort de Marcel Gonstran* (1971), illustrates the multiple alienations brought about by assimilationism (see ASSIMILATION/INTÉGRATION/INSERTION). *L'Eau-de-mort guildive* (1973) consolidated his literary reputation in France, but showed the tension between the complexity of his artistic vision and the radical simplicity of his political standpoint. *Frères volcans* (1983) is written from the point of view of a liberal slave-owner at the time of emancipation in 1848. With the play *Dessalines* (1983), he turns to Haïtian history. *Une journée torride* (1991) was awarded the Prix Franz FANON shortly before his death. (**Denise Ganderton**)

Polisario   The army which fought the four-year Mauritanian occupation of the WESTERN SAHARA that ended in 1979, and currently fights the Moroccan occupation which began in 1975. Polisario was founded by Mustapha Ouali in 1973, to prevent the Western Sahara's annexation by MOROCCO, before Spain relinquished its colonial control. It declared the territory to be the Saharan Democratic Arab Republic in 1976. The result of the 1988 UN peace plan gave Morocco *carte blanche* in the region, and the proposed referendum on Western Sahara's future has been repeatedly postponed. See also ABDEL AZIZ. (**Susan Fox**)

Further reading

Mohsen-Finan (1997).

Politics, Canada   The principal native groups in Canada were until the arrival of the Europeans, and remain the Cree, the Odawa, the Inuit and the Migmaw. In the 1530s, the French started colonising the Atlantic and St-Lawrence valley regions. The English took control of these colonies in 1760. Canada was founded as a confederation in 1867, with Ottawa as its capital. It has 10 provinces and 3 territories. It is a constitutional monarchy with the English queen, who is represented in Canada by the Governor-General. The governing federal party chooses a new governor-general every five years. The federal government, elected every five years, implements foreign, monetary, cultural and economic policies. The provinces manage educational, health and regional development issues. Their areas of responsibility are enshrined in the Canadian Constitution.

Canada continues to be a nation of immigrants. Federal services are offered in French and English and there is also an official policy on multiculturalism. Most Canadians speak at least two languages. QUEBEC and NEW BRUNSWICK are officially bilingual provinces. The majority of the French Canadian population resides in these provinces and in the east and mid-north of ONTARIO. The French–English factor has always challenged the Canadian *realpolitik*. The most successful governments have had a French-Canadian prime minister as leader.

Canada is a vibrant modern society, always in transition, due to its constant influx of immigrants. It specialises in communications, tourism, resource development, hydro infrastructures and other energy sectors. It is an active member of the Commonwealth nations, *la FRANCOPHONIE*, and works in peacekeeping activities sponsored by the United Nations. It is an active member of the Group of 8, the Organisation of American States and a founding member of the NORTH AMERICAN FREE TRADE ASSOCIATION (NAFTA). (**Raymond Lalonde**)

Further reading

For a guide to Canadian history, see Taylor/Owram (1994); also Jackson and Jackson (2001); Francis and Smith (1998).

Pol Pot   1925–98. Cambodian KHMER ROUGE leader. Originally named Saloth Sar, he came from a well-off family, related to the Cambodian royal family through his aunt's marriage to the king and his own marriage to IENG SARY's sister-in-law. After studies in France, he returned to CAMBODIA in 1953. He worked with the Vietnamese Communists for a number of years, but, under the influence of Mao Tse Tung, he embarked on a campaign of purging the Vietnamese (seen as puppets of Moscow) from the Cambodian Communist Party and then the country. Having gained power in 1975, he lived an obscure clandestine existence. His sole strategy for changing society appears to have been the physical elimination of all class and culturally contaminated enemies, coupled with the ethnic cleansing of foreigners, especially Vietnamese.

Polynesia *La Polynésie française* is one of the two remaining *territoires d'outre mer* (TOMs) in the Pacific Ocean and a reminder of the great influence France once held over this region. The colonial history of the area is characterised by a struggle for control between France and Britain, which only came to an end when French Oceania became a French protectorate in 1843 and a colony in 1880. The Territory is currently made up of around 130 volcanic islands and coral atolls, scattered across an area as large as Europe and divided into five separate archipelagos: Iles du Vent (Windward Islands) – including Tahiti, Iles sous le Vent (Leeward Islands), Marquesas Islands, Austral or Tubuai Islands, and Tuamotu Archipelago. The Territory is administered by a Council of Ministers, and represented in France by two deputies and one senator. However, new statutes (1984 and 1996) are currently in place to allow the region greater autonomy, although not total independence from France. French Polynesia remains dependent on outside sources for energy, although a solar energy programme is being developed. Its main exports are fish, coconut oil (copra) and pearls, although the region has a large trade deficit and relatively high unemployment rate since it imports heavily from elsewhere. Nuclear testing took place in the Tuamotu Archipelago from 1966 to 1996, but the activities of the Pacific Testing Centre (CEP) were stopped in response to mounting local and international protest (including a demonstration in 1995 during which the airport on Tahiti was very badly damaged). Nuclear testing and independence dominated political debate throughout the 1980s. The end of testing led to major ecological benefits, but meant that much-needed jobs were lost. Tourism has now become the main industry, with approaching 200,000 tourist arrivals each year. In the half-century or more since Polynesians voted to support the Free French, the region has undergone both great changes (especially with the improvement of its communications with France) and continued upheaval (including six cyclones in 1982–83). (**Charles Forsdick**)

Further reading

Aldrich (1993) provides the best account in English of French Polynesia in the post-war period; see also Belorgey and Bertrand (1994), pp. 84–9.

Pondicherry Former French colony, on the Coromandel coast of India, 160 km south of Chennai (Madras), ruled by France for 300 years and still showing clear signs of French influence today in its architecture, language, food and ambiance. It was the administrative capital of French India under colonisation until it was handed over to India in 1954, though still remains the capital of the Union Territory of Pondicherry, which, with the exception of Chandernagore, groups together the geographically separated former French outposts: Karaikal, just south of Pondicherry; Yanam (Yanaoun), further north on the Andra Pradesh coast; and Mahe, on the western Malabar coast. Pondicherry is most known today for the Sri Aurobindo Ashram, established in 1926, with the Mother, Mirra Alfassa, by the revolutionary-turned-yogic philosopher-sage Aurobindo Ghosh, who had taken political refuge in the city, along with other independence fighters. It is also visited for the ashram's offspring, the utopian international community of Auroville.

Pontecorvo, Gillo   Born Pisa, Italy, 1919. Film director. His film *The Battle of Algiers* (1966, 120 minutes) is an Algerian–Italian co-production, with music by Ennio Morricone, photography by Marcello Gatti, and screenplay by Franco Solinas). It focuses on the Algerian urban guerrilla struggle against French colonialism 1954–57, emphasising the suffering of ordinary people in the war. The film is a realistic cinematographic recreation of history, presented as a pseudo-documentary. The meticulously researched screenplay, use of non-professional actors, authentic locations and gritty, black and white photography gives the film the appearance of newsreel footage. This anti-imperialist film won several awards including a Golden Lion at the Venice Festival, 1966. See also BATTLE OF ALGIERS. (**Marianne Durand**)

Further reading

Pontecorvo (1967) – interesting and useful article by Pontecorvo, where he explains his direction of the film and the challenges he faced whilst making it. It also includes a paragraph about the author.

Popular culture, Indian Ocean   The popular cultural forms in the region are most often those of the various ethnic and religious groups that make up the diverse population of the islands. The CREOLE peoples of the SEYCHELLES, MAURITIUS, Rodrigues and REUNION sustain a heritage of folk-tales, with its accompanying tradition of storytelling, and riddles, called 'sirindanes'. There is also a somewhat occult survival of animist rituals involving trance-inducing music and dance on the islands, referred to as a '*kabar*' in Reunion, where the accompanying musical form of the Maloya has become well known. The origins of these lie probably in MADAGASCAR, where the tradition of the '*kabary*', a kind of oratorical jousting spectacle, is part of the popular entertainment called '*hira-gasy*'. Madagascar's animist heritage is based on ancestor-worship, featuring the well-known rituals of 're-burial' of the bodies of deceased relatives. In many of the islands, this animist heritage has coloured the local Catholic beliefs, leading to the creation of unofficial saints, such as 'Saint-Expédit' and the cult of the 'Black Virgin' in Reunion. The Indian populations of Reunion and Mauritius have maintained many of their Hindu festivals, such as Dipavali, which are often shared by the whole island community, and in Reunion and Mauritius the ritual of 'fire-walking' on hot coals is still widely practised. In Mauritius, a major focus of Hindu religious observance is the pilgrimage to the holy shrine of Grand Bassin, in the hills to the south of the island. A more secular popular culture of trade unionism and political resistance has grown up in the islands with the increasing urbanisation of the population; this has led to major demonstrations and sometimes serious rioting in the urban centres of Reunion, Mauritius and Madagascar, leading on occasion to major changes and even the collapse of the political regime, as in Madagascar in 1991. (**Peter Hawkins**)

Popular culture, Sub-Saharan Africa   The popular cultures of Francophone Sub-Saharan Africa are as diverse as the continent itself, but they may be categorised under a variety of headings: music, dance, ritual, theatre, sport. These naturally overflow into each other to some extent, which is typical of popular cultural manifestations in Africa. Thus African dance is present in most communities, and usually associated with either drumming, in a rural setting, or more westernised electric dance music in an urban context. In rural settings both drumming and music are usually bound up with the celebration of a festival or a ritual, and these often have a theatrical aspect as well. Naturally, popular urban theatre tends to combine all these elements and this is the inspiration for well-known forms such as the 'concert party' in the coastal states of West Africa such as BÉNIN, TOGO, Ghana and Nigeria; it also features in the more avant-garde theatre of WEREWERE LIKING's Ki-Yi company, based in CÔTE D'IVOIRE. Even local forms of sport, such as wrestling in SENEGAL, have a theatrical and ritual quality, and are not dissociated from dance, music and drumming. African urban dance music is now quite familiar to Western 'World Music' audiences and much of it emanates from Francophone African countries such as Senegal, MALI, the CONGO or CAMEROON, with artists such as Youssou N'DOUR, Baba Maal, Salif KEITA, Papa Wemba and many more having achieved the status of international stars. Popular theatre is less often experienced outside Africa, but African football is a hugely popular sport which is beginning to acquire an international following on television, thanks to the exploits of teams such as Cameroon in recent World Cup competitions. Popular culture is thus an increasingly familiar aspect of Francophone Africa as perceived in the rest of the world. (**Peter Hawkins**)

Postcolonialism　　The term used to describe the body of academic work concerned with theorising the links between different experiences of colonialism. Postcolonial critics analyse the social, historical and ethnic context in which literature, and other cultural forms, are produced within the former colonial possessions of the European empires. However, postcolonial theory is not simply a matter of chronology, concerning itself with the period after colonialism. Consequently, postcolonial criticism has sought to reassess colonial culture, and also to challenge notions of European identity, from a 'postcolonial' standpoint. Postcolonial theory and criticism have evolved rapidly since the late 1980s – amongst the leading scholars in the field are Edward Said, Homi Bhabha and Neil Lazarus. Far from being a monolithic and hegemonic discourse, postcolonial theory groups together many heterogeneous thinkers (from Marxists to feminists to poststructuralists), some of whom are, in fact, deeply sceptical about 'postcolonialism' itself as a concept, viewing it as reductive and schematic.

　　Most critical works engaging with postcolonial issues have emerged from the English-speaking world, and relatively few of these works have been translated into French. It is ironic that the French have been reluctant to engage with 'postcolonial' issues, as Francophone writers such as Aimé CÉSAIRE, Frantz FANON and Albert MEMMI are generally considered to have launched the postcolonial debate, and French theorists such as Lacan, Derrida and Foucault are central to the writings of many postcolonial critics. The French have grouped 'postcolonial' literatures together under the heading of 'Francophone literatures'. Although many French and Anglophone critics of 'Francophone literatures' deal with what might be considered 'postcolonial' issues, there has as yet been no concerted effort to develop a theoretical reflection of Francophone postcolonial studies. (**David Murphy**)

Further reading

McLeod (2000) – excellent introduction to postcolonialism; Moura (1999) – first overview of postcolonialism in relation to Francophone literatures.

Postmodernity   Postmodernity refers to the contemporary period in which the projects and ideologies of MODERNITY have been subjected to a critical gaze. If modernity was epitomised by the spirit of enlightenment, in which a new version of 'Man' would be built on the foundations of science and rationality, then postmodernity is more sceptical of the power of science and rationality to deliver their proclaimed promise of a 'brave new world'. The horrors of the Holocaust, colonialism and Stalinist communism – all fashioned at the heart of modern Europe – are a major reason for this profound reconsideration of the ideas of modernity, and in particular its version of 'Man' and civilisation. Today the hierarchies and binary oppositions which defined modernity (man/woman, white/black, civilisation/barbary, West/non-West, and so on) have been challenged so that values and 'truths' appear more relative, boundaries more porous and former certainties more ambivalent. Some see this as the chance for a new democratic pluralism in which formerly oppressed voices can be liberated and a new ethics of hospitality towards differences can be forged. Others view it simply as the end of ideology and values, the triumph of amoral Western liberalism and the end of all opposition to globalised capitalism. It should be noted that postmodernity is itself a disputed term. Some commentators argue that we are living through a period of late modernity, rather than postmodernity, in which the ideas which informed modernity are still prevalent but are now being refashioned in line with a more pluralist age. Others suggest that postmodernity is not a term which is universally applicable since it defines the evolution of Western societies but fails to appreciate the different development of the non-Western world. (**Max Silverman**)

Further reading

Lyotard (1979) – seminal text defining the major features of postmodernity in terms of 'the end of grand narratives'; Silverman (1999) – survey of contemporary French thinking on postmodern developments and critique of the republican tradition.

Poulin, Jacques   Born Saint-Georges-de-Beauce, 1937. Published his first book in 1967 and has since been one of QUEBEC's leading novelists. In all his novels, Poulin analyses the conditions of love and happiness in the relationship between man and woman. His fifth novel, *Volkswagen Blues* (1984; Eng. trans., 1988) was a major success, with the reading public as well as in the academic world. This story about a Quebecer and his hitch-hiking *metisse* companion crossing North America from Gaspé to San Francisco has become a standard work representing the tendency for '*américanité*' in Quebec literature. Poulin is now living in Paris. (**John Kristian Sanaker**)

Further reading

Hébert (1997) – an interesting synthetic reading of Poulin's novels as love stories.

Pouvanaa a Oopa   Born Huahine; 1895; died 1977. Tahitian politician. He is considered the founding father (*Metua*) of the Polynesian independence movement. He received his political education in part as a volunteer in World War I. After volunteering with the Free French in World War II, he returned to TAHITI to create the pro-independence RDPT (*Rassemblement Démocratique du People Tahitien*) in 1949. He was elected deputy to the French National Assembly in 1951, and again in 1956, as well as controlling the local territorial assembly. After campaigning for a No vote in de Gaulle's 1958 referendum, he was perceived as an unacceptable threat by the French authorities, especially in the light of plans to move the NUCLEAR TESTING site to POLYNESIA. He was sacked by DE GAULLE, under emergency powers, accused of planning to burn down Papeete, and sentenced to eight years in prison and fifteen years in exile. The RDPT in turn was outlawed in 1963. After Pouvanaa a Oopa's release in 1968, he was allowed to return in 1970. He was elected senator in 1971 until his death in 1977.

Further reading

Saura and Gobrait (1998).

PPA *Parti du Peuple Algérien*   (Algerian People's Party). Founded in 1937 by Messali HADJ to replace the ENA, the PPA was a nationalist party with a strong working-class following both in France and ALGERIA. Its programme was less aggressive and less secular than that of the ENA, but it still advocated national independence and PAN-ARABISM (Arab unity). Its emphasis on agrarian and economic reforms as well as its opposition to the *Code de l'Indigénat* attracted discontentented youth, workers, students and soldiers serving in the French army. Dissolved in 1939, it was forced to go underground until the amnesty of 1946, when it re-emerged under a new name, MTLD (*Mouvement pour le Triomphe des Libertés Démocratiques*). (**Naaman Kessous**)

PQ *Parti Québécois*   One of the two major political parties in QUEBEC, the other being the *Parti Libéral*. Founded in 1968 by René LÉVESQUE (Quebec Prime Minister 1976–85). Government party 1976–85 and again from 1994. Lucien BOUCHARD, Quebec Prime Minister from 1996, resigned in 2001 and was succeeded by Bernard Landry. The PQ has always promoted – with greater or lesser enthusiasm – the independence of Quebec, losing two referendums on this question (1980, 1995). The PQ is the main instigator of the linguistic laws defending the position of French (versus English) in Quebec (see LAW 101). (**John Kristian Sanaker**)

Présence Africaine   Cultural journal and publishing house based in Paris, founded in 1947 by Aimé CÉSAIRE, Léopold SENGHOR, Léon DAMAS and Alioune Diop, and supported by Richard Wright, André Gide, Jean-Paul Sartre, Albert CAMUS and Michel Leiris. Both the publishers and the journal are still operating today. The publishing house has played a central role in bringing African, mainly Francophone, literature, politics and culture to a wide European audience, through writers' conferences (especially the Black writers' congresses of 1956 and 1959) and its impressive list of publications. Africa's greatest Francophone writers – SEMBENE, DADIÉ, Cheikh Anta DIOP – are on its list, as are those from the Caribbean, such as CÉSAIRE.

Indeed its publication policy has been dominated by theories of *NÉGRITUDE* and PAN-AFRICANISM, amalgamating the Black world from, and outside of, Africa, into a unified political and cultural project. Though predominantly French-speaking, the journal and the publication lists have not been impervious to Anglophone, Hispanophone, Lusophone nor Dutch-speaking Black writers, from all over the world – see, for example, the 1966 special number (no. 57), called *Nouvelle somme de poésie du monde noir*. This universalisation of Africanism, to cover all corners of the globe, has been criticised recently by theorists of *CRÉOLITÉ* for its mirroring of French and colonialist UNIVERSALISM.

The predominance of the publishing wing has been challenged recently in two ways. First by the wave in the 1970s of new publishers actually based in Africa (NEA in Dakar, CEDA in Abidjan, and many others), and then by more recent enterprises based in Paris (L'Harmattan, Karthala, Silex). Nevertheless, its age and importance almost guarantee publisher and journal alike a healthy future. (**Andy Stafford**)

Press, Sub-Saharan Africa   Most of the former French colonies of West and Central Africa possess at least one daily newspaper, often more or less dominated by the government, particularly in those states still under the rule of a single party or a military dictatorship. A good example would be *Fraternité-Matin*, for many years the only national newspaper in CÔTE D'IVOIRE under the long, autocratic rule of President Félix HOUPHOUËT-BOIGNY, and notorious for its bland official discourse and endorsement of the government line. Movements towards DEMOCRATISATION in the 1990s often led to the creation of an independent, underground press, which has gradually become more or less legitimate in the countries that have finally embraced political pluralism. This oppositional press has remained vulnerable to sudden movements of repression and censorship, however, when the regime in power has felt under threat, as has happened in countries such as TOGO. These daily papers usually use French, but there is often a concession to local African languages in some of the pages of local news and comment. Quite apart from the daily press, news magazines such as the well-known weekly *JEUNE AFRIQUE*, published in Paris, are widely available, and there is a growing local magazine press, particularly in the more affluent urban centres such as Abidjan in Côte d'Ivoire, catering to the new African ruling classes. This often takes the form of economic and business magazines, women's magazines, children's comics etc. Its content is often bland and uncontroversial and reflects the often westernised aspirations of its audience, as do the glossy advertisements for expensive consumer goods. In general the Francophone African press still suffers from its dependency and vulnerability to repression and censorship by autocratic governments, yet is one of the more hopeful signs of the general move towards political accountability in Francophone Africa. (**Peter Hawkins**)

Printemps Berbère   See BERBER SPRING.

Quebec Quebec is the major French-speaking area of Canada, with a population of 7.3 million, of whom 82 per cent are Francophone. There are Francophone communities elsewhere in Canada, notably in NEW BRUNSWICK (the historic ACADIE), which is 50 per cent Francophone, ONTARIO and other provinces. Although still viable, these are much smaller than Quebec, and to some extent depend on the critical mass of Quebec for survival.

Survival has been the central concern of Quebec itself since the foundation of New France in 1608, but especially since 1759, when the French colony was defeated by Wolfe's British army and became a British possession. Although the French Canadians were given rights to continue to use their own language, they had legitimate fears for their future under Anglophone rule in an overwhelmingly Anglophone continent. These fears led to the armed uprising of *les Patriotes* in 1837–38, which, although unsuccessful, has retained a great symbolic importance. The Catholic Church, which preached faith and language as indissoluble, was for long their major bastion against ASSIMILATION.

In the 1960s, however, Quebec (the term now preferred to French Canada) launched a series of initiatives for social, economic and cultural development, originally dubbed the RÉVOLUTION TRANQUILLE (Quiet Revolution), which have transformed its situation. These included measures to protect the French language (see CHARTER OF THE FRENCH LANGUAGE) and a quest for greater political autonomy. Referendums on a form of separation from Canada (see René LÉVESQUE) failed in 1980 but almost succeeded in 1995. Occasional strained relations with the rest of Canada have resulted from these events (see LAKE MEECH ACCORD), without affecting Quebec's continuous progress. Whatever its ultimate constitutional status may be, Quebec's future as a thriving Francophone society in North America now seems assured. See also CINEMA; LITERATURE; THEATRE. (**Ian Lockerbie**)

Further reading

Lacoursière (2000) is an up-to-date, attractively presented history.

Quiet Revolution See RÉVOLUTION TRANQUILLE.

Qur'an See KORAN.

Rabéarivelo, Jean-Joseph 1903–37. Malagasy poet and novelist. Rabéarivelo was a pioneer of Francophone writing in MADAGASCAR, torn between loyalty to the ancestral poetic traditions of the Malagasy language and the desire to conquer new literary horizons in France. In *Presque-songes* (1934) and *Traduit de la nuit* (1935; *Translations from the Night*, 1975), he composed poetry in French strongly marked by a delicate Malagasy musicality, which he claimed were translations, also giving his own Malagasy versions. He also drafted a posthumously published novel, *L'Interférence* (1931/1987). He committed suicide in 1937. (**Peter Hawkins**)

Rabémananjara, Jacques   Born 1913. Malagasy poet, essayist and dramatist. His poetry, such as *Lamba* (1956), is a militant celebration of Malagasy identity and independence, and he was included in SENGHOR's famous *Anthologie de la poésie nègre et malgache* (1948). He has also composed historical dramas such as *Les Dieux malgaches* (1947). After a period in prison because of his opposition to French colonial domination, he returned to MADAGASCAR at its independence in 1960, served as a government minister and eventually became Vice-President of the Republic. After 1972, he was forced into exile by a military *coup* and has since lived in France, working for the publishing house PRÉSENCE AFRICAINE. (**Peter Hawkins**)

Race/ethnicity   Terms denoting group categories and affiliations often regarded as taboo in contemporary France, especially among official representatives of the state. Ideas of a biologically based racial hierarchy, with a superior white race at the top and inferior coloured races below, were prevalent during the colonial period. Similar distinctions were drawn between Aryans and Jews within France by the anti-Semitic Vichy regime (1940–44). After the horrors of the Holocaust and the collapse of the colonial system, theories of racial difference became scientifically discredited and unwelcome reminders of unpalatable episodes in recent French history. Hence their disappearance from official French discourses.

Ethnicity, a form of group consciousness based more on cultural than on biological differences, has never enjoyed favour in the thinking of French officials, mainly because it has been seen as a challenge to the cohesion of the nation-state. The only form of collective identity officially recognised in the so-called 'republican' mode of thinking dominant among state actors is that of nationality. Within this optic, the ethnic identities of regional or immigrant minorities have no legitimacy.

In contrast with this official stance, racial and ethnic consciousness is in reality widely present in France at both popular and élite levels. It has been sharpened in particular by the settlement of immigrant minorities originating in former African, Caribbean and Asian colonies whose cultural traditions and physical appearance mark them as apparently different from the mainly white majority ethnic population. Racial and/or ethnic discrimination in employment, housing and other fields has become recognised in France as a major problem leading to significant policy initiatives by the Socialist-led government elected in 1997. In seeking to measure the scale of discrimination and the effectiveness of attempts to combat it, French researchers and public officials are gradually becoming more willing to use racially and/or ethnically based categories. (**Alec G. Hargreaves**)

Further reading

Dewitte (1999) offers an up-to-date view of this field.

Race/population, Caribbean   The population of the French Caribbean territories is noted for its diverse origins, even though, apart from GUIANA, the original Amerindian inhabitants of the islands were largely wiped out. In MARTINIQUE (pop. 350,000), there are three main groups: the black population of African descent forming the majority, with a white (*BÉKÉ*) upper class and a significant mulatto (or mixed race) middle class. In GUADELOUPE (pop. 350,000), both the white élite and the mulattoes are fewer in number and importance. East Indians, brought in originally as indentured labourers after the abolition of slavery in 1848, form a significant percentage of the population of Guadeloupe (about 17 per cent), though only around 3 per cent in Martinique. Guiana (pop. *c.* 100,000) has the most diverse population, with the descendants of African slaves, Creoles and Maroons, sharing the country with a mixture of Amerindians, Europeans, Chinese, Cambodians, Javanese, Syrians, and Lebanese. It is a lively pole for immigration from other Caribbean countries, as well as Brazil. All the territories have a significant number of metropolitan French, who usually come to stay for short spells only. Moreover, a large proportion of the territories' population (as much as one-third) currently reside outside the Caribbean – about 400,000 people of French Caribbean origin live in France. Journeys to and fro across the Atlantic have become a normal feature for these '*négropolitains*', as they are often called.

Unlike some other parts of the Caribbean, tensions between different racial groups remain latent rather than overt. However, notwithstanding the NÉGRITUDE movement, there are clear lines of racial stratification, with a hierarchical order largely dependent on skin colour, and East Indians, known as *Coulis*, generally disparaged. Traditionally, class structures have corresponded with racial divisions, though these barriers have increasingly been broken down, with greater social mobility. Some resentment and animosity towards metropolitan whites also surfaces from time to time. One of the main features of the CRÉOLITÉ movement is that it attempts to transcend these divisions, in a celebration of the strengths of DIVERSITY, racial or otherwise.

Further reading

Burton and Reno (1995).

Racism   Traditionally defined as a doctrine based on the notion of a hierarchy of 'RACES', racism relies on racialisation, a process by which boundaries between human groups are created and then fixed in terms of supposed 'differences', as part of racism's attempt to justify and/or implement political domination. Racialisation operates according to two logics. Firstly, there can be *autoracisation* (racialisation of the self) – within Nazi ideology with reference to 'Aryans', for example. The second logic, *hétéroracisation* (racialisation of the other), attributes negative properties to stigmatise supposedly inferior groups (the colonised, 'Jews') on the grounds of skin colour, religion, ethnicity or culture (Taguieff, 1987). Both *autoracisation* and *hétéroracisation* are intricately related: declaring the colonised as 'inferior' presumed the 'superiority' of the 'white' metropolitan French. Most post-1960s racism, often termed 'neo-racism' (Barker, 1981) or 'cultural racism', has focused less overtly on the concept of 'race', a pseudo-scientific category elaborated in the nineteenth century. Instead, this 'newer' racism has increasingly relied on the supposedly immutable 'cultural' or 'ethnic' differences between human groups, notably in relation to postcolonial migrants and their descendants (FRONT NATIONAL discourse, for example) (see ANTIRACISM, *BEURS*, ISLAM, *SANS-PAPIERS*). The development of this 'cultural racism' has been facilitated by considerable earlier overlapping between 'race' and 'culture' in colonial social discourses (politics, journalism, fiction) and governance (Fanon, 1952/1975; Said, 1978). In the Francophone context, there are strands of racism (anti-black, anti-North African) stemming from slavery and colonialism, in addition to a well-established tradition of anti-semitism (House, 2002). Wieviorka (1991) usefully distinguishes between different levels of racism (from diffuse ideas within society to state racism). Racism is often articulated with forms of gender differentiation. Racism can be produced and carried by different vectors (e.g. the state, political organisations, associations) and has to be understood within local, regional, national and transnational contexts. (**Jim House**)

Further reading

Wieviorka (1998) – an excellent introductory discussion of the theories of racism; Balibar (1992) – a fully contextualised analysis of the historical development of racism in postcolonial France.

Radio Beur   A Parisian radio station operating from 1981 to 1992, *Radio Beur* served mainly as a media outlet for North African cultures. The station was founded by Nacer KETTANE and other leaders of the *BEUR* movement in 1981, the year that the Socialists gained power and loosened restrictions on ethnic minority and foreign organisations. Derderian (1997) describes notable programmes, including 'La tribune de Radio Beur' (a talk show with invited guests), 'Les Beurs et la plume' (literature) and 'Paroles de femmes' (women's issues). The show vigorously promoted RAÏ and KABYLE culture, but also featured PIED-NOIR, Jewish and Caribbean music. (**Mark McKinney**)

Raï   This Arabic word for 'opinion' refers to a musical genre originating in Oran, ALGERIA, and is a hybrid of different traditions: the Bedouin, who sang in everyday language about the trials of daily life; the much more codified and literary Arabo-Andalousian music, and the '*meddahates*' – female singers whose repertoire included romantic songs, and others praising God. CHEIKHA RIMITTI is the doyenne of *raï*, which has added influences from Lebanese, Egyptian, and Moroccan music, jazz, reggae and rap, to expresses the emotions of young Maghrebians on both sides of the Mediterranean. KHALED, CHEB MAMI and CHEB HASNI have ensured *raï*'s international success. (**Samantha Neath**)

Further reading

Daoudi and Miliani (1996); Virolle (1995).

Rainbow Warrior   Ship of the Greenpeace environmental campaigning NGO, was named after a Native American Cree warrior prophecy that 'when the world is sick and dying, the warriors of the Rainbow will rise up to protect it'. The ship, launched in 1978, was the first diesel electric one of its kind to be built in Britain, and was originally a fishery research vessel. Its purpose was to campaign against whaling in the North Atlantic, to protest against ships carrying nuclear waste and to prevent the massacre of 6000 grey seals by hunters in the Orkney Islands. The first campaign against whaling was jointly financed by Greenpeace and the World Wildlife Fund. The *Rainbow Warrior* was rammed by a French navy vessel in 1980 after it sailed into Cherbourg to protest against the unloading of nuclear waste from Japan. In 1985, the *Rainbow Warrior*, anchored in New Zealand waters, was blown up by agents of the French Secret Service, the DGSE, to prevent its protest voyage to the NUCLEAR TESTING site of Mururoa in French POLYNESIA. One crewmember was killed during the explosion. Despite initial official denials by the French government, the Prime Minister, Laurent Fabius, was forced to hold an official investigation, following an international outcry.

In 1989, the new *Rainbow Warrior* sailed into Papeete, TAHITI, and Mururoa again, to protest against the effects of nuclear testing and to take water samples for radio-activity checks. A year later, shortly after the *Rainbow Warrior* was impounded and its crew expelled from French Polynesia, the French government announced a year's moratorium on nuclear testing, to be extended if other countries followed suit. The purpose of recent *Rainbow Warrior* campaigns has been to protest against genetic engineering in poultry rearing in New Zealand. (**Susan Fox**)

Further reading

Charpentier (1991).

Rakotoson, Michèle Born 1948. Malagasy novelist and dramatist. Michèle Rakotoson first came to prominence as a promising playwright, winning the Radio France International prize in 1989 for *La Maison morte*. More recently she has worked in Paris as a radio journalist, and has published well-received novels, such as the prize-winning *Dadabe* (1984), and *Le Bain des Reliques* (1988), about the conflict between the modern media and traditional Malagasy beliefs, and *Elle, au printemps* (1996), about the unhappy experiences of economic migrants in France. (**Peter Hawkins**)

Ramdane, Abane Born Azouza, ALGERIA, 1920; died MOROCCO, 1957. One of the most outstanding, yet least known, figures of the ALGERIAN REVOLUTION, Abane Ramdane was among the earliest victims of struggles within the Revolutionary movement. His political career began in 1945 and was brief but eventful. From 1943 he was active as head of The Friends of the Manifesto and Liberty (AML) and survived the test represented by the events of 1945, when more than 45,000 Algerians were massacred by the French Army in response to anticolonial demonstrations in Guelma, SETIF and Kharata. In 1950 the colonial authorities sentenced him to six years' imprisonment. On leaving prison he continued his anticolonial struggle and drafted the platform of the Congress of Soummam, the first meeting that led Algeria towards independence. He was assassinated in 1957. (**Kamal Salhi**)

Further reading

Mammeri (1988).

Rassemblement démocratique africain   See RDA.

RCD Rassemblement pour la culture et la démocratie   Algerian BERBER political party, founded by Saad SAADI in 1988, as a splinter movement from the FFS. This move temporarily isolated Saadi and his supporters from the Berber Cultural Movement (MCB). The RCD would like a constitutionally secular ALGERIA and equal status for the repressed Berber language and culture with Arabic. Berbers also face discrimination in employment and housing. The RCD pulled out of BOUTEFLIKA's government in 2001 following the latter's failure to contain violence against Berbers in KABYLIA. (**Susan Fox**)

Further reading

Ouerdane (1993).

RDA Rassemblement démocratique africain   (African Democratic Union). See DIORI; HOUPHOUËT-BOIGNY.

Reclus, Onésime   Born Orthez, France, 1837; died 1916. A geographer who specialised in France and North Africa and who sought to classify peoples by the languages that they spoke in official contexts and within their families. It was Reclus who coined the term '*Francophonie*' in *France, Algérie et Colonies*, published in 1880, to describe the notion of a common grouping sharing the FRENCH LANGUAGE. It was not until Léopold SENGHOR used the term in an article in *Esprit* in 1962 that Reclus' term started to gain the currency that it now enjoys. (**Antony Walsh**)

Religion   See SECULARISM and RELIGION.

Religion, Indian Ocean   The island peoples of the south-west Indian Ocean practise a kaleidoscope of different religions, which arise principally from their diverse origins, and usually with a great degree of mutual tolerance. The experience of French colonisation that they all share left a widespread legacy of Catholic beliefs in all the islands, but with varying levels of support. It is probably strongest in the SEYCHELLES and REUNION, but coloured by some local animist influences from the occulted African religions of the island's early slave population. In MADAGASCAR, traditional animist beliefs of ancestor worship are dominant, and among the Christian minority, as well as Catholicism, there is a strong presence of Protestant beliefs, such as Anglicanism, arising from British missionary activity in the nineteenth century. In MAURITIUS the Hindu influence is most strongly felt, with a less important presence of mainly Catholic and some Protestant Christian churches. The Hindu presence in Reunion is less strong, but highly visible even so. All the islands have a small minority of Muslims, usually the descendants of traders who emigrated from northern India; the Islamic influence is dominant in the COMOROS archipelago, however, as a result of the early Arabic trading routes along the east coast of Africa. The Chinese immigrant populations of Mauritius and Reunion brought Buddhism to the islands, and this is still practised by a very small minority. In general, across the region, religious conflicts have been rare, although in some islands, such as Mauritius, the religious and ethnic groups tend to maintain a separate social identity. (**Peter Hawkins**)

Religion, Sub-Saharan Africa   The indigenous forms of religious belief in Sub-Saharan Africa can be considered as animist, characterised by the worship of ancestors and spirits who inhabit the natural environment, and may influence the lives of living human beings in powerful ways. The particular nuances of these beliefs may vary considerably from one community to another, but most correspond recognisably to this general model. Over this substratum, more or less visible and dominant in different regions and countries, have been overlaid other beliefs imported from the West and the Middle East. The Sahelian regions of West Africa were Islamised from the eleventh century onwards: Islam was brought from the Middle East along the trading routes across the SAHARA, and led to the development of specifically West African forms of Islam. A renowned centre for Islamic scholarship grew up during the Middle Ages at Timbuktu in present-day MALI. This Sahelian Islamic culture still dominates SENEGAL, MAURITANIA, Mali and NIGER, and is strongly present in Burkina Faso, GUINEA and CHAD, and in the northern parts of CÔTE D'IVOIRE, TOGO, BÉNIN and CAMEROON. There are aspects of it, however, such us the magic powers attributed to *marabouts* or Islamic holy men, which probably have their roots in pre-Islamic animism. Western colonisation brought with it Christian missionaries, in the future French colonies predominantly Catholic priests, permeating inland from the coastal regions from the mid-nineteenth century onwards. This has led to a relatively high proportion of Catholics in the population of countries such as Ivory Coast, Cameroon, CENTRAL AFRICAN REPUBLIC, GABON, Republic of CONGO (ex-Congo-Brazzaville), DEMOCRATIC REPUBLIC OF CONGO (ex-Zaire), RWANDA and BURUNDI, but often overlapping with those professing traditional animist beliefs. Protestantism in a wide variety of forms, both European and North American, is a minority presence particularly in the strongly Christian areas of Central Africa. This rich tapestry of different beliefs often leads to some unusual varieties of religious syncretism, such as the Harrist church popular along the West African seaboard from Bénin to Ivory Coast. (**Peter Hawkins**)

Renaud, Jacques   Born 1943. QUEBEC novelist, known especially for *Le Cassé* (1964; *Flat Broke and Beat*, 1969; *Broke City*, 1984), the first literary work to be written extensively in JOUAL, the Montreal working-class dialect. See Gauvin (1975) and Major (1979) for the wider literary movement *Parti Pris*, championing the use of *joual* in literature, with which Renaud was loosely linked. (**Ian Lockerbie**)

Reunion   Island in the south-west Indian Ocean, population 705,072, administered as a DOM, an overseas department of the French Republic, since 1946. Despite its small size and mountainous terrain (the *Piton des Neiges* is over 3000m high), with an active volcano (*Piton de la Fournaise*), Reunion island exerts a considerable influence as a prosperous showcase for French culture in the region. First inhabited in 1647, the island is home to a very mixed-race population of diverse origins: MADAGASCAR, metropolitan France, Sub-Saharan Africa, southern India, Pakistan and China. As well as the Catholicism of the majority, various other beliefs are practised on the island, such as Hinduism, Protestantism, Islam, Buddhism and a vestigial African animism. Although heavily dependent on French support, the economy of the island still relies on sugar cane, with a range of other local agricultural products: tropical fruits, vanilla, etc. The island has recently developed as a centre for high-tech distribution and information technology and has a growing tourist industry, based as much on the attraction of its spectacular mountains as on its coastline. Reunion boasts a large, well-endowed university, a lively theatrical life now administered by the *Centre Dramatique de l'Océan Indien*, a distinctive and varied musical output, and an improbably thriving culture of cartoons and animation film. Its literary heritage goes back to the late eighteenth century, producing internationally celebrated poets such as Parny, Bertin and Leconte de Lisle. Most locally born Reunionese speak CREOLE before they learn French, and since the 1970s there has been a growing body of literature written in Creole, published locally, but most influential in oral forms such as theatre and popular song. There are many social, cultural and economic links with its Francophone neighbours, MAURITIUS and Madagascar, as well as with the smaller islands of the region, such as MAYOTTE, the SEYCHELLES and the COMOROS. It has also established growing exchange contacts with the major powers of the area, South Africa and India. (**Peter Hawkins**)

Révolution tranquille   A period of major transformation of QUEBEC society during the 1960s, often referred to in English as the 'Silent' or 'Quiet Revolution'. To understand the impact of these changes, one must keep in mind that Quebec, for a very long time, differed from other Western societies by the fact that until the 1950s it remained a rural society, strongly influenced by the Catholic Church and clerical authority. With the death of the last traditionalist political leader, Maurice DUPLESSIS, in 1959, Quebec was ready for the changes which were realised during the Liberal government of Jean Lesage.

The *Révolution tranquille* covers a period of less than ten years, during which Quebec turned into a modern Western welfare state. The changes were political and economic as well as cultural. The most important political changes consisted in creating a state school system (the first Quebec ministry of education was created in 1963) and a public health system. Both these sectors were formerly controlled by the Church. There was also a considerable growth in other public services, creating a new Quebecois, Francophone middle class, which was necessary in order to turn Quebec into the French-speaking society it was to become in the 1970s (see LAW 101).

The economic base for the modernisation of society realised during this period was provided by the nationalisation programme introduced by the Lesage government (affecting especially the hydroelectric industry).

A remarkable cultural boom accompanied the political and economic changes. In literature as well as in music and cinema, the idea of IDENTITY became crucial. In fact, the Silent Revolution meant a transformation of the old French-Canadian (rural and

Catholic) identity into a modern Quebecois (urban and secular) identity. (**John Kristian Sanaker**)

Further reading

Belanger, Comeau and Metivier (2000) – papers from retrospective university conference evaluating the period and its impact.

Rhizome   See ROOTS/RHIZOME.

Ringuet   Pseudonym of Philippe Panneton. Born Trois-Rivières, 1895; died Lisbon, 1960. QUEBEC writer. Working first as a medical doctor and a university professor, then in Canadian foreign affairs, Ringuet is also the author of three novels. His fame is entirely due to *Trente arpents* (1931; *Thirty Acres*, 1940), a penetrating portrayal of the transformation of traditional Quebec rural society during the first decades of the twentieth century. Considered as one of the first realistic novels in French-Canadian literature, *Trente arpents* is the story of a peasant who is ruined by a series of disasters and ends his days miserably in exile in New England. (**John Kristian Sanaker**)

Rithy Panh   Born Phnomh Penh, 1964. Cambodian film-maker, living in France. He experienced the re-education camps from 1975, until he managed to escape to Thailand in 1979, from where he made his way to Paris a year later, entering the film school, IDHEC. Work includes *Gens de la rizière* (1994), set in the time of the KHMER ROUGE.

Roblès, Emmanuel   Born Oran, ALGERIA, 1914; died 1995. French PIED-NOIR writer. His parents were second generation settlers. He received his primary education in Oran, and in 1931 he joined *l'Ecole Normale* of Algiers, where he met his fellow-student and friend Mouloud FERAOUN. In 1937 he met CAMUS and Audisio, among others, who established the *Ecole d'Alger* literary group. In the following year he published his first novel, *L'Action*, which was followed in 1943 by *Cela s'appelle l'aurore* (*Dawn on Our Darkness*, 1954), a novel that describes a plane accident he survived in Sardinia during the Second World War, and *Les Hauteurs de la ville* (1948). Roblès was known for his support for the Algerian cause, calling for the abolition of colonialism. (**Zahia Smail Salhi**)

Further reading

Astre (1987); Chèze (1979).

Rochereau, Tabu Ley   Born Congo, 1940. Musician. See MUSIC, SUB-SAHARAN AFRICA.

Roots/rhizome   These botanical terms provide metaphors for two different understandings of origins. Whereas the root grows downwards from a single central point, the rhizome (a term first popularised by the theorists Deleuze and Guattari) grows randomly and from many different points at the same time. Postcolonial thought has used the rhizome to challenge, with a more complex model of cultural interaction, the monolithic understandings of culture and identity on which the CENTRE–PERIPHERY view of the colonial relationship depends. The principal reflection on this subject is

Edouard Glissant's work, in which the Martinican author contrasts the often oppressive, essentialist, fixed nature of *identité-racine* (root-identity) with the more open-ended, plural, dynamic, 'rhizomatic' idea of an *identité-relation* inherent in creolised cultures. (**Charles Forsdick**)

Further reading

For a more detailed discussion, see Glissant (1990; 1996).

Roumain, Jacques   1907–44. Haitian novelist, poet and essayist. He is principally remembered for his masterpiece *Gouverneurs de la rosée* (1944; *Masters of the Dew*, 1947), a peasant novel which dramatises village conflicts around the search for water as a Marxist-inspired allegory of the need for solidarity. Written in a poetic style inflected with popular turns of phrase, it is a major precursor of the creolised narratives of Simone Schwarz-Bart and Patrick Chamoiseau, as well as the subsequent work of his fellow Haitian writers Jacques-Stephen Alexis and René Depestre. Roumain's idealistic and committed poetry, such as *Bois d'Ebène* (1945; *Ebony Wood*, 1972), is also celebrated in Senghor's *Anthologie de la Poésie Nègre et Malgache* (1948). (**Peter Hawkins**)

Roy, Gabrielle   Born Saint-Boniface, Manitoba, 1909; died Quebec, 1983. Quebec writer. She worked initially as a primary teacher in western Canada. After some time living in Europe, she settled in Montreal. Her novels break with the rural tradition of the Quebec novel to explore urban life in Montreal, as in *Bonheur d'occasion* (1945; *The Tin Flute*, 1948) and *Alexandre Chenevert* (1954; *The Cashier*, 1956). She also writes about her childhood and native province in *La Petite Poule d'eau* (1950; *Where Nests the Waterhen*, 1952), *La Montagne secrète* (1961; *The Hidden Mountain*, 1962) and *Les Enfants de ma vie* (1977; *Children of My Heart*, 1979). Classical in form, her work demonstrates a tremendous sensitivity towards people and their suffering, as well as great concern for precision in the description of places and atmosphere. (**Kamal Salhi**)

Roy, Jules   Born Rovigo, Algeria, 1907; died Vézelay, France, 2000. French Algerian writer. He was a close friend of Albert Camus. Rovigo, where he grew up, was a small town in the Mitidja, south of Algiers, which became the setting for his critical history of France's colonisation of Algeria – *Les Chevaux du soleil*. After France's defeat in 1940, he joined the RAF as a bomber pilot, and he was with the French army in Indochina when the Algerian independence struggle began in 1954. He resigned his command and was one of the first to criticise France's conduct in the Algerian War. Later he retired to Vézelay in France and continued to write and publish. (**Kay Adamson**)

Further reading

Roy (1972) – Roy's response to the publication by the paratroop commander General Massu of his defence of the use of torture by French forces in Algeria; Roy (1995) – Roy's attempt to put the history of France's colonisation of Algeria into a popular perspective, note Book 4: *Le Maître de la Mitidja*; Calmette (2001) – biography of Roy's life from the 1940s to 2000.

RPCR *Rassemblement pour la Calédonie dans la République* Major anti-independence (or 'loyalist') party in NEW CALEDONIA. Formed (under a different name) in 1977, the party, headed by Jacques Lafleur, draws support largely from Caldoche (ethnically European) residents and Polynesian migrants worried about their future in an independent Melanesian-dominated state. During the 1980s, the party engaged in a militant combat with the pro-independence FLNKS, allegedly condoning racist attitudes and violent tactics. In 1988, it signed an accord with the FLNKS for a ten-year moratorium, and in 1998 another agreement foreshadowed New Caledonia's accession to an imprecise 'sovereignty' between 2013 and 2018 at the latest. (**Robert Aldrich**)

Rwanda A small, landlocked country with a population of about 6 million. Subsistence level agriculture supports 92 per cent of the population. Two-thirds of the state's revenue is international aid, with the rest based upon coffee and tea production. Under Belgian colonisation, from 1916 until independence on 1 July 1962, French became the official administrative language and the precolonial ethnic groups of Hutu, Tutsi and Twa were redefined as distinct racial groups.

The First Republic's multi-party DEMOCRACY was preceded by the 'social revolution' of 1959 in which the colonial Tutsi ÉLITE was forcibly removed by a Hutu élite, supported by the Belgians and the *PÈRES BLANCS*. In 1966, President Grégoire Kayibanda abolished the multi-party democracy and transformed Rwanda into a one-party state. In 1973, a *coup d'état* by General Habyarimana created a Second Republic ruled by a single party, the *Mouvement Révolutionnaire National pour le Développement* (MRND). In 1975, he signed a military assistance agreement with France. In 1990, after an attack by the Rwandan diaspora of the *Front Patriotique Rwandais* (RPF), the MRND launched a programme of mass arrests. Under international pressure, it began a process of transition towards democracy. In 1992, a transitional government was formed which opened negotiations with the RPF, leading to the Arusha Accords of 1993. During this period, the MRND and Habyarimana tried to obstruct and undermine the operation of the transitional government and, with the signature of the Accords, began to plan the implementation of a genocide. This began on 6 April 1994, lasting until the RPF took power in July 1994 and leading to the death of about 1 million people and the creation of 2 million refugees. Since 1998, the war in the Gaullist DEMOCRATIC REPUBLIC OF CONGO has led the RPF's army to take control of the principal positions of power. (**Peter Langford**)

Further reading

Period up to independence – Chrétien (1999); postcolonial period up to 1994 genocide – Africa Rights (1994), Vidal (1995), Prunier (1995), Mamdani (2001); postcolonial period after 1994 genocide – Prunier (1997), *Réseau documentaire sur la région des Grands Lacs africains.*

S

Saadi, Saad Algerian politician. Leader of RCD.

Sadji, Abdoulaye Born Rufisque, SENEGAL, 1910; died 1961. Senegalese writer. Best known as the author of the novels *Maïmouna* (1953) and *Nini, mulâtresse du Sénégal* (1954). In these works, the young African woman represents the nation being tempted by rampant Western individualism and 'immorality'. Essentially a moralist, Sadji uses these cautionary tales to preach the virtues of traditional customs and practices. A teacher, who later worked in radio, Sadji was closely associated with SENGHOR and *NÉGRITUDE*, serving on the editorial board of *PRÉSENCE AFRICAINE* from its launch in 1947. (**David Murphy**)

Sahara The Sahara, in North Africa, is the largest desert in the world, covering an area of about 9,065,000 sq. km. It spans ten countries, and extends from the Atlantic in the west to the Red Sea in the east. In recent years, it has been increasing its southerly advance into the Sahel. The spread of the Sahara is part of a process that began at least 8000 years ago, when the area was still fertile. It has a harsh climate, with temperatures often exceeding 50 degrees centigrade by day, but heat loss under cloudless skies brings the temperature down dramatically at night.

Its massive size splits Africa into two regions. The WESTERN SAHARA is rocky with varied elevation and contains underground rivers, tributaries of the Niger and Nile, which penetrate the surface into oases, where dates and other fruits are grown. The central Sahara has peaks such as Emi Koussa and Tahat, and although the area lacks rainfall, these peaks are snow-capped in winter. The main mountain ranges are the Hoggar, the Aïr/Azbine and the Tibesti. The Eastern part, the Libyan Desert, is dry with few oases. There are four main land routes through the Sahara.

The Sahara has a population of 2 million, with many indigenous tribes inhabiting parts of the desert, but the majority of dwellers comprise Arabs and BERBERS, who live chiefly in ALGERIA, MOROCCO and MAURITANIA. Important cities are Ghat, Nouakchott and Tamanrasset. The desert is rich in mineral deposits, especially iron, natural gas, oil and uranium, and there remain French and Spanish economic interests, which have strategic aspects (oil routes). The argument for the liberation of former Spanish Sahara (Western Sahara) began in the 1950s, but the decolonisation process has been protracted because of French, Moroccan and Spanish economic and strategic interests. (**Susan Fox**)

Further reading

Moorhouse (1986).

Said, Amina Born TUNISIA, 1953. Tunisian writer. She immigrated to Paris in 1978, and studied language and literature at the Sorbonne. She has taught English literature and worked as a journalist for various publications, running literature workshops, giving poetry readings and taking part in literary debates in France and abroad. She is perhaps best known for her poetry. She has published collections of poems, *fables* and *contes,* and translated a number of works. Most of her work explores cross-cultural issues deriving from her divided heritage. Her publications include *Demi-coq et compagnie: Fables de Tunisie* (1997), *Gisements de lumière* (1998), *Le Secret et autres histoires* (1994), *Marcher sur la terre* (1994), *Métamorphose de l'île et de la vague* (1985), *Paysages, nuit friable* (1980) and *Sables funambules* (1988). (**Kamal Salhi**)

Saint Augustine Born Thagaste (now Souk-Ahras, ALGERIA), 354; died Hippone (Bône during colonisation, Annaba from 1962), 430. Christian theologian, author of *Soliloques* (386–7), *La Cité de Dieu* (413–27), *Confessions* (397–401), known today in the Francophone world as Augustin de Thagaste, African bishop. His origins and presence on African soil, his truly African sources of inspiration and his efforts to promote the then revolutionary religion of Christianity have made writers, intellectuals and some present-day politicians, open to historical and cultural DIVERSITY, see him as a key founding father of Algerian culture and history. KATEB YACINE entitled an early work *Soliloques* (1946) and later engaged in a critical dialogue with Augustine, reproaching him for dismissing Donatist thought, in spite of its closer links with mystical African reality. Assia DJEBAR also prefaced *L'Amour, la fantasia* (1985) with excerpts from the *Confessions*, characteristic of Augustine's BERBER memory. A major international conference on Augustine and Algeria, held in Algiers in 2001, attracted the participation of President BOUTEFLIKA. (**Beïda Chikhi**)

Further reading

For more extensive treatment of the role of Saint Augustine in the history of Algerian thought, see Chikhi and Berehi (2002); see also Mandouze (1998); Kébir (1999, 2001).

Saint-John Perse (Pseudonym of Alexis Saint-Léger Léger.) Born St-Léger-les-Feuilles, GUADELOUPE, 1887; died Presqu'île-de-Giens, France, 1975. A leading French-language poet of the twentieth century, winner of the Nobel Prize for Literature in 1960. Perse was also a distinguished career diplomat, posted notably to China where he wrote *Anabase* (1924; *Anabasis*, 1930), but forced into American exile under Vichy. After 1940, he began to publish long, rhythmical, highly innovative prose poems: *Exil* (1944; *Exile*, 1953), *Vents* (1946; *Winds*, 1961), and *Amers* (1957; *Seamarks*, 1958). Perse was born in Guadeloupe, but moved to France at the age of twelve; there has been considerable interest in his work from GLISSANT and other writers linked to the contemporary Caribbean CRÉOLITÉ movement, and a resultant re-emphasis of the poet's own Creole roots. (**Charles Forsdick**)

Further reading

For an excellent introduction to Perse, see R. Little (1973). Gallagher (1998) reconsiders the poet in his Caribbean context.

Saint-Pierre-et-Miquelon (SPM) These two small islands (242 sq. km, about 6000 inhabitants) close to the south coast of Newfoundland are all that remains of the

French territories in North America. Today officially called *Collectivité territoriale de la République* (from 1985), SPM send one representative to the National Assembly. The islands were originally frequented by French fishermen (sixteenth century), before they became a colony in the seventeenth century. Alternating several times between French and English domination, the islands definitively became French by the Treaty of Paris in 1814.

The main reason for the great interest England and France took in these tiny territories with their harsh climate was the rich cod fisheries on the Newfoundland banks. After restrictions on cod fishery, there was a serious controversy with Canada in the 1980s about fishing quotas (by arbitration in New York 1990, SPM was accorded the right to establish an exclusive economic zone of 24 nautical miles). Due to the fishery crises, fishing and the fishing industry were of variable economic importance till the end of the twentieth century. At present, SPM represent a negative balance in French global economy (a commercial deficit of 321 million francs in 1999). The islands have some tourism during the short summer season (10,000 visitors in 1999).

SPM have been of great political and military interest to France (occupied by General DE GAULLE's forces from 1941 during World War II) and they are still important as part of the strategic presence of France outside Europe, along with REUNION, NEW CALEDONIA and ANTILLES-GUYANE).

A considerable number of the islanders are European French, working there for a limited time (e.g. teachers, policemen, customs officers), and the French spoken is that of France, not that of Canada. (**John Kristian Sanaker**)

Further reading

Belorgey (1993) – an introduction to the history of the islands as well as to their present political and economic situation (and not just about fishery).

Salan, Raoul   Born Roquecourbe, Tarn; 1899; died Paris, 1984. French army officer. He was the most senior figure in the April 1961 putsch by the generals in ALGERIA which aimed to prevent Algerian independence. Nominated 1952 as army chief in VIETNAM, he experienced France's defeat at DIEN BIEN PHU in March 1954. He returned to Algeria as army chief in 1956 and took over civilian affairs in 1958. He resigned his command in October 1960, having declared his support for a French Algeria. His support and his ability to rally the French settlers helped to legitimate the putsch. However, also implicated in the assassination of Camille Blanc, the mayor of Evian and the Kabyle writer Mouloud FERAOUN (see KABYLIA), he was sentenced to life imprisonment in May 1962, but amnestied and released in 1968. (**Kay Adamson**)

Sam-Long, Jean-François   Born 1949. Reunionese poet, novelist and literary critic. His early poems celebrated the idea of *Créolie*, which he champions along with Gilbert AUBRY, but he is better known for his historical novels, such as *Madame Desbassayns* (1985) and his imaginative fiction, such as *L'Arbre de Violence* (1994). He has also published several guides and anthologies of Reunionese literature in both French and CREOLE. (**Peter Hawkins**)

Sankara, Thomas   1950–87. Army officer and former president of BURKINA FASO. After taking power in a *coup d'état* in 1983, Sankara commenced an anti-corruption drive, attempted to implement policies to assist the country's poor, and espoused women's rights. He also granted equal rights to the formerly oppressed Mossi tribe. Such policies inevitably earned him enemies. Sankara gave the country its present name, which translates as 'land of honest men'. He also tried to resolve the African debt crisis. Sankara, a popular leader, was deposed and shot in a *coup* allegedly staged by the current president. (**Susan Fox**)

Further reading

Jaffré (1997).

Sans-papiers   The term *sans-papiers* (formerly CLANDESTINS, and meaning undocumented residents) refers to those foreigners whom the French state judges not to fulfil the conditions for legal residency status. Popularised due to a 1996 social movement culminating in a hunger strike (St Bernard church, Paris), the term in fact describes a problem going back several decades. French law distinguishes very carefully between nationals and non-nationals, the latter being subject to specific rules governing entry and residency (Noiriel, 1988). In the post-1945 period, French governments encouraged cheap labour from developing countries. After 1971, however, successive governments applied existing rules more harshly and introduced many further restrictions. *Sans-papiers* protests have been frequent since 1972 (Siméant, 1998), challenging official policy that is seen to discriminate against non-Europeans. Furthermore, the evolution of European Union (EU) law has introduced much stricter legislation for non-EU than EU non-French nationals. Most participants in the 1996 movement had been directly affected by the restrictive 1993–4 immigration laws ending the 'automatic' renewal of ten-year residency cards.

The 1996 *sans-papiers* movement, supported by a diverse coalition (far-left, antiracist, church and humanitarian groups, labour organisations, intellectuals and artists), initially comprised mostly Chinese, Malian, Moroccan and Senegalese residents, many of whom were women (cf. Cissé, 1999). The protestors sustained a lengthy, six-month mobilisation maintaining autonomy and demanding that all *sans-papiers* be regularised rather than having cases examined on an individual basis. The violent security-force removal of all St Bernard hunger-strikers and their supporters (23 August 1996) drew widespread protests, and in 1997 the right-wing government had to withdraw further plans for restrictive legislation after mass mobilisation from civil society. *Sans-papiers* mobilisations have continued, as the law has not been substantially changed. These protests have revived calls for a new CITIZENSHIP, drawn attention to the problems faced by the most marginalised groups within French society, and revealed the effects of GLOBALISATION on MIGRATION. (**Jim House**)

Further reading

Cissé (1999) – a first-hand account of the 1996 mobilisation by one of the *sans-papiers*' key spokespeople; Fassin, Morice and Quiminal (1997) – edited volume containing useful analyses of legal developments, migration policy, and *sans-papiers* mobilisations.

Sassine, Williams 1944–97. Guinean novelist. He was of mixed-race background and lived in exile in various neighbouring states in West Africa for most of his life. His novels, such as *Saint Monsieur Baly* (1973), *Wirriyamu* (1976; Eng. trans. 1980), *Le Jeune Homme de sable* (1979) and *Le Zéhéros n'est pas n'importe qui* (1985) all depict in different ways the difficulties of outsider figures to come to terms with the post-independence situations of African countries. (**Peter Hawkins**)

Schwarz-Bart, André Born Metz, France, 1928. French Jewish resistance activist and novelist, whose *Le Dernier des justes* (1959; *The Last of the Just*, 1960) won the Prix Goncourt, causing a lively polemic for its 'fictional' account of Jewish history and myth, focusing on self-sacrifice in the Holocaust. With his Guadeloupean wife Simone Schwarz-Bart he then produced *Un Plat de porc aux bananes vertes* (1967). This was followed by another novel of historic and tragic proportions, *La Mulâtresse Solitude* (1972; *A Woman Named Solitude*, 1973), tracing the slave trade across the Atlantic and celebrating female MARRONNAGE (marooning) in the Caribbean. (**Andy Stafford**)

Schwarz-Bart, Simone Born France, 1938. French writer. She was brought up in GUADELOUPE, where she now lives, after having spent much of her life in Europe and in Africa. Schwarz-Bart is the author of *Pluie et vent sur Télumée Miracle* (1972; *The Bridge of Beyond*, 1974), a novel of multigenerational feminine survival, *Ti-Jean L'Horizon* (1979; *Between Two Worlds*, 1981), a quest novel in magic realist mode, and an innovatory play, *Ton beau capitaine* (1987), about Haitian migrant workers in Guadeloupe. *Un plat de porc aux bananes vertes* (1967) is a novel co-authored with André Schwarz-Bart. While not indebted to any particular ideological movement, her writing affirms the poetry of the black spirit, the beauty of Caribbean space, and CREOLE turns of mind and of speech. Her emphasis on survival as resistance lends her lyrical work a certain political undercurrent. (**Mary Gallagher**)

Science and technology Science and technology are considered as two vital ingredients for the economic and social development of modern nations. A vast literature shows they have largely been missing and badly managed in less developed countries, often as a result of poor policies. A host of issues are related to their proper integration into economic development, ranging from scientific education at schools, vocational training centres and universities, to organising research and development and innovation. In the Maghreb countries, namely ALGERIA, TUNISIA and MOROCCO, they have gradually become a growing area of interest both at the academic and policy-making level, though still limited to a relatively small circles of researchers. The first impetus started from Algeria in the early 1970s as a result of its early choice of a development model based primarily on industrialisation and a massive acquisition of technology from abroad. The other Maghreb countries came to grips with these issues in the late 1980s and (mostly) in the 1990s. Francophone studies in the field can be divided into three major categories. They reflect the stages Maghreb countries have been going through. The first set of studies dealt exclusively with the issues of transfer of technology to Maghreb countries, the second set of studies relates to the issue of technology management and the third stage, which is the current stage, relates to the issues of technology accumulation and innovation. (**Abdelkader Djeflat**)

Further reading

Yachir (1983) shows how science and technology raised a variety of issues both internally and from an external point of view. His merit is to show for the first time the complex links with the international market and its structure. Djeflat and Zghal (1995) show how the classical beliefs and approaches came into crisis in the 1980s, mainly as a result of the transition Maghreb countries have been going through.

Sebbar, Leïla Born 1941. Writer of Algerian and French parentage. She grew up in ALGERIA and studied in France. During the 1980s Sebbar worked on *Sans frontière*, a multiculturalist, pro-immigrant magazine produced in Paris, and published several novels documenting multiculturalism in France: e.g. *Fatima ou les Algériennes du square* (1981); *Les Carnets de Shérazade* (1985); *Le Chinois vert d'Afrique* (1984). Their protagonists are usually Maghrebi-French runaways who explore the colonial and immigrant inheritances of French society. More recently, she has written novels about death and exile (*Le Silence des rives*, 1993; *Silence on the Shores*, 2000) and the massacre of Algerians by French police on 17 OCTOBER 1961 (*La Seine était rouge*, 1999). (**Mark McKinney**)

Sebti, Youcef 1943–93. Algerian poet. He was assassinated by Islamic extremists at the National Institute for Agronomy, where he taught rural sociology. His poetry survives in the collection *L'Enfer et la folie*, published in 1981.

Secularism and religion Secularism, or LAÏCITÉ, is an integral part of French Republicanism, which provided the ideological basis for Third Republic imperialism in the nineteenth and early twentieth centuries. The French concept of secularism, unlike other types elsewhere, supposes religion to be a private matter, with no bearing on the political rights and equality of CITIZENS, and does not allow for any special status for particular religious groups or institutions. Secularism is a key tenet of a public education system, in which religion is supposed to play no part. French institutional and cultural practice has, in fact, often deviated from this principle. This was especially true in the colonies, where the principles of secularism were not applied with any great consistency. Christian religious bodies were often closely associated with the colonial authorities. Moreover, religion itself was used as a discriminatory principle for differentiating 'Muslim' Algerians from settlers of European origin, as a basis for their unequal juridical status.

It is not surprising that, given colonial discrimination against Islam in the Maghreb, it should be used as a unifying, rallying cause for the national liberation movement, particularly in ALGERIA. In the postcolonial period, however, differences have arisen regarding the role which religion should play, particularly with regard to state institutions and the legal system, the rights of individuals and of women. On the one hand, dissatisfaction with the position of women, codified in an unequal status (see FAMILY CODES), in the name of religious law and social tradition, has given rise to movements campaigning for equal rights and individual freedoms (see WOMEN'S

MOVEMENTS IN THE MAGHREB). On the other hand, discontent with the poor performance of post-independence regimes and the lack of real economic and social progress, because of a variety of local and global factors, has also led to an upsurge of dissident movements, which use a fundamentalist approach to religion as their main social and political ideology (see ISLAM, MAGHREB).

Different issues have arisen in Quebec, where the dominance of the Catholic Church has been eroded since the 1960s (see QUEBEC and RÉVOLUTION TRANQUILLE). Contradictions arising from the notion and application of secularism have also come to the fore in France itself (see HEADSCARF AFFAIR; LAÏCITÉ). See also RELIGION, SUB-SAHARAN AFRICA; RELIGION, INDIAN OCEAN.

Further reading

Baubérot (1996) – on the French debates concerning *laïcité*; Westerlund (1996) – on the global resurgence of religion in politics; Arkoun (1992) – on Islam and society.

Sefrioui, Ahmed   Born Fès, 1915. Moroccan writer. Attended Koranic and French schools. In 1956 became inspector for the *Service des Arts et Métiers marocains*, then Directeur du Tourisme (Rabat). Received the *Grand Prix littéraire du Maroc* for his collection of novellas, *Le Chapelet d'ambre* (1949) – the first indigenous Moroccan author so honoured. *La Boîte à merveilles* (1954) was one of the first Moroccan novels written in French. *La Maison de servitude* was published in ALGERIA in 1973. Sefrioui's interest in the fairytale dimension of MOROCCO is also evident in his collection of short stories, *Le Jardin des sortilèges ou le parfum des légendes* (1989). (**Susanne Heiler**)

Further reading

Mouzouni (1985) – analyses the importance of Sefrioui's work for Moroccan literature in French.

Sembene, Ousmane   Born Zilguinchor, SENEGAL, 1923. Senegalese writer and film director. Sembene has used his work to provide scathing critiques of social injustices in colonial and postcolonial Senegal. A committed Marxist, he began writing while a docker in Marseilles in the 1950s. Since the early 1960s, he has led a dual career as writer and film-maker, directing 11 films and publishing 10 books. He turned to cinema in order to reach a wider African audience, and he is often referred to as 'the father of African cinema', credited with a number of 'firsts': first film by a Black African, *Borrom Sarret* (1962); first feature film, *La Noire de ...* (1966); first film in an African language, *Le Mandat* (1968).

Sembene is best known for his novel *Les Bouts de bois de Dieu* (1960; *God's Bits of Wood*, 1962), in which he weaves an epic story around an historical railway strike. Anger at the failures of DECOLONISATION mark many of his later works, and, in particular, the film *Xala* (1974), adapted from his 1973 novel of the same title (Eng. trans. 1976), in which he criticises a parasitic African bourgeoisie and the hypocrisy of SENGHOR'S *NÉGRITUDE*. Similar ideas are examined in *Le Mandat*, the novella (1966; *The Money Order*, 1972) and film (1968), and in *Guelwaar* (novella, 1996; film, 1992). He has made three historical films about Senegal: *Emitaï* (1972) and *Camp de Thiaroye*

(1988) deal with colonialism, while *Ceddo* (1976) examines slavery and the rise of Islam. His positive representation of women has been a central feature of all his work. Although generally acclaimed for their political commitment, some of his major works are now considered by many critics to be masterpieces of African literature and cinema. (**David Murphy**)

Further reading

Murphy (2000) – first overview of Sembene's work both as film-maker and author.

Sénac, Jean   Born Benisaf, western Algeria, 1926. Algerian poet. His parents were French settlers of Spanish origin. His career as a poet started at the early age of fifteen, when he had his first poems published in the daily *Oran-Républicain*. He discovered other Algerian-born French authors, whom he befriended, including CAMUS. After the outbreak of the ALGERIAN WAR OF INDEPENDENCE in 1954, Sénac joined the FLN, announcing the rupture with many of his French friends. He devoted his poetry to the Algerian cause, chanting its glories and predicting the dawning of independence. His collections of poetry include: *Le Soleil sous les armes* (1957), *Matinale de mon peuple* (1961) and *Aux héros purs* (1962). Sénac was mysteriously murdered in his Algiers flat in 1973. (**Zahia Smail Salhi**)

Further reading

Belamri (1989); Péroncel-Hugoz (1983).

Senegal   A West African country on the Atlantic coast. It surrounds the Gambia and is bordered by MAURITANIA to the north, MALI to the east, GUINEA and Guinea-Bissau to the south. Capital: Dakar. The first French settlement in Senegal was at Saint-Louis, where a fort was built in 1659 at the mouth of the Senegal River. French companies traded in gum arabic, slaves and gold from along the river, as well as ivory, millet and salt from further inland. The town was captured by the British during the Napoleonic wars but returned to France under the 1814 Treaty of Paris. As French colonial ambitions took shape in the 1850s, Louis Faidherbe (Governor of Senegal 1854–61, 1863–5) initiated French expansion into the interior. Initially, there was widespread resistance, but by 1892 only the southern province of Casamance (south of the Gambia) was not fully under French control. Export of groundnuts, the staple of the Senegalese export economy, began in the 1890s. The assimilationist tradition in French West African politics has its origins in Senegal. From 1848, except during the Second Empire, Senegal sent a *député* to the National Assembly in Paris. Four *communes de plein exercice* with elected town councils were set up in Saint-Louis, Gorée, Rufisque and Dakar between 1872 and 1887, French schools were established and in 1914 citizens of the Four Communes elected Blaise Diagne as their first black African *député*. Political rights were extended from the Four Communes to the whole of French West Africa at the end of the Second World War. After the War, Léopold Sédar SENGHOR emerged as the territory's leading political figure. In 1947 he left the French Socialist Party and founded his own political party, the *Bloc Démocratique Sénégalais*. He led the country to independence on 20 August 1960, following the collapse of the short-lived Mali Federation involving the former territory of Soudan and Senegal, and remained President until he stood down in January 1981. His successor, Abdou Diouf, remained President until his defeat in the 2000 presidential elections by Abdoulaye Wade. Throughout the postcolonial period, Senegal has been a key French ally in West Africa. It has maintained close relations with its former colonial power and a French garrison of some 1000 men is permanently stationed at Dakar. It is one of the world's poorest countries with a GDP per capita of $520 (1998) and is very dependent on western aid. Its main foreign currency earnings come from groundnuts, fish, phosphates and tourism. However, the latter has been undermined in recent years by the sometimes violent activities of the separatist movement in Casamance. (**Tony Chafer**)

Senghor, Léopold Sédar   Born Joal, Senegal, 1906; died 2001. President of Senegal, 1960–80, Senghor is also the chief theorist and poet of négritude. He attended university in Paris, where he encountered Aimé Césaire, with whom he developed the concept of *négritude*. In critically acclaimed poetry collections such as *Chants d'ombre* (1945) and *Ethiopiques* (1956), he seeks a form of expression for the simplicity and beauty of African culture. Senghor rejected the idea that colonial subjects should become 'assimilated Frenchmen', instead promoting the notion of *métissage* (HYBRIDITY), whereby 'Black' and 'European' identities would create a new hybrid culture (his ideas on *négritude* and *métissage* are contained in the five-volume *Liberté* series: Editions du Seuil, Paris, 1964–93). Senghor's *négritude* was the dominant vision of African culture in the Francophone world until the 1970s when it was challenged and rejected by younger generations.

Senghor entered politics in 1945, quickly forming his own party, which became the dominant force in Senegalese politics. He was a late convert to the cause of independence, long favouring a close-knit confederation of African states with France. As President of Senegal, he became an advocate of 'African socialism', the adaptation of Marxism to African conditions. He also played a vital role in creating an institutional Francophonie in the 1960s, forging a partnership between Francophone nations. However, political opponents accused him of a NEO-COLONIAL relationship with France, as Senegal relied heavily on French economic aid and French troops remained stationed on Senegalese soil. By the late 1960s, Senegal had become a one-party state, although other parties were gradually authorised. Senghor retired in 1980, leaving behind a poor but nonetheless stable and democratic country. (**David Murphy**)

Further reading

Hymans (1971) – a sympathetic account of Senghor's career as poet and politician; Sembene (1981) – a left-wing, fictionalised critique of Senghor's Senegal.

Senghor University   See Université Senghor.

Serfaty, Abraham   Born 1926. Moroccan dissident and political activist, writer and academic. He was imprisoned for seventeen years by the Moroccan regime, after the failed *coup* of 1972, alongside Abdellatif LAÂBI, as a co-editor of SOUFFLES. He became a *cause célèbre* for human rights groups and opponents of MOROCCO's repressive political system. Stripped of his Moroccan citizenship in 1991 (for allegedly not being fully Moroccan) and exiled to France, he was recently allowed to return to Morocco. He has not however renounced his opposition to Morocco's continued occupation of WESTERN SAHARA. (**Andy Stafford**)

Serhane, Abdelhak   Born Sefrou, 1950. Moroccan writer. He formerly taught psychology at the University of Kenitra. In his politically committed novels he exposes the dark side of Moroccan society: poverty, corruption, homosexuality, the oppression of women, and the lack of perspectives for young people. In his poems, however, he also praises love. Novels: *Messaouda* (1983; Eng. trans., 1986); *Les Enfants des rues étroites* (1986); *Le Soleil des obscurs* (1992); *Le Deuil des chiens* (1998). Poetry: *L'Ivre poème* (1989); *Chant d'ortie* (1993); *La Nuit du secret* (1992); *Le Silence est déjà trop tard* (2000). Essays: *L'Amour circoncis* (1995); *Le Massacre de la tribu* (1997). Short stories: *Les Prolétaires de la haine* (1995). (**Susanne Heiler**)

Further reading

Chikhi (1996) – pp. 165-8, for an analysis of Serhane's '*romans à option psychopathologique*'; Gontard (1993) – pp. 151–5 for an account of Serhane's writing techniques.

Setif Uprising   On 8 May 1945, thousands of Algerians, spurred by an air of optimism for freedom, celebrated in the streets of Setif. Accounts of how events unfolded differ; shots were fired, followed by some French casualties. In reprisal, in the triangle between Setif, Guelma and Kherrata in the north-east of the country, thousands were slaughtered – some crushed under the wheels of tanks. The French were confident that, through this massive reprisal, they had broken the signs of rebellion. Less than a decade later, events proved them wrong. An armed uprising took place, engulfing the whole country, a very bloody episode from which independent Algeria emerged. Setif 1945 was the last warning, and the trigger too. (**Salah Zaimeche**)

Seychelles   A tropical archipelago made up of 32 granite and 83 coral islands, situated in the southern Indian Ocean to the north of MADAGASCAR. Capital: Victoria, on the island of Mahé. The population of 78,680, is of mixed European, African and Indian descent and speak CREOLE, the official language of the country, and some English and French. Although originally settled by the French, the Seychelles are a former British colony and member of the Commonwealth. The principal exports of the islands were formerly coprah and vanilla, but in recent times the tourist industry provides the vast majority of the country's earnings. Fishing and the fishing rights to its extensive territorial waters represent another substantial source of revenue, and the islands enjoy a high standard of living relative to their limited natural resources. The islands' culture is centred on the Creole language, which is celebrated in the songs of Jean-Marc Volcy; the islands also boast a Francophone poet, Antoine Abel (b. 1934), author of collections such as *Paille en queue* (1969) and poetic tales in prose such as *Coco sec* (1969) and *Une tortue se rappelle* (1977). (**Peter Hawkins**)

Sherazade (Shéhérazade)   The heroine of the ARABIAN NIGHTS continues her story-telling through the pages of the Francophone literature of the Maghreb. Through her mastery of feminine strategy, the name of Sherazade has come to signify the origin of the redemptive power of the female word. Just as the sultana was saved through her amazing story-telling capacity, so many writers claim to be the natural or spiritual heirs of the 'Sultana of the dawn', including Assia DJEBAR in *Ombre sultane* (1987; *A Sister to Scheherazade*, 1988). Indeed, the title, *Les Mille et une nuits* (A Thousand and One Nights') in its French form, lent itself readily to a further instalment. This sequel, *La Mille et deuxième nuit*, by Mostafa Nissaboury, presents us with the unexpected vision of a Sherazade who has lost her charms and powers. Other '*Nights*' have been produced, all different in character: nostalgic, searching or critical versions, such as Rachid BOUDJEDRA's *Les Mille et une années de la nostalgie* (1979); tinged with suspicion in Abdelkebir KHATIBI's *De la mille et troisième nuit* (1980), which questions the ethical principle of the *Nights*; Leïla SEBBAR's *Shérazade, 17 ans, brune, frisée, les yeux verts* (1982; *Sherazade: Missing, aged 17, dark curly hair, green eyes*, 1991) portrays the typical figure of the rebellious, young immigrant girl from the Paris suburbs. Thus Sherazade, the product of a monumental work of oriental literature, constitutes a *motif* in today's writing, as well as a focus for reflection and nostalgia about the past. (Beïda Chikhi)

Sihanouk, Norodom   Born 1922. Cambodian leader, as King (1941–55), Prime Minister (1955–60), Head of State (1960–70), and again as King (1993–). Studied in Saigon and Paris. He led the country to independence from France in 1953, then attempted to preserve CAMBODIA's neutrality in the VIETNAM War in the 1960s, although he broke relations with the Americans after the killing of Cambodians. After his overthrow by Lon Nol in 1970, he took refuge in China and set up a government in exile. Although he returned to Cambodia in 1975, when the KHMER ROUGE took power, he soon fell foul of the regime and eventually returned to exile, though he allied himself with the Khmer Rouge following the Vietnamese invasion of 1978. He returned to power in 1993, following the peace settlement. A skilful politician, he has been seen as one of history's great 'survivors'. Sihanouk was one of the initial founders of the notion of a Francophone community and contributed to the 1962 issue of *Esprit* which launched the Francophone idea.

Further reading

Sihanouk (1973) – for his own account of the early period of his rule.

Silent Revolution   See *RÉVOLUTION TRANQUILLE*.

Smaïl, Paul   French writer. A certain mystery surrounds the identity of the successful author who goes under this name. He is said to be of Moroccan origin and hold a DEA in French literature. However, one literary critic and journalist claims to have spotted Alain Jack Léger, a fellow journalist, from *Libération*, hiding behind the mask of Paul Smaïl. She claims that, since he could not make it as a French writer, he chose '*BEUR* literature' as the route to success in Francophone literary circles. Whatever the truth may be, his dynamic writing and use of top-notch BANLIEUE imagery, backed up by a university education, complete with cultural and literary references, contrive to subvert the stereotypical image of the dislocated *banlieusard*. The autobiographical-style writing is akin to the *Diwan* style, as a sort of conglomerate of diverse texts and fragments, drawing on all possible genres and both eastern and western sources. According to him, *Diwan* represents best the identity-mosaic of the migrant writer. His texts are increasingly dense and complex: *Vivre me tue* (1997; *Smile*, 2000), *Casa, la casa* (1998), *La Passion selon moi* (1999), *Ali le Magnifique* (2001). (**Beïda Chikhi**)

Smaïn, Fairouz Born ALGERIA, 1958. Maghrebi-French comedian and actor. Abandoned as a child and brought up by social services and a foster family in France. After a succession of menial jobs, he began doing stand-up in café-theatres, aged 22. His third show, '*Comme ça se prononce*' ('As it's pronounced'), won him a Molière award for best one-man show in 1992. Of 20 films, some have been award-winners, others flops. Owner of two successful restaurants in Paris, Smaïn considers father-hood his most important role. He returned to the small screen in 2001 as a police inspector in *Commissariat Bastille* for TF1. Films include *L'œil au beur(re) noir*, by Meynard (1987); *Les 2 papas et la maman*, co-written and produced with J-M. Longval (1997). (**Samantha Neath**)

Socé, Ousmane (Also known as Ousmane Socé Diop.) Born Rufisque, 1911; died 1973. Senegalese writer and politician. Socé's two novels, *Karim* (1935) and *Mirages de Paris* (1937), belong to a transitional, pre-NÉGRITUDE moment of Francophone African literature. The first describes a young Senegalese protagonist's first contact with French culture in an African city. The second recounts the character Fara's journey to France, at the time of the 1931 Exposition Coloniale. It explores the hero's relationship with a Frenchwoman and seems to advocate MÉTISSAGE, although its stark conclusion shows the exile's ultimate alienation from his host culture. In 1938, Socé published *Contes et légendes d'Afrique noire*. While a student in France, he co-founded the journal *L'Etudiant noir* with SENGHOR, DAMAS and CÉSAIRE. Socé was a Senegalese representative in the French parliament from 1937, and later became a senator. (**Charles Forsdick**)

Further reading

For a useful discussion of Socé's work, see Blair (1976), and of *Mirages de Paris* in particular, see Miller (1998).

SONATRACH *Société Nationale pour la Recherche, la Production, le Transport, la Transformation et la Commercialisation des Hydrocarbures* Since 1963 the Algerian state oil and gas company, Sonatrach, has been the main source of foreign exchange earnings for the country (97 per cent of foreign exchange revenue in 1996). As well as developing 35 major oil fields and gas and condensate production, especially at Hassi R'Mel, Sonatrach has developed gas liquefaction at its Arzew and Skikda plants and has pioneered two sub-Mediterranean pipelines to export gas directly to Italy and Spain. Restructuring in the early and mid-1980s under the Chadli government has decentralised Sonatrach into several *entreprises nationales*. The 1990s saw several joint ventures with international oil companies covering exploration and production. A 1998 modernisation and expansion programme seeks to place Sonatrach in the front rank of international hydrocarbons companies, while maintaining its close integration with the Algerian state. (**Keith Sutton**)

Further reading

Entelis (1999).

Sony Lab'ou Tansi (Pseudonym of Marcel Sony.) Born Kimwanza, Belgian Congo (now DEMOCRATIC REPUBLIC OF CONGO), 1947; died Foufoudou, 1995. Congolese novelist and dramatist. Sony's first novel, *La Vie et demie* (1979), is a farcical, grotesque satire on the violent politics of post-independence African regimes, setting the tone for the majority of his subsequent prolific production of plays and novels, where the influence of Latin-American magic realism is evident. His plays, such as *Qui a mangé Madame d'Avoine Bergota* (1989), usually first performed by his company the Rocado Zulu Théâtre in Brazzaville, were often showcased in Paris and at festivals such as the *Festival des Francophonies* at Limoges. After a short-lived foray into politics in 1992–3, he died of AIDS in 1995. (**Peter Hawkins**)

Sony, Marcel See SONY LAB'OU TANSI.

SOS-Racisme Youth antiracist movement. Founded in late 1984 by a group of Paris-based former student political activists led by Harlem DÉSIR and Julien Dray, SOS-*Racisme* became the largest mass youth antiracist movement of the 1980s, organising rock concerts, cultivating celebrity endorsements and distributing a badge stating *Touche pas à mon pote!* (Hands off my mate!). SOS-*Racisme* combined celebrations of 'pluricultural' France with calls for INTEGRATION, and attracted widespread criticism and lost its support because of a perceived lack of political autonomy due to links with MITTERRAND and the Socialist Party (PS) (Bouamama, 1994). Power battles within the PS and internal conflicts further weakened the association, which nonetheless remains active. (**Jim House**)

Further reading

Désir (1985) – an accessible description of the first few years of the association, related by one of its founders.

Souffles Important Moroccan journal published between 1966 and 1972, it mixed a MODERNIST, and often violently avant-gardist, literary vision with a deeply political critique of the situation in MOROCCO. Its animators, Tahar BEN JELLOUN, Abdellatif LAÂBI, Abdelkebir KHATIBI, Mostafa Nissaboury, Mohammed KHAÏR-EDDINE and Abraham SERFATY, were either imprisoned after the 1972 *coup* attempt against the regime, or forced into exile, and the journal was subsequently suppressed. Originally publishing in French, it began to arabise its content at the same time as supporting the Palestinian cause in 1970. (**Andy Stafford**)

Soundiata   Founder of the MALI empire. He fought the tyrant Soumangourou in about 1235, organising the clans so that each had specific roles. This organisation is to a certain extent respected even today. The *Epic of Soundiata* (*Son-Jara*), also called *L'Epopée mandingue* ('Mande epic'), is still recited and known far beyond the borders of Mali. (**Ingse Skattum**)

Further reading

Niane (1960) – the classic French prose version, with good annotations by a well-known historian; DIABATÉ (1986) – a French prose version recorded and translated by a nephew of the *griot* who recited it, contains a good introduction.

Souphanouvong   See LAOS.

Soustelle, Jacques-Emile   Born Montpellier, 1912; died Paris, 1999. Ethnologist and politician. He was a member of the *Académie Française*. An anti-fascist, Soustelle joined DE GAULLE's Free French forces in 1940, continuing to serve Gaullism after 1945 as minister, general-secretary of the RPR (Rally of the French People) (1947–51) and parliamentary deputy until 1958. As Governor-General of ALGERIA 1955–56, Soustelle became a defender of French Algeria. He supported de Gaulle's re-election in 1958 but broke with Gaullism in 1960, resigning in protest over de Gaulle's 'betrayal' of French Algeria. Fearing arrest after a failed army 'putsch', he went into exile (1961–68), later returning to politics. (**Marianne Durand**)

Further reading

Soustelle (1968) – this book presents a polemic but useful overview of Soustelle's relations with Charles de Gaulle; Talbott (1980) – an English-language account of the Algerian War with particular reference given to Jacques Soustelle.

South Pacific Forum   See PACIFIC ISLANDS FORUM.

Souvanna Phouma   See LAOS.

Souza, Carl de   Born 1949. Mauritian novelist. Carl de Souza came to prominence with his first novel, *Le Sang de l'Anglais* (1993), a social and psychological drama reflecting the complex social and cultural conflicts of MAURITIUS. Similar themes inspired his successful second novel, *La Maison qui marchait vers le large* (1996), set in the suburbs of Port-Louis with dialogues written in CREOLE. His third novel, *Les Jours Kaya* (2000), is an oneiric account of the recent inter-community riots during which the celebrated Creole singer Kaya died in prison. (**Peter Hawkins**)

Sow Fall, Aminata   Born SENEGAL, 1941. Senegalese novelist. She is also currently director of Khoudia publishing house and CAEC (*Centre Africain d'Animation et d'Echanges Culturels*) in Dakar. Three of her six novels have been selected for prestigious literary prizes in Africa and in Europe. Her second and most famous novel, *La Grève des Bàttu* (1979; *The Beggars' Strike, or The Dregs of Society*, 1981), confronts social inequality in contemporary Senegal and draws parallels with Ousmane

SEMBENE's *Xala*. Whereas most of her novels are social commentaries, *Le Jujubier du patriarche* (1993) signals a change in direction, drawing more specifically on the African oral tradition than Sow Fall's earlier texts. (**Nicki Hitchcott**)

Further reading

Hitchcott (2000) – comprehensive chapter on Sow Fall.

Sport, Maghreb   Sport, which involves competitions based on the nation-state system and described by Vidacs (2000: 110) as the vehicle *par excellence* for national sentiments, has known different stages in the Maghreb Union. During the colonial period it contributed, as did cinema, theatre and literature, to the consolidation of the solidarity and unity of the Maghreb in its struggle against the common colonial power. The FLN (Algerian National Liberation Front) football team was supported by TUNISIA and MOROCCO. Indeed, the Moroccan federation was simply excluded from FIFA following a demand from the French Federation after Morocco's friendly match against the FLN team. In the post-independence era, apart from some initiatives such as the launch of the first Maghreb games in May 1967, which aim to develop interstate partnership and cultural exchanges, sport was transformed into an arena of ultra-nationalism, popular chauvinism and political manipulation. It was used (and still is) by different regimes (as in countries in Latin America and Eastern Europe) as a privileged site for the mobilisation of masses and the legitimisation of a specific state model of political administration.

Today, the search for glory and international recognition at any cost has provoked in many sports competitions between ALGERIA, Tunisia, Morocco and Libya (supposedly members of the Maghreb Union) the development of certain regrettable tendencies that seriously threaten the solidarity and the sense of unity between Maghreb populations. Sometimes these arise amongst the population of the same country due to the fragmentation of the Maghreb region for political and economic reasons and as a consequence of the re-emergence of restricted tribal and *inter-quartier* dogmas in the streets of Tunis, Algiers and Casablanca that have transformed sport into a source of violence and destruction rather than fraternity and social emancipation. (**Mahfoud Amara**)

Further reading

Buell (1994); Chevallier, Guellouz and Miquel (1991) – helpful overview of the historical development of Arab identity and Islamic civilisation in relation to other occidental and non-occidental cultures, from both Arab and Western (Orientalists) point of view; Vidacs (2000) – talks about how football, which is a global culture, could affect local identity, and result in the unity or fragmentation of the imagined community; Stora (1999).

Sport, Sub-Saharan Africa   Football is, undoubtedly, the most popular sport in Sub-Saharan Africa. The African Nations Cup of football was established as early as 1957, when there were very few independent African countries (only three teams took part in the first competition). The competition, which takes place every two years, has now become the main event on the African sporting calendar. Amongst Francophone nations from Sub-Saharan Africa, CAMEROON has been by far the most successful country, winning the competition on four occasions. Cameroon has also had great success in other competitions, qualifying for the quarter-finals of the 1990 World Cup, and winning the gold medal at the 2000 Sydney Olympics. At club level, there are thriving leagues in most Sub-Saharan countries, as well as a number of international club competitions. Most African footballers ply their trade in Europe, some adopting the nationality of the host nation, as is the case with one of Africa's most famous footballers, Patrick Vieira, a World Cup winner with France, but born in SENEGAL.

Other sports have an important place in African life. Athletics has become increasingly popular, but Francophone nations have not made the same breakthrough as their Anglophone counterparts have done in disciplines such as long-distance running (dominated by Ethiopia and Kenya). Growing access to cable television has helped to promote basketball, which appears attractive to many young Africans because it is exciting, fast-paced, and presents a glamorous image of (mainly) black sportsmen. As in so many other areas of life, the chief problem of sport in Africa is the lack of infrastructure (football, athletics and basketball are all sports which do not require expensive equipment). 'Traditional' sports are often very popular: for example, in Senegal, wrestling attracts huge live and television audiences. (**David Murphy**)

Further reading

Ricci (2001) – a comprehensive set of facts and figures about African football from 1957 to 2001.

Stephens, Jimmy VANUATU rebel leader, head of MANH (New Hebrides Autonomy Movement), who led a short-lived attempt to establish a secessionist 'Republic of Vemarana' at Espiritu Santo, after independence in 1980.

Sub-Saharan Africa See AUDIO-VISUAL MEDIA; CINEMA; EDUCATION; LITERATURE; MUSIC; POPULAR CULTURE; PRESS; RELIGION; SPORT; VISUAL ARTS.

Syria Syrian Arab Republic. Capital: Damascus. Population: 16 million, mainly Arab with Kurdish and Armenian minorities. Official language: Arabic. After World War I, Syria was under French mandate from 1920 to independence in 1945. However, there is little residual French influence.

Tadjo, Véronique Born France, 1955. Writer of mixed French and Ivorian parentage. She was brought up in CÔTE D'IVOIRE and now lives in London. Along with authors such as Tanella BONI and WEREWERE LIKING, she produces hybrid texts which cross generic boundaries. Best known for her first 'novel', *A vol d'oiseau* (1986; *As the Crow Flies*, 2001), she has recently published *L'Ombre d'Imana: Voyages au bout du*

Rwanda (2000), following a 'writers in residence' group visit to Rwanda in 1998. (**Nicki Hitchcott**)

Further reading

D'Almeida (1994) – includes useful analysis of *A vol d'oiseau.*

Tahiti   The principal island in French Polynesia and the location of its capital (Papeete) as well as of its main airport (Tahiti-Faa'a, opened in 1961). Of volcanic origin and with peaks of over 2000 metres, it is situated in the *Iles du Vent* (Windward Islands) and has a population of *c.* 150,000 (over half of whom live in Papeete). Tahitian, a Polynesian language, is accepted as a *lingua franca* throughout the TOM and, with French, has been adopted as the official language. Official documents are now printed in both languages. Since it was first visited in 1768 by the French traveller de Bougainville (who dubbed the island the 'New Cythera'), Tahiti has become a privileged, even legendary site in the French imagination and transformed, through the processes of exoticism, into an earthly paradise. Throughout the twentieth century, however, this idealised representation has been slowly eroded as Tahiti has been subject to rapid urbanisation and the pressures of international tourism. In the post-war period, there have been greater demands for autonomy and the Polynesian independence movement has been centred on activity in Tahiti. It is also on Tahiti that the power and wealth of French Polynesia are concentrated and most tourist attractions are situated. However, the island suffers from marked poverty, with the inhabitants of its numerous shantytowns regularly augmented by the victims of cyclones on other islands or simply by those seeking a better standard of living.

Although earlier French literature on Tahiti focused on the island's supposedly idyllic aspects, twentieth-century authors (such as Victor Segalen) have emphasised the harmful effects of contact with Western civilisation on indigenous cultures. This trend has continued amongst post-war writers (such as Jean Reverzy), although the island continues to attract travellers seeking a radically different way of life (Bernard Moitessier). In the late twentieth century, a specifically Tahitian literature (written by poets such as Henri Hiro) has begun to emerge. (**Charles Forsdick**)

Further reading

For a study of the state of contemporary Tahiti, see Cizeron and Hienly (1983); Margueron (1989) provides a comprehensive account of French literary representations of Tahiti, whereas Scemla (2001) explores the emergence of contemporary Tahitian literature.

Taleb Ibrahimi, Ahmed   Born Setif, 1932. Algerian politician and doctor. Under Boumedienne he held the post of Minister of Education (1965–70), responsible for 'Algerianisation' and Arabisation of the system; Minister for Information and Culture (1970–77), and various other positions.

Tamazight, Morocco   Moroccans have predominantly Berber origins (Ayache, 1964; Laroui, 1977; Chafik 1987); *Tamazight* (Berber) is Morocco's oldest language. A Hamito-Semitic language (Basset, 1952; Galand, 1966; Sadiqi, 1990), it used to be written, but is now exclusively oral, without its own alphabet, though it may be written using Arabic or Latin characters. Morocco has three major Berber dialects (*Tashelhit* – south, *Tamazight* – centre, *Tarifit* – north), sharing an overall syntactic structure but somewhat different lexicons and phonologies, hindering their inter-comprehensibility (Cadi, 1997; Ennaji, 1997; Sadiqi, 1997).

Mother tongue of almost 50 per cent of Moroccans (Boukous, 1995; Ennaji, 1997; Sadiqi, 1997), *Tamazight* is not the language of education or commerce, but has survived thanks to the vitality that characterises mother tongues. *Tamazight* is more used in rural areas. In urban areas, it is mainly used in informal/intimate situations, with family and friends. It is also allocated limited space in the audio-visual media. On a wider level, *Tamazight* functions as symbol of Moroccan identity and difference from Middle Eastern Arab and other Islamic countries. A typical indigenous language, *Tamazight* embodies a huge oral culture (songs, dances, folktales, proverbs, riddles), in which women have an important place.

The intermingling of '*Tamazight*' and 'Arab' components in Moroccan history is complex. Although *Tamazight* dynasties ruled Morocco (e.g. Berghuatas, Almohavids, Almohads), the official language has always been Standard Arabic. This may be due to the non-existence of a holy book in Berber. Nowadays, official policy on *Tamazight* is promising. In 1994 HASSAN II advocated *Tamazight* teaching in primary schools. This was followed by TV news broadcasting in the three *Tamazight* dialects. In October 2001, Mohamed VI created the 'Royal Institute of Tamazight', which will boost the language's position. However, other factors discourage its growth, such as ARABISATION, which has not profited Berbers with barely sufficient knowledge of Standard Arabic.

Given its status, *Tamazight* has the lowest share in the linguistic market at the symbolic level, although it is preserved as the language of local Moroccan identity. Its cultural strength is attested in the fact that, to break Arab/Berber cultural/linguistic solidarity during colonisation, the French issued the 'Berber Decree' in 1935, which allowed Berbers to attend schools where only *Tamazight* and French, not Arabic, were taught. Nationalists reacted by establishing private Islamic schools, teaching French as a foreign language. (**Fatima Sadiqi**)

Further reading

Boukous (1995); Laroui (1977); Sadiqi (1997).

Tati-Loutard, Jean-Baptiste   Born CONGO, 1938. Congolese writer, mainly known for his poetry. After studies in Bordeaux, he returned to Brazzaville, where he has taught in higher education and participated in government, with various ministerial portfolios. Works include: *Poèmes de la mer* (1968; *Poems of the Sea*, 1990); *L'Ordre des Phénomènes* (1996); *Chroniques Congolaises* (1974); *Nouvelles Chroniques Congolaises* (1980); *Fantasmagories* (1998); *Le Palmier-lyre* (2000). Prizes include: Grand prix du rayonnement de la langue française (1992, Académie française); Grand prix littéraire de l'Afrique noire (1987), ADELF, for his novel *Le Récit de la mort* (1987); All Africa Okigbo Prize for poetry (1987), Nigeria Writers Association, for poetry collection *La Tradition du songe* (1985).

Tchicaya U Tam'si, Gérald-Félix 1931–88. Congolese poet, novelist and drama-tist. One of the best-known and widely respected African poets of the post-independence years, Tchicaya's hermetic and elliptical style did not preclude oblique political and social commentary, as in *Epitomé* (1962). In his later years he concen-trated on novels – *Les Méduses ou les Orties de la mer* (1982; *The Madman and the Medusa*, 1989) – and theatre, achieving notable popular successes with *Le Destin glo-rieux du maréchal Nnikon Nniku, prince qu'on sort* (1979; *The Glorious Destiny of Marshal Nnikon Nniku*, 1986), a rambunctious farce satirising the excesses of African military dictatorships, and *Le Bal de N'Dinga* (1987), a tribute to the resilience of African popular culture, both successfully performed in Paris at the Théâtre International de Langue Française. (**Peter Hawkins**)

Temaru, Oscar Leader of the Tahitian independence movement, *Tavini Huiraatira*, mayor of Faa'a and anti-nuclear campaigner.

Tengour, Habib Born Mostaganem, 1947. Algerian writer. Habib Tengour made his literary début with a narrative poem, *Topapakitaques, la poésie-île*, published in 1977. After publishing collections of poetry, he began, like many Algerian writers before him, to flirt with the mixing of genres and heterogeneous writing. His texts after 1983, such as *Le Vieux de la montagne* (a tale in which the poet-narrator is pro-pelled through time and space to meet up with Omar Khayyam, Hassan As Sabah of the 'hachichiyuns' or 'Assassins' sect, and Abou Ali Nizam el Moulk) and *Sultan Galiev*, invite the reader to look at literature as a whole made up of simultaneous effects: poetic, fictional narrative, historical and mythical. *Les Gens de Moṣta* (1999) and *Le Poisson de Moïse* (2001) are more clearly anchored in the tormented reality of present-day ALGERIA. (**Beïda Chikhi**)

Theatre, Indian Ocean The Francophone islands of the Indian Ocean have a long-established and vibrant theatrical tradition, particularly in recent years. In MAURITIUS, contemporary popular theatre is dominated by the CREOLE dramas of Dev VIRAHSAWMY, who since 1980 has staged and published a series of plays, many of which are freely adapted from Shakespeare. Among the most successful is *Toufann*, a Creole version of *The Tempest*, recently translated ino English and performed in London in 1999. In REUNION, two locally-based theatre companies dominate the scene: the Théâtre Vollard and the Théâtre Talipot. The Vollard troupe, founded in 1979 by Emmanuel Genvrin and Jean-Luc Trulès, takes its name from the Reunionese art dealer Ambroise Vollard, a friend of French dramatist Alfred Jarry. The company's first production was a controversial version of Jarry's *Ubu roi* and in 1995 they staged an adaptation of Vollard's sequel *Ubu colonial* under the title *Votez Ubu colonial*. This farcical political satire was condemned by the local authorities and led to their sub-sidy being withdrawn in 1999. In the intervening years, Genvrin and Pierre-Louis Rivière wrote many original plays for the company, based around the popular histor-ical culture of Reunion and making extensive use of Creole, such as *Lepervenche chemin de fer* (1992), a chronicle of the Popular Front period in Reunion and the birth of trade unionism on the island. Both the aforementioned shows were successfully performed in Paris and at various French theatre festivals. The Théâtre Talipot, founded in 1993 by Philippe Pelen, practise a multi-lingual theatre which draws on the myths and legends of the diverse cultures of the region. Their most notable productions have been *Mâ* (1995) and *Les Porteurs d'Eau* (1997); the latter toured extensively in Africa and Europe, winning many festival awards including an Edinburgh Fringe First in 1998. MADAGASCAR has a strong theatrical tradition, beginnning with its own indigenous form of theatre, the *hira-gasy*, a popular form of oratorical jousting. More conventional theatre has been illustrated by such writers as Michèle RAKOTOSON, who won the Radio France International Prize in 1990 with her radio play *La Maison morte*. (**Peter Hawkins**)

Theatre, Quebec   Apart from infrequent visits by theatrical companies from France, there was little significant theatrical activity in French Canada until the midtwentieth century. It was in the 1930s that Les Compagnons de Saint-Laurent began to perform an international repertory of plays, but the first major plays by Quebec dramatists did not appear until after the war. The most important of these, *Tit-Coq* by Gratien Gélinas, *Zone* (1953) and *Un Simple Soldat* (1958) by Marcel Dubé, are among the first striking expressions of the mood of social frustration which was to fuel the RÉVOLUTION TRANQUILLE of the 1960s (see QUEBEC). Part of the impact of these plays came from their use of everyday Quebec French to which audiences could easily relate, rather than the more formal speech hitherto associated with the theatre. But it was Quebec's most celebrated dramatist, Michel TREMBLAY, who in 1968 brought *le JOUAL* fully into the theatre and made it into a powerful dramatic medium. His initiative inspired a generation of dramatists, including Jean-Claude Germain, Michel Garneau and Marie Laberge, who used various forms of the vernacular to express the distinctive sense of identity of Quebec.

Since the mid-1980s, new forms of theatre have appeared which distance themselves from overt social and political concerns and concentrate on formal experimentation. Drama is combined with mime, music, dance and cinematic use of light and space to produce choreographed stage events in which spoken text is but one of the threads, and where the producer's role tends to overshadow the playwright's. Jean-Pierre Ronfard, with numerous productions like his play cycle *Vie et mort du roi boiteux* (1982), performance companies like Carbone 14, as well as the ubiquitous Robert LEPAGE, are among those who have given Quebec an international reputation for this kind of innovative theatre. But this trend has not prevented the emergence of individual dramatists creating text-centred plays. Normand Chaurette, Daniel Danis, Michel-Marc Bouchard, Wajdi Mouawad and Carol Fréchette are among the many new voices who have given contemporary Quebec theatre a remarkable vitality. (**Ian Lockerbie**)

Further reading

Godin and Mailhot, I & II (1988) together with Godin and Lafon (1999) give the most comprehensive overview, particularly of individual dramatists. The less text-based visual theatre of Lepage, Carbone 14 and others has not yet been adequately studied.

Théâtre Talipot   See THEATRE, INDIAN OCEAN.

Théâtre Vollard   See Theatre, Indian Ocean.

Tirolien, Guy   1917–88. A Guadeloupean-born poet and short-story writer, Tirolien came to Paris in the mid-1930s to train as a colonial administrator. Although the War intervened, he did leave France for Africa in 1944. He was posted to Guinea, then Niger, and the Ivory Coast, working later on for the UN in Mali and Gabon. He returned in 1977 to the Caribbean, where he became involved in politics until illness forced him to retire. His writing is informed by his non-conflictual feeling for Africa. Although he was close to the négritude movement in Paris, his work is not marked by surrealism. Its appealing simplicity is well illustrated by the much anthologised, anti-assimilation poem 'Prière d'un petit enfant nègre'. His collection of poems, *Balles d'or* (1961), and of short stories, *Feuilles vivantes au matin* (1977), were both published by Présence africaine. (**Mary Gallagher**)

Tjibaou, Jean-Marie   Born Tiendanite, New Caledonia, 1936; died Ouvéa, 1989. *Kanak* independence leader. He was ordained as a priest, but, after a period of study in France, he abandoned the priesthood in 1971. He then organised the 'Melanesia 2000' Festival with Jacques Iekawé, highlighting *Kanak* identity. Elected Mayor of Hienghène in 1977, he became Vice-President of the Union Calédonienne. In 1979, he was elected a Territorial Councillor for the newly formed Independence Front, then Vice-President of the Governing Council in 1982, until the boycott of territorial elections in 1984 by independence supporters. On the formation of the FLNKS the same year, he became President of the provisional government of *Kanaky*. After the 1988 Ouvéa drama, he signed the Matignon Accords, which set out a staged timetable for independence. However, he did not live to see it fulfilled, as he was assassinated less than a year later, along with Yeiwene Yeiwene, by rival independence supporters. A Centre for *Kanak* culture, designed by Rienzo Piano, has been built in his memory near Nouméa. (See also New Caledonia.)

Togo   A small Francophone West African country with a population of around 5 million. Originally a German protectorate, Togoland was partitioned after the First World War, with Britain acquiring the western segment (now part of Ghana) and France receiving the eastern part (present-day Togo). It became a UN trusteeship territory in 1946, a semi-autonomous republic in 1956 and an independent state in 1960.

Togo's first President, Sylvanus Olympio, was elected in 1961 but was unpopular with France due to his apparent Marxist sympathies and his support for Algerian independence. He was assassinated in 1963 and was replaced initially by Nicolas Grunitzky, then, in 1967, by his alleged assassin, General Gnassingbé Eyadéma.

Togo prospered under Eyadéma's autocratic government, benefiting from high prices for its main export, phosphates, and from a period of stability which earned the country its nickname: 'the Switzerland of Africa'. By the 1980s, however, over-ambitious economic policies had led to debts, IMF recovery programmes and Togo's reclassification from low-income to least developed country. Togo came to rely increasingly on the support of France, which remained the largest donor and which intervened militarily in 1986 to defend Eyadéma's regime.

Togo's relations with Paris cooled in the early 1990s when Eyadéma's party, the Rally for the Togolese People, rejected demands for political reform and withdrew from the national conference on DEMOCRACY. Togolese intransigence led Paris to suspend COOPÉRATION, but this was resumed in 1994 largely because of Eyadéma's friendship with France's political leaders and his donations to French electoral campaigns (Verschave, 2000).

Togo is again facing sanctions after the 1998 presidential elections were marred by allegations of manipulation and state-sponsored executions (Amnesty International, 1998). The regime has nonetheless survived thanks to a deal – brokered by President CHIRAC – in which Eyadéma has promised to stand down in 2003. (**Gordon Cumming**)

Further reading

Africa South of the Sahara – the chapter on Togo covers domestic politics and foreign relations; Amnesty International (1998); Decalo (1996) – compilation of political, economic and cultural entries on Togo; Verschave (2000).

Tombalbaye, François Ngarta   Born Bessada, CHAD, 1919; died 1975. Politician. He came from Christian/animist southern Chad. After assuming the presidency of newly independent Chad in August 1960, his urge to consolidate power throughout the country led to dictatorship and repression. Opposed both by the population of the Islamic north and increasingly by elements within his own ethnic group, he spent most of his time in power fighting off rebellion. He was killed (or possibly executed) during a *coup d'état* carried out by one of his former generals. (**Simon Massey**)

Further reading

Azevedo and Nnadozie (1998) – Chapter 3 gives a concise overview of the Tombalbaye era.

Tonton Macoutes   A paramilitary force of thugs, who served as the private militia of both François Duvalier and then his son Jean-Claude in Haiti. They are credited with the murder of many thousands of opponents of the Duvalierist regime. The name derives from a bogeyman character in Haitian folktales. See HAITI; DUVALIER, FRANÇOIS.

Toubon, Jacques   Born Nice, France, 1941. French politician. Since 1981 he has been a member of the RPR (Rally of the French People). Held ministerial office as Minister for Culture and *FRANCOPHONIE* (1993–95) and Minister for Justice (1995–97). In 1994 he was responsible for introducing a major piece of linguistic legislation, known as the *Loi Toubon*. The law, intended to protect consumers and employees, makes the use of French compulsory in official documents, work contracts, consumer information, the media and education. (**Marie-Anne Hintze**)

Touré, Ahmed Sékou   Born Faranah, GUINEA, 1922; died 1984. Guinean politician. He is chiefly remembered as the man who led the Guinean people to vote 'no' (for independence) in the 1958 referendum in which DE GAULLE's France offered its Sub-Saharan African territories the choice of either complete independence or autonomy within a 'French Community' (see COMMUNAUTÉ FRANÇAISE). Touré came to politics via trade unionism and his *Parti Démocratique de Guinée* rose to prominence in the 1950s by challenging ethnic rivalries and the power of the tribal chiefs. Although Guinea was the sole colony to opt for independence, its rejection of France prompted all the other Sub-Saharan French colonies to achieve independence by 1960, and Sékou Touré became a hero of anticolonial resistance. Touré himself was keen to take on the mantle of African leader, writing numerous books on African solidarity, and becoming a leading advocate of PAN-AFRICANISM, alongside Ghana's Kwame Nkrumah, and they were both key players in the founding of the Organisation of African Unity (OAU) in 1963.

However, Touré's autocratic one-party rule increasingly came to be seen as oppressive. Detention camps, including the infamous Camp Boiro, were set up to house those perceived as enemies of the state, and torture and executions were rife, leading thousands of Guineans to seek exile abroad, including the novelist Camara LAYE, who criticises Touré's regime in *Dramouss* (1978). Although condemning the excesses of his regime, some commentators argue that his paranoia was fed by French attempts to destabilise the country: already in 1958, de Gaulle's anger at Guinea's defiance of his will had led him to withdraw the entire French administrative structure immediately and also to withdraw all financial aid to the fledgling state. Touré died in 1984 after 26 uninterrupted years in power, leaving behind a poor and divided country. (**David Murphy**)

Further reading

Rivière (1977) – balanced overview of Touré's regime.

Touré Kunda   African pop group. One of the first African groups to reach an international audience, Touré Kunda was founded by three brothers, Sixu, Ismaïl and Amadou Touré from Ziguinchor in southern SENEGAL. (Amadou died suddenly in 1983 and was replaced by another brother, Ousmane). They moved to Paris in the late 1970s, recording a number of albums which fused rhythms from their native Casamance with electro-funk, rock and reggae. These records were relatively successful, making a name for the band, particularly in France. However, some critics have attacked their work as 'commercial', abandoning Senegalese musical traditions in favour of international success. (**David Murphy**)

Toussaint   See NOVEMBER 1ST 1954.

Tradition   See MODERNITY and TRADITION.

Tran Anh Hung   Vietnamese film-maker living in France. Films include *L'Odeur de la papaye verte* ('The smell of green papaya', 1993) and *Cyclo* (1995), about the poverty of a cycle-rickshaw driver in Ho Chi Minh City.

Tran Duc Thao   Born VIETNAM, 1917; died France, 1993. Philosopher, whose interests spanned phenomenology and dialectical materialism. After studying in Paris at the Ecole Normale Supérieure, he became involved in ANTICOLONIALIST movements, and was linked to the *Temps Modernes* group. He returned to Vietnam in 1951, where he became Dean of History at the new national University of Hanoi, but was forced from this post, after criticism of the Party. Thereafter he worked in the publishing house Su That and lived a life of isolation, until his situation began to improve in the 1980s. He was allowed to travel to France again and awarded the Ho Chi Minh prize posthumously in 2001. His most important work is *Phénoménologie et matérialisme dialectique* (1951; *Phenomenology and Dialectical Materialism*, 1971).

Traoré, Moussa See MALI; KONARÉ; LY.

Tremblay, Michel Born Montreal, 1942. QUEBEC writer. He is famous for having given spoken Quebec language (*le* JOUAL) its dignity in modern literature, initially in his play *Les Belles-Soeurs* (1968; *Belles-Soeurs*, 1974, or *Guid Sisters*, 1988). He practises the same language realism in a great number of novels presenting images of popular, urban life, particularly in his own quarter, the Plateau Mont-Royal (*Chroniques du Plateau Mont-Royal*, 2000). Tremblay has also published a series of novels with homosexual themes – *Le Coeur découvert* (1986; *The Heart Laid Bare*, 1989, or *Making Room*, 1990), *Le Coeur éclaté* (1989) – and nostalgic memories about his own growing up in Montreal – *Les Vues animées* (1990; *Bambi and Me*, 1998). (**John Kristian Sanaker**)

Further reading

David and Lavoie (1993) – texts by leading Quebec academics.

Trudeau, Pierre Elliot Born Montreal, 1919; died, 2000. Canadian politician and statesman; Prime Minister 1968–79 and 1980–82. He trained as a lawyer and was called to the QUEBEC Bar in 1943. In 1950 he was one of the founders of *Cité Libre*, a journal opposed to the separatist policies of Maurice DUPLESSIS, then Prime Minister of Quebec. He urged the reform of the educational and electoral systems and the separation of church and state in Quebec. Trudeau was also active in *Rassemblement*, a group of left-wing opponents of Duplessis. After four years as a law academic, he became an MP for the Liberal Party. In 1967, as Minister of Justice and Attorney-General, Trudeau opposed the separation of Quebec from the rest of Canada. The next year, he succeeded Lester Pearson as leader of the Liberal Party and federal Prime Minister. In the ensuing general election, the Liberal Party secured a landslide victory. In 1969, the Trudeau government championed the Official Languages Act and other measures to improve the position of French-speaking Canadians (see LANGUAGE/LANGUAGE POLICIES IN QUEBEC). Pursuing independence from US influence, Trudeau recognised the People's Republic of China in 1970 and promoted Canadian control of its own economy. Following terrorist activities by the *Front Libération de Québec* in 1970, he controversially instituted temporary anti-terrorist measures. When the Liberal Party was returned to power in 1980 and the *Parti Québécois* proposition was defeated in the referendum of that year, Trudeau proposed a new constitution for Canada independent of the British Parliament, with a Charter of Rights.

In international affairs, Trudeau encouraged a dialogue between the wealthy industrialised and the developing nations, and fostered a debate about reducing nuclear weapons and Cold War tensions. Trudeau was a charismatic and flamboyant figure, who dedicated his political life to preserving and enhancing Canada's federalism. (**Susan Fox**)

Further reading

Clarkson and McCall (1994).

Tunisia   Country on the North African coast, between Algeria and Libya. The capital is Tunis. The population of 9,705,102 comprises 98.2 per cent Arabs, 1.2 per cent Berbers, 0.2 per cent French, and 0.1 per cent Italian, with a literacy rate of 64.7 per cent; 99.4 per cent of the population is Sunni Muslim with 0.3 per cent Christian and 0.1 per cent Jewish. The official language is Arabic, but French is widely spoken, with many Tunisians being linguistically flexible between the two languages.

Phoenicians settled on the coast in 1000 BC and Carthage was founded here in 814 BC. Berber caravans travelled to the region to exchange produce for imports and subsequently settled in the country's interior. Jews arrived in the period before the Babylonian Captivity in 586 BC. The region was absorbed into the Roman Empire and was held by Vandals in the fifth century and the Byzantines in the sixth. The Berbers gave way to successive invasions of Muslim dynasties. The Ottoman Turks established a dynasty of governors or *beys* in 1612, which lasted throughout the duration of the French protectorate from 1881, until 1957.

Nationalist activity from 1920 to 1955 culminated in independence, with Habib Bourguiba as President and the Neo-Destour as sole political party. The government's refusal to introduce social reform policies led to outbreaks of civil unrest in the 1970s and 1980s. Bourguiba, who was removed from power in 1988 by Ben Ali, established rights for women and repressed Islamic fundamentalism.

Tunisia has a free market economy, of which the oil industry is the key. It has natural gas reserves offshore and its mineral production includes iron ore, lead, phosphate and zinc. Agriculture employs one-third of the population, and produces cereals, fruit and olives. The export of fish is threatened by pollution. Tourism plays an important part in the economy. (**Susan Fox**)

Further reading

Findlay, Findlay and Lawless (1982) – bibliography; Zartman (1991).

Tunisia, cinema   See Cinema, Tunisia.

TV5   Claiming to be the biggest French language TV channel in the world in terms of number of viewers, TV5 was an early and increasingly successful attempt by the French state to use satellite broadcasting to promote French language and culture in the world. Its prime purpose is cultural rather than commercial: as a defence against the threat of American television programmes broadcast from 'Coca-Cola satellites'. Founded in 1984 as an international collaborative project, showing compilations from French, Belgian and Swiss public service television, it was soon joined by Quebec.

The signals are both carried by cable systems and broadcast direct by satellites. In 2001 it was received in 135 million homes worldwide (500 million viewers), third only to MTV and CNN as global channels. It broadcasts 24 hours a day to five continents. From Paris, Satellimages-TV5 sends its programming to Europe, Africa, Asia and the Arab world, while, in Montreal, CTQC controls programming for Canada, the USA, Latin America and the Caribbean. Digitalisation has brought five different signals, now allowing greater differentiation of time zones, cultural backgrounds and sub-titling language.

TV5 schedules are composed of an hour of news every four hours (some produced internally, and some re-broadcasting the news programmes of its major partner channels), over 2000 hours per year of French cinema and TV films, and magazine programmes including documentaries. Its website (http://www.tv5.org) offers a pedagogical apparatus accompanying the programmes.

In Paris, TV5 is owned by a consortium of France 2, France 3, la 5ᵉ and Arte (between them owning 60 per cent of shares); a further third is controlled by SSR (Swiss Romande), RTBF (Belgium), CTQC (Quebec). Over 80 per cent of TV5's income is from the French Ministry for Foreign Affairs (total budget 448 million francs in 2000). Since 1999 it has carried a small amount of advertising. (**Geoff Hare**)

Further reading

Kuhn (1995).

UGTA *Union Générale de Travailleurs Algériens* (General Union of Algerian Workers). Constructed along the lines of French trade unions like the CGT and the CFDT with which it also had historic links; it was, however, a direct creation of the nationalist movement and of the FLN. Its compromised beginnings in 1954 meant that its role after independence was often to act as the enabling agent for government policy. This was particularly so after BEN BELLA unilaterally removed its secretariat at the UGTA's first congress in January 1963. Individual members and sections were involved in the *autogestion* movement but with a government-nominated secretariat and no power base of its own, it proved difficult for it to act independently. (**Kay Adamson**)

Ulama' See OULEMA.

UMA *Union du Maghreb Arabe* (Arab Maghreb Union). The UMA was set up in 1989 after three decades of pan-Maghreb rhetoric. It links ALGERIA, Libya, MAURITANIA, MOROCCO and TUNISIA. After a decade of ministerial meetings and occasional head-of-state summits, a limited practical economic integration has been achieved, constrained by the fact that trade between the Maghreb countries is low, all of them being rivals for trade with the European Union. Political differences over the future of WESTERN SAHARA have threatened co-operation with Morocco. In 1995 the UMA signed a free trade agreement with the European Union – the BARCELONA AGREEMENT. This aimed to remove all barriers to bilateral trade by the year 2010. Proposals to add Egypt to the UMA have been made. (**Keith Sutton**)

Further reading

Aghrout and Sutton (1990).

Union française   (1944–58). The constitutional structure devised by France to oversee the post-Second World War evolution of the French colonial empire. Its shape emerged from the conference that took place in Brazzaville, the administrative capital of the AEF, in January 1944, at which colonial administrators and African ÉLITES proposed ideas for the future relationship of the colonies with the metropole (see BRAZZAVILLE DECLARATION).

It featured a president (by default, that of France), an advisory council made up of representatives of the overseas states, and French government representatives, together with a consultative assembly featuring members from France's parliament and elected representatives from France's colonies.

The constitution was motivated by two principles: firstly the introduction of federalism and secondly a greater degree of autonomy. Part of the principle of federalism was that its peoples would become citizens (see CITIZENSHIP) of a greater France rather than colonial subjects on the way to independence at a later date. (**Antony Walsh**)

Union Générale de Travailleurs Algériens   See UGTA.

Universalism   The name given to practices and ideas whose values are deemed to be common to and shared by the whole of humanity. The opposite of universalism is particularism, which refers to practices and ideas whose values are deemed to be common only to a specific group of people. This opposition suggests that the universal is neutral and favours no single group, whilst the particular is an expression of specific values and beliefs. In the modern era, the opposition between universalism and particularism was exploited to equate Western values with the shared universal aspirations of humanity – for example, the '*droits de l'Homme*' (Rights of Man) propounded at the time of the French Revolution – and to devalue the particular values of other peoples, which were considered backward, parochial and uncivilised in comparison. Nineteenth-century colonialism could consequently be justified as a mission to civilise unenlightened and barbarous peoples ('*la mission civilisatrice*'). In the twentieth century ANTICOLONIAL movements, such as NÉGRITUDE in the 1930s and 1940s, or the more politically motivated FLN in Algeria in the 1950s, and the thinkers behind these movements such as Léopold SENGHOR, Frantz FANON and Albert MEMMI, exposed the hypocrisy at the heart of the opposition between universalism and particularism. Universalism was attacked as the means by which the West justified its hierarchical view of humanity, imposed its own values on the rest of the world and oppressed other peoples. In *Peau noire, masques blancs* (1952; *Black Skin, White Masks*, 1967) Fanon reflects on the ways in which black men and women are profoundly enslaved by the unremitting gaze and judgement of whites whose values are unquestioningly accepted as the universal norm. In today's postcolonial world, it is more commonly accepted that all values are particular and relative and that the supposed neutrality of universalism was always a Western myth. (**Max Silverman**)

Further reading

Fanon (1975) – classic anticolonial text dissecting the enslaving ideologies of white imperialism; Lévi-Strauss (1952) – exposé of the ethnocentrism at the heart of Western universalism and plea for cultural diversity.

Université Senghor d'Alexandrie   Senghor University, an operating agency of the OIF, was created by the Dakar Francophone Summit in 1989 and is based in Alexandria. It aims to provide training at doctoral level for high-level officials and educators/trainers, in areas which prioritise the development needs of African countries in particular.

Further reading

See the university's website: http://www.usenghor-Francophonie.org/

Upper Volta   Former name of Burkina Faso. A French colony (*Haute Volta*) 1919–60, part of AOF (*Afrique Occidentale Française*), developed from French protectorates around the River Niger. French investment in the colony was always low and exploitation of human and natural resources high; indigenous resistance to colonisation was strong. Upper Volta gained independence in 1960. The immediate post-independence regime was authoritarian and had major economic difficulties. Military *coups* followed. Some of these installed more liberal regimes. In 1983, Captain Thomas Sankara took power, renaming the country Burkina Faso and attempting radical social and economic reforms. (**Rachael Langford**)

UREF   See AUF.

Vanuaaku Pati   See VP.

Vanuatu   A group of 80 islands in the South Pacific Ocean, formerly known as the New Hebrides. The British and French jointly administered the islands as an Anglo-French condominium from 1906 until independence in 1980. Population: approx.

200,000. Capital: Port-Vila. Languages: Bislama English, French. Main resources: manganese, timber, fish. Exports: copra, kava, beef, cocoa, timber, coffee. Main trading partner: Japan. Established since 1971 as an international finance centre and offshore tax haven.

Vaulx-en-Velin   A suburb of Lyon typical of the urban areas known in France as the BANLIEUES. The literal meaning of this word, 'suburbs', has been narrowed in recent years to refer more specifically to socially disadvantaged areas containing dense concentrations of minority ethnic groups, housed typically in high-rise appartment blocks. Rioting in Vaulx-en-Velin in 1990 helped to focus media attention on these areas, where tensions often run high between the police and disaffected youths suffering from high levels of unemployment and racial discrimination. (**Alec G. Hargreaves**)

Further reading

A sympathetic portrait of Vaulx-en-Velin is drawn by its mayor, former Communist Maurice Charrier (1995).

Vaxelaire, Daniel   Born 1948. Reunionese journalist, historian and novelist. Vaxelaire was the general editor of the seven-volume *Mémorial de la Réunion*, and this provided him with the material for a series of historical novels set in the islands of the south-western Indian Ocean and dramatising various key moments of their population and development. The first, *Chasseur de noirs* (1982), is the fictitious autobiography of an early hunter of runaway slaves, and the second, *L'Affranchi* (1984), the story of a successful emancipated slave. *Chasseur d'épices* (1990) recounts the exploits of Pierre Poivre, the French botanist of eighteenth-century MAURITIUS, and *Grand-Port* (1992) and *Cap Malheureux* (1993) centre around the British conquest of Mauritius during the Napoleonic wars. *Les Mutins de la Liberté* (1986) tells the story of the mutineers and pirates who established the utopian community of Libertalia in northern MADAGASCAR; and *Bleu nuit* (1996) playfully celebrates the ghosts of pioneer settlers of the Mascarene islands. (**Peter Hawkins**)

Veil   The belief of the average non-Muslim that women are required by Islamic Law to wear a veil and cover their faces in public, is a gross simplification of a complex subject. The KORAN exhorts both women and men to dress modestly, which is defined by some scholars as a means of not drawing unnecessary attention to oneself, so a woman wearing baggy trousers, jumper and a headscarf in a Western country could be perceived as being in accordance with Islamic Law. The wearing of the veil, however, as a face covering, is much more controversial. Traditional dress codes vary sharply in Muslim societies. In matriarchal Islamic societies like the Bedouin and Tuareg, it is traditional for women to go unveiled, whereas the veil is worn as a face covering in patriarchal Islamic societies.

The mistaken belief of Islamic fundamentalists that the Koran prescribes the covering of women's faces is largely a political statement, and is attributable to their rejection of European colonial domination and Western materialism. The revival of the veil as an Islamic practice has become part of the fundamentalist ideology, in an attempt to restore Islamic identity.

On the other hand, however, Muslim women who wear the veil from choice, regard it as a sign of modesty with the purpose of protecting them from threat of sexual abuse, quoting the Koranic dictum that a man who falsely accuses a woman of immorality will be punished. Chastity, modesty and piety are fostered by wearing the veil, which is therefore not a form of oppression, but represents liberation from the shackles of male scrutiny and standards of attractiveness.

Most Muslim women stress that culture and religion shape their lives, whatever their particular position on the veil. (**Susan Fox**)

Further reading

El Fadwa (1998).

Verlan French backslang (*ver/lan* = *l'envers*, 'backwards' with syllables transposed) originating in the criminal underworld but now mainly associated with working-class youths of the Paris BANLIEUES. Like Cockney backslang, it articulates sub-cultural play, marginality and resistance. Therefore, when a *verlan* term gains currency in mainstream culture (e.g., through rap music, LA HAINE and other *banlieue* films), practitioners often *re-verlanise* it (e.g. BEUR becomes *rebeu*). Other common *verlan* terms, found by Goudaillier (2001) in rap, film and novels, are significant to Francophone studies: *babtou* (white person); *Beurette*; *cainf* (African); *céfran*, *gaulois* (French person); *greune*, *renoi* (black person); *zoreil'land* (metropolitan France). (**Mark McKinney**)

Viet Cong See HO CHI MINH.

Viet Minh See HO CHI MINH; PHAM VAN DONG; VO NGUYEN GIAP; DIEN BIEN PHU; INDOCHINA WAR.

Vietnam, Socialist Republic of Country in South-east Asia, and former French colony originally divided into three regions, Tonkin, Annam and Cochinchine, joined with CAMBODIA and LAOS after 1887 to form the colony of Indochina, and occupied by Japan during World War II French control of the territory was finally lost after the battle of DIEN BIEN PHU in 1954 which ended the (first) INDOCHINA WAR, the first stage of Vietnam's independence drive led by HO CHI MINH. American concerns about the spread of Communism across the sub-continent led to the Vietnam (or second Indochina) War.

Though an important strategic area for France in the nineteenth century, aiming to rival British economic interests in China, Vietnam (and Laos and Cambodia) were never penetrated by French culture and language, in the same way as Francophone Africa for example. Firstly, Vietnam already had a romanised alphabet (thanks to the Frenchman Alexandre de Rhodes in 1651). Secondly, France was interested primarily in exploiting economically, rather than 'civilising', the region. Indeed rural poverty, exploitation and deep resentment led to many revolts against French control in the 1930s. After France's withdrawal in the 1950s, Northern Vietnam went through a 'cultural revolution', to remove French influence.

Today's Vietnam retains very little of its French past, and, with the exception of the older generation, the country can barely be described now as 'Francophone'. At best Vietnam is 'francotectural' – roads, buildings, citiscapes, designed during French colonial control, are the last, if not permanent, vestiges of France's presence. Paradoxically northern Vietnam, especially Hanoi, still retains a French flavour, whereas Ho Chi Minh City (aka Saigon) in the south is distinctly more Americanised and Anglophone. Important Francophone writers include the philosopher TRAN DUC THAO, and novelist PHAM VAN KY. Marguerite Duras's novel *L'Amant* paints a lively picture of colonial Vietnam. Alexandre Yersin, discoverer of the Bubonic plague bacillus in the nineteenth century, lived and worked in Nha Trang. (**Andy Stafford**)

Further reading

Brocheux and Hémery (1994) – definitive and in-depth study of the colonial period; Cooper (2001) – interdisciplinary re-evaluation of colonial and postcolonial significance of the region for France.

Vigneault, Gilles Born 1928. QUEBEC singer, poet, composer and storyteller. His music and songs have become a quintessential expression of Quebec identity. Coming from the remote rural area of Natashquan, he identifies strongly with the French Canadian past and its rich folklore, and, like Pauline JULIEN, he is a passionate nationalist. His song 'Mon Pays' has become an unofficial national anthem for Quebec, closely followed in public affection by 'Les Gens de mon pays'. His mesmeric stage performances have been captured in many widely available video recordings and audio CDs. The texts of his songs are included in his many published volumes of poetry. (**Ian Lockerbie**)

Virahsawmy, Dev Born MAURITIUS, 1942. Writer, politician (1969–86), linguist and teacher. A militant, organic intellectual he is the most prolific creative writer using Mauritian, with over 40 published oeuvres. Many of his plays have been translated and internationally acclaimed (*Li*, 1977; *The Prisoner of Conscience*, 1982; *Toufann*, 1991; *The Tempest*, 2001). His literary dedication, which aims at forging Mauritian into a standard language, is informed by his belief in the link between national language and socio-economic, cultural and political development. Described by anthropologist T. H. Eriksen (1998: 21) as a 'cultural one-man movement', his name is associated with the first (1967) and latest (1999) writing system for Mauritian. (**Roshni Mooneram**)

Further reading

See his personal website: http//pages.intnet.mu/develog

Visual arts, Sub-Saharan Africa The status and practice of the visual arts in this vast portion of Africa testify to the wealth of creativity, talent and historical richness of this crucial element of African culture. However, the economic reality of Africa today means that the potential is never realised, the vitality skewed by the Western trading in the art market, and the links with the past undermined by continued post-colonial pillage. For these reasons, account must be taken of the political economy of the art world and of radical anthropology, as Bidima (1997) begins to do. A brilliant documentary commissioned by PRÉSENCE AFRICAINE in 1952 and made by French film-maker Alain Resnais, *Les Statues meurent aussi* (1953), was banned for many years because it showed, as the title suggests, the effect of colonialism on Africa's cultural heritage.

Any account must also include the desire for emancipation, illustrated in the last sixty years by political posters and photography (see Enwezor, 2001). Finally, visual arts in Africa must be seen as independent from, though not blind to, external developments; the perceived function of arts objects within African societies (fetishism, rituals, cookery, etc.) need not detract from the wealth of abstract and non-functional creations. Schools have emerged in the decades since independence: the eclectic 'Vohou-Vohou' in CÔTE D'IVOIRE, in which Kra N'guessan plays a leading role and the 'Ecole de Dakar' set up by Lods in 1961, are good examples. Individuals are also represented: Paul Ahyi in TOGO, Iba Ndiaye and Papa Ibra Tall in SENEGAL.

Three phenomena currently threaten the vitality of African visual arts: the international art market, economic destitution and war, art historians and art criticism. With respect to the last of these, Bidima (1997) sets out the pitfalls (pp. 83–96), ranging from postcolonial myths and stereotypes, to Afrocentric and male-centred viewpoints. (**Andy Stafford**)

Further reading

Phillips (1996) – esp. Chapters 4–6, authoritative and well-illustrated, based on the '*Africa 95*' exhibition at the Royal Academy of Arts; Bidima (1997) – brief but sophisticated discussion and overview of aesthetic and political dimensions, from a deconstructionist point of view; Enwezor (2001) – excellent pictorial history, with photographs, posters and bibliography.

Vo Nguyen Giap   Born 1912. Vietnamese military leader. He studied law at Hanoi University and joined the Vietnamese Communist Party. He led the Viet Minh army against the French, leading to the decisive defeat of the French army at DIEN BIEN PHU in 1954. As deputy prime minister and defence minister of North VIETNAM, Giap masterminded the military strategy that forced US forces to leave Vietnam, which led to the country's reunification in 1975. As a member of the Politburo until 1982, he opposed the 1978 invasion of CAMBODIA. He is a prolific military historian. (**Susan Fox**)

Further reading

McDonald (1994).

VP   *Vanuaaku Pati*   (Party of our land). Political party in VANUATU.

Wade, Abdoulaye   Born Kébémer, SENEGAL, 1926. Senegalese politician. A lawyer by profession, Wade has been a central figure in post-independence Senegalese politics.

In 1974, he founded the *Parti Démocratique Sénégalais*, which became the leading opposition party throughout the 1970s and 1980s. He eventually entered government in 1991 as part of a 'national' government, under President Abdou Dᴏᴜꜰ. Wade finally beat his old adversary Diouf in the presidential elections of March 2000, standing under the slogan of '*sopi*' ('change' in Wolof), advocating economic liberalism after forty years of socialist rule. A year later, his party won a landslide victory in legislative elections. (**David Murphy**)

Wallis & Futuna   A group of islands in the South Pacific, which has been a French protectorate since 1842 and a French overseas territory (see DOM-TOM), with its own Territorial Assembly since 1961. Capital: Mata-Utu. Population: 14,500. Official language: French. It advertises its potential (as yet undeveloped) as an offshore financial centre, with its situation on the International Dateline and as the only French territory with its own flag of convenience for shipping.

Werewere Liking   Born 1950. Cameroonian writer, painter and musician, now living in Cᴏᴛᴇ ᴅ'Iᴠᴏɪʀᴇ, and whose initiate name is Eddy Njock. She is director of the Abidjan-based Kiyi Mbock theatre company. Her best-known published works are her *chants-romans* (song-novels), particularly *Elle sera de jaspe et de corail: journal d'une misovire...* (1983; *It Shall be of Jasper and Coral*, 2000). Like Tanella Bᴏɴɪ and Véronique Tᴀᴅᴊᴏ, Werewere Liking's writings blur generic categories, mixing poetry and prose, and are largely rooted in the traditional mythology and rituals of the Bassa ethnic group. (**Nicki Hitchcott**)

Further reading

Hitchcott (2000) – contains the only substantial analysis of *Elle sera de jaspe et de corail*.

Western Sahara   A large, empty and arid territory on the Atlantic coast of NW Africa between Mᴏʀᴏᴄᴄᴏ and Mᴀᴜʀɪᴛᴀɴɪᴀ, and bordering on Aʟɢᴇʀɪᴀ. Its population of Arabs and Bᴇʀʙᴇʀꜱ numbered 252,146 in 1994. The economy is based on nomadic pastoralism, dates, fishing and phosphates – the latter developed by Spanish colonial power and exported through the capital, Laayoune. The 1970s saw guerrilla fighting and pressure on Spain to decolonise. King Hᴀꜱꜱᴀɴ II of Morocco led a 'Gʀᴇᴇɴ Mᴀʀᴄʜ' to occupy the territory. Spain withdrew in 1976 and Morocco and Mauritania divided the territory up. The guerrilla Pᴏʟɪꜱᴀʀɪᴏ group resisted with support from Algeria, Libya and much of the OAU. Mauritania withdrew in 1979 and Morocco extended its occupation behind a defensive wall, which pushed the Polisarios eastwards into Algeria and exile around Tindouf. From 1988 Algerian support for the guerrillas lessened and a UN-sponsored referendum on the territory was offered but repeatedly delayed. There is no agreement on who is qualified to vote. Territory is being increasingly integrated into Morocco. (**Keith Sutton**)

Wilaya   A term designated by the FLN in 1954 to identify the regional areas of Aʟɢᴇʀɪᴀ for administrative purposes. There are currently 48 *wilayate* in Algeria, under the direction of a *wali* and an elected assembly, with legal powers; responsibility for public services; regional cultural, economic, and social development; and environmental protection. The 1969 Charter of the *Wilaya* emphasised the notion of the *wilayate* comprising a unit state, rather than a federal state of Algeria. The 1990 Constitution specified that the *wilaya* was a region of the state with financial autonomy. (**Susan Fox**)

Further reading

Entelis and Naylor (1992).

Women   See Gender issues.

Women's Movements in the Maghreb   The history of Women's Movements in the Maghreb goes back to the protectorate era during which male leaders of the *Islah* (Reform) trend argued for women's emancipation within the cultural/religious values of Maghrebian societies. This led women to start organising and claiming their rights, at first through associative movements, loosely affiliated to political parties. These associations never problematised women's participation in politics, but made women aware of their social importance and trained them in the public organisation of their demands. They also constituted a platform for liberation movements and produced many female nationalist militants, including Touria Sekkat, Malika Al-Fassi, Djamila Bouhired.

After independence, the shift from an ideology of liberation to one of state-building meant that women's position and concerns were not considered a priority. Family and personal codes (see Family codes, Maghreb) relegated women to 'minor' legal status. In Morocco and Algeria, the family/personal codes were regarded as a betrayal, given women's participation in the independence struggle. Only in Tunisia did the Family Code give women some basic rights.

In the early 1980s, the question of women's role in development surfaced in the three countries, because of four major factors: literacy, the law of the job-market, democratic political values and international pressure. In the 1990s, the democratisation process consolidated the debate on women and politics, enhanced by factors such as Islamism, the Berber question, the Beijing Conference, civil society and women's social promotion. These interacted to create a duality of reference for Women's Movements: Islamic law, enforcing complementarity between the sexes, and international conventions, stipulating sexual equality. Tunisia is far ahead of Morocco and Algeria in balancing the two references – polygamy is abolished in the former, but still allowed in the latter. On the other hand, Islamism is not as threatening to Women's Movements in Morocco as in Algeria – the Moroccan constitution stipulates that the king has supreme religious power.

Maghrebian women's status and lifestyle have radically changed over the last four decades; gains in terms of health, education, jobs, etc. have greatly benefited their societies. However, women face serious challenges: Maghrebian societies are still heavily gendered and hierarchical; illiteracy affects women more than men; the law is still harsher on them and they are more targeted by social sanctions than men in times of crisis, are more victims of totalitarian and fundamentalist trends, and are still absent from decision-making. (**Fatima Sadiqi**)

Further reading

Lazreg (1994); Sadiqi (2002); Naamane-Guessous (1991); Mernissi (1990).

World Cup, France 1998   On a July day in 1998, France lived its third most glorious day, after the taking of the Bastille and the Liberation: the victory in the football World Cup final over Brazil. Hundreds of thousands of Frenchmen and women all over the country celebrated that great sporting achievement. It was seen as the victory of players whose parents had come from all corners of the world, giving the country of their adoption great joy and proving the power of a multitude of faiths, cultures and origins coming together. Throughout the 1980s and 1990s, France had led the way in propelling forward a party of bigots, the *Front National*. France 1998 had given the completely opposite image. France 1998 was, possibly, the greatest footballing victory ever. (**Salah Zaimeche**)

Yaoundé Convention   The Yaoundé Convention was a collective aid and trade agreement between the six founder members of the European Community (EC) and 18 of their former African colonies. The first five-year convention was signed in 1963 and the second in 1969. Both offered trade preferences and economic assistance to African signatories. Both were initially hailed as a model for the economic and social development of 'associated states'. However, the main beneficiary turned out to be France, which was able, through her dominance in EC institutions, to gain privileged access to African raw materials, to guarantee markets for her over-priced exports and to channel European aid to former French colonies. (**Gordon Cumming**)

Yeiwene Yeiwene   See T~JIBAOU~.

Youth culture   Francophone youth cultures in France are simultaneously a vibrant source of innovative ideas, styles and cultural products that feed capitalist production (e.g. cinema, recording, publishing and clothing industries), and of opposition to racist oppression and economic exploitation. Similarly, the GLOBALISATION of youth cultures favours international profit-taking by corporations (African-American clothing styles sold in France; rap by MC SOLAAR distributed in the USA), but also the creation of resistant identifications and communication (Rock Against Police concerts in the UK, then in France). Ancestral cultural shards nonetheless remain as irreducible relics in post-immigrant cultural formations (Certeau, 1994: 266–8): e.g.

North African words, gestures and symbols (hand of Fatma) in BANLIEUE youth cultures.

Hip-hop culture exemplifies the stakes and forces at issue in Francophone youth cultures in France. Imported from the USA in the early 1980s, hip-hop culture quickly produced local breakdance (*smurf*), rap and graffiti groups across France. The hip *Actuel* magazine spun off *Zoulou*, a magazine to reflect new youth cultures, especially Francophone ones. But mainstream publications later sensationalised the threat to society of *banlieue* hip-hop gangs (*bandes de zoulous*), much as French newspapers exploited fears of working-class delinquents, called *Apaches*, in the early twentieth century. Rap music's commercial success in France fuels record company profits, but sometimes threatens the establishment: 'Sacrifice de poulets', by Ministère Amer, issued on an album in conjunction with *La Haine*, was the object of legal proceedings.

New images and narratives from Francophone youth cultures have had an impact through prose fiction and comics by minority novelists (BELGHOUL, CHAREF, KETTANE and SEBBAR) and cartoonists (Boudjellal, Monpierre, Séra), as well as ethnic majority ones. (**Mark McKinney**)

Z

Zaïre   See DEMOCRATIC REPUBLIC OF CONGO.

Zebda   A Toulouse-based rap group, composed of both white and BEUR members. Their songs have often engaged with French politics, dealing with issues such as social EXCLUSION in the suburbs, and immigration. One of their most famous songs, 'Le Bruit et l'odeur', features a 'sample' of an infamous speech by Jacques CHIRAC, in which he speaks of the 'legitimate' concerns of the French working classes, forced to live with the 'smell' and the 'noise' of immigrant families. The band gained a much wider audience when their song 'Tomber la chemise' became the most successful song of the summer in 1999. (**David Murphy**)

Zemmouri, Mahmoud   Born ALGERIA, 1946. Algerian film-maker and actor. He has worked mainly in France and is known for his humorous approach to cinema. Films include: *Prends 10 000 balles et casse-toi* (1980); *Les Folles Années du Twist* (1983), set during the ALGERIAN WAR; *De Hollywood à Tamanrasset* (1991); *L'Honneur de la Tribu* (1993); *100 per cent Arabica* (1997), featuring RAï singers KHALED and CHEB MAMI.

Zeroual, Liamine   Born Batna, 1941. Algerian soldier and politician. He was the first President of ALGERIA to be elected in nationwide elections in November 1995. This provided Zeroual, a former general and defence minister under Redha MALEK, with a legitimacy which his initial appointment to the presidency in January 1994 by the military Higher Executive Council had not given him. He established the RND, with which he won the June 1997 general election. However, he became increasingly frustrated by the limited nature of his power and resigned in 1998, when he was replaced by Abdelaziz BOUTEFLIKA. Zeroual achieved some success in negotiations with the FIS but it was not sufficient to bring to an end the violence. (**Kay Adamson**)

Zidane, Zinedine   Born Marseilles, 1972. Maghrebi-French footballer. On 6 May 2001, in one of the deciding games for the Italian championship, Juventus were two goals up on Roma, the first made by Zidane, and the second scored by him. This was the last illustration of how crucial a player he was, always rising to the great occasions. In France 1998, his two goals stunned Brazil and offered France the victory in the final. In a very tense game against Portugal in the Euro Semi-Finals of 2000, it was Zidane, again, who scored the goal that sent France to the final and to victory. In Italy, with Juventus, Zidane had already won the Italian title, the Inter-Continental Cup, and trophies for best world player and European player of the year twice. Not much is left for him to win. (**Salah Zaimeche**)

Zobel, Joseph   Born MARTINIQUE, 1915. Martinican writer. The bildungsroman *La Rue Cases-Nègres* (1955; *Black Shack Alley*, 1980), made into a successful film by Euzhan PALCY), is a classic of Antillean literature. The novel charts the development of the narrator from rural to urban Martinique, and from the oral tradition (represented by Médouze, the elderly storyteller who dies in the course of the novel) to the written. The experience of French schooling is presented as *the* means of escaping the exploitation and misery established by slavery and perpetuated in the plantation system. *Diab'là* (1942), which deals with the occupation and ownership of land, was banned by the Vichy administration in Martinique. (**Maeve McCusker**)

Zone   See LA ZONE.

Zoreille   Term used to describe metropolitan French visitors to the islands. It is used in the Caribbean as well as in parts of the South Pacific.

Appendix:
The Institutions of *Francophonie*

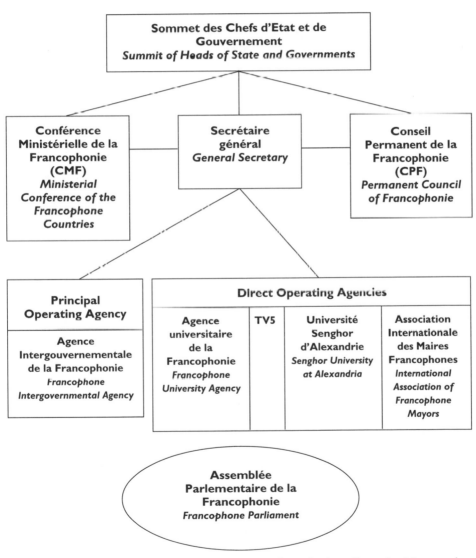

Sommet des Chefs d'Etat et de Gouvernement
Summit of Heads of State and Governments

Conférence Ministérielle de la Francophonie (CMF)
Ministerial Conference of the Francophone Countries

Secrétaire général
General Secretary

Conseil Permanent de la Francophonie (CPF)
Permanent Council of Francophonie

Principal Operating Agency

Agence Intergouvernementale de la Francophonie
Francophone Intergovernmental Agency

Direct Operating Agencies

Agence universitaire de la Francophonie
Francophone University Agency

TV5

Université Senghor d'Alexandrie
Senghor University at Alexandria

Association Internationale des Maires Francophones
International Association of Francophone Mayors

Assemblée Parlementaire de la Francophonie
Francophone Parliament

Source: http://www.francophonie.org/francophonie/structure.htm

259

Bibliography

Abbas, F. (1931) *Le Jeune Algérien: De la colonie vers la province*, Paris: La Jeune Parque.

Abbas, F. (1962) *La Nuit coloniale*, Paris: Julliard.

Abdel Haleem, M. (2001) *Understanding the Qur'an: Themes and Style*, London/New York: I. B. Tauris.

Abenon, L.-R. (1992) *Petite Histoire de la Guadeloupe*, Paris: L'Harmattan.

Abu-Lughod, J. (1991) 'Going beyond global babble', in D. King (ed.), *Culture, Globalisation and the World System*, London: Macmillan and Department of Art and Art History, State University of New York at Birmingham, pp. 131–8.

Adda, J. and Smouts, M.-C. (1989) *La France face au Sud*, Paris: Karthala.

Adelaïde-Merlande, J. (1994) *Histoire générale des Antilles et des Guyanes*, Paris: Editions Caribéennes/L'Harmattan.

Adotévi, S. (1971) *Négritude et négrologues*, Paris: Editions 10/18.

Africa Rights (1994) *Rwanda: Death, Despair and Defiance*, London: Africa Rights.

Africa South of the Sahara (Annual), London: Europa.

Afrique Contemporaine (1994) 'Les crises de l'éducation dans un contexte d'ajustement structurel', special issue, 172, Oct.–Dec. (La Documentation française).

Ager, D. (1996) *Francophonie in the 1990s: Problems and Opportunities*, Clevedon: Multilingual Matters.

Ageron, C. R. (1979) *Histoire de l'Algérie contemporaine*, Paris: Presses Universitaires de France.

Aghrout, A. (2000) *From Preferential Status to Partnership: The Euro-Maghreb Relationship*, Aldershot: Ashgate.

Aghrout, A. and Sutton, K. (1990) 'Regional economic union in the Maghreb', *Journal of Modern African Studies*, 28:1, pp. 115–39.

Agir ici et Survie (1995) *Jacques Chirac et la Françafrique*, Paris: L'Harmattan.

Agir ici et Survie (1996) *Dossiers Noirs de la politique africaine de la France*, 1–5, Paris: L'Harmattan.

Ahmed, L. (1992) *Women and Gender in Islam: Historical Roots of a Modern Debate*, New Haven: Yale University Press.

Aicardi de Saint-Paul, M. (1993) *De la Haute Volta au Burkina Faso: tradition et modernité au pays des hommes intègres*, Paris: Editions Albatross.

Aït Ahmed, H. (1983) *Mémoires d'un combattant*, Paris: Messinger.

Aït Ahmed, H. (1989) *L'Affaire Mécili*, Paris: La Découverte.

Ait Mansour, F. (1968) *Histoire de ma vie*, Paris: Maspero.

Aldrich, R. (1993) *France and the South Pacific since 1940*, Basingstoke: Macmillan.

Aldrich, R. and Connell, J. (1992) *France's Overseas Frontier: Départements et Territoires d'Outre-Mer*, Cambridge: Cambridge University Press.

Alleg, H. (1958) *La Question*, Paris: Editions de Minuit.

Alleg, H. *et al.* (1981) *La Guerre d'Algérie*, 3 vols, Paris: Temps Actuels.

Alomes, S. and Provis, M. (eds) (1998) *French Worlds, Pacific Worlds*, Port Melbourne: Institute for the Study of French–Australian Relations.

Amnesty International (1998) *Togo, Etat de terreur*, London: Amnesty International.

Amondji, M. (1984) *Félix Houphouët-Boigny et la Côte d'Ivoire: l'envers d'une légende*, Paris: Karthala.

Amrane, D. (1991) *Les Femmes algériennes dans la guerre*, Paris: Plon.

Ancelet, B. (1991) 'Music and musical instruments', in Ancelet, B., Edwards, J. and Pitre, G. (eds), *Cajun Country*, Jackson and London: University Press of Mississippi, pp. 149–70.

Anderson, B. (1983) *Imagined Communities: Reflections on the Origin and Spread of Nationalism*, London: New Left Books.

Arkoun, M. (1992) *L'Islam, religion et société*, Paris: Cerf.

Arnaud, G. and Vergès, J. (1957) *Pour Djamila Bouhired*, Paris: Editions de Minuit.

Arnaud, J. (1986) *La Littérature maghrébine de langue française: origines et perspectives*, Paris: Publisud.

Astre, G.-A. (1987) *Emmanuel Roblès ou le risque de vivre*, Paris: Grasset.

Auracher, T. (2001) *Gabon: une démocratie bloquée? Reculs et avancées d'une décennie de lutte*, Paris: L'Harmattan.

Ayache, A. (1964) *Histoire ancienne de l'Afrique du Nord*, Paris: Editions Sociales.

Azevedo, M. and Nnadozie, E. (1998) *Chad: A Nation in Search of Its Future*, Boulder, CO and Oxford: Westview Press.

Azodo, A. U. (1993) *L'Imaginaire dans les romans de Camara Laye*, New York: Lang.

Baker, A. (1998) *Voices of Resistance: Oral Histories of Moroccan Women*, Albany, NY: State University of New York Press.

Balibar, E. (1992) *Les Frontières de la démocratie*, Paris: La Découverte.

Balibar, E. and Wallerstein, I. (1997) *Race, nation, classe: les identités ambiguës*, Paris: La Découverte.

Barbadzan, A. (1982) *Naissance d'une tradition*, Paris: ORSTOM.

Barbara, A. (1993) *Les Couples mixtes*, Paris: Bayard Editions.

Barker, M. (1981) *The New Racism*, London: Junction Books.

Barrat, J. (1997) *Géopolitique de la Francophonie*, Paris: Presses Universitaires de France.

Barry, D. (1989) 'The French literary renaissance in Louisiana: Cultural reflections', *Journal of Popular Culture*, 23, pp. 47–63.

Basset, A. (1952) *La Langue Berbère*, London: International African Institute.

Baubérot, J. (1990) *Vers un nouveau pacte laïque?* Paris: Editions du Seuil.

Baubérot, J. (ed.) (1996) *La Laïcité: Évolutions et enjeux*, Paris: La Documentation française.

Bauman, Z. (1991) *Modernity and Ambivalence*, Cambridge: Polity.

Bauman, Z. (1998) *Globalization: The Human Consequences*, Cambridge: Polity Press.

Beaudoin, R. (1996) *Une Etude des poésies d'Emile Nelligan*, Montreal: XYZ.

Beauvoir, S. de and Halimi, G. (1962) *Djamila Boupacha*, Paris: Gallimard, trans. P. Green, London: André Deutsch/Weidenfeld & Nicolson (1962).

Bebey, F. (1975) *African Music: A People's Art*, trans. by Josephine Bennett, Westport, CT: Lawrence Hill.

Begag, A. (1986) *Le Gone du Chaâba*, Paris: Editions du Seuil.

Begag, A. (1989) *Béni ou le paradis privé*, Paris: Editions du Seuil.

Begag, A. (1995) *Les Chiens aussi*, Paris: Editions du Seuil.

Begag, A. and Chaouite, A. (1990) *Ecarts d'identité*, Paris: Editions du Seuil.

Bekri, T. (1986) *Malek Haddad, l'oeuvre romanesque. Pour une poétique de la littérature mahgrébine de langue française*, Paris: L'Harmattan.

Belamri, R. (1989) *Jean Sénac, entre désir et douleur*, Algiers: OPU.

Belanger, Y., Comeau, R. and Metivier, C. (eds) (2000) *La Révolution tranquille: 40 ans plus tard: un bilan*, Montreal: VLB.

Belorgey, G. (1993) *Saint-Pierre-et-Miquelon et le droit de la pêche dans l'Atlantique nord-ouest*, Paris: La Documentation française.

Belorgey, G. and Bertrand, G. (1994) *Les DOM-TOM*, Paris: La Découverte.

Ben Jelloun, T. (1997) 'La mémoire déroutée', *Dédale*, 5/6, Spring, pp. 159–63.

Benaissa, S. (1997) *Théâtre en exil*, Morlanwelz, Belgium: Editions Lansman.

Benaissa, S. (1999) *Les Fils de l'amertume*, Paris: Plon.

Benguigui, Y. (1997) *Mémoires d'immigrés*, Paris: Canal Plus.

Berchadsky, A. (1994) '*La Question*' *d'Henri Alleg: un livre-événement dans la France en guerre d'Algérie*, Paris: Larousse.

Bernabé, J. (1983) *Fondal-Natal*, Paris: L'Harmattan.

Bernabé, J., Chamoiseau, P. and Confiant, R. (1989) *Eloge de la créolité*, Paris: Gallimard.

Bernal, M. (1987) *Black Athena*, London: Free Association Books and New Brunswick: Rutgers University Press.

Berque, J. (1978) *Structures sociales du Haut Atlas*, 2nd edn, Paris: Presses Universitaires de France.

Bertin, J. (1987) *Félix Leclerc: le roi heureux*, Paris: Arléa.

Bhabha, H. (1994) *The Location of Culture*, London: Routledge.

Bidima, J.-G. (1997) *L'Art négro-africain*, Paris: Presses Universitaires de France.

Blair, D. (1976) *African Literature in French: A IIistory of Creative Writing in French from West and Equatorial Africa*, Cambridge: Cambridge University Press.

Blank, D. (1999) 'A Veil of Controversy: The Construction of a "Tchador Affair" in the French Press', *Interventions. International Journal of Postcolonial Studies*, 1:4, pp. 536–54.

Bolduc, Y. (1994) *L'Etoile mythique: lecture de l'Etoile pourpre d'Alain Grandbois: essai*, Montreal: L'Hexagone.

Bonn, C. (1990) *Anthologie de la littérature algérienne, 1950–1987*, Paris: Hachette.

Bonnet, A. (2000) *Anti-Racism*, London: Routledge.

Borgomano, M. (2000) *Des Hommes ou des bêtes. Lecture de 'En attendant le vote des bêtes sauvages', d'Ahmadou Kourouma*, Paris: L'Harmattan.

Bottomore, T. B. (1993) *Élites and Society*, London: Routledge.

Boualit, F. (1999) 'La Littérature algérienne des années 90: "Témoigner d'une tragédie", in Bonn, C. and Boualit, F. (eds), *Paysages littéraires des années 90: témoigner d'une tragédie?*, Paris: L'Harmattan/Université Paris-Nord, pp. 25–40.

Bouamama, S. (1994) *Dix ans de marche des Beurs. Chronique d'un mouvement avorté*, Paris: Desclée de Brouwer.

Bouamama, S. (2000) *J'y suis, j'y vote. La lutte pour les droits politiques aux résidents étrangers*, Paris: L'Esprit frappeur.

Bouchard, C. (1998) *La Langue et le nombril: Histoire d'une obsession québécoise*, Montreal: Fides.

Bougchiche, L. (1997) *Langues et littératures berbères des origines à nos jours, Bibliographie internationale*, Paris: Ibis.

Boukous, A. (1995) *Société, langues et cultures au Maroc*, Rabat: Publications de la Faculté des Lettres et des Sciences Humaines.

Bounfour, A. (1999) *Introduction à la littérature berbère. 1. La poésie*, Paris/Louvain: Peeters.

Bourqia, R. and Miller, S. G. (eds) (1999) *In the Shadow of the Sultan: Culture, Power and Politics in Morocco*, Cambridge, MA: Harvard University Press.

Brand, L. (1998) *Women, the State and Political Liberalization: Middle Eastern and North African Experiences*, New York: Columbia University Press.

Brett, M. and Fentress, E. (1996; paperback, 1997) *The Berbers*, Oxford: Blackwell.

Britton, C. (1999) *Edouard Glissant and Postcolonial Theory*, Charlottesville, VA: University Press of Virginia.

Brocheux, P. and Hémery, D. (1994) *Indochine. La colonisation ambiguë, 1858–1954*, Paris: La Découverte.

Brochu, A. (1985) *L'Evasion tragique: essai sur les romans d'André Langevin*, Ville LaSalle (Montreal): Hurtubise HMH.

Brochu, A. (1999) *Saint-Denys Garneau: le poète en sursis*, Montreal: XYZ.

Bromberger, S and M., Elgey, G. and Chauvel, J.-F. (1960) *Barricades et colonels, 24 janvier 1960*, Paris: Fayard.

Brooks, J. (1999) 'Challenges to writing literature in Creole: the cases of Martinique and Guadeloupe', in S. Haigh (ed.), *An Introduction to Caribbean Francophone Writing*, Oxford/New York: Berg, pp. 119–34

Brouillard, M. (1994) *Félix Leclerc: l'homme derrière la légende*, Montreal: Québec/Amérique.

Brown, B. (1997) 'The development of a Louisiana French norm', in A. Valdman (ed.), *French and Creole in Louisiana*, New York: Plenum Press, pp. 215–35.

Bruézière, M. (1983) *L'Alliance française 1883-1983, histoire d'une institution*, Paris: Hachette.

Brunel, S. (1993) *Le Gaspillage de l'aide publique*, Paris: Editions du Seuil.

Brunet, J.-P. (1999) *Police contre FLN : Le drame d'octobre 1961*, Paris: Flammarion.

Buell, F. (ed.) (1994) *National Culture and the New Global System*, London: Johns Hopkins University Press.

Bulliet, R. W. (1994) *Islam: The View from the Edge*, New York: Columbia University Press.

Burnell, P. (1997) *Foreign Aid in a Changing World*, Buckingham: Open University Press.

Burton, R. D. E. and Reno, F. (eds) (1995) *French and West Indian: Martinique, Guadeloupe and French Guiana Today*, London and Basingstoke: Macmillan.

Cachin, O. (1996) *L'Offensive rap*, Paris: Gallimard/'Découvertes'.

Cadi, K. (1997) 'Constance et variabilité syntaxiques interdialectales en Berbère', *International Journal of the Sociology of Language*, 123, pp. 147–62.

Callaloo 18:3 (1995) Special issue dedicated to Maryse Condé.

Calmette, G. (2001) *Jules Roy, le barbare de Vézelay*, Saint-Cyr-sur-Loire: Christian Pirot.

Carton, D. (2001) *La deuxième vie de Charles Pasqua*, Paris: Flammarion.

Célestin, R. (1995) *From Cannibals to Radicals: Figures and Limits of Exoticism*, Minneapolis and London: University of Minnesota Press.

Certeau, M. de (1994) *La Prise de parole et autres écrits politiques*, ed. Luce Giard, Paris: Editions du Seuil.

Césari, J. (1994) *Etre musulman en France: associations, militants et mosques*, Paris and Aix-en-Provence: Karthala/IREMAM.

Césari, J. (1998) *Musulmans et républicains: les jeunes, l'islam et la France*, Brussels: Complexe.

Chafik, M. (1987) 'La Poésie Amazigh et la résistance armée dans le Moyen Atlas et l'est du Grand Atlas' (in Arabic), *Al kaadimiyyah*, 4, pp. 69–99.

Chaker, S. (1989) *Berbères aujourd'hui*, Paris: L'Harmattan.

Challe, M. (1968) *Notre révolte*, Paris: Presses de la Cité.

Chamoiseau, P. and Confiant, R. (1991) *Lettres créoles. Tracées antillaises et continentales de la littérature. Haïti, Guadeloupe, Martinique, Guyane 1635–1975*, Paris: Hatier.

Chamoiseau, P., Delver, G., Glissant, E. and Juminer, B. (2000) 'Manifeste pour refonder les DOM', *Le Monde* (21 January).

Charef, M. (1989) *Le Harki de Meriem*, Paris: Mercure de France.

Charpentier, J. (1991) *L'Affaire Rainbow Warrior et la responsabilité des états*, Saarbrücken: Europainstitut der Universität des Saarlandes.

Charrier, M. (1995) 'Une Petite Ville en France', *Le Monde* (10 October).

Chatwin, B. (1980) *The Viceroy of Ouidah*, London: Jonathan Cape.

Chaudenson, R. (1995) *Les Créoles*, Paris: Presses Universitaires de France.

Chaulet-Achour, C. (1994) *Jamel Eddine Bencheikh: Présentation et choix de textes critiques et poétiques*, Paris: L'Harmattan.

Chaulet-Achour, C. (ed.) (1998) 'Cahiers Jamel Eddine Bencheikh: Savoir et imaginaire', *Etudes littéraires maghrébines*, 13.

Chevallier, D., Guellouz, A. and Miquel, A. (1991) *Les Arabes, L'Islam et L'Europe*, Paris: Flammarion.

Chèze, M.-H. (1979) *Emmanuel Roblès: Témoin de l'homme*, Sherbrooke, Quebec: Naaman.

Chikhi, B. (1989) *Problématique de l'écriture dans l'oeuvre romanesque de Mohamed Dib*, Algiers: Office des Publications Universitaires.

Chikhi, B. (1996) *Maghreb en textes: écriture, histoire, savoirs et symboliques*, Paris: L'Harmattan.

Chikhi, B. (1997) *Littérature algérienne: désir d'histoire et esthétique*, Paris: L'Harmattan.

Chikhi, B. and Berehi, A. (eds) (2002) *L'Algérie, ses langues, ses lettres, et ses histoires*, Blida (Algeria): Editions Mauguin.

Chipman, J. (1989) *French Power in Africa*, Oxford: Blackwell.

Chouraqui, A. (1998) *Histoire des Juifs en Afrique du Nord*, 2 vols, Monaco: Editions du Rocher.

Chrétien, J.-P. (1997) *Le Défi de l'ethnisme: Rwanda et Burundi 1990–1996*, Paris: Karthala.

Chrétien, J.-P. (1999) 'Hutu et Tutsi au Rwanda et au Burundi', in J.-L. Amselle and E. M'Bokolo (eds), *Au Coeur de l'ethnie: ethnie, tribalisme et Etat en Afrique*, Paris: La Découverte, pp. 129–65.

Chrétien, J.-P. and Guichaoua, A. (1988) 'Burundi, d'une république à l'autre: bilans et enjeux', *Politique Africaine*, 29, March, pp. 87–94.

Chrétien, J.-P., Guichaoua, A. and Le Jeune, G. (1988) 'La crise politico-ethnique du Burundi: l'ombre de 1972', *Politique Africaine*, 32, December, pp. 105–10.

Cissé, M. (1999) *Parole de sans-papiers*, Paris: La Dispute.

Cissé, M. (2000) 'The Sans-Papières: an interview with Madjiguène Cissé', in J. Freedman and C. Tarr (eds), *Women, Immigration and Identities in France*, Oxford: Berg, pp. 29–38.

Cizeron, M. and Hienly, M. (1983) *Tahiti côté montagne*, Papeete: Haere po no Tahiti.

Clarkson, S. and McCall, C. (1994) *Trudeau and Our Times*, 2 vols, Toronto: McClelland & Stewart.

Clegge, I. (1971) *Workers' Self-Management in Algeria*, London: Allen Lane.

Clerc, J.-M. (1997) *Ecrire, transgresser, résister*, Paris: L'Harmattan.

Clifford, J. (1988) *The Predicament of Culture: Twentieth-Century Ethnography, Literature and Art*, Cambridge, MA: Harvard University Press.

Collectif (2000) *L'Année Francophone Internationale 2001*, Ste-Foy, Quebec: AFI.

Condé, M. and Cottenet-Hage, M. (eds) (1995) *Penser la créolité*, Paris: Karthala.

Confiant, R. (1993) *Aimé Césaire. Une traversée paradoxale du siècle*, Paris: Stock.

Cooper, N. (2001) *France in Indochina: Colonial Encounters*, Oxford: Berg.

Corcoran, P. (2001) *Oyono: 'Une vie de boy' et 'Le Vieux nègre et la médaille'*, London: Grant & Cutler.

Cot, J.-P. (1984) *A l'épreuve du pouvoir. Le tiersmondisme pour quoi faire?*, Paris: Editions du Seuil.

Corcoran, P. (2002) *Le Pleurer-Rire*, Glasgow: Glasgow Introductory Guides to French Literature.

Côte, M. (1996) *L'Algérie*, Paris: Masson.

Coubba, A. (1995) *Le Mal djiboutien: rivalités ethniques et enjeux politiques*, Paris: L'Harmattan.

Coulombe, M and Jean, M. (eds) (2000) *Le Dictionnaire du cinéma québécois*, Montreal: Boréal.

Courrière, Y. (2001) *La Guerre d'Algérie*, 2 vols, Paris: Fayard (originally 4 vols, 1969–1971).

Croutier, A. L. (1989) *Harem: The World Behind the Veil*, London: Bloomsbury.

Cumming, G. (2001) *Aid to Africa: French and British Aid Policies from the Cold War to the New Millennium*, Aldershot: Ashgate.

Dadié, B. (1959) *Un Nègre à Paris*, Paris: Présence Africaine.

Daeninckx, D. (1998) *Cannibale*, Paris: Verdier.

D'Almeida, I. A. (1994) *Francophone African Women Writers: Destroying the Emptiness of Silence*, Gainesville: University Press of Florida.

Daninos, G. (1987) *Comprendre 'Tribaliques' d'Henri Lopes*, Paris: Les Classiques Africaines.

Daoudi, B. and Miliani, H. (1996) *L'Aventure du Raï: Musique et société*, Paris: Editions du Seuil.

Dash, M. (1995) *Edouard Glissant*, Cambridge: Cambridge University Press.

Dauncey, H. and Hare, G. (eds) (1999) *France and the 1998 World Cup*, London: Frank Cass.

David, G. and Lavoie, P. (eds) (1993) *Le Monde de Michel Tremblay*, Montreal: Cahiers de Théâtre Jeu.

Davis, G. (1997) *Aimé Césaire*, Cambridge: Cambridge University Press.

Decalo, S. (1996) *Historical Dictionary of Togo*, Lanham, MD: Scarecrow Press.

Decalo, S. (1997) *Historical Dictionary of Niger*, Lanham, MD: Scarecrow Press.

Delvert, J. (1983) *Le Cambodge*, Que sais-je? Paris: Presses Universitaires de France.

Demers, F. (1999) *Céline Dion et l'identité québécoise*, Montreal: VLB.

Derderian, R. (1993) 'Daughters in conflict: the brother/sister relationship in Ferrudja Kessas's "Beur's Story"', *Journal of Maghrebi Studies*, 1:1–2, pp. 72–8.

Derderian, R. (1997) 'Broadcasting from the margins: minority ethnic radio in contemporary France', in A. G. Hargreaves and M. McKinney (eds), *Postcolonial Cultures in France*, London: Routledge, pp. 99–114.

Derive, J. (1979–80) 'L'Utilisation de la parole traditionnelle dans *Les Soleils des indépendences* d'Ahmadou Kourouma', *L'Afrique littéraire* (Paris), 54–5:4, pp. 103–110.

Derradji, A.-R. (1997) *The Algerian Guerrilla Campaign, Strategy and Tactics*, New York: Edwin Mellen Press.

Désir, H. (1985) *Touche pas à mon pote*, Paris: Bernard Grasset.

Dewitte, P. (1985) *Les Mouvements nègres en France 1919–1939*, Paris: L'Harmattan.

Dewitte, P. (ed.) (1999) *Immigration et intégration: l'état des savoirs*, Paris: La Découverte.

Diabaté, M. M. (1986) *Le Lion à l'arc*, Paris: Hatier, Coll. Monde noir.

Dib, M. (1996) 'A. Djemaï's *Sable Rouge*', *Le Nouvel Observateur*, 1669, 30 Oct.–6 Nov., pp. 129.

Diop, A.-B. (1981) *La Société wolof: tradition et changement, les systèmes d'inégalité et de domination*, Paris: Karthala.

Diop, M. C. and Diouf, M. (1990) *Le Sénégal sous Abdou Diouf*, Paris: Karthala.

Djebar, A. (1989) *Fantasia: An Algerian Cavalcade*, London: Quartet.

Djeflat, A. and Zghal, R. (ed.) (1995) *Science, Technologie et Croissance au Maghreb*, Sfax: Biruni.

Ducrocq-Poirier, M. *et al.* (eds) (1996) *Anne Hébert, parcours d'une oeuvre*, Montreal: Hexagone.

Durmelat, S. (1998) 'Petite histoire du mot *beur*: ou comment prendre la parole quand on vous la prête', *French Cultural Studies*, vol. 9, pp. 191–207.

Einaudi, J.-L. (2001) *Octobre 1961: Un massacre à Paris*, Paris: Fayard.

Elbaz, R. (1996) *Tahar Ben Jelloun ou l'inassouvissement du désir narratif*, Paris: L'Harmattan.

El Fadwa, G. (1998) *Veil: Modesty, Privacy and Resistance*, Oxford: Berg.

Englebert, P. (1996) *Burkina Faso: Unsteady Statehood in West Africa*, Oxford: Westview Press.

Ennaji, M. (1988) 'Language planning in Morocco and changes in Arabic', *International Journal of the Sociology of Language*, 74, pp. 9–39.

Ennaji, M. (1997) 'The sociology of Berber: change and continuity', *International Journal of the Sociology of Language*, 112, pp. 97–111.

Ennaji, M. (2001) 'De la diglossie à la triglossie', *Languages and Linguistics*, 8, pp. 49–64.

Ennaji, M. and Sadiqi, F. (1994) *Applications of Modern Linguistics*, Casablanca: Afrique Orient.

Entelis, J. (1989) *Culture and Counter-Culture in Moroccan Politics*, Boulder, CO: Westview Press.

Entelis, J. (1999) 'Sonatrach: the political economy of an Algerian state institution', *Middle East Journal*, 53:1, pp. 9–27.

Entelis, J. and Naylor, P. (eds) (1992) *State and Society in Algeria*, Boulder, CO: Westview Press.

Enwezor, O. (ed.) (2001) *The Short Century: Independence and Liberation Movements in Africa, 1945–1994*, London: Prestel.

Eriksen, T. H. (1998) *Common Denominators, Ethnicity, Nation-building and Compromise in Mauritius*, Oxford: Berg.

Erwin, R. (1994) *The Arabian Nights: A Companion*, London: Allen Lane.

Etudes françaises (1999) 'Gaston Miron: un poète dans la cité', special issue, 35:2/3 (L'Université de Montréal).

Ewens, G. (1991) *Africa O-Ye! A Celebration of African Music*, Enfield: Guinness.

Fabian, J. (1983) *Time and the Other: How Anthropology Makes Its Object*, New York: Columbia University Press.

Fabre, M. (1985) *Rive noire: de Harlem à la Seine*, Paris: Lieu commun.

Fanon, F. (1975) *Peau noire, masques blancs*, Paris: Editions du Seuil (originally published 1952).

Fanon, F. (1991) *Les Damnés de la terre*, Paris: Editions du Seuil (originally published 1961).

Fanon, F. (2001a) *L'An V de la révolution algérienne*, Paris: La Découverte (originally published 1959).

Fanon, F. (2001b) *Pour la révolution africaine: Écrits politiques*, Paris: La Découverte (originally published 1964).

Fassin, D., Morice, A. and Quiminal, C. (eds) (1997) *Les Lois de l'inhospitalité: Les politiques de l'immigration à l'épreuve des sans-papiers*, Paris: La Découverte.

Ferdi, S. (1981) *Un enfant dans la guerre*, Paris: Editions du Seuil.

Ferguson, C. F. (1959) 'Diglossia', *Word*, 15, pp. 325–40.

Findlay, A., Findlay, A. and Lawless R. (1982) *Tunisia*, Oxford: Clio.

Francis, R. Douglas and Smith, Donald B. (1998) *Readings in Canadian History. Pre-Confederation, Vol I*; *Post-Confederation, Vol II*, Toronto: Harcourt.

Freeman, E. (1971) *The Theatre of Albert Camus: A Critical Study*, London: Methuen.

Freyss, J. (1995) *Economie assistée et changement social en Nouvelle-Calédonie*, Paris: Presses Universitaires de France.

Gadant, M. (1995) *Le Nationalisme algérien et les femmes*, Paris: L'Harmattan.

Gaid, M. (1995) *Les Berbères dans l'histoire*, Algiers: Editions Mimouni.

Galand, L. (1966) 'La construction du nom complément du nom en Berbère', GLECS, pp. 166–72.

Galand-Pernette, P. (1998) *Littératures berbères, des voix, des lettres*, Paris: Presses Universitaires de France.

Gallagher, M. (1994) 'Whence and whither the French Caribbean "créolité" movement?' *ASCALF Bulletin* 9, pp. 3–19.

Gallagher, M. (1998) *La Créolité de Saint-Jean Perse*, Paris: Gallimard.

Gallays, F. and Laliberté, Y. (1997) *Alain Grandbois, prosateur et poète*, Orléans (Ont.): Editions David.

Gallimore, R. B. (1997) *L'Œuvre romanesque de Calixthe Beyala: le renouveau de l'écriture féminine en Afrique francophone*, Paris: L'Harmattan.

Gaspard, F. and Khosrokhavar, F. (1995) *Le Foulard et la République*, Paris: La Découverte.

Gauvin, L. (1975) *Parti pris littéraire*, Montreal: Presses de l'Université de Montréal.

Geesey, P. (1996) 'Exhumation and history: Tahar Djaout's *Les chercheurs d'os*', *The French Review*, 70:2, December, pp. 271–9.

Gellner, E. (1983) *Nations and Nationalism*, Ithaca: Cornell University Press.

Giesbert, F.-O. (1995) *Jacques Chirac*, Paris: Editions du Seuil.

Giesbert, F.-O. (1996) *François Mitterrand: Une Vie*, Paris: Editions du Seuil.

Gilroy, P. (1993) *The Black Atlantic: Modernity and Double Consciousness*, Cambridge, MA: Harvard University Press/London: Verso.

Giono, J. (1990) *Entretiens avec Jean Amrouche et Taos Amrouche*, Paris: Gallimard.

Givanni, J. (ed.) (2000) *Symbolic Narratives/African Cinema*, London: BFI Publishing.

Glissant, E. (1989) *Caribbean Discourse: Selected Essays*, Charlottesville: University Press of Virginia.

Glissant, E. (1990) *Poétique de la Relation*, Paris: Gallimard.

Glissant, E. (1996) *Introduction à une poétique de la Relation*, Paris: Gallimard.

Godin, J.-C. and Lafon, D. (1999) *Dramaturgies Québécoises des années quatre-vingt*, Montreal: Leméac.

Godin, J.-C. and Mailhot, L. (1988) *Théâtre Québécois* (I and II), Montreal: Bibliothèque Québécoise.

Godin, P. (1995/8) *René Lévesque, héros malgré lui* (Vols 1 and 2), Montreal: Boréal.

Golsan, R. J. (ed.) (2000) *The Papon Affair: Memory and Justice on Trial*, New York and London: Routledge.

Gontard, M. (1981) *La Violence du texte: La littérature marocaine de langue française*, Paris: L'Harmattan.

Gontard, M. (1993) *Le Moi étrange: Littérature marocaine de langue française*, Paris: L'Harmattan.

Gordon, A. A. (1996) *Transforming Capitalism and Patriarchy: Gender and Development in Africa*, Boulder, CO: Lynne Rienner.

Gordon, L. R., Sharpley-Whiting, T. D. and White, R. (eds) (1996) *Fanon: A Critical Reader*, Oxford: Blackwell.

Goudaillier, J.-P. (2001) *Comment tu tchatches!: Dictionnaire du français contemporain des cités*, pref. C. Hagège, 3rd edn, Paris: Maisonneuve et Larose.

Grandguillaume, G. (1991) 'Arabisation et langues maternelles dans le contexte national au Maghreb', *International Journal of the Sociology of Language*, 87, pp. 45–54.

Gray, C. (1989) *Conceptions of History in the Work of Cheikh Anta Diop and Théophile Obenga*, London: Karnak.

Grésillon, M. (1986) *'Une si longue lettre' de Mariama Bâ: étude*, Issy les Moulineaux: Editions Saint-Paul.

Grosser, A. (1967) *French Foreign Policy under de Gaulle*, Connecticut: Greenwood Press.

Guénif Souilamas, N. (2000) *Des Beurettes aux descendantes d'immigrants nord-africains*, Paris: Bernard Grasset.

Guettat, M. (1980) *La Musique classique du Maghreb*, Paris; Sindbad.

Guttman, A. (1993) 'The sport process: the diffusion of sports and the problem of cultural imperialism', in R. G. Dunning, J. A. Maguire and E. R. Pearton (eds), *The Sport Process: A Comparative and Developmental Approach*, Leeds: Human Kinetics Publisher, pp. 125–39.

Hall, S. (1990) 'The local and the global: globalisation and ethnicity', in D. King (ed.), *Culture, Globalisation and the World System*, London: Macmillan and Department of Art and Art History, State University of New York at Birmingham, pp. 19–41.

Hamel, R. (1997) *Panorama de la littérature québécoise contemporaine*, Montreal: Guérin.

Hamody, M. (1995) *Bibliographie Générale de la Mauritanie*, Nouakchott: Centre Culturel Français.

Hamoumou, M. (1993) *Et ils sont devenus harkis*, Paris: Fayard.

Hannerz, U. (1991) 'Scenarios for peripheral cultures', in D. King (ed.), *Culture, globalisation and the world system*, London: Macmillan and Department of Art and Art History, State University of New York at Birmingham, pp. 107–28.

Harbi, M. (1980) *FLN: mirage et réalité*, Paris: Jeune Afrique.

Harbi, M. (1981) *Les Archives de la révolution algérienne*, Paris: Editions Jeune Afrique.

Harbi, M. (1984) *La Guerre commence en Algérie*, Brussels: Editions Complexe.

Harbi, M. (2001) *Une Vie debout. Mémoires politiques*, Vol. I: *1945–1962*, Paris: La Découverte.

Hargreaves, A. G. (1992) *La Littérature beur: Un guide bio-bibliographique*, New Orleans: CELFAN.

Hargreaves, A. G. (1995) *Immigration, 'Race' and Ethnicity in Contemporary France*, London: Routledge.

Hargreaves, A. G. (1996) 'A deviant construction: the French media and the *banlieues*', *New Community*, 22:4, pp. 607–18.

Hargreaves, A. G. (1997) *Immigration and Identity in Beur Fiction: Voices from the North African Community in France*, 2nd edn, Oxford and New York: Berg.

Hassan II (1976) *Le Défi*, Paris: Albin Michel.

Hazaël-Massieux, M.-C. (1987) *Chansons des Antilles, comptines, formulettes*, Paris: CNRS.

Hazaël-Massieux, M.-C. (1993) *Ecrire en créole*, Paris: L'Harmattan.

Hébert, P. (1997) *Jacques Poulin: la creation d'un espace amoureux*, Ottawa: Les Presses de l'Université d'Ottawa.

Heiler, S. (1996) '*Le Miroir du silence* de Aïcha Bouabaci: une poétique silencieuse, chantée et réfléchie', *Bulletin of Francophone Africa*, 5:9, pp. 57–70.

Hennebelle, G. and Schneider (eds) (1990) *Cinémas métis de Hollywood aux films beurs*, Paris: CinémAction; Hommes et Migrations.

Henningham, S. (1992) *France and the South Pacific: A Contemporary History*, Sydney: Allen & Unwin.

Henry, J. (1993) 'Le CODOFIL dans le mouvement francophone en Louisiane', *Espace Francophone*, 43, pp. 25–46.

Henry, J. (1997) 'The Louisiana French movement: actors and actions in social change', in A. Valdman (ed.), *French and Creole in Louisiana*, New York: Plenum Press, pp. 183–213.

Henry, T. R. (1955) *Wilderness Messiah: Story of Hiawatha and the Iroquois*, New York: W. Sloane Associates.

Hergé (1982) *Les Aventures de Tintin reporter du Petit Vingtième au Congo*, Paris and Tournai: Casterman (first published 1931).

Hervo, M. (2001) *Chroniques du bidonville. Nanterre en Guerre d'Algérie 1959–1962*, Paris: Editions du Seuil.

Hesmondhalgh, D. (1998) 'Globalisation and cultural imperialism: a case study of the music industry', in R. Kiely and P. Marfleet (eds), *Globalisation and the Third World*, London: Routledge, pp. 163–84.

Heurgon, M. (1994) *Histoire du PSU. 1: La fondation et la guerre d'Algérie*, Paris: La Découverte.

Hitchcott , N. (1997a) 'Calixthe Beyala and the postcolonial woman', in A. G. Hargreaves and M. McKinney (eds), *Postcolonial Cultures in France*, London: Routledge.

Hitchcott, N. (1997b) 'Female sexuality and family romance: Tanella Boni's *Une vie de crabe*', in J. P. and R. Little (eds), *Black Accents: Writing in French from Africa, Mauritius and the Caribbean*, London: Grant & Cutler.

Hitchcott, N. (2000) *Women Writers in Francophone Africa*, Oxford: Berg.

Hobsbawm, E. (1990) *Nations and Nationalism since 1780*, Cambridge: Cambridge University Press.

Hordern, P. and Purcell, N. (2000) *The Corrupting Sea: A Study of Mediterranean History*, Oxford: Basil Blackwell.

Hornblower, M. (1990) 'A rebel named Désir', *Time* (26 November), pp. 70–1.

Horne, A. (1987) *A Savage War of Peace. Algeria 1954–1962*, London: Macmillan (originally published 1977).

Hornug, A. and Ruhe, E. (eds) (1998) *Postcolonialisme et autobiographie*, Amsterdam and Atlanta, GA: Rodopi.

Houlihan, B. (1994) 'Hegemonisation, Americanisation and creolisation of sport: Varieties of Globalisation', *Sociology of Sport Journal*, 11, pp. 356–75.

House, J. (1996) 'Muslim communities in France', in G. Nonneman, T. Niblock and B. Szajkowski (eds), *Muslim Communities in the New Europe*, Reading, MA: Garnet, pp. 219–39.

House, J. (2001) 'Antiracist memories: the case of 17 October 1961 in historical perspective', *Modern and Contemporary France*, 9:3, pp. 355–68.

House, J. (2002) 'Antiracism in France, 1898–1962: modernity and beyond', in F. Anthias and C. Lloyd (eds), *Re-thinking Antiracism*, London: Routledge.

Hovannisian, R. C. and Sabagh, G. (1997) *The Thousand and One Nights in Arabic Literature and Society*, Cambridge: Cambridge University Press.

Hughes, S. O. (2000) *Morocco under King Hassan*, Reading, MA: Ithaca.

Hussein, M. (1997) 'L'Individu postcolonial', *Dédale*, 5/6, Spring, pp. 164–76.

Hymans, J. L. (1971) *Léopold Sédar Senghor: An Intellectual Biography*, Edinburgh: Edinburgh University Press.

Ibrahim, S. E. (1996) Discussion Paper No. 10: *Management and Mismanagement of Diversity: The Case of Ethnic Conflict and State-Building in the Arab World*, http://www/unesco.org/most/ibraeng, November 2000.

Icheboudene, L. (1997) *Alger: Histoire et Capitale de Destin National*, Algiers: Casbah Editions.

Ireland, S. and Proulx, P. J. (eds) (2001) *Immigrant Narratives in Contemporary France*, Westport, CO: Greenwood Press.

Isaak, R. A. (2000) *Managing World Economic Change*, Upper Saddle River, NJ: Prentice-Hall.

Jack, B. (1996) *Francophone Literatures*, Oxford: Oxford University Press.

Jackson, R. J. and Jackson, D. (2001) *Politics in Canada: Culture, Institutions, Behaviour and Public Policy*, 5th edn, Toronto: Prentice-Hall.

Jaenen, C. J. (ed.) (1993) *Les Franco-Ontariens*, Ottawa: Les Presses de l'Université d'Ottawa.

Jaffré, B. (1997) *Biographie de Thomas Sankara*, Paris: L'Harmattan.

James, C. L. R. (1980) *The Black Jacobins: Toussaint L'Ouverture and the San Domingo Revolution*, London: Allison & Busby (first published 1938).

Jarreau, P. (1997) 'Bruno Mégret, le mutant du Front National', *Le Monde* (4 February).

Joffé, G. (1997) 'Maghribi Islam and Islam in the Maghreb: the eternal dichotomy', in D. Westerlund and E. E. Rosander (eds), *African Islam and Islam in Africa*, London: Hurst, pp. 55–78.

Jouanny, R. (ed.) (1992) *Lectures de l'oeuvre d'Hampaté Bâ*, Paris: L'Harmattan.

Judge, A. (1993) 'French: a planned language?' in C. Sanders, *French Today*, Cambridge: Cambridge University Press, pp. 7–26.

Julien, C. A. (1979) *Histoire de l'Algérie contemporaine: conquête et colonisation, 1830–1871*, Paris: Presses Universitaires de France.

Kaddache, M. (1980) *Histoire du nationalisme algérien*. Vol. II: *Question nationale et politique algérienne 1919–1951*, Algiers: Société Nationale d'Edition et de Diffusion (SNED).

Kadra-Hadjadji, H. (1986) *Contestation et révolte dans l'oeuvre de Driss Chraïbi*, Paris: Publisud.

Kapil, A. (1994) 'Algeria', in Frank Tachau (ed.), *Political Parties of the Middle East and North Africa*, Westport, CO: Greenwood Press, pp. 3–68.

Kateb, K. (2001) *La Fin du mariage traditionnel en Algérie? 1876–1998*, Saint-Denis: Editions Bouchène.

Kaur, P. (2000) *Federalism and Political Separatism*, New Delhi: South India Press.

Kazi-Tani, N.-A. (2001) *Pour une lecture critique de 'L'Errance' de Georges Ngal*, Paris: L'Harmattan.

Kébir, A. (1999) *Thagaste*, La Tour d'Aigues: Editions de l'Aube.

Kébir, A. (2001) *Sur les pas de Saint Augustin*, Paris: Presses de la Renaissance.

Kepel, G. (1987) *Les Banlieues de l'Islam: naissance d'une religion en France*, Paris: Editions du Seuil.

Kettane, N. (1986) *Droit de réponse à la démocratie française*, Paris: La Découverte.

Khaled (1998) *Derrière le sourire*, Paris: Editions Michel Lafon.

Khatibi, A. (1968) *Le Roman maghrébin*, Paris: Maspero; 2nd edn (1979), Rabat: SMER.

Kibbee, D. A. (ed.) (1998) *Language Legislation and Linguistic Rights*. Amsterdam-Philadelphia: John Benjamins Publishing.

Kidd, W. and Reynolds, S. (2000) *Contemporary French Cultural Studies*, London: Arnold.

King, A. (1980) *The Writings of Camara Laye*, London/Ibadan: Heinemann.

Konaré, K. (ed.) (2001) *Le Mali des talents*, Saint-Paul: Cauris Editions.

Krop, P. (1994) *Le Génocide franco-africain: faut-il juger les Mitterrand?*, Paris: J.-C. Lattès.

Kuhn, R. (1995) *The Media in France*, London: Routledge.

Labat, S. (1995) *Les Islamistes algériens: entre les urnes et le maquis*, Paris: Editions du Seuil.

Lacoste-Dujardin, C. (1986) *Des Mères contre les femmes: Maternité et patriarcat au Maghreb*, Paris: La Découverte.

Lacoursière, J., Provencher, J. and Vaugeois, D. (2000) *Canada-Québec 1534–2000*, Montreal: Septentrion.

Lacouture, J. (1986) *De Gaulle*, 3 vols, Paris: Editions du Seuil.

Laffifi, W. (1989) 'La Mort d'un juste', *Actualité de l'émigration*, no. 175, 10 May, pp. 11–15.

Lallaoui, M. (1995) *Du bidonville aux HLM*, Paris: Au nom de la mémoire/Syros.

Lamchichi, A. (1991) *L'Algérie en crise: 1954–1991*, Paris: L'Harmattan.

Laroche, M. (1978) *Le 'Romancero aux étoiles' et l'oeuvre romanesque de Jacques-Stéphen Alexis*, Paris: Nathan.

Laroui, A. (1977) *Les Origines culturelles du nationalisme marocain*, Paris: Maspero.

Lawrence, M. (1992) *Chrétien*, Toronto: Lester.

Laye, C. (1980) *The Guardian of the Word*, trans. by James Kirkup, London: Fontana.

Lazreg, M. (1994) *The Eloquence of Silence: Algerian Women in Question*, London: Routledge.

Le Boucher, D. (2000) 'Jean Pélégri l'Algérien ou Le Scribe du caillou', *Algérie Littérature Action* 37–8, Paris: Edition Marsa.

Lechervy, C. (1993) 'Cambodge: de la paix à la démocratie?' *Problèmes politiques et sociaux*, 716 (Dec.), La Documentation Française.

Leclerc, G. (2001) *Lionel Jospin: l'énigme du conquérant*, Paris: J.-C. Lattès.

Lecomte, H.-B. (1999) *Lomé V et le commerce ACP-UE*, London: Overseas Development Institute.

Lefebvre, D. (2001) *Guy Mollet face à la torture en Algérie 1956-1957*, Paris: Bruno Leprince.

Lefort, C. (1988) *Democracy and Political Theory*, Cambridge: Polity.

Leiner, J. (1977) 'René Depestre ou du surréalisme comme moyen d'accès a l'identité haïtienne dans *Arc-en-ciel pour l'Occident chrétien*', *Romanische Forschungen*, 89, pp. 37–50.

Leiris, M. (1950) 'L'Ethnographe devant le colonialisme', *Les Temps Modernes*, 6:58, pp. 357–74.

Lemarchand, R. (1970) *Rwanda and Burundi*, London: Pall Mall Press; (1979) New York: Praeger.

Lemarchand, R. (1994) *Burundi: Ethnocide as Discourse and Practice*, Cambridge: Cambridge University Press.

Lesbet, D. (1985) *La Casbah d'Alger*, Algiers: Office des Publications Universitaires.

Letwidge, B. (1982) *De Gaulle*, London: Weidenfeld & Nicolson.

Levine, M. V. (1990) *The Reconquest of Montreal*, Philadephia: Temple University Press; French edition (1997) *La Reconquête de Montréal*, Montreal: VLB.

Lévi-Strauss, C. (1952) *Race et histoire*, Paris: Gallimard/Folio.

Linden, I. (1977) *Church and Revolution in Rwanda*, Manchester: Manchester University Press.

Little, J. P. (2000) *Cheikh Hamidou Kane: 'L'Aventure ambiguë'*, London: Grant & Cutler.

Little, R. (1973) *Saint-John Perse*, London: Athlone.

Lloyd, C. (1998) *Discourses of Antiracism in France*, London: Ashgate.

Lodge, R. A. (1993) *French: From Dialect to Standard*, London: Routledge.

Long, M. (ed.) (1988) *Etre Français aujourd'hui et demain. Rapport de la Commission de la nationalité*, 2 vols, Paris: Union Générale d'Editions.

Looseley, D. (1995) *The Politics of Fun: Cultural Policy and Debate in Contemporary France*, Oxford and New York: Berg.

Lyotard, J.-F. (1979) *La Condition postmoderne*, Paris: Minuit.

Macey, D. (2001) *Frantz Fanon: A Life*, London: Granta.

Mailafia, O. (1997) *Europe and Economic Reform in Africa*, London: Routledge.

Maillet, A. *et al.* (1984) *Les Acadiens, piétons de l'Atlantique*, Paris: ACE.

Maillet, M. and Hamel, J. (eds) (1990) *La Réception des oeuvres d'Antonine Maillet. Actes du Colloque International organisé par la chaire d'Etudes Acadiennes les 13, 14 et 15 octobre 1988*, Moncton: Chaire d'Etudes Acadiennes.

Major, R. (1979) *Parti pris: idéologies et littérature*, Montreal: HMH.

Majumdar, M. A. (2000) 'Language and history in Franco-Algerian Relations', in K. Salhi (ed.), *Francophone Studies: Discourse and Identity*, Exeter: Elm Bank, pp. 105–20.

Majumdar, M. A. (2001) 'Lutte, parole et résistance dans les textes antillais', in B. Chikhi (ed.), *Passerelles Francophones. Pour un nouvel espace d'interprétation*, Vol. II: *Vives Lettres*, 11 (Strasbourg), pp. 133–56.

Makward, C. P. (1999) *Mayotte Capécia*, Paris: Karthala.

Malkmus, E. and Armes, R. (1991) *Arab and African Film-making*, London and New Jersey: Zed Books.

Mamdani, M. (2001) *When Victims Become Killers. Colonialism, Nativism and the Genocide in Rwanda*, London: James Currey/Princeton University Press.

Mammeri, K. (1988) *Abane Ramdane – Héros de la guerre d'Algérie*, Paris: L'Harmattan.

Mandouze, A. (1998) *Mémoires d'outre siècle: d'une résistance à l'autre*, Paris: Viviane Hamy.

Marçais, W. (1930–31) 'La diglossie: un pèlerinage aux sources', *Bulletin de la Société Linguistique de Paris*, 76:1, pp. 61–98.

Marchal, H., Boulay, R. and Kasarhérou, E. (eds) (1990) *De Jade et de nacre: Patrimoine artistique kanak*, Paris: Réunion des musées nationaux.

Marcus, J. (1995) *The National Front and French Politics: The Resistible Rise of Jean-Marie Le Pen*, New York: New York University Press.

Marfleet, P. (1998) 'Globalisation and the Third World', *International Socialism Journal*, 81 (Winter), pp. 91–130.

Margueron, D. (1989) *Tahiti dans toute sa littérature*, Paris: L'Harmattan.

Marshall, B. (2001) *Quebec National Cinema*, Montreal/Kingston: McGill-Queen's University Press.

Martin, V. (1996) *Toulon la noire*, Paris: Denoël.

Marty, E. (1998) *Entretiens Gide-Amrouche*, Tournai: La Renaissance du livre.

Maspero, F. (1990) *Les Passagers du Roissy-Express*, Paris: Editions du Seuil.

Mathieu, J.-L. (1993) *Histoire des DOM-TOM*, Paris: Presses Universitaires de France.

Maugey, A. (1993) *Le Roman de la francophonie*, Paris: Jean-Michel Place.

Mauriac, F. (1981) *Souvenirs retrouvés: entretiens avec Jean Amrouche*, Paris: Fayard.

McDonald, P. (1994) *Giap: The Victor in Vietnam*, London: Warner.

McFarland, D. M. and Rupley, L. A. (1998) *Historical Dictionary of Burkina Faso*, Lanham, MD: Scarecrow Press.

McIlvanney, S. (1998) 'Female identity in process in Soraya Nini's *Ils disent que je suis une beurette*', *Modern and Contemporary France*, 6:4, pp. 505–17.

McLeod, J. (2000) *Beginning Postcolonialism*, Manchester: Manchester University Press.

McMurray, D. A. (1997) 'La France Arabe', in A. G. Hargreaves and M. McKinney (eds), *Postcolonial Cultures in France*, London and New York: Routledge, pp. 26–39.

McNulty, M. (1999) 'The collapse of Zaïre: implosion, revolution or external sabotage?' *Journal of Modern African Studies*, 37:1, 55–82.

McRoberts, K. (1997) *Misconceiving Canada: The Struggle for National Unity*. Toronto: Oxford University Press.

Méliani, A. (1993) *Le Drame des harkis. La France honteuse*, Paris: Perrin.

Memmi, A. (ed.) (1964) *Anthologie des écrivains maghrébins d'expression francaise*, Paris: Présence Africaine.

Merahi, Y. (1998) *Tahar Djaout ou les raisons du cri*, Tizi Ouzou: TOP Sarl.

Mernissi, F. (1985) *Beyond the Veil: Male–Female Dynamics in Modern Muslim Society*, London: Al Saqi.

Mernissi, F. (1988) *Doing Daily Battle: Interviews with Moroccan Women*, London: Women's Press.

Mernissi, F. (1990) *Le Monde n'est pas un harem*, Paris: Albin Michel.

Mernissi, F. (1993) *Islam and Democracy*, translated by Mary Jo Lakeland, London: Virago.

Mernissi, F. (1994) *The Forgotten Queens of Islam*, Cambridge: Polity Press.

Mernissi, F. (1995) *The Harem Within*, Toronto and London: Bantam.

Messaoudi, K. (1995) *Une Algérienne debout* (with E. Schemla), Paris: Flammarion.

Miller, C. L. (1998) *Nationalists and Nomads: Essays on Francophone African Literature and Culture*, Chicago and London: University of Chicago Press.

Minces, J. (1992) *L'Algérie de Boumedienne*, Paris: Presses de la Cité.

Mohsen-Finan, K. (1997) *Sahara Occidental: les enjeux d'un conflit régional*, Paris: CNRS Editions.

Moorhouse, G. (1986) *The Fearful Void*, Harmondsworth: Penguin.

Moreira, P. (1987) *Rock métis en France*, Paris: Souffles.

Mortimer, M. (1990) *Journeys Through the French African Novel*, London: James Currey.

Moura, J.-M. (1999) *Littératures francophones et théorie postcoloniale*, Paris: Presses Universitaires de France.

Mouzouni, L. (1985) *Réception critique d'Ahmed Sefrioui*, Casablanca: Afrique Orient.

Mouzouni, L. (1987) *Le Roman marocain*, Paris: Publisud.

Mudimbe-Boyi, M. E. (1992) *L'Oeuvre romanesque de Jacques-Stéphen Alexis*, Montreal: Humanitas.

Murphy, D. (2000) *Sembene: Imagining Alternatives in Film and Fiction*, Oxford: James Currey; Trenton, NJ: Africa World Press.

Mworoha, E. (1995) *ACCT 1970–1995: 25 ans au service du développement et de la coopération francophone*, Paris: ACCT

Naamane-Guessous, S. (1991) *Au delà de toute pudeur: La sexualité féminine au Maroc*, Casablanca: Eddif.

Nafziger, E. W. (1988) *Inequality in Africa: Political Elites, Proletariat, Peasants and the Poor*, Cambridge: Cambridge University Press.

Nair, S. (1994) *Lettre à Charles Pasqua*, Paris: Editions du Seuil.

Nandjui, P. (1995) *Houphouët-Boigny, l'homme de la France en Afrique*, Paris: L'Harmattan.

Naudin, M. (1996) 'Tahar Djaout: paysage métaphorique de l'Algérie', *The French Review*, 70:1, October, 81–9.

Ndagano, B. (1994) *La Guyane entre mots et maux. Une lecture de l'œuvre d'Elie Stephenson*, Paris: L'Harmattan.

Ngal, G. (1975) *Aimé Césaire: un homme à la recherche d'une patrie*, Dakar: Nouvelles Editions Africaines; 2nd edn (1994), Paris: Presence Africaine.

Niane, D. T. (1960) *Soundiata ou l'épopée mandingue*, Paris: Présence Africaine.

Nicholls, D. (1996) *From Dessalines to Duvalier: Race, Colour and National Independence in Haiti*, London and Basingstoke: Macmillan.

Nicolaïdis, D. (1994) *Oublier nos crimes: l'amnésie française – une spécificité française?*, Paris: Autrement.

Noiriel, G. (1988) *Le Creuset français: histoire de l'immigration XIXe–XXe siècles*, Paris: Editions du Seuil.

Nolutshungu, S. (1996) *Limits of Anarchy: Intervention and State Formation in Chad*, Charlottesville and London: University Press of Virginia.

Notre Librairie (1984) 'Littérature malienne. Au carrefour de l'oral et de l'écrit', 75–6 (July–Oct.).

Notre Librairie (1995) Special number on Bénin, 124 (Oct.–Dec.).

Nouvelles questions féministes (1985) 'Antillaises', 9–10 (Spring).

Oliver, D. (1989) *Oceania: The Native Cultures of Australia and the Pacific Islands*, Honolulu: University of Hawaii Press.

Orlando, V. (1997) 'Who's covering who in the postmodern 90s? Subverting the Orientalist image in the contemporary North African Francophone text', *Romance Languages Annual*, 8, pp. 97–103.

Oufreha, F.-Z. (1998) 'Femmes algériennes: la révolution silencieuse?' *Monde Arabe. Maghreb Machrek*, 162 (Oct.–Dec.), pp. 57–68.

Ouerdane, A. (1993) *La Question Berbère dans le mouvement national algérien 1926–1980*, Algiers: Editions Epigraphe/Dar El Ijtihad.

Ouvrage collectif (1997) *En Mémoire du futur pour Abdelkader Alloula*, Paris: Sindbad–Actes Sud.

Owram, D. (ed.) (1994) *Canadian History – A Reader's Guide*. Vol. II: *Confederation to the Present*, Toronto: University of Toronto Press.

Oyeronke, O. (1997) *The Invention of Women: Making an African Sense of Western Gender Discourses*, Minneapolis: University of Minnesota Press.

Parker, G. (1996) 'French language policy in Sub-Saharan Africa', *Modern and Contemporary France*, NS, 4:4, pp. 471–81.

Paulin, M. (1998) *Félix Leclerc: filou, le troubadour*, Montreal: XYZ.

Péan, P. (1994) *Une Jeunesse française: François Mitterrand 1934–1947*, Paris: Fayard.

Peju, P. (2000) *Ratonnades à Paris*, précédé de, *Les Harkis à Paris*, Paris: La Découverte.

Péroncel-Hugoz, J. P. (1983) *Assassinat d'un poète*, Marseille: Editions du Quai.

Peronnet, L. (1993) 'La situation du français en Acadie', in D. de Robillard and M. Beniamino. (eds), *Le Français dans l'espace francophone*, Vol. I, Paris: Champion, pp. 101–16.

Perrault, G. (1990) *Notre Ami le Roi*, Paris: Gallimard.

Perrineau, P. (1997) *Le Symptôme Le Pen: radiographie des électeurs du Front National*, Paris: Fayard.

Pérusse, D. (1994) *L'Homme sans rivages: portrait d'Alain Grandbois*, Montreal: L'Hexagone.

Pettinger, A. (ed.) (1998) *Always Elsewhere: Travels of the Black Atlantic*, London: Cassell.

Pfaff, F. (1995) *Entretiens avec Maryse Condé*, Paris: Karthala.

Phillips, T. (ed.) (1996) *Africa: The Art of a Continent*, Munich/New York: Prestel.

Pineau, G. (1995) 'Ecrire en tant que Noire', in Maryse Condé and Madeleine Cottenet-Hage (eds), *Penser la créolité*, Paris: Karthala, pp. 289–95.

Pleven, R. (1996) 'La Conférence de Brazzaville', *Revue juridique et politique – indépendance et coopération*, 4, pp. 749–66.

Plourde, M. (2000) *Le Français au Québec: 600 ans d'histoire et de vie*, Montreal: Fidès/Les Publications du Québec.

Poirine, B. (1992) *Tahiti: Stratégie pour l'après-nucléaire*, Arue, Tahiti: PK4.

Pontecorvo, G. (1967) 'The Battle of Algiers: an adventure in film-making', *American Cinematographer*, Los Angeles, April, pp. 266–8.

Post, K. (1989) *Revolution, Socialism and Nationalism in Vietnam*, Aldershot: Dartmouth Publishing.

Prévost, N. (2001) *La Mort indigne de Malik Oussekine*, Paris: Barrault.

Prunier, G. (1995) *The Rwanda Crisis, 1959–1994. History of a Genocide*, London: Christopher Hurst.

Prunier, G. (1997) *Rwanda: The Social, Political and Economic Situation. June 1997, Réseau documentaire sur la région des Grands Lacs africains*: www.grandslacs.net/index.html

Ravenhill, J. (1985) *Collective Clientelism: The Lomé Convention and North–South Relations*, New York: Columbia University Press.

Regaud, N. and Lechervy, C. (1996) *Les Guerres d'Indochine*, Que sais-je? Paris: Presses Universitaires de France.

Renault, F. (1994) *Cardinal Lavigerie: Churchman, Prophet and Missionary*, London: Athlone Press.

Réseau documentaire sur la région des Grands Lacs africains: www.grandslacs.net/index.html

Reyntjens, F. (2000) *Burundi: Prospects for Peace*, London: Minority Rights Group International.

Ricci, F. M. (2001) *ProSports African Football Yearbook 2001*, Rome: Filippo Maria Ricci.

Rickard, P. (1989) *A History of the French Language*, London: Routledge.

Rivière, C. (1977) *Guinea: The Mobilization of a People*, Ithaca, NY: Cornell University Press.

Roberts, E. (2000) 'Close Encounters: French women of Vietnamese origin and the homeland in *Retour à la saison des pluies* and *Les Trois Parques*', in J. Freedman and C. Tarr. (eds), *Women, Immigration and Identities in France*, Oxford: Berg, pp. 121–34.

Rosanvallon, P. (1992) *Le Sacre du citoyen: Histoire du suffrage universel en France*, Paris: Editions du Seuil.

Rosello, M. (2001) *Postcolonial Hospitality: The Immigrant as Guest*, Stanford: Stanford University Press.

Rossatanga-Rignault, G. (2000) *L'Etat au Gabon: histoire et institutions*, Libreville: Editions Raponda-Walker.

Rossillon, P. (ed.) (1995) *Atlas de la langue française*, Paris: Bordas.

Roy, J. (1972) *J'accuse le général Massu*, Paris: Editions du Seuil.

Roy, J. (1995) *Les Chevaux du soleil. La saga de l'Algérie de 1830 à 1962*, Paris: Omnibus (originally published 1968).

Rühn, C. (ed.) (2000) *Le Foot: The Legends of French Football*, London: Abacus.

Ruscio, A. (1987) *La Décolonisation tragique: une histoire de la décolonisation française 1945–1962*, Paris: Messidor/Editions Sociales.

Sadiqi, F. (1990) 'The notion of comp in Berber', in *Linguistics in the Maghreb*, Rabat: Okad.

Sadiqi, F. (1997) *Grammaire du Berbère*, Paris: L'Harmattan.

Sadiqi, F. (2002) *Women, Gender and Language in Morocco*, Leiden: Brill.

Said, E. W. (1978) *Orientalism: Western Conceptions of the Orient*, New York: Pantheon.

Saigh Bousta, R. (1999) *Lecture des récits de Tahar Ben Jelloun*, Casablanca: Afrique Orient.

Saint-Denys Garneau (1960) Documentary film, Montreal: Office National du Film du Canada/National Film Board of Canada, directed by L. Portugais, screenplay A. Hébert.

Salhi, K. (1999) *The Politics and Aesthetics of Kateb Yacine*, Lampeter: Mellen Press.
Salhi, Z. S. (1999) *Poetics, Politics and the Algerian Novel*, Lampeter: Mellen Press.
Saura, B. and Gobrait, V. (eds) (1998) *Pouvanaa a Oopa: Père de la culture politique polynésienne*, Papeete: Au Vent des îles.
Sayad, A. with Dupuy, E. (1995) *Un Nanterre algérien, terre de bidonvilles*, Paris: Autrement
Scemla, J.-J. (2001) 'La littérature dans le Pacifique: le cas tahitien', *Notre Librairie*, 143, pp. 112–23.
Schousboe, E. (1991) *Albert Bensoussan*, Paris: L'Harmattan.
Scott, C. V. (1995) *Gender and Development: Rethinking Modernization and Dependency Theory*, Boulder, CO: Lynne Rienner.
Segalen, V. (1986) *Essai sur l'exotisme*, Paris: Livre de Poche.
Segarra, M. (1997) *Leur Pesant de poudre: romancières francophones du Maghreb*, Paris: L'Harmattan.
Sembene, O. (1981) *Le Dernier de l'empire*, Paris: L'Harmattan.
Senghor, L. S. (1948) *Anthologie de la poésie nègre et malgache*, Preface 'Orphée noir', by J.-P. Sartre, Paris: Presses Universitaires de France.
Sharpley-Whiting, T. D. (1998) *Frantz Fanon: Conflicts and Feminisms*, New York and Oxford: Rowman & Littlefield.
Shelling, V. (1998) 'Globalisation, Ethnic Identity and Popular Culture in Latin America', in R. Kiely and P. Marfleet (eds), *Globalisation and the Third World*, London: Routledge, pp. 141–62.
Shohat, E. and Stam, R. (1994) *Unthinking Eurocentrism: Multiculturalism and the Media*, London and New York: Routledge.
Signaté, I. (1994) *Med Hondo, cinéaste rebelle*, Paris: Présence Africaine.
Sihanouk, N. (1973) *My War With the CIA*, London: Penguin.
Silverman, M. (1992) *Deconstructing the Nation: Immigration, Racism and Citizenship in Modern France*, London and New York: Routledge.
Silverman, M. (1999) *Facing Postmodernity: Contemporary French Thought on Culture and Society*, London and New York: Routledge.
Siméant, J. (1998) *La Cause des sans-papiers*, Paris: Presses de Sciences-Po.
Simon, S. (1985) 'Speaking with authority: the theatre of Marco Micone', *Canadian Literature*, 106, pp. 57–63.
Smith, D. (1995) *Jacques Godbout: Du roman au cinéma*, Montreal: Québec/Amérique.
Souchard, M., Wahnich, S., Cuminal, I. and Wathier, V. (1997) *Le Pen, les mots: analyse d'un discours d'extrême droite*, Paris: Le Monde Editions.
Soustelle, J. (1968) *Vingt-huit ans de gaullisme*, Paris: La Table Ronde.
Soyinka, W. (1976) *Myth, Literature and the African World*, Cambridge: Cambridge University Press.
Spleth, J. (2000) 'African intellectuals in France: echoes of Senghor in Ngandu's memoirs', in M.-P. Le Hir and D. Strand (eds), *French Cultural Studies: Criticism at the Crossroads*, Albany: SUNY Press.
Stora, B. (1993) *Histoire de la Guerre d'Algérie*, Paris: La Découverte.
Stora, B. (1999) 'Nous nous dirigeons vers un Maghreb des régions', interview by Sylvain Cypel, *Le Monde* (21 December).
Stora, B. (2001) *Histoire de l'Algérie depuis l'indépendance*, Paris: La Découverte.

Stovall, T. (2001) 'From Red Belt to Black Belt: Race, class and urban marginality in twentieth-century Paris', *L'Esprit Créateur*, 41.3, pp. 9–23.

Sutton, K. (1996) 'The Casbah of Algiers – a World Heritage site?' *Journal of Algerian Studies*, 1, pp. 65–83.

Sutton, K. (1999) 'Army administration tensions over Algeria's *Centres de Regroupement*', *British Journal of Middle Eastern Studies*, 26:2, pp. 243–70.

Sutton, K. and Aghrout, A. (1992) 'Multi-party elections in Algeria: problems and prospects', *Bulletin of Francophone Africa*, 2, pp. 61–85.

Taguieff, P.-A. (1987) *La Force du préjugé. Essai sur le racisme et ses doubles*, Paris: La Découverte.

Talbott, J. (1980) *The War Without a Name: France in Algeria 1954–1962*, London: Faber & Faber.

Tarr, C. (1997) 'French cinema and postcolonial minorities', in A. G. Hargreaves and M. McKinney (eds), *Postcolonial Cultures in France*, London: Routledge, pp. 59–83.

Taylor, M. B. (ed.) (1994) *Canadian History – A Reader's Guide.* Vol I: *Beginnings to Confederation*; Owram, D. (ed.) Vol II: *Confederation to the Present*, Toronto: University of Toronto Press.

Tcheuyap, A. (1998) *Esthétique et folie dans l'oeuvre romanesque de Pius Ngandu Nkashama*, Paris: L'Harmattan.

Tétu de Labsade, F. (revised edn, 2000) *Le Québec: un pays, une culture*, Montreal: Boréal.

Thody, P. (1961) *Albert Camus, 1913–1960*, Basingstoke: Macmillan.

Tibi, B. (1981) *Arab Nationalism: A Critical Enquiry*, edited and translated by F. M. and P. Sluglett, London: Macmillan.

Titley, E. B. (1997) *Dark Age: The Political Odyssey of Emperor Boukassa*, Liverpool: Liverpool University Press.

Todorov, T. (1993) *On Human Diversity: Nationalism, Racism, and Exoticism in French Thought*, Cambridge, MA and London: Harvard University Press.

Toumi, M. (1989) *La Tunisie de Bourguiba à Ben Ali*, Paris: Presses Universitaires de France.

Touraine, A. (1992) *Critique de la modernité*, Paris: Fayard.

Towa, M. (1971) *Essai sur la problématique philosophique dans l'Afrique actuelle*, Yaoundé: Editions Clé.

Tribalat, M. (1996) *De l'Immigration à l'Assimilation*, Paris: La Découverte/INED.

Ukadike, N. F. (1994) *Black African Cinema*, Berkeley: University of California Press.

UNDP (1998) *Human Development Report*, New York: United Nations.

Valdman, A. (1997) *French and Creole in Louisiana*, New York: Plenum Press.

Verschave, F.-X. (2000) *Noir silence, qui arrêtera la Françafrique?* Paris: Les Arènes.

Vidacs, B. (2000) 'Football in Cameroon: a vehicle for the expansion and contraction of identity', in P. T. Finn and G. Giulianotti (eds), *Football Culture: Local Contests, Global Visions*, London: Frank Cass, pp. 100–17.

Vidal, C. (1995) 'Les Politiques de la haine', *Les Temps Modernes*, 583 (July–Aug), pp. 6–23.

Viollette, M. (1931) *L'Algérie vivra-t-elle?* Paris: F. Alcan.

Virolle, M. (1995) *La Chanson raï*, Paris: Karthala.

Wake, C. (1965) *An Anthology of African and Malagasy Poetry*, London: Oxford University Press.

Warnier, J.-P. (1999) *La Mondialisation de la culture*, Paris: La Découverte.

Wauthier, C. (1995) *Quatre Présidents et l'Afrique*, Paris: Editions du Seuil.

Westerlund, D. (ed.) (1996) *Questioning the Secular State: The Worldwide Resurgence of Religion in Politics*, London: Hurst.

Whiteman, K. (1987) '"*Francophonie*", culture and development: the experience of the ACCT', in O. Akinrinade and J. K. Barling (eds), *Economic Development in Africa*, London: Pinter Publishers, pp. 174–98.

Wieviorka, M. (1991) *L'Espace du racisme*, Paris: Editions du Seuil.

Wieviorka, M. (1998) *Le Racisme, une introduction*, Paris: La Découverte.

Wieviorka, M. *et al.* (eds) (1996) *Une Société fragmentée? Le multiculturalisme en débat*, Paris: La Découverte/Syros.

Wihtol de Wenden, C. (1988) *Les Immigrés et la politique: cent cinquante ans d'évolution*, Paris: Presses de la Fondation nationale des sciences politiques.

Wihtol de Wenden, C. and Leveau, R. (2001) *La Bourgeoisie: les trois âges de la vie associative issue de l'immigration*, Paris: CNRS Editions.

Willame, J.-C. (1999) *L'Odyssée Kabila: trajectoire pour un Congo nouveau?*, Paris: Karthala.

Wood, N. (1999) *Vectors of Memory: Legacies of Trauma in Postwar Europe*, Oxford and New York: Berg.

Wyczynski, P. (1999) *Emile Nelligan: biographie*, Montreal: Bibliothèque québécoise.

Xenakis, D. K. and Chryssochoou, D. N. (2001) *The Emerging Euro-Mediterranean System*, Manchester/New York: Manchester University Press.

Yachir, F. (ed.) (1983) *Technologie et industrialisation en Afrique*, Algiers: Office des Publications Universitaires.

Yeager, J. A. (1987) *The Vietnamese Novel in French: A Literary Response to Colonialism*, Hanover, NH and London: University Press of New England.

Youssi, A. (1995) 'The Moroccan triglossia: facts and implications', *International Journal of the Sociology of Language*, 112, pp. 29–43.

Zartman, W. I. (1982) *Political Elites in Arab North Africa: Morocco, Algeria, Tunisia, Libya and Egypt*, London: Longman.

Zartman W. I. (ed.) (1991) *Tunisia: the Political Economy of Reform*, Boulder, CO: Lynne Rienner.

Zeiler, T. W. (1999) *Free Trade, Free World: The Advent of GATT*, Chapel Hill and London: University of North Carolina Press.